BAUDELAIRE

BAUDELAIRE

by Claude Pichois

Additional research by Jean Ziegler

Translated by Graham Robb

HAMISH HAMILTON

HAMISH HAMILTON

Published by the Penguin Group
27 Wrights Lane, London W8 5TZ, England
Viking Penguin Inc, 40 West 23rd Street, New York, New York 10010, U.S.A.
Penguin Books Australia Ltd, Ringwood, Victoria, Australia
Penguin Books Canada Ltd, 2801 John Street, Markham, Ontario, Canada L3R 1B4
Penguin Books (N.Z.) Ltd, 182–190 Wairau Road, Auckland 10, New Zealand

Penguin Books Ltd, Registered Offices: Harmondsworth, Middlesex, England

First published in Great Britain 1989 by
Hamish Hamilton Ltd

Copyright © 1987 by Julliard
Translation copyright © 1989 by Graham Robb
1 3 5 7 9 10 8 6 4 2

British Library Cataloguing in Publication Data
Pichois, Claude
Baudelaire

Library of Congress Number
89–83912

ISBN 0241 124581

Typeset by Butler & Tanner Ltd

Printed and bound in Great Britain by
Butler & Tanner Ltd, Frome and London

CONTENTS

TRANSLATOR'S NOTE

Over half a century since T. S. Eliot acclaimed Baudelaire as 'the greatest exemplar in *modern* poetry in any language', English is still one of the few major languages which lacks an edition of Baudelaire's complete works. There are of course several translations of *Les Fleurs du Mal* available, many of which have the advantage of being in prose and accompanied by the French text. There are also two excellent illustrated volumes of Baudelaire's art criticism, translated by Jonathan Mayne, and an annotated translation of Baudelaire's *Selected Letters* by Rosemary Lloyd.

The English-speaking reader might piece together most of Baudelaire's work by referring also to translations of the prose poetry, literary criticism and other essays. Many of these are out of print. Partly, therefore, for the sake of consistency, I have used my own translations throughout. Verse poems are quoted in French, with prose translations at the bottom of the page. Translating Baudelaire's poetry into English when he himself despaired of rendering the 'powerful monotony' of 'The Raven' is clearly an act of indiscretion and the translations should be read with Baudelaire's warning in mind: 'A translation of poetry ... may be an enticing dream, but can only ever be a dream.'

Having had the pleasure of working with Claude Pichois and of following the writing of this biography, I have been able to appreciate fully the difficulty of abridging a work which satisfies Baudelaire's dual criterion of coherence and suggestiveness. I have tried wherever possible to perform a manicure rather than a surgical operation, to summarise rather than omit, in the hope that this translation, which takes account of a small number of revisions and details which came to light after the publication of the French edition, might preserve the richness of the original.

I would like in particular to thank my father, Gordon Robb, and my wife, Margaret, for reading the manuscript at various stages and for their many indispensable suggestions.

G. M. R.
Oxford
May 1988

LIST OF ILLUSTRATIONS

FOREWORD

The first scholarly biography of Baudelaire dates back a century. It was the work of a man of letters called Eugène Crépet who, when compiling an anthology in the late 1850s, had invited Baudelaire to contribute some introductory articles. Their business relationship was difficult and sometimes acrimonious; nevertheless, in 1887, Crépet published a detailed and impartial study of the poet which laid the foundations of all that was subsequently written on Baudelaire's life.

Crépet's *Etude biographique* was the culmination of a remarkable series of studies and editions which quickly gave Baudelaire an important place in contemporary literature. For a *poète maudit*, convicted of obscenity by the criminal courts, and plagued throughout his life by what he called his *guignon* – the evil spirit of misfortune and disaster – it was an enviable fate.

Baudelaire, who was so severe, even tyrannical in his dealings with other people, owed his literary good fortune to a few true friends who recognised his genius and devoted themselves to making his work more widely known. It is in fact the very legend which Baudelaire built up around himself or allowed his contemporaries to create – a legend which we shall see as part of his poetic work – that has inspired writers and scholars over the years to discover or rediscover the man behind the mask. The decadent blasphemer and *poseur*, condemned, even in this century, by certain sections of the press and academe, was hailed shortly after his death as a highly original poet and critic by his friend, Charles Asselineau. In his affectionate biography, *Charles Baudelaire, sa vie et son œuvre*, Asselineau gave a certain amount of space to significant aspects of the Baudelaire legend, whilst warning the reader: 'In this biography of a mind, I cannot allow myself to be sucked down into the quicksand of anecdote and gossip.'

When Asselineau's work appeared at the end of 1868, the first two volumes of Baudelaire's *Œuvres complètes* had just been published; they contained Baudelaire's art criticism, collected for the first time, and the third edition of *Les Fleurs du Mal*, with an introduction by Théophile Gautier in which Baudelaire was acclaimed as one of the greatest poets of his time. By 1870, the seventh and last volume had appeared, thus completing an edition which included three volumes of translations from Edgar Allan Poe. The ban on the six poems condemned by the criminal court in 1857 was not lifted until after the Second World War; but they resurfaced in

Belgium as early as 1869, thanks to the selfless efforts of Baudelaire's friend and publisher, Poulet-Malassis. Five years after the poet's death, most of his work had been brought together and published.

The work carried out by Baudelaire's friends was continued with equal devotion by Eugène Crépet, who, in the 1870s, began to assemble an impressive collection of the poet's unpublished manuscripts. Little is known of Crépet's work on Baudelaire until 1886. Tracing Baudelaire's footsteps, he travelled that summer to Brussels, where he took a room at the Hôtel du Grand Miroir. This was the hotel in which, two decades before, Baudelaire had written his last poems and notes. During his stay there, Crépet paid a visit to the collector and scholar, Spoelberch de Lovenjoul, and after a five-and-a-half-hour conversation, left the Viscount's home, 'dazzled and wonder-struck' at all he had seen. Several mysteries concerning details of Baudelaire's life had been cleared up, and he held in his hand a letter of recommendation for the only man in Brussels who had known both Baudelaire and Poulet-Malassis, his publisher. Crépet's investigations also led him to interview many writers who could still recall the distant days when they had been friends of the young poet in the Latin Quarter. For the time, his research was unusually thorough and it enabled him to bring to life an age that already belonged to history.

Twenty years after Baudelaire's death, Eugène Crépet was able to publish his remarkable edition of Baudelaire's *Posthumous Works and Unpublished Correspondence Preceded by a Biographical Study*. It included the plans Baudelaire had drawn up for a preface to *Les Fleurs du Mal*, as well as sketches of plays, novels and short stories, fragments of his inflammatory book on Belgium and, most importantly, the notes that make up *Fusées* and *My Heart Laid Bare*. There were also letters to Poulet-Malassis and Sainte-Beuve, and a copious appendix, including documents relating to the trial of *Les Fleurs du Mal*.

Crépet's monument to the memory of Baudelaire was not a commercial success: one and a half thousand copies were printed costing ten francs each. Twelve years after Crépet's death in 1892, seven hundred were still waiting to be sold. But the *Œuvres posthumes* had some important readers – Paul Bourget and Nietzsche among them.

In 1906, the *Etude biographique* was published separately with revisions and additions. It now contained details which had been discreetly omitted from the earlier edition, some of them concerning women whom Baudelaire had known and who were now no longer living. The biography had been revised by the author's son, Jacques Crépet. Born in 1874, he had tried his hand at several trades, including journalism, but was not particularly keen in his younger days to apply his skill as a writer to the study of Baudelaire. His decision to republish his father's work was an act of filial piety; but it was also the first act of a long career devoted to Baudelaire.

The 1906 biography has been reprinted many times, but has never been replaced: Eugène Crépet's *Etude biographique*, revised by Jacques Crépet, has until now been the only reliable biography of Baudelaire.

In the last forty years, Baudelaire research has made considerable progress, sometimes in quality, more often only in quantity: the W. T. Bandy Center for Baudelaire Studies at Vanderbilt University – the largest collection of its kind in the world – has now recorded nearly 50,000 titles, from short articles of a few lines, to large studies of 500 pages or more.

Close as we both were to Jacques Crépet, Jean Ziegler and I felt that it was time to write a new biography of Baudelaire. Not that we can claim to have solved every mystery: large areas of Mme Aupick's family history have yet to be discovered and explored; Jeanne Duval's origins (and even her real surname) are still unknown, as is the identity of the woman to whom Baudelaire dedicated *Les Paradis artificiels* and the poem, 'L'Héautontimo-rouménos' – a woman known only by the mysterious initials 'J. G. F.' Nevertheless, one century after the publication of Eugène Crépet's masterly work, there are many new facts to be presented and new interpretations to be advanced.

We decided to adopt the English formula, 'Life and Letters', and to quote extensively from the important texts, so as to allow the reader to form his own impressions and opinions. Asselineau's work was the 'biography of a mind'. Our own ambition has been to tell the story of a mind and a body, to write the biography of a man of flesh and blood.

A biography is only a biography. It cannot claim to offer explanations of a poet's work, even though that work may sometimes call for biographical interpretation, as Baudelaire seemed to suggest when writing to his mother after the publication of *Les Fleurs du Mal*:

> You didn't notice, then, that there are two poems in *Les Fleurs du Mal* which are about you, or which contain allusions to intimate details of our former life together – that period of your widowhood which left me with such strange and sad memories? One of them is 'Je n'ai pas oublié, voisine de la ville ...' (Neuilly), and the other is the following poem: 'La servante au grand coeur dont vous étiez jalouse ...' (Mariette). I left those poems untitled and without any clear indication because I hate prostituting private family affairs.

It may be that biography says more about the biographer than it does

about its subject. The writer projects himself into the work and his own
shadow rises from the page to meet him. Perhaps the fact that there were
two of us has made it possible to avoid excessive partiality; or perhaps
neither of us was really hoping to avoid it. One is reminded of the phrase
which Julian Barnes used as the epigraph of *Flaubert's Parrot*: 'When you
write the biography of a friend, you must do it as if you were taking *revenge*
for him.' And also of Baudelaire's own description of criticism in the *Salon
de 1846* – a description which might also be applied to the way in which he
himself practised the art of biography: 'In order to be just, and thus to earn
its *raison d'être*, criticism must be partial, passionate and political, in other
words, it must be written from an exclusive point of view, but from the
point of view which opens up the greatest number of horizons.'

                                                        Claude Pichois

PART ONE

FAMILY PORTRAITS

'My ancestors, idiots or maniacs, in grand apartments, all of them victims of terrible passions.'[1] Editing Baudelaire's *Journaux intimes*, Jacques Crépet described these words as a biographer's nightmare, 'for Baudelaire's ancestors on his father's side were smallholders, and his mother's forebears have been searched for in vain'. Since then, the enigma of Baudelaire's *Fusée* has remained intact, though the field of inquiry has been narrowed by the discovery of several documents, notably the mother's marriage contract, which states that her father was a soldier who 'perished in the Quiberon Affair' in 1793. Soon, perhaps, we shall know whether Baudelaire was aware of a darker side to his family history – or whether the 'victims of terrible passions' were the protagonists of a novel that was never written.

The life stories of Baudelaire's immediate forebears are certainly more comforting and virtuous than the poet might have wanted to suggest.

François Baudelaire, the father, rose from humble origins in the provinces to become a student of philosophy in Paris, where he was ordained. After the Revolution, he became a civil servant and although he never attained the highest honours, he rubbed shoulders with those who had.

His second wife, the poet's mother, lost both her parents before she reached the age of seven and, despite being of higher birth than François, spend most of her childhood in poverty. As the wife of François Baudelaire, she belonged to the bourgeoisie; as the wife of General Aupick, she attained a form of military aristocracy.

Aupick, the stepfather, had an astonishing career. He, too, was an orphan, entered the army and climbed the ranks with the aid of friends in high places. He became French Ambassador to Turkey and Spain, and was offered the embassy in London. At the time of his death, he was a senator under the Second Empire.

The family history seems to have been one of social ascent, interrupted for a time by the Revolution, but eventually bringing the three main characters to Paris, where they enjoyed middle-class respectability and even brilliant success.

Charles Baudelaire, the black sheep, would descend in the social hierarchy, partly as the result of conscious choice. In a bourgeois world which had lost its faith in such things, poetry was a close companion of decadence and disgrace, and to be called to the priesthood of Poetry was to find oneself placed under a curse:

Lorsque, par un décret des puissances suprêmes,
Le Poète apparaît en ce monde ennuyé,
Sa mère épouvantée et pleine de blasphèmes,
Crispe ses poings vers Dieu, qui la prend en pitié:

—'Ah! que n'ai-je mis bas tout un noeud de vipères,
Plutôt que de nourrir cette dérision!'*

* 'When, by decree of the powers supreme, / The Poet appears in this world of *ennui*, /
His Mother, appalled and full of blasphemy, / Raises her clenched fists towards God, who
takes pity on her:

"Oh! I would rather have spawned a whole nest of vipers, / Than nurture this mockery of
a child!" ' ('Bénédiction')

CHAPTER 1

The Father

The happy event occurred in Paris on April 21, 1821. At the age of twenty-six, Caroline Baudelaire gave birth to a son, Charles-Pierre, at number 13, rue Hautefeuille, in the heart of the Latin Quarter. The street still exists, but the house itself, in which the Baudelaires owned an apartment, was demolished in the poet's lifetime to make way for the Boulevard Saint-Germain. On the 23rd, Charles-Pierre Baudelaire was held over the baptismal font of the nearby Eglise Saint-Sulpice by the godparents, M. and Mme Pierre Pérignon, who signed the register with the baby's father, a 'painter', François Baudelaire.

The father came from a village on the edge of the Argonne forest – La Neuville-au-Pont. He was born within a few weeks of his future friend, Pierre Pérignon, on June 7, 1759, into a family whose ancestors included wine growers, farm labourers and a few smallholders, as well as village craftsmen such as coopers and clog-makers. The family name – Baudelaire or Beaudelaire – occurred in several parishes of the Marne valley. In the Meuse, it seems to have been written generally without the first 'e', which would have pleased the poet who hated to see his name misspelt. The noun *'baudelaire'* or *'badelaire'* is defined by Pierre Larousse as a 'straight sabre with a double-edged blade, hooked and widened at the tip'. Baudelaire himself declared that his name was a 'barbarian noun' derived from the Latin for 'baldric-maker'.[2] Whatever the true origin, the scimitar described by Larousse is the most apposite meaning – Baudelaire's contemporaries often suffered from his aggressive behaviour and cutting remarks.

As an only child, François Baudelaire received a solid education at the nearby Collège de Sainte-Menehould.[3] The prospectus drawn up by the principal, a cleric called Nicolas François Buirette, assured parents of his commitment to producing 'men of letters', 'useful citizens' and 'enlightened Christians'. In 1775, François Baudelaire was enrolled in the top class with thirteen other boys, including Pierre Pérignon. It was the start of a long and fruitful relationship: besides being the godfather of Charles-Pierre, Pérignon would also be responsible for bringing up the poet's orphaned mother; and after the death of François, Pérignon's son Paul became a member of the young Baudelaire's board of guardians.

At the end of their first year at Sainte-Menehould, the two friends went their separate ways – Pierre Pérignon to Reims where he studied law and François Baudelaire to Paris. A scholarship, probably secured for François by the Abbé Buirette, enabled the promising young scholar to join the Catholic community of Sainte-Barbe whose boarders followed courses given at the Collège Du Plessis. For two years, he read philosophy at the University of Paris, whilst continuing to live at Sainte-Barbe, where one of his fellow students was René Desgenettes, later to become chief physician in Napoleon's Grande Armée. After receiving his master's degree and being tonsured, François continued his studies at the Sorbonne, where his academic success assured him a job as rhetoric tutor. During this time, he was taking minor orders and, in 1784, the man who was to be the father of Charles Baudelaire was ordained a priest.

The Abbé Baudelaire had almost certainly not entered the priesthood out of any strong convictions: in September 1785, he elected to leave the ministry for teaching and was taken on as a private tutor by Count Antoine de Choiseul-Praslin. He then went to live with his two young pupils, Félix and Alphonse, in the rue du Bac, not far from the Hôtel Praslin. It was there, and at the Count's country home in Auteuil on the outskirts of Paris, that François Baudelaire spent the next ten years of his life.

He took his job seriously and proved to be an excellent teacher. In order to instruct the boys in the rudiments of Latin, he composed and illustrated a manual, *La Langue latine démontrée par des figures*. Most of its 153 pages are covered with ink sketches, embellished with watercolours in the style of eighteenth-century illustrators. Each object and person – attired in modern dress instead of the usual toga – is labelled with the corresponding Latin word, including its gender and genitive ending.

The family was delighted with the new tutor. Letters to François from the Count and Countess speak of their 'inviolable affection' for him. François himself was very attached to his employers, as he showed on May 18, 1791, when he declined a call to the curacy of Dammartin-sous-Hans – a parish close to his native village.

During the Terror, Choiseul-Praslin, having become the head of his illustrious family after the death of his father the Duke, took the precaution of removing the family to Auteuil. But these were dangerous times: Condorcet, who was one of their neighbours, was arrested and imprisoned under the Law against Suspects promulgated by the Committee for Public Safety. Several other aristocratic inhabitants of the suburb followed him to prison, including Lefebvre-Laroche, who had come to warn Condorcet of his imminent arrest. Amongst the victims were the Duc de Praslin and his wife; they were placed under arrest in the Bonnet-Rouge guardhouse in the rue de Sèvres and their property was confiscated.

Their children, now bereft of all support, remained in the care of François Baudelaire, who tried to provide for them by giving drawing lessons and selling some of his work.[4] For the parents, too, he did what he could to make life a little easier and made courageous attempts to have them freed from prison. In short, as Mme Aupick wrote much later: 'When the Revolution broke out, M. Baudelaire showed himself to be a man of very fine character. He was heroic ... Twenty times he risked his life for the Duke and Duchess ... Having run into some school friends who were influential in the revolutionary party ... he made use of them in the interest of his friends, even as he condemned their policies, reproached them for their excesses, and denounced their aims, all with an eloquence which commanded their attention ... He was untiring in his endeavours; day and night he went from prison to court. But in spite of all his efforts, he was unable to save Condorcet's life, and rescued him only from the scaffold, as you know.'[5]*

Mme Aupick had clearly been given a rather romanticised version of her husband's role in the affair. François Baudelaire was not alone in attempting to rescue Condorcet and was not quite so opposed to the new regime as perhaps he led his wife to believe. On November 19, 1793, six days after the signing of the decree which set up the administrative machinery for 'depriestification', he prudently resigned his priesthood. Mme Aupick probably never heard the whole story – and there was a very good reason for François's discretion. His 'valiant' and 'zealous' action on behalf of Condorcet's widow had not been entirely disinterested. According to her biographer, Sophie Condorcet harboured 'tender feelings' for two of her intimate circle: a writer called Mailla Garat and a former priest called François Baudelaire. When the biography of La Marquise de Condorcet was published in 1896, it was reviewed by a friend of Charles Baudelaire who claimed to have heard the poet say of his father that 'he became angry at having to share his mistress, and she found his behaviour quite extraordinary.' This certainly has the ring of truth to it. In her Lettres sur la sympathie, Sophie expresses the opinion that it ought to be possible, 'as in

* Condorcet was arrested as a member of the moderate Girondin party. He escaped execution by poisoning himself.

Rome, to form brief liaisons which the Law would not condemn'.

With the fall of Robespierre in July 1794, the Terror came to an end and the family was reunited. François Baudelaire contined to work for the Duke and Duchess, and on May 9, 1797, he married a relative of the Condorcet family, Rosalie Janin. Both partners are described in the marriage contract as 'painters', a description which is confirmed by the inventories drawn up after Rosalie's death in 1815 and that of François in 1827.[6]

During their first year of marriage, the couple's only source of income appears to have been their painting, supplemented by a pension of 1,200 francs from the Duc de Choiseul-Praslin. François Baudelaire then decided at the age of thirty-eight to seek a post in the civil service and applied to the Directeur Général de l'Instruction Publique, Ginguené, describing himself as a man 'whose tastes have always inclined him towards literature and the arts':

> Being convinced that if a gentleman may desire and seek a position, he owes it to himself to perform his functions with honour rather than calculating the profit he might have of it, Citizen Baudelaire would prefer a position in which he might with some degree of success give to his country what little knowledge and experience he has to offer.

Citizen Baudelaire added that if evidence of his patriotism were required, references might be taken up with the 'enlightened republicans with whom he has the good fortune to be acquainted'.[7] François's note is neither signed nor dated and is clearly incomplete – perhaps some compromising remark was carefully deleted? Its vagueness and rather casual tone would appear to suggest that François either knew or had been recommended by a friend to the Director. Unfortunately, Ginguené was despatched in December 1797 as Ambassador to the Court of Turin and it was not until June 1798 that François Baudelaire was appointed 'Assistant Commissioner for the selection of books from the libraries of convents, émigrés or condemned people', with a salary of 1,800 francs.

His new colleagues included Antoine Alexandre Barbier, a defrocked priest who later became Napoleon's bibliographer and librarian, and a painter, Jean Naigeon, who introduced Baudelaire to his friend, the sculptor Claude Ramey. The job, by definition, was temporary, but on January 6, 1800, Baudelaire had the good fortune to be elected 'Private Secretary to the Senate Administrative Commission', which included five senators, one of whom was the Duc de Choiseul-Praslin. It was an important position, with a starting salary of 4,000 francs. Having made such a good start in the civil service, the former private tutor continued to rise steadily in the ranks, working in collaboration with several important senators and dealing with the artists commissioned by the Senate. Professional relations with Naigeon led to friendship and, on January 18, 1805, along with Claude Ramey, they went to the townhall of the eleventh arrondissement to declare the birth of François and Rosalie's first child, a son, Alphonse.

One of the artists known to François at that time was the famous painter, Jean-Baptiste Regnault. It was Regnault who painted the only known portrait of François Baudelaire – the 'eternally silent' portrait which the poet carried around with him from hotel room to hotel room until he sent it to his mother in Honfleur in July 1861.

With the strong nose, penetrating eyes, dark, bushy eyebrows, pursed lips and determined expression, the portrait seems to reveal a rugged and irascible personality. It matches the description given by René Desgenettes, François Baudelaire's classmate at Sainte-Barbe: he 'dominated lofty circles with his gruffness, his caustic wit, and the intransigence of his republicanism'[8] – like father, like son. And yet at other times, François could strike those who met him as a pleasant and charming person, and when he came visiting the Pérignons' home, this was the Baudelaire who was to make such an impression on young Mlle Dufaÿs.

CHAPTER 2

The Mother

François Baudelaire's family tree had all its roots in the same region of France and his ancestors can be traced back to the early seventeenth century. The origins of Caroline Dufaÿs, on the other hand, are shrouded in mystery: even the correct spelling of her surname is unknown.

Caroline's mother, Julie Foyot, belonged to a family which came from the same area of France as the Baudelaires.[1] Julie's father, the poet's great-grandfather, was a solicitor and a Freemason, and it was through his professional and masonic connections that Didier Foyot made the acquaintance in 1786 of François Baudelaire's friend, Pierre Pérignon. Julie Foyot was the middle of three sisters. The eldest, Charlotte, married the explorer and naturalist, François Levaillant, and had three children by him. She died prematurely in 1798. About the early life of Julie, very little is known, except that she married and emigrated to England in 1792.

The baptismal register for the parish of Saint Pancras, Middlesex, contains the following entry for 1794:

> Jan[ry] f[st], Caroline Archenbant, Daughter of Charles and Juliet Defayis, [born on] sept. 27th [1793].[2]

When recording the birth, the vicar should have written 'Caroline Archenbaut-Defayis', since Archenbaut (or Archimbaut) was part of the surname. The origin of this second name is unknown and the identity of Charles Defayis himself is a complete mystery. His name appears on only one other document – a statement drawn up in 1819 to replace Caroline's missing birth certificate at the time of her marriage to François Baudelaire: Caroline, it says, 'was born during her parents' emigration, the parents themselves having been married in England' and 'her father, who was a soldier, perished in the Quiberon Affair'. (This was the counter-revolutionary expedition of Royalist émigrés to Brittany in July and August 1795; the Royalists were defeated and those who failed to escape onto the British ships were slaughtered.) Whether Charles Defayis was already an officer when he fled to England, or whether he became a soldier by joining the regiment of émigrés funded by the British Government, we can only guess.

His widow and baby daughter, Caroline, were supported by the French and British Relief Committees which shared out funds allocated to the émigrés.[3] Each month, Julie received a little over two pounds for herself and her baby daughter. From January 1, 1796, being too ill to manage on her own, she was allowed one extra pound for the upkeep of an English servant. In the spring, her renewed application for the additional grant had first to pass through the hands of the doctor assigned to the French committee, who would then have sent the claimant with her medical certificates to his English counterpart, Mr Hollings, at 120, Mount Street, Berkeley Square. This man, 'who had behind him a fair amount of experience with émigrés, was not one to treat matters concerning the public coffers lightly', writes Pierre Christophorov in his book on Chateaubriand in exile. Julie's allowance was renewed for a period of two or three months. Her next petition was signed 'Lacombe Dufaiz' – another name, another mystery. Perhaps Lacombe was a pseudonym which Julie adopted after her husband's death.

Mother and daughter spent another two years' exile in London – years during which the mother's health continued to decline. At the end of October 1800, happy news reached the émigrés in England: Napoleon had signed a decree which granted many of them, women in particular, permission to return home. Julie successfully applied for a passport and sailed for France. She arrived in Paris around November 13, probably with her daughter and in the company of other returning exiles. One of her fellow travellers must have offered to take care of Caroline whilst Julie, very ill and nearly destitute, went off in search of her family. No doubt she hurried to the family home in Chaillot, where she learned that her father and elder sister had both passed away, and that her mother and brother-in-law had moved to Champagne. There were other relatives on her mother's side still living somewhere in Paris, but her failing health prevented her from reaching them. Julie died alone in a Paris hotel room on November 23, 1800, 'from a chest complaint', according to the death certificate. She was thirty-two years old. A search of her luggage revealed no clue as to her little girl's civil status. Caroline's name had not been added to the passport.

The orphan, now seven years old, was taken in by M. and Mme Pérignon, who lived close to the hotel in which Julie had just died, at number 8, rue Neuve-Saint-Augustin. 'When I made the acquaintance of M. Baudelaire,' she wrote many years later, after the poet's death, 'it was in the home of M. Pérignon, my guardian, in whose house his wife brought me up with his daughters. There were also some sons. It was a large and very wealthy family, living luxuriously in a palatial residence.'

Pérignon had come a long way since the days when he sat on the school benches at the Collège Sainte-Menehould with François Baudelaire. He was now a very successful lawyer, with four daughters. Caroline was extremely lucky to be adopted by such a well-to-do family. One might suppose that Pérignon owed a debt of gratitude to Caroline's grandfather for some assistance in the early stages of his career; or perhaps he was acting out of a sentimental attachment to the memory of Julie Foyot.

Caroline became a boarder at a *'pension pour demoiselles'* in the Marais district of Paris, run by two Irish Benedictine nuns, friends of the Pérignon family. Caroline spent her holidays and days out with Mme Pérignon, reading or doing embroidery, except on those occasions when Mme Pérignon was hostess at an important dinner or reception to which high-ranking officers, civil servants and lawyers were invited.

The eldest daughter of the family, Apolline, was engaged to be married to an artillery general, Louis Tirlet, whom Pérignon and his friend François Baudelaire already knew, by reputation at least. Fortunately for us, Louis Tirlet was away for many long months fighting in the Spanish wars. The letters he received from his young wife, which are now in the Bibliothèque Nationale, are a rich source of information on the Pérignons' family life.

François Baudelaire and his wife Rosalie appear regularly in Apolline's correspondence, for they often came to visit the Pérignons, bringing with them their son, Alphonse. When there was a reception, the couple would arrive in a carriage which bore the coat-of-arms of the Senate. According to the custom of the time, François was served by his own footman: young Caroline was tremendously impressed and later recalled how M. Baudelaire struck her at the time as being 'a great lord'. Mme Baudelaire, who was not in the best of health, was much liked by Apolline, and her admiration was apparently shared by Caroline, who told the poet's first biographer in 1868 that M. Baudelaire was 'married to an intelligent woman, his intellectual equal'.

Apolline's letters from 1811 to 1813 are missing. Her correspondence takes up the family story again at the beginning of 1814. The French Empire was in its last days and, on April 6, 1814, Napoleon abdicated. 'He has accepted the Island of Elba,' wrote Apolline, 'and six millions for himself and his family. The constitution is signed, and Louis XVIII is to be recognised.'

François Baudelaire and Pierre Pérignon weathered the change of regime, the former becoming 'Head Clerk of the Internal Administration of the Palais de la Chambre des Pairs'. But Baudelaire had other worries: both he and his wife were in poor health. Their friends would come to see them in their charming house on the corner of the rue de Vaugirard, by one of the gates leading into the Luxembourg Gardens. 'When I was a little girl,' wrote Caroline in 1868, 'I often dined there with the Pérignon family, and it was delightful to run about after the retreat had sounded in the Jardin du Luxembourg, when everyone had gone.'

At the end of 1814, Rosalie Baudelaire died, leaving François alone with a ten-year-old son. He remained a close friend of the Pérignon household, as Caroline recalled: 'I was always hearing his praises sung. I liked that old man (to me he looked old – I was so young! – with his curly grey hair and his eyebrows black as ebony) because of his very original mind. I remember they often used to say in the family: "Baudelaire, with his brilliant wit, also has the *naïveté* and bonhomie of La Fontaine." '

During the Hundred Days, after Napoleon's landing at Fréjus, Baudelaire had the sense and foresight to remain at his post. Pérignon and his son-in-law, Louis Tirlet, experienced a few contretemps: Pérignon saw fit to withdraw to England and General Tirlet was denounced to the Emperor for making defeatist remarks. After sending his written disavowal to Napoleon, he was restored to his former position.

On June 18, 1815, the battle at Waterloo was fought. The exiles returned and Louis XVIII was firmly re-established on the throne. For François Baudelaire, however, life was becoming more and more difficult, as Caroline remembered: 'M. Baudelaire, whose probity was so strict, and who was so careful with State money, had no desire to yield to the demands of all the new favourites who now surrounded him.' Baudelaire's superior hinted 'that he was not well thought of, that he was suspected of pining for the old order, and also of being a Bonapartist, and that his best course of action would be to retire'.

It was in these circumstances – ill health and an unpleasant atmosphere at the Luxembourg – that François Baudelaire handed in his resignation on August 3, 1816. His co-operative behaviour was rewarded with a pension of 4,000 francs. He left the house at the Luxembourg (which was government property) and took an apartment at number 13, rue Hautefeuille. There he lived alone with his son until September 9, 1819, on which date, at the grand age of sixty, he married the orphan he had known since she was a little girl, Caroline Dufaÿs. Caroline was only twenty-six. Perhaps this unconventional match should be seen as the joining together of two lonely people. Caroline herself never explained the story behind her marriage; but whatever the case, Pierre Pérignon must have been relieved to see his ward assured of a comfortable future and was probably glad to provide his old friend with a youthful companion.

The marriage took place at the townhall of the eleventh arrondissement. (As an unfrocked priest, François was not allowed to marry in church.) Maybe the couple spent their honeymoon in Neuilly, just outside Paris, where François owned some properties left to him by Rosalie; or perhaps they travelled to the Marne to visit his cousins in La Neuville-sur-Pont, before returning to Paris and the apartment in the rue Hautefeuille. There it was that Charles-Pierre Baudelaire was born to François and Caroline on April 9, 1821.

The home in which the poet spent the first six years of his life with his parents, half-brother and two servants emerges in some detail from the inventory drawn up after François Baudelaire's death. Even after many years, he remembered the scenes of his earliest childhood quite vividly:

> *Childhood*: Old Louis XVI furniture, antiques, Consulate, pastels, 18th-century life ... A permanent taste since childhood for all plastic representations.[4]

The furniture, much of which came from Rosalie's mother, was indeed Louis XVI, as were the plaster statues and statuettes, though they were cast in the time of the Consulate. These must either have been models used by François Baudelaire, who painted in the Classical style, or gifts from his friend Claude Ramey or from the sculptors who entered the competitions organised by Baudelaire and the architect Chalgrin to select artists for the Imperial Senate.

The apartment consisted of an antechamber, kitchen, dining room and drawing room, which, with the elder brother's bedroom, looked onto the courtyard. The garden was overlooked by Charles' small bedroom, Mme Baudelaire's room, and a large study which also served as M. Baudelaire's library and bedroom. The Baudelaires' home was filled with furniture, except perhaps for the drawing room, much of which was taken up with an old style billiard table, and two small English pianos. The drawing room walls disappeared under the paintings of François Baudelaire and those of his first wife. Most of François's works, contrary to what Charles remembered, were gouaches.

Charles' room contained a tall mirror with a grey wooden frame, a small bunk bed in cherry wood, a white marble-top table and a small rosewood chiffonier. In his mother's room, the bed and chairs were covered in yellow velvet with a flower pattern which matched the curtains of the bed and windows. An opaline water service and two flower vases in Japanese porcelain betrayed the occupant's weakness for ornaments, and in particular for old ceramics.

The adjoining room was François Baudelaire's study. Nothing in the inventory suggests that Charles' cot stood against the 'dark Babel' of the bookshelves (as he wrote in the poem, 'La Voix'), though it does mention, under lot 72, a 'child's armchair'. The bookshelves contained, among other works, the *Encyclopédie* of 1772, Lavater's *L'Art de connaître les hommes par la physionomie*, Piranesi's album, Voltaire, Crébillon[5] and Rabelais, probably also the copy of *Les Antiquités d'Herculanum* which the Duchesse de Praslin had bequeathed to her sons' tutor as a token of gratitude. As in Caroline's room, there was a clock under a glass cover. In the evening, the study was lit only by two brass candlesticks.

Here, François Baudelaire painted his last gouaches,[6] when his illness gave him some respite. It was here, too, that he died, watched over by his wife or a nurse who occupied the trestle-bed mentioned in the inventory.

Because of the husband's poor health and the birth of the baby, the Baudelaires rarely left the rue Hautefeuille. Sometimes, François would go out walking in the Luxembourg Gardens with his very young son, pointing out the statues to him. He was fortunate in having his friends close at hand and enjoyed unrestricted admission to the nearby Odéon Theatre. For several years, he had been a member of the theatre reading committee, 'spending much time on examining the plays submitted and on the reports that were made of them'.

Charles' half-brother was still living with the family and getting on very well with his stepmother. Alphonse was studying law, and after presenting his theses on French and Roman Law in 1824, did his articles in the Cour Royale de Paris. In 1832, he would decide to enter the magistracy and become a judge at Fontainebleau, where he remained until his death in 1862.

On February 10, 1827, at three o'clock in the afternoon, François Baudelaire died, perhaps from the illness which had been plaguing him since 1814. That same day, without having been taken to the parish church, the body was buried in the Montparnasse Cemetery in a 'separate grave' – number twenty-six in the third row, according to the admissions register.[7]

CHAPTER 3

Major Aupick

Caroline remained a widow for less than two years. Her second husband was an officer in the French army, an orphan like herself, whose origins are no less mysterious.

We know from his service record that his father, Jacques Joseph Aupick, was born in Ireland on October 1, 1735.[1] Following what was probably a family tradition, Aupick joined the Berwick Infantry regiment in France. He climbed the ranks slowly, becoming a lieutenant only in 1791. Three years later, he died a captain as a result of wounds received at the Battle of Hondschoote. His son was five years old. The mother, who may or may not have been his legal wife, was probably an English woman called Amelia Talbot.

The son, Jacques Aupick, had no birth certificate and what little we know of his family comes from a replacement document drawn up in Gravelines on July 10, 1808. The signatories of the document declared that the young man, Jemis (Jacques) Aupick, had been known in that town since his earliest childhood when the Berwick-and-Irish regiment was garrisoned there in 1790, 'and that the said Aupick was brought there by Mr. Jacques Joseph Aupick, officer ... in the aforementioned regiment, and Mrs. Amelia Talbot, both held to be lawfully married ... that the said Mr. Jacques Joseph Aupick and the said Mrs. Amelia Talbot died without having provided or left behind any information as to the place or date of birth of the said child. Several inquiries, moreover, conducted with an aim to discovering these have so far been fruitless. Everything leads us to believe that he was born in some small township on the path of the aforementioned regiment which is known to have changed garrison frequently around that time.'

The service record of the future General Aupick states more positively that he was born in Gravelines on February 28, 1789. As for the curious Christian name, Jemis (or Jémis), it may reflect a French pronunciation of

James or Seamus. To most people, except for those closest to him, he was known simply as Jacques.[2]

The man responsible for having the 1808 certificate drawn up was Louis Baudart, a Gravelines magistrate who considered Aupick his adopted son. Baudart was an excellent fellow, distinguished by the sort of *sensibilité* in favour at the end of the eighteenth century. This he passed on to young Jemis so successfully that even their wills are very much alike – the same religious lyricism, the same humility and gratitude towards providence which raised them both from a lowly estate to a comfortable or outstanding social position, the same forgiveness of insult, even the same request for a discreet funeral.

Napoleon Bonaparte, as First Consul, was to visit Gravelines in June 1803. Baudart composed a speech of welcome which gives some idea of the atmosphere in which the boy was raised:

> That day will be forever memorable on which your presence graced our peaceful climes, close by the waters of the North once plied by the warlike fleets of *Fingal's* son. Inspired with righteous gratitude for all the blessings men will owe you, Posterity will say that the shade of *Erin's hero*, pursued by his phantom warriors of noble heart and Bards with their Romantic songs, was seen hastening over the clouds to behold the restorer of religious morality (that true philosophy of feeling), the protector of Science and the Arts, the friend and Father of Frenchmen. She will say that the shade of *great Ossian* was seen there smiling on *great Bonaparte*, regenerator of his Land and Pacifier of the world.

In later years, Aupick himself expressed his feelings on public occasions with similar enthusiasm.

The young orphan studied first in Gravelines and then at the military school of Saint-Cyr where not a year went by without his winning some award. The prize list in 1807 praised him for his leading role in the school play, *Fortunas* – a dramatisation of the siege of Danzig, acted out against a backdrop of Napoleonic splendour:

> One pupil who has constantly distinguished himself by his success in studies, by his love of order, and by firm and proper vigilance in the field of discipline, which qualities have earned him the confidence of M. le Général Commandant and of his civilian and military superiors, being one year ahead of the other pupils in the various classes he has attended, tactfully decided not to enter into competition with his comrades. It is he who has just enacted the role of Fortunas – a character perfectly suited

to his qualities. We felt him worthy of a distinction. That pupil is young *Aupick-Baudart*, born in Gravelines, Département du Nord.

In 1808, some of the pupils were transferred to the 'Ecole Impériale Spéciale Militaire' which had been moved from Fontainebleau to Saint-Cyr and which is still known today as 'Saint-Cyr'. In order to matriculate, students were required to be conversant with arithmetic and geometry, and to be able to write and speak French correctly. Aupick was more ambitious and sat the entrance examination for the Ecole Polytechnique. His results were good, but the '*Admissible*' he received was not enough to ensure him a place; he had to settle for Saint-Cyr. This nevertheless was the important step from classroom to battlefield. Aupick achieved rapid promotion, becoming a sub-lieutenant by March 1809. He then enlisted in the 105th Regiment at Neufbrisach.

Napoleon's campaigns took the young soldier to Austria, Spain (1812) and Saxony (1813). Under the First Restoration, he remained on the active list and was even decorated in March 1815 by the dying Duc d'Angoulême. However, this did not prevent him from rallying to Napoleon during the Hundred Days. Shortly before Waterloo, he took part in the Battle of Fleurus and was wounded by a bullet which lodged in his left knee. The chronic infection produced by the wound was to cause him considerable pain for the rest of his life. He was able to take refuge after the battle with his adoptive father and, temporarily discharged, was put on half-pay for two years. This was the only period in which fortune failed to smile on Jemis Aupick.

After the fall of Napoleon, and as early as July 25, 1815, he asked to be reinstated, but it was not until August 5, 1817 that his urgent protestations of loyalty to His Majesty were given a hearing. Aupick re-entered the French army as a major and, the following year, became the aide-de-camp of General Durrieu, and then of Generals Barbanègre, Fririon and Meynadier, under whose orders he served in Spain.

His star was shining bright once more in the clear skies of loyalty rediscovered; but never did it shine so bright as when he was specially chosen as an aide-de-camp by the Prince de Hohenlohe after the expedition undertaken by Louis XVIII to re-establish Ferdinand VII on the Spanish throne. Hohenlohe's reports on his new aide-de-camp are full of glowing praise; those dating from 1827 and 1829 contain such expressions as: robust constitution, agreeable physique, pleasant company, steadfast and full of discernment, master of himself in all his actions, hard-working and studious, never dismayed, excellent military knowledge in all that concerns infantry

and staff, speaks English, Spanish and German (rare qualities at the time),
would make an excellent leader. Hohenlohe did not forget to mention that
in collaboration with A.-M. Perrot, Aupick had produced the *New Atlas
of the Kingdom of France*, published in instalments from 1823 to 1827. On
the title page of this large and attractive album, containing maps, articles
and statistics, J. Aupick was described as a 'superior officer of the Corps
Royal d'Etat-Major' and as a 'member of the Société de Géographie'.

One might wonder whether the Major had even the slightest imper-
fection. Yet he owes his fame, not to this marvellous catalogue of virtues,
but to the hate his stepson was to bear him.

The report on Aupick for March 24, 1829 noted under the section
entitled, 'Morals, conduct, and principles': 'Noble in his comportment, a
good husband.' Major Aupick had indeed taken a wife over four months
before; or perhaps one should say that she had taken him.

CHAPTER 4

The Marriage of Major Aupick and Mme Baudelaire

François Baudelaire had died on February 10, 1827. Three days later, a board of guardians was set up, consisting notably of the son of Charles' godfather, Paul Pérignon, the Duc de Choiseul-Praslin and François Baudelaire's friends, Jean Naigeon and Claude Ramey. The inventory after death was prepared, and, at the request of Alphonse, who may already have been contemplating marriage, the father's estate was settled and divided between the two half-brothers. Three experts were appointed to assess the value of the property and to propose a division of the land at Les Ternes, then part of Neuilly, now part of the seventeenth arrondissement.

Like most widows, Mme Baudelaire found her income drastically reduced – no more pension from the Chambre des Pairs, nor from the Duc de Praslin. Her only source of money now was the 2,000 franc annuity with which François had provided her in the marriage contract. Forced to cut back on expenses, she would have to find a new apartment before the end of October and sell off the furniture that was no longer needed. The summer brought some relief from these pressing concerns. She borrowed or rented a house in Neuilly, and lived there alone for a time with Charles and a maidservant. This was the little house evoked in one of the earliest poems of *Les Fleurs du Mal*:[1]

> Je n'ai pas oublié, voisine de la ville,
> Notre blanche maison, petite mais tranquille;
> Sa Pomone de plâtre et sa vieille Vénus
> Dans un bosquet chétif cachant leurs membres nus,
> Et le soleil, le soir, ruisselant et superbe,
> Qui, derrière la vitre où se brisait sa gerbe,
> Semblait, grand oeil ouvert dans le ciel curieux,
> Contempler nos dîners longs et silencieux,

> Répandant largement ses beaux reflets de cierge
> Sur la nappe frugale et les rideaux de serge.*

It was also the period to which Baudelaire referred in the moving letter he sent to his mother on May 6, 1861:

> There was in my childhood a period of passionate love for you; listen and read without fear. Never before have I said so much to you about it. I remember a ride in a cab; you were leaving a nursing home in which you had been cooped up, and to prove you had been thinking of your son, you showed me some ink drawings you had done for me. I have a terrific memory, don't I? Later on, there was the place Saint-André-des-Arcs and Neuilly. Long walks and constant affection! I remember the *quais*, so sad in the evenings. Ah! for me, those were the good days of maternal affection. I apologise for calling *good* those days which, for you, were probably bad.

August and September 1827 passed very quickly. Charles and his mother returned from Neuilly to the rue Hautefeuille, but not for long. At the end of September or the beginning of October, they moved out with Alphonse, leaving behind a few pieces of furniture, various objects, paintings, drawings, prints – and also the old clothes which had belonged to the deceased. These were all sold at public auction and brought in more than 1,000 francs.

The new home was close to the river on the Left Bank, at number 30, rue and Place Saint-André-des-Arcs (now Saint-André-des-Arts). Charles was happy; he had his mother all to himself. The 'days of maternal affection' would last for a few months more. Mme Baudelaire had had some teaching experience in her final years at boarding school and perhaps she taught her son to read. Unbeknownst to Charles, however, this 'period of passionate love' was drawing to a close. From the spring of 1828, his mother would leave him from time to time under the watchful eye of Mariette, the servant, to go out in the evening with a handsome officer who came to the house strapped up in his uniform. Mme Baudelaire was a widow of thirty-five and, in those days, thirty-five was not an age at which one could expect a second youth. For Caroline, it was now or never.

---

* 'I have not forgotten, close to the town, / Our white-walled house, small but serene; / Its plaster Pomon and its agèd Venus / Hiding their naked limbs in a scraggly grove, / And the sun which, in the evening, streaming down and superb, / Behind the pane on which its shower of light did break, / Seemed, like a great eye opened in the curious sky, / To watch our long and silent meals, / Spreading abundantly its candle reflections / On the frugal cloth and the curtains of serge.'

We know nothing of the circumstances which brought her and Major Aupick together. We do know, however, that they must have met towards the beginning of 1828. Aupick was away from Paris on manoeuvres, probably from May until September. After returning briefly to Paris, he set off again almost at once for Lunéville, where he was received in the château by the Prince de Hohenlohe in October 1828. From the Prince, he obtained a letter addressed to the minister requesting permission to marry. Mme 'Bodelaire' was described in the letter as a widow possessing 'all the qualities called for by the regulations . . . as well as those of age, fortune, and social proprieties'. The Prince concluded by begging the minister to have the matter dispatched without delay in the interests of Major Aupick. With all possible speed, the Major returned to Paris, left the letter with the ministry and, on October 20, permission was granted. The couple-to-be immediately attended to the other administrative formalities. The British Consulate authenticated the certificate delivered to Caroline in 1821 by William Sallofield, Vicar of Saint Pancras; the board of guardians appointed the Major joint guardian of Charles; and finally, on November 8, Aupick, who had just been made a Chevalier of the Order of Saint Louis, married 'Caroline Archenbaut Defayis' at nine o'clock in the morning at the townhall of the tenth arrondissement. The religious ceremony followed at Saint-Thomas d'Aquin. A single ban had been published, a dispensation from the other two having been accorded by the Archbishop of Paris. The witnesses were four friends, including Marc-Antoine Dufour, whom Aupick had met in one of the military masonic lodges to which he once belonged.

This discreet and expeditious marriage caused some astonishment in Paris as well as in Gravelines, where people continued to follow with interest the career of the boy they still called Jemis. Why did he go and marry a thirty-five-year-old widow with no fortune and why was it all done on the quiet?

The newlyweds settled for a time at number 17, rue du Bac; but duty called. The Major set off for Lunéville, leaving his wife in the country at Creil with a widow recommended by his friend Dufour – Mme Hainfray. Scrutiny of the register of births, marriages and deaths at Creil reveals the reason for the couple's haste and discretion in seeing the marriage through:

> . . . the lady Caroline Dufay, currently at Vaux, in the home of Monsieur Hainfray, residing ordinarily in Paris, rue du Bac, number 17, wife of M. Jacques Aupick, major, aide-de-camp of the Prince de Hohenlohe, gave birth to a still-born child of the female sex on the 2nd inst [December 1828] at 3 o'clock in the morning.

Even if Caroline remained in bed for the usual twenty-one days, she would have returned home in time to spend Christmas with Charles. Perhaps the boy was taken by Mariette to meet the coach from Creil and rode home with his mother in a cab to the rue du Bac. Maybe this is the cab-ride mentioned in the 1861 letter. Had Mme Aupick turned her secret delivery into a short stay in a 'nursing home'? But when Baudelaire added, 'I have a terrific memory, don't I?' the irony was probably unintended. It seems unlikely that he ever found out about his still-born sister.

After Christmas, Caroline wrote to Alphonse, who had remained behind in the rue Saint-André-des-Arcs: 'If your business ever brings you to the rue du Bac, come and have a chat with us, come and dine with the family. Your little brother talks about you all the time and will be very happy to see you.'[2] Alphonse was in fact rather busy with arrangements for his forthcoming marriage to his friend's sister, Félicité Ducessois.

The wedding of Alphonse and the eighteen-year-old Félicité took place on April 30, 1829 in the church of Saint-Etienne-du-Mont. The bride's brother, Théodore, who had left the bar to take over the family printing shop, produced a song sheet for the occasion consisting of verses written by friends and relatives. The Aupicks seem to have approved of this marriage, and the mother-in-law and daughter-in-law formed a friendship which blossomed after the death of Alphonse in 1862, and particularly during Charles' final illness in 1866 and 1867.

Shortly after the wedding and the death of his protector, the Prince de Hohenlohe, the Major was placed on the reserve list. This situation was not at all to his liking, but at least it gave him a chance to be with his wife and stepson for nine months. Charles was probably attending a primary school nearby, close to an army barracks and the Seine:

La diane chantait dans les cours des casernes...*

The Major was finally called up in March 1830 and attached to the expeditionary force sent to Algeria the following June. His distinguished service did not pass unnoticed and he was promoted to the rank of lieutenant-colonel. Only on July 1, 1831, after fifteen months' absence, did he return to France and his family. Once again, he was placed on the reserve list; but this time, new orders would not be long in coming.

In the meantime, there were 'two red eyes'[3]: on October 3, 1831, Charles started school at the Collège Royal de Charlemagne in *septième* (equivalent to the last year at primary school). He was also sent as a boarder to an institution run by a M. Bourdon, who was renowned for his success at

---

* 'The bugle sang out in the barracks square...' (First verse of the early *Fleur du Mal*, 'Le Crépuscule du matin')

getting pupils through the entrance examinations for the government Ecoles – amongst which was the Ecole Militaire known as Saint-Cyr. Perhaps Aupick, as an old Saint-Cyrian, was hoping to make an officer or a civil servant of his stepson.

The glowing memory related much later by Baudelaire in *Morale du joujou* dates from this period. It concerns a visit made with his mother to the home of Mme Panckoucke, wife of the writer and printer, Charles Panckoucke, who had been one of the signatories of Alphonse's marriage contract.

> I remember very clearly that the lady was dressed in velvet and fur. After a while, she said: 'Here's a little boy I want to give something so he'll remember me.' She took me by the hand, and we passed through several rooms. Then she opened the door of a chamber in which an extraordinary and magical sight presented itself to the eye. The walls were so covered in toys that they could not be seen. The ceiling had disappeared under a flowering of playthings which hung like miraculous stalactites. The floor scarcely offered a narrow path on which to place one's feet. It was a whole world of toys of every sort, from the most expensive to the humblest, from the simplest to the most complex.
>
> 'Here,' she said, 'is the children's treasure-trove. I have a small allowance to spend on them, and when a nice little boy comes to see me, I bring him here so that when he leaves he can take away some memory of me. Choose one.'
>
> With that wonderful, clear-sighted spontaneity characteristic of children, in whom desire, thought and deed might be said to form part of one and the same function, by which they distinguish themselves from degenerate men, who, by contrast, find nearly all their time devoured by deliberation, I immediately took hold of the finest, dearest, brightest, newest, and most bizarre of all the toys. My Mother exclaimed at my indiscretion, and obstinately opposed my taking it away with me. She wanted me to be happy with an infinitely inferior object. But I could not agree, and, in order to settle everything, I resigned myself to a *juste-milieu*.
>
> I have often conceived a desire to know all the 'nice little boys' who, having lived now through a large part of this cruel life, have long been handling other things than toys, and who once in carefree childhood drew a *souvenir* from Mme Panckoucke's treasure-trove.

This was one of the few happy memories from Baudelaire's youth.

Charles remained with M. Bourdon for only one term. On November 25, 1831, Lieutenant-Colonel Aupick was enjoined to leave for Lyons and to place himself at the disposal of the Minister of War, Marshal Soult. He was ordered to travel '*en poste*', meaning that he was to stop at each stage only for as long as it took to change the horses. He arrived in Lyons at the end of November. His wife and ten-year-old stepson would join him there in February 1832. The coach-journey via Auxerre took three and a half days.

Little did Charles know that he would be stuck in Lyons almost without interruption for four long years and that soon he would be missing Paris, 'the boulevards and the sweets from Berthellemot, the Giroux "universal store", and the rich bazaars in which one finds in such abundance such beautiful New Year gifts'. Neither did he know what was taking his stepfather to that big city in the provinces.

When he arrived in Lyons, Charles was ten and a half years old. We know of no feelings or opinions which mark him out from other boys his age. He appears spontaneous and affectionate in relations with his parents; and there is no sign of any hostility towards Aupick. But what did he think of the man who was his real father?

Surely the child cannot have failed to notice that his parents were an ill-assorted pair. His friends had mothers and fathers of a similar age, but he was the son of an old man and, in the minds of people then (and even now), that meant that he must in some way be stunted.[4] François Baudelaire must have appeared to be more of a grandfather than a father. The Lieutenant-Colonel, on the other hand, was a very presentable substitute. Psychological studies of the poet have always failed to take this social aspect of the question into account.

Later, in his intricate game of resentment and remorse (including the remorse he hoped to inspire in others), he would sometimes denigrate his father whilst proving that he had always remained loyal to his memory. He piously kept the portrait by Regnault and thanked his mother in 1863 for having sent him some letters written by his father, adding, 'These old papers have something magical about them.' The expression recalls the letter of December 30, 1857, in which Baudelaire describes his discovery in a shop of a painting by his father; he decided not to buy it: 'My father was a detestable artist; but those old things all have a moral value.' It was a harsh judgement, but Charles was writing to his mother, whom he liked to treat rather roughly. Perhaps he was annoyed with his father for having failed to be a great artist – François Baudelaire's gouaches tend to confirm his son's opinion. In any case, his feelings were ambivalent and it would be a great mistake to imagine Baudelaire cherishing fond memories of walks in the Luxembourg Gardens with that lovable old gentleman. Nostalgia is not affection.

If Baudelaire grew to hate the General his stepfather, it was without a doubt because Aupick tried to stand in the way of his vocation and especially because he robbed him of some of his mother's love. Even if François had been the same age as Caroline, nothing proves that their son would have loved him either. Only one person really counted in the life of Charles Baudelaire – his mother.

PART TWO

THE SCHOOLBOY

CHAPTER 5

Lyons

1832–1836

The poetess Marceline Desbordes-Valmore lived in Lyons from 1827 to 1832. During her stay there she witnessed two important events. First, the 1830 Revolution, concerning which she wrote to a friend: 'Not a drop of blood, not a single calamity to lament. One thought sustained a hundred thousand souls. One voice cried to heaven, and heaven's justice now reigns supreme.' Her letter ended with the words, 'The colours of freedom are flying in every part.'[1]

Unfortunately, the political change wrought by the July days heralded no improvement in social conditions. During the autumn of 1831, the silk workers were reduced to poverty and even starvation. At the end of October, they were scouring the city for food, still peaceable and silent. Meetings took place and the workers were granted the slight increase they had requested. 'Jubilant cries were heard,' wrote Marceline. 'In the evening, those poor men lit fires as a sign of gratitude. They serenaded the authorities and the businessmen. Eight days later, their claim was rejected; they were laughed at. A manufacturer was stupid enough to point a pistol at one of the claimants, saying as he did so, "Here's your wage!" And then the flames rose in the heads and hearts of that formidable part of Lyons, and the insurrection began.'

> Politics played no role in that immense uprising. It was a hunger riot ... Women shouted as they threw themselves in front of the shots, 'Kill us! End our hunger!'
>
> [The workers and the people] have been the masters of Lyons for five days now, and order reigns as ever before. Amid the tocsin, drums, and gunfire, and the lamentable cries of the dying men and the women, we waited for the looting and burning to begin if they won. Nothing! Not a single brutal crime after the struggle ... Ten or twenty foolhardy soldiers of the National Guard opened fire ... Then everything grew

muddled and confused – women, children, in fact all the common people, who had gone over onto the side of the workers – they whose courage is all the more extraordinary for their being exhausted with hunger and in rags.

It was not until December 3 that the troops led by the Duc d'Orléans entered the city. 'I have seen this riot,' wrote Marceline, 'stamped out by guns and order, as they put it. Underneath, hunger and despair live on, whilst in the streets people come and go, visiting one another, buying things, giving presents. Things are just as they were. Only the dead have learnt their lesson. Those who survive have failed to see. It will happen again, perhaps more dreadful than before, for in the triumph of their despair and in their five days' reign, the people, whom they call the scum of the earth and the dregs, were sublime in their clemency, their discipline, and their generosity.'

The atmosphere remained tense. The insurrection had been stamped out, but hunger had not been appeased.

This suppression of a popular uprising was a great stroke of luck for Jémis Aupick and a turning-point in his brilliant career. Shortly after his arrival in Lyons, he was appointed Chief of Staff of the 7th Division and it was there that he served under the orders of the Duc d'Orléans. Aupick was an excellent organiser and his shining qualities were fully appreciated by his superiors.

In January 1832, the Lieutenant-Colonel decided to have his wife and stepson join him in Lyons, as Charles told Alphonse in his earliest known letter on January 9. After arriving in Lyons, Charles wrote again on February 1, to tell his brother all about the journey:

> We climbed into the stagecoach, and set off at last. In the first few moments, I myself was very out of humour because of the hand-muffs, water bottles, foot-muffs, men's hats, women's hats, pillows, blankets (lots of those), bonnets of every shape and size, shoes, fur-lined slippers, boots, baskets, preserves, beans, bread, napkins, gigantic poultry, spoons, forks, knives, scissors, thread, needles, pins, combs, dresses, skirts (lots of them), woollen stockings, cotton stockings, corsets all higgledy-piggledy, biscuits, and I can't remember what else.
>
> You can well imagine, dear brother, that I who am always active, always hopping from one foot to the other, couldn't move, and I could *scarcely* look out of the window.
>
> Soon I was happy again as usual. We changed horses at Charenton, and continued on our way. I can hardly remember now where we

stopped, and so I'll go on to the evening. With night coming on, I saw a very fine sight – it was the setting sun. That reddish colour contrasted strangely with the mountains which were as blue as the darkest pair of trousers. Having put on my little silk cap, I reclined on the back of the coach, and thought how travelling all the time would be the sort of life I'd enjoy very much. I'd like to write some more, but an *accursèd prose* forces me to end my letter here.

> Your little brother,
> Charles Baudelaire

At the beginning of their stay in Lyons, M. and Mme Aupick took up temporary residence on the Place Henri IV, now the Place Carnot. Charles was lodged a few minutes' walk away in a boarding house run by a young couple. Their few boarders went to the nearby Collège Royal. According to the system then in force, Charles, coming from a Paris school, was put up a year into *sixième* (first form) despite having spent only one term in *septième*. There were about forty-five pupils in his class and the new boy's marks were 'very mediocre', as he told Alphonse on April 1. Notwithstanding a slight improvement and a merit at the end-of-year prizegiving, his education in *sixième* was, as he himself admitted, 'very sketchy'.

The first-form master, Charles Bobet, was well known for his strictness and for the facility with which he inflicted punishments. After some parents had lodged a complaint, the school board set a limit on the number of impositions a pupil could be made to do in any given period. Bobet nevertheless gave young Baudelaire fifty lines for talking in class, to be handed in on Monday, August 6. 'Luckily', Charles told his brother in a letter, 'he forgot to ask me for them.' As usual, Charles promised to improve and to be less of a chatterbox; and to give more weight to his promise he added, 'I've just done my first communion.'

The ceremony took place on Sunday, July 8, 1832 in the college chapel. Baudelaire's memory of the event is not recorded, but the chapel itself stuck in his mind. In 1865, he wrote a letter to Sainte-Beuve from Belgium in which he mentioned 'that monstrous Jesuit style I'm so fond of, and which I really knew only from the chapel of the Collège de Lyon, which is made of variegated marble'.[2] For Baudelaire, this discovery of baroque architecture was one of the few things that would count in Lyons' favour.

At the end of the 1831–32 school year, having become a boarder in the Collège itself, Charles sent Alphonse the list of his marks in composition, asking his brother not to be too hard on him and pointing out how much time he had lost in preparing for his first communion. In fact, this aspect

of his education had been sadly neglected, to judge by a report from the
school inspectors: the chaplain was in poor health and as a result there was
a regrettable lack of religious instruction in the school. 'The word of the
gospels in his sermons – when they are given – carries no power of
persuasion nor strength of communication.'[3]

The inspectors were always full of praise, on the other hand, for Joseph
Noirot – an abbé whose philosophy lectures were attended by large and
enthusiastic classes. Baudelaire was too young to have been his student; but
Noirot's thought was disseminated by his pupils and books, and it was
Noirot, among others, who came to mind when, around 1860, Baudelaire
made notes for a study on 'L'Art philosophique':

> Lyons is a philosophical city. There is a Lyons philosophy, a Lyons
> school of poetry, a Lyons school of painting, and lastly, a Lyons school
> of philosophical painting.
>
> A strange town, bigoted and mercantile, Catholic and Protestant, full
> of mist and soot; ideas disentangle themselves in Lyons only with the
> greatest difficulty. Everything that comes from Lyons is painstaking,
> laborious, and indecisive. Abbé Noireau [sic], Laprade, Soulary, Chena-
> vard, Janmot. It's as if everyone's brain were congested.

In school, Charles was bored and very unhappy: 'It's filthy, poorly kept,
and untidy; the pupils are nasty and dirty like all Lyonnais. Out of five
Parisians in the boarding house, there are only two I could be friends with,
and even then the second one has spent nearly all his life in Marseille.'
Things did not improve with the end of the school year. On September 6,
he wrote sadly: 'I'm on holiday now, but it's just as if I weren't. They've
had the horrible idea of keeping me in school like the rest of the year. The
worst thing is that Papa promised we'd travel, but now he doesn't have the
time.' One wonders why Charles was not allowed to spend the summer
with his mother. The Aupicks had moved that July to the rue d'Auvergne
where they owned an apartment which Charles described as 'enchanting':
'We've got one of the finest views in Lyons and I'm not exaggerating. You
can't imagine how beautiful, how magnificent, and how beautiful [sic] it is,
how rich and green the hillside is.'

By October 15, 1832, Charles was a little more cheerful. He went up into
cinquième and was now allowed to wear the school uniform. Even the food
was good: 'I'm very happy to be at the *lycée*,' he told Alphonse on November
9. 'I'm quite certain that our ancestors didn't have in school the way we
do, jam, compotes, pâtés, pies, chicken, turkey, compotes [sic], and all the
other things I haven't eaten yet.'

Baudelaire's English master was Joseph Jackson, born in Lancaster in 1794. An official tour of inspection in June 1833 found Jackson's students reading 'Walther Scott' and answering questions in English. The teacher gave a satisfactory performance; but in the following years, reports were less favourable. In 1835, he was described as 'sickly' and lacking in energy. In 1836: 'This teacher may be familiar with his mother tongue, but he has neither the control nor the energy needed to make his pupils progress.' This was the master who first taught English to Baudelaire in November 1832. Having dropped the subject for a few months, Charles found it very difficult to start again and his work in other subjects suffered as a result: 'I daren't stop doing English, which takes up a lot of time, because since I started it once before and gave it up last year, I feel it would be a disgrace not to finish. But I'm very weak in my class this year [1834], and I really want to get back up to the level of those who were on a par with me last year.'[4]

In 1833, Charles spent the summer holidays alone with his mother. His stepfather was away at Compiègne with the army, still awaiting promotion, but proud to be serving at the side of the Prince (the Duc d'Orléans), 'dining at his table, living in the palace, and working with him at conference time'. This was how Aupick described his duties to a friend of his. He ended his letter with a comment which shows his affection for Charles: 'I found my wife in good health as well as my youngster who has just gone up into *quatrième*. He's a source of great satisfaction and will contribute to our happiness in years to come.'

The 1833–34 school year began well, despite a sprained ankle which prevented Charles from enjoying his latest pastime: 'Just think what a cruel torture that is for me – that little sprain which stops me dancing – I who never miss a single quadrille. And then during the holidays, I acted in a comedy! And I'm going to be acting again in a *proverbe*.'

As in 1832, Charles spent his holidays at school; but during one of those dismal Lyons summers (perhaps the summer of 1833), he met the little girl mentioned in the poem written down a few years later at Louis-le-Grand. The same incident is recounted in the short story, *La Fanfarlo*, which Baudelaire was to publish in 1847. His autobiographical hero, Samuel Cramer, one day in Paris meets the young woman (now enslaved to a husband), whom he had known 'in the vicinity of Lyons, when she was young, lively, playful, and more slender'. In an unsuccessful attempt to seduce her, he reminds her, as they sit in the Luxembourg Gardens, of the happy days they spent together: 'Do you still recall, Madame, the enormous haystacks we slid down so quickly, the old nursemaid, so slow in pursuit, and the clock so prompt to call you back under the eye of your aunt in the big dining room?'

At the end of the summer of 1833, Aupick brought back a '*phénakisticope*' for his 'youngster' – a toy which was a by-product of the latest experiments with light. Charles described the mechanism in great detail to his brother: 'Then you turn it, and you look through the little holes in the glass where you can see some very pretty designs.' This letter, written on November 23, 1833, also contained some more promises to work hard and win prizes. But the promises were not kept. On New Year's day, 1834, Charles admitted to Alphonse that he had become discouraged: 'How bored one gets at school – especially at the Collège de Lyon. The walls are so dreary, so grimy and dank, the classrooms so dark, and the Lyons character so unlike that of Parisians! But at last the day is drawing near when I shall be back in Paris ... and I hope that Mother and Father will follow close behind.'

Little did he know that his wish would not be granted so soon. Doubtless his parents wanted to send him to Paris, where the schools had a better reputation, but the family remained for another two years in Lyons – 'that city black with coal smoke'. Charles continued to waste his time. 'I've been weak-willed, cowardly, and idle,' he told his parents in a long letter on February 25, but 'I want to convince you that you should not despair of me.' Sure enough, on March 24, he was able to send Mme Aupick some good reports and asked her to show them to his father.

The Collège de Lyon was about to live through some of the most difficult days in its history. Just after the end of the Easter holidays, the silk workers rebelled and the school, finding itself between the rioters on the one hand and the forces of law and order on the other, came under fire from both sides. The headmaster, Bedel, drew up a report for the Minister of Education[5]:

> The insurgents began their insurrectionary movement last Wednesday on the 9th inst [April] at 11 in the morning. From that moment on, with communications interrupted, classes could be held only for the boarders. But what classes they were! taught to the sound of cannon and gunfire, whilst all the time the bullets fired from the neighbouring streets and houses struck the windows and flew into the classrooms ... Yesterday ... a sinister-looking band of men presented itself at one of the gates, crying out that they wanted the weapons they claimed we possessed. I opened the gate to four of their number, declared with the utmost conviction that the school had no weapons, and invited them to leave. I had just been relieved of this inopportune visit, when I received the

terrible news that a house standing hard by the school was in flames.
What could we do in that horrible situation? ...

Finally a pump arrived from the townhall ... But what made our
position more dreadful yet was that the troops posted at Les Broteaux
and at the head of the Lafayette Bridge mistook the workers on the roofs
for insurgents, and rained projectiles down upon them, so that for a
moment we found ourselves faced with the cruel choice of either being
killed or burnt alive. No, I believe there can be no position more horrible
for a man entrusted as I am with such immense responsibility. However,
with the extraordinary protection of Providence, we suffered no casual-
ties, though we were constantly picking up musket-shot and shrapnel
which had fallen in the courtyard, and, thanks to the quick-witted courage
which everyone displayed, this fine institution was preserved from the
blaze, and our schoolboys worked like men to extinguish the fire on the
neighbouring houses ... Today [April 11], the shooting continues. A
barricade has gone up in front of the school, and we are redoubling our
resolve, M. le Ministre, to brave fresh calamities, should they threaten.
Each one of us will remain at his post, vying to justify the confidence of
the Government.

Bedel continued his letter the following day at noon since no mail had
been able to leave the city. The workers had returned, as the headmaster
feared, demanding arms. 'Having remained outside as a sort of hostage, I
declared once more that we had no weapons, and prevailed upon them, as
did the Rector, to respect our establishment.'

Nothing at this hour indicates any end to this terrible crisis. Our boys
are mournful and dismayed. Fortunately, we have a few provisions in
the store-rooms so that refectory service can be maintained.

5 am
The Place du Collège has been evacuated. The troops are in control
of it. People are beginning to circulate again in the streets. Long live the
King!

I beg you, M. le Ministre, to excuse the haste and disorder of my letter.
I thought it my duty above all to inform Your Excellency of the events
which concerned the institution in my keeping. Every man has done his
duty.

On Sunday the 13th, peace had returned to the city. The boys were sent
home to their families whilst the most urgent repairs were completed. On
Friday, the school gates would open again.

These terrible days ended with repression more savage yet than in 1831. Marceline Desbordes-Valmore, who had returned to Lyons in March 1834, described events in a letter: 'six nights and six and a half days of terror, houses collapsing in flames, and the wretched temptation to look out of the window punished everywhere with death ... We found ourselves after this great calamity amazed or almost sad to be alive amongst so many victims.'

Marceline's words form a bitter contrast to Bedel's patriotic homilies, even more so in the poems she published in 1839 under the title, *Pauvres Fleurs*. Her compassionate indignation was such that one poem – the lament of a Lyons woman – could not be published until after her death. Even then, Sainte-Beuve was careful not to quote the last four lines:

> Les vivants n'osent plus se hasarder à vivre.
> Sentinelle soldée, au milieu du chemin,
> La mort est un soldat qui vise et qui délivre
> Le témoin révolté qui parlerait demain.*

Baudelaire would not have known this poem, but as an admirer of Marceline, he certainly read the Lyons poems of *Pauvres Fleurs*, as he wrote in his 1861 article, 'with the eyes of adolescence'. Indoctrinated at the Collège de Lyon by the party which stood for order at any price, he would have realised only much later that this had been a revolt of *misérables*, not of murderers. Though nothing is known of his reactions at the time, it is easy to guess that his opinions did not differ greatly from those of his headmaster and parents. When cholera reared its head the following year not far away in Vienne, Charles wondered in a letter if it would come and 'purge the city of Lyons'. But, he added, 'we haven't yet sunk that low.'

Aupick did not have long to wait for his reward. On April 29, he was promoted to the rank of Colonel. Had he not shown 'the greatest vigour' and acted with 'unfailing zeal and devotion'? When in 1857 Baron Lacrosse delivered the funeral oration in praise of his friend, his remarks contained more than a hint of unintended irony: 'As you can see, Messieurs les Sénateurs, each step in his career became a reward for a military action.'

Alphonse Baudelaire sent his congratulations. Mme Aupick wrote to thank him on June 30 and in passing on news about Charles described what might be called her son's procrastination:

---

* 'The living now no longer dare to live. / Standing like a sentry in the middle of the street, / Death is a mercenary who takes aim and delivers / The horrified witness who would talk the next day.'

On our return we were delighted to hear that Charles had performed miracles – he has been first or second out of fifty on each occasion ... He is far from being an ordinary child, but he's so frivolous, so light-headed, and loves playing so much! As for his heart and character, he leaves nothing to be desired. He is charming to be with, as sensitive as can be and very loving. The only thing for which he might be scolded is that he plays in class instead of working, and has got into the bad habit of always putting his homework off until the last minute. When you write to him, do say something to him about it. Tell him how important it is in life to do *what one has to do*, and that *always putting things off* is a fault which has very serious consequences.

The 'miracles' his parents were so pleased about were officially rewarded on August 31, 1834 – prize-giving day. Charles' name appeared five times among 'those who came closest to winning prizes'. It was a fairly good performance, though not exactly spectacular. Once again, Aupick was away at Compiègne and could not attend the ceremony.

On October 26, Charles entered *troisième*. His progress was 'fair', but by the end of the year, his good resolutions had come to naught. He was gated and, during her visit to the school, his mother accused him of ingratitude. The 'insult', as he called it, stung him deeply: 'I, ungrateful. Even if I hadn't made some excellent resolutions at the beginning of the year, that word alone would convert me.' (December 21)

Apart from detentions, and those 'accursèd lines', there were also other forms of punishment. Charles recorded the following exchange:

> Pupil: Hey, friend, lend me your homework so that I can copy it.
> Master: You, Monsieur, half-an-hour of *arrêt*.
> Pupil: Ah! the rat!
> Master: For muttering, Monsieur, you'll do a double *arrêt*.
> Pupil: But wh...
> Master: Triple.

To be in *arrêt*, as Charles told Alphonse, meant 'being stuck like a statue against a wall or a tree, and freezing (in winter) for as long as the tyrant demands it'. These were the complaints of the student who incessantly talked in class. Nonetheless, his marks were good – 7th, 4th, 4th, 3rd and 2nd – and at the end of the 1834–35 school year, to his father's delight, he won five 'merits' and a second prize in drawing.

One of Charles' friends, Henri Hignard, described the schoolboy as he knew him in 1835: 'More refined and distinguished than any other of our classmates, one could imagine no more charming adolescent. We were bound by strong affection, which our common tastes and sympathies sustained – a precocious love for fine works of literature, the cult of Victor Hugo and Lamartine, whose poems – our favourites – we used to recite to one another during those monotonous breaks in the playground and those dreary walks in the quartier. We even wrote some verses, which, thank goodness, have not survived.'[6]

After the summer holidays, which he probably spent in Lyons with his parents, Charles went up into *seconde* in October 1835. His literature teacher was well-thought-of by the inspectors, though chided for 'presenting his pupils all year long with nothing but *Homer* for Greek explication'.

When sending Christmas greetings to his brother that December, Charles said nothing of his masters. 'As for myself,' he wrote, 'I'm quite well. I'm big and fat, and I'm very bored. But I'm working and swotting up, and I've been fourth, second, tenth, first, second, sixth, and first – first twice, and second twice: I think that's quite a good showing.' Charles was also hoping 'to find a new source of pleasure' by learning to skate. In September, a friend of the Colonel had offered to teach him how to swim, but the Rhône was too icy; and he still had not been hunting, because, as he told Alphonse, 'my Father is virtually locked up the whole time ... and Mothers are scared of gunpowder. You will probably be the one who has the honour of introducing me to the pleasures of that particular sport.'

At the end of 1835, he was still expecting to leave for Paris in time for the next school year. Mme Aupick had told him that she would be going up to the capital with him next Easter – 'a little maternal trick', as he said, to make her son work hard up until the last moment. But then the joyful news arrived on January 9 that Colonel Aupick had been appointed Chief of Staff for the First Division based in Paris.

Apart from the chapel at the Collège de Lyon, that city later evoked in Baudelaire's mind only dark and bitter memories, which might explain his rather unfair remarks on the Lyons school of painting.[7] Lyons meant the smell of soot, the closed society in which his parents found few friends, the prison life of school and even 'that sinister wailing' which descends in the evening 'from the black Hospice des Antiquailles'[8] – the lunatic asylum which stood on the Fourvière hill. Having been cheated of his holidays and shut up in a city that was built in the shadow of madness and smoke, Charles must have thought that the Paris school he was about to enter would be idyllic by comparison.

CHAPTER 6

Louis-le-Grand

1836–1838

Aupick left for the capital in January 1836. A few weeks later he was joined at the luxurious Hôtel des Ministres by his wife and stepson. Charles was to start school at Louis-le-Grand on March 1.

Full of enthusiasm for his stepson's abilities, Aupick took him along to see the headmaster, Pierrot, and introduced him with the words, 'Here's a present for you – a pupil who will do honour to your school.'[1] Despite the Colonel's recommendation, the new boy was placed in *troisième*, the reason being that the level of Paris schools was thought to be higher than that of their provincial counterparts and, as Charles himself pointed out, 'they start mathematics one year early in Paris.'

The absence of any other letter from this period suggests that Charles settled in, got down to work and lost none of his days out. In fact, the list of prizes awarded on August 17, 1836 is a clear indication that he had been wrong to worry about coming bottom of the class. He made a very good showing indeed:

> 1st prize for Latin verse;
> 2nd prize for Greek unseen;
> 3rd *accessit* for Latin prose;
> 3rd *accessit* for Greek prose;
> 3rd *accessit* for drawing;
> 1st *accessit* for English language.

No less than six awards! And to crown his achievement there was a first *accessit* (or merit) for Latin verse in the *Concours général*. The subject which candidates had been asked to develop was 'Philopemen at the Nemean Games'. Charles turned out an eloquent eulogy of the Greek hero, inspired perhaps by the example of his own stepfather.[2]

In October, he went up a year into *seconde*. Thanks to an article published in 1917 by a former history master at Louis-le-Grand, something is known of Baudelaire's school reports.[3] One should bear in mind, however, that these require a certain amount of interpretation: 'Term reports under Louis-Philippe,' wrote the history master, 'listed each pupil's religious duties, assessed his morals, conduct, character, work, progress and position, and gave the total number of pupils in the class.' The usual comments were apparently not always remarkable for their originality: *morals* were usually 'good'; *conduct* 'satisfactory', 'erratic', or 'frivolous'; *character* 'irresponsible', 'weak', 'orderly', 'docile' or 'bizarre'; *work* 'inadequate' or 'sustained'; *progress* 'mediocre' or 'noticeable', 'normal', 'slow', or sometimes 'nil'.

Charles' main teacher during his first year at Louis-le-Grand was Achille Chardin – the man responsible for the Juvenal edition which Alphonse had given his brother in 1833. Chardin's comments on his pupil in December 1836 were as follows: 'Much frivolity; not very conversant with ancient languages; too lax to correct his faults.' A few months later, he noted: 'Very unpredictable and inconsistent in his work. An erratic thinker; lacks vigour in composition, but has made noticeable progress.'

It seems extraordinary that Chardin was able to say of a boy who had just won four awards in Latin and Greek that he was not very conversant with ancient languages. The explanation lies in a letter Charles wrote to his mother after the 1837 Easter holidays. He claimed to be discouraged by a feeling that he was not very good at Latin verse any more, adding that that was why he had let things slide in that subject. 'The teacher went so far as to say in that way he has, "You must work at your Latin verse; you're severing a tie with the future." That made me laugh. In the end, thinking how little time was left before the *concours,* I got down to some hard work again, and now he's delighted with my poems – not so much for me as for himself of course, because I've noticed that if I write bad verse, he's very unhappy, but if I neglect Greek or anything else, he hardly points it out at all.'

In short, Pierrot and Chardin saw Baudelaire as examination fodder – one of the prize pupils who were expected to bring glory to the school. 'Preparatory lectures,' wrote the former history master, 'were held between 10 and 11 in the evening, three or five times a week.' The pupils – boarders or dayboys – were divided into groups of fifteen or eighteen. 'Teachers were specially recruited from the Ecole Normale, and even the headmaster himself participated in the teaching of Latin to the cream.'

Baudelaire was placed in one of these groups of supposedly 'extra-gifted' children. Towards the end of June 1837, he and his classmates rebelled and asked to be excused from the evening lectures. In response, the headmaster put them all in detention. Charles decided to capitulate, as he told his mother: 'For me, it's another reason to work hard, in all subjects if I can, so as to avoid any unpleasantness with the headmaster, because he was furious about our request ... Anyway, it might be a long time before he lets us go out ... So now I'm prevented from seeing him [Aupick] until God knows when because of this M. Pierrot who thinks it odd that anyone should want to sleep an hour extra instead of trying to win some good places for him in the *concours*.'

Mme Aupick, who always wanted her son to be first in everything, had the satisfaction of seeing him presented that August with four awards in Latin and Greek. Also, the results of the *Concours général* were in. Baudelaire had come second in Latin verse and won the second *accessit* for the unseen. The headmaster and Chardin were delighted. The latter, in fact, kept a copy of some of Baudelaire's prize-winning verse. It was a piece entitled *The Exile*. In 1864, two of Chardin's former students published it in an anthology along with other work produced under the guidance of M. Chardin.[4] The subject was drawn from Chateaubriand's *Génie du christianisme* and concerned a Frenchman forced to flee from the Terror. Living with his family in a boat, he sails from one bank of the Rhine to the other, turned away each time he tries to land, but wishing still to breathe the air that has passed over the fatherland.

Charles' *maître d'étude* (roughly equivalent to an English housemaster) was J.-B. Riton. He seems to have been fair in his treatment of students, but he and Baudelaire were unable to establish any good rapport: 'Undisciplined character. His behaviour is more than frivolous. His work, as a consequence, is not what it should be.' Shortly after writing this, he noted against Baudelaire's name in the register, 'Still very unruly.' When he returned to school in October 1837, Charles entered *Rhétorique* (the Lower Sixth). The year began well. He was top of the class. But then when out riding one day with his stepfather he fell from his horse and was sent to the infirmary. According to Baudelaire, all he had was a bad bruise on the knee; but the school doctor and surgeon – those 'two old fools' – thought otherwise and diagnosed 'an aqueous dropsy'. Exasperated at having to languish in bed wasting his time, Charles managed to obtain a second opinion from the doctor of Aupick's regiment, who confirmed the patient's diagnosis.

Nevertheless, for a month and a half, he was confined to the infirmary, where he kept up with classes, wrote compositions and did a lot of reading. His mother came quite often to keep him company and he enjoyed a visit from his stepfather. There was also one of his masters, M. Rinn, who was very popular with the boys and who had acquired an excellent reputation as a teacher. The headmaster asked and obtained for Rinn the Cross of the

Légion d'Honneur, which, in those days, was still meted out with some discretion.[5]

Rinn was to exert a considerable influence on Baudelaire's education. Mme Aupick first heard of him when Charles wrote from the infirmary in December. He wanted to read Victor Hugo's *Last Day of a Condemned Man*, probably so that he could discuss the book with his teacher when they met in two days' time. It was the first of many meetings. 'Very often,' he told Aupick on July 17, 1838, 'I go and talk with M. Rinn, my teacher, about the books I've read, about ideas to do with literature, Latin writers, about what's being done today, and what to do with one's life, etc. When he realised I was very keen on modern writers, he told me he'd be glad if one day he could do a long analysis with me of a modern work, to show me what was good and what was false in it, and that I should go then to his place one Thursday. M. Rinn is an oracle to me.' Baudelaire had finally met a teacher he could like.

Dupont-Ferrier – the history master who recorded some of Baudelaire's marks – unfortunately says nothing about the Louis-le-Grand school magazine. No copy has ever come to light, though its existence is confirmed by a letter written many years later by one of Baudelaire's contemporaries: 'We all worked together on *The Chameleon* – a paper as silly as they come which was published in 1837 in the *rhétorique* section of Louis-le-Grand. Some of the *rhétoriciens* who worked on that chaotic paper became remarkable men, poor old Baudelaire among them...'[6] Baudelaire was probably one of the editors or must at least have contributed an article to *The Chameleon*.

On Monday, December 18, 1837, Charles was finally released from the infirmary. Two days before, he had imparted, or rather proclaimed the good news to Mme Aupick, and begged her to come and collect him on Sunday morning at 7.30. 'Ah! I assure you I need to see you and Papa for a whole day. I need to get back into life. I'm mad with delight. Tomorrow evening, I'll be back in the study room, reimmersed in the paternal home, and hard at work.'

For the first few months of 1838, he stuck to his resolution. In March, he told his brother that he was top in Latin discourse, but added, 'The closer I come to the day when I'll have to leave school and start on life, the more scared I become; for then I shall have to work, and seriously, it's a terrifying thought.' In the meantime, Baudelaire was causing his teachers some concern: Rinn and his colleague both found him inventive, but unwilling to use his abilities; and his personality was appreciated even less by the *maître d'étude*, who noted: 'Falseness and lying. Attitude occasionally cavalier and shocking in its affectation.' The history master, who, unlike his colleagues, had had a lively career as a journalist and writer before becoming a schoolmaster, was just as indignant: 'This pupil seems convinced that History is perfectly useless,' and he confined Baudelaire to the school for a whole month. Charles had asked his mother to send him Hénault's *New Chronological Summary of History*, but did he ever read it? Even as late as 1864, he admitted to Mme Aupick that he knew absolutely nothing at all about history and hated it anyway.[7] One should note, however, that none of his classmates received any awards in this subject in 1838.

At the beginning of June, the Aupicks went to take the waters at Barèges. Charles was sad to see them leave and wrote long letters. In return, he received only a few and complained to his parents about their slowness in writing. He described his time alone in the following way: 'I read books which they let me take from the library, I work, I write verses, but now they are awful. Despite all that, I'm bored. The main reason is that I don't see you any more. There are other reasons too. The conversations we have at school are usually quite pointless and very boring; and so I often stop going around with the friends I'm close to, sometimes to go off and walk by myself, sometimes to go and try out other groups and other conversations. My frequent absences shocked my friends, and so as not to vex them any more, I returned; but conversation with them is never anything more than chit-chat. I prefer our long silences, from 6 o'clock to 9 o'clock, when you are working and Papa is reading.'

Baudelaire apparently quite enjoyed his solitude after all and only rarely appreciated visits from friends of the family. Claude Ramey, the sculptor friend of François Baudelaire, was an exception. Mme Jaquotot was less favoured: when she invited Charles to come and spend the day with her, he inventively informed her that he was confined to the school for the rest of the year. M. Emon was treated with caution – perhaps Baudelaire sensed that future relations with him would be far from amicable.

On July 17, 1838, writing to his stepfather, Charles gave a long account of the school trip to Versailles. After dinner and a tour of the palace, the King had arrived and conducted the boys to the theatre, where 'he apologised for being unable to offer us a spectacle to provide a fitting end to the day'. For Charles, the high point of the visit was the magnificent collection of paintings – historical scenes by Horace Vernet and Henri Scheffer, and Delacroix's *Battle of Taillebourg*. 'All the paintings from the time of the Empire, which are said to be very fine,' he told Aupick, 'often appear so monotonous and so cold. The people in them are often stacked up like the trees or extras in an opera. It's probably ridiculous for me to be speaking in this way about the Empire painters who have been praised so highly.

Perhaps I'm talking gibberish; but I'm just recording my impressions' (a cautious remark for the benefit of his conformist reader). 'Perhaps also,' he went on, 'it's the result of reading *La Presse*, which praises Delacroix to the skies.' This, then, was Baudelaire's first encounter with Théophile Gautier who had just reviewed the 1838 Paris Salon and included in his review a retrospective eulogy of Delacroix, mentioning the painting Baudelaire saw at Versailles, as well as those he was later to admire: *The Death of Sardanapalus, The Massacres of Scio* and *Algiers Women*.

On August 3, Charles wrote his fifth letter to Mme Aupick (he was numbering each one). He urged her to stay at the spa as long as possible so that the Colonel might take full advantage of the healing waters. Charles had talked to a man just back from Barèges where he had seen Mme Aupick on horseback looking very happy. 'Ah! you're so lucky to be having fun,' he wrote. 'With me, it's just the opposite; I'm so bored that I cry without knowing why.'

The empty days at the end of the school year were filled with reading – modern writers only. Eugène Sue, he told his mother, bored him to tears. 'Only the plays and poems of Victor Hugo and a book by Sainte-Beuve (Volupté) gave me any pleasure. I'm completely disgusted with literature; and in fact, ever since I've been able to read, I've never found a work that pleased me entirely, which I could enjoy from beginning to end, and so I've stopped reading. I'm stuffed full. I don't talk any more; I think of you. At least *you* are a perpetual book.'

In the same letter, Charles expressed his fears about school work: 'No matter how philosophical I try to be, telling myself that success at school means nothing, that it proves very little and so on, the fact remains that prizes bring a great deal of pleasure.' His fears were unfounded. At the prize-giving on August 21, Baudelaire appeared among the winners four times, with two first prizes in French discourse and Latin verse. He was rewarded with copies of Villemain's *Mélanges* and the same critic's course on eighteenth-century literature.

There was all the more reason to rejoice since he was soon to join his parents in the Pyrenees, travelling down from Paris on his own. 'Here I am, forced to behave like a man,' he wrote, 'to take care of myself, keep account of expenses, see the sights, climb hills, and walk about Toulouse.' Charles decided to stay at the inn in Toulouse rather than spend the night with Aupick's friend, General Durrieu. He had no desire 'to chat and be pleasant'.

Once at Barèges, he spent a fortnight running about and going horseback riding. 'The day was filled with visits, and we went back only to sleep,' he later reported to Alphonse.[8] From Barèges, he journeyed with his parents to Bagnères and then on to discover the Western parts of the country: Tarbes, Auch, Agen, Bordeaux, the Gironde estuary, Royan, Rochefort, La Rochelle, Nantes, the banks of the Loire (which 'scarcely deserve their reputation'); then back to Paris via Blois and Orléans. By mid-October, he was back at Louis-le-Grand for his last year at school.

Bagnères, 'the most beautiful region in France', had provided Baudelaire with the Lamartinian and Hugolian theme of the poem later to be known under the incorrect title of 'Incompatibilité'. The lake in question is probably Escoubous, above Barèges:

> Tout là-haut, tout là-haut, loin de la route sûre,
> Des fermes, des vallons, par-delà les coteaux,
> Par-delà les forêts, les tapis de verdure,
> Loin des derniers gazons foulés par les troupeaux,
>
> On rencontre un lac sombre encaissé dans l'abîme
> Que forment quelques pics désolés et neigeux;
> L'eau, nuit et jour, y dort dans un repos sublime,
> Et n'interrompt jamais son silence orageux.*

The schoolboy who was composing these 'Flowers of Good' felt no such 'incompatibility' – neither between himself and nature, nor between himself and his parents. Having turned seventeen and with a good classical education, he had now discovered the mountains, rivers and shores of France. One senses his happiness. He had also discovered modern art in the paintings of Delacroix, and modern literature in the poetry of Victor Hugo and in Sainte-Beuve's novel, *Volupté*. From within the school, he followed literary events in the outside world. Recent developments in science also attracted his attention – magnetism, theories of evolution and other new domains.

Nothing seemed to cloud his affection for his mother and stepfather. His letters bear not the slightest hint of dissimulation; spontaneity was the dominant feature of his character – a trait which would soon be making life difficult for him.

The only aspect of this refreshingly open young man which might cause

---

* 'Way on high, higher still, far from the steady path, / From farms and valleys, beyond the hills, / Beyond the forest and carpets of green, / Far from the last grass and grazing flocks,

One finds a sombre lake hemmed in by the abyss / Formed by a few desolate and snowy peaks; / The water, night and day, sleeps there in sublime repose, / And never breaks its stormy silence.'

mild concern is his procrastination (nothing unusual in that) and, more especially, his feeling of distaste or disgust. The word *dégoût* often appears in his letters. Sometimes he gives no reason for this feeling, suggesting thus that it was a general *ennui*, a part of his very being.

On his return to school in 1838, he would meet with active constraints which would force him to discover his true identity. Without these, he might have been no more than happy.

CHAPTER 7

Expulsion from Louis-le-Grand

1839

'Now I'm in *philosophie*. It's a terrible class, and I've had a lot of trouble getting through. Once again, the headmaster wanted to make me repeat the year. – I got out of it.' This is how Alphonse heard about his brother's successful start to the school year. Mme Aupick had received the following report: 'I'm delighted with all my teachers. Everything is going well. As for the prep master, that's different. I can't stand him – and neither can anyone else.'[1]

Why such revulsion? In the two reports he wrote on Baudelaire, the master in question, Achille Carrère, comes across as a good, impartial judge:

> 4th term, 1838. Baudelaire. Well-behaved in religious duties. Good conduct. Character a little unusual and sometimes bizarre, but, following my advice, has made a laudable effort to behave like everyone else. Works steadily and with no lack of enthusiasm.

> 1st term, 1839. Baudelaire. Well-behaved in religious duties. Good conduct in quarters. Had much to do to achieve normal and acceptable standards of behaviour. He has succeeded, which seems to me very commendable. Works, but a little erratically.

Before putting his name to this satisfactory report, Carrère had second thoughts and jotted in the margin, 'See page 4'. There, he recorded his disappointment: 'For a few days now, Baudelaire has started behaving in a very peculiar manner again. I have been forced to inflict a number of very severe penalties on him. It is unfortunate that this pupil, who has fallen into line since the beginning of the year, now delights in setting a bad example.'

Baudelaire's philosophy teacher was Valette, described by a junior colleague as the 'veteran of a vanished order of philosophical things'.[2] At the end of the first term of the 1838–39 school year, he was well-pleased with his students. Baudelaire earned a 'quite good'. In the second term, 'Baudelaire does not take enough care over his compositions. Many ideas. Not much order.'

As might be expected, Baudelaire's achievements in the sciences fell short of the mark. In elementary mathematics, fourth term of 1838: 'Conduct fair; his work has been fruitless, to judge by his unsatisfactory answers.' First term of 1839: 'Work mediocre. A weak student.' In physics, his reports were no better: 'Very inattentive; his work is hopeless.' 'He does not work and talks in class when he thinks no one is looking.'

Baudelaire was busy with other things. One of his classmates in '*philosophie*', Emile Deschanel, who, as a dayboy, was able to bring his friend the latest novels, plays and poetry of Lamartine, Hugo, Musset, Vigny and Sainte-Beuve, later spoke of his friendship with the poet in an article published in 1864 by the *Journal des Débats*. In 1866, he expanded on this article in a lecture delivered in Paris. His lecture notes have never before been published.* They are particularly interesting in that they contain an early poem by Baudelaire of which, until now, only a few verses were known. Commenting on the poem, Deschanel wrote: 'Baudelaire had not yet begun to compose "Flowers of Evil", but, curiously enough, one can already detect a few Byronic affectations of premature decay: "N'est-ce pas qu'il est doux, maintenant que nous sommes / Fatigués et flétris comme les autres hommes..."† Schoolboys of eighteen!' Baudelaire's poem also reveals traces of his brief romance in Lyons and prefigures part of *La Fanfarlo*, in which the hero meets the little girl with whom he used to play near Lyons.

In mathematics, Baudelaire wrote poems. In art, he apparently 'does not do as well as he could'. He has 'ability', but his work is 'weak'. Baudelaire rather gracefully got his own back on one of his art masters – Léon Cogniet – in the *Salon de 1845*, describing him as 'one of those whose talent is complete in its moderation and who defy criticism'.

Baudelaire claimed to have an enemy in the person of the *sous-directeur* – the man responsible for school discipline – who deprived him of his days out for misbehaving in art. 'The *sous-directeur* I used to make fun of a lot last year,' he explained to his mother, 'took the earliest opportunity this year to punish me, and when I was being noisy one day, he said that I'd been tormenting him for three years, and that he'd ask that I be given some exceptional punishment...'

During the holidays, Charles wrote to his brother to wish him a happy

---

* See Appendix 2, p. 383
† 'Is it not a sweet delight, now that we / Like other men are tired and worn...'

Christmas. Full of good intentions, he added: 'I want more than anything else to have a good year in *philosophie*, I'm so afraid of having to take it again, because at home they think I'm very young. It seems I don't look at all like a philosopher. I got out of doing *rhétorique* again by the skin of my teeth. No matter how hard I try to look serious, my Father and Mother persist in seeing me as a child. Defend my interests and convince them that I'm the very spirit of reason. Make them think of me as a proper Cato, perfectly capable of studying Law.' At the time, 'studying Law' was more often than not a euphemism for having no particular vocation in mind.

On February 26, 1839, he sent a letter to Colonel Aupick which suggests that he was indeed a little confused about what to do:

> I am writing to ask you for something that will surprise you very much. You promised me fencing and riding lessons. Instead of that, I'd like to ask you, if you agree, if it's possible, and if you don't mind, for a *tutor* . . .
>
> I don't need help with following the class itself, and what I would ask from my tutor would be some extra philosophy – the things that aren't covered in class, in other words, *religion*, which is not included in the University syllabus, and Aesthetics or the philosophy of art, which our teacher will certainly not have time to demonstrate to us.
>
> The other thing I'd ask him for would be some Greek – yes, I'd like him to teach me Greek, which, like everyone else who learnt it in school, I don't know at all, and which I'll be hard put to learn all by myself when I'm swamped with so many other things . . .
>
> Wouldn't that fit in with what I want to be – science, history, philosophy – who knows? Studying Greek might make it easier to study German . . .
>
> I'd choose a very distinguished young teacher who has recently come from the Ecole Normale and who is known at Louis-le-Grand – M. Lasègue. If he couldn't give me lessons, I'd rather do without a tutor . . .
>
> Lately I examined myself, and asked myself what I knew – a rather large number of things on every subject, but vague, confused, lacking order, each detrimental to the other – nothing clear, definite, or systematized, which amounts to saying that I know nothing – even though I'm about to enter life. I need some store of very precise knowledge.

It seems unlikely that Charles won his case. The moods of apprentice philosophers were not the sort of thing to soften a parent's heart – especially when one's parents, like the Colonel and Mme Aupick, had not had the benefit of an easy childhood.

Two months later, on April 18, 1839, a letter arrived for Colonel Aupick from the headmaster of Louis-le-Grand. It ran as follows:

Monsieur,

This morning, your son, having been called on by the *sous-directeur* to hand in a note which one of his classmates had just passed to him, refused to surrender it, tore it up and swallowed it. Summoned to my office, he asserted that he would suffer any punishment rather than divulge his classmate's secret. When urged to explain himself for the sake of his friend whom he was exposing thus to the most regrettable suspicions, he answered me with sneers and impertinence which I cannot allow myself to brook. I am therefore sending back to you this young man who was remarkably gifted, but who has ruined everything with his very bad attitude which has undermined school discipline on more than one occasion.

Charles Cousin, who knew Baudelaire in his days at Louis-le-Grand, claimed to know the reason for Baudelaire's sudden and untimely disappearance. 'Here it is in Latin . . . or rather, no, if you want to know, read Virgil's second *Eclogue*.' It is quite possible that the boy who loyally swallowed the note had some homosexual tendencies – for lack of anything else – and that the note in question was compromising in that respect. Cousin, however, had reason to bear Baudelaire some ill will. (It should be remembered that when Cousin was writing in the 1870s, male homosexuality was still considered a serious crime.)[3]

The headmaster's letter is clear enough. The episode of the secret message was the straw that broke the camel's back. Baudelaire had been tormenting his teachers for some time and this flouting of the rules was the first manifestation of what he was later to call '*la conscience dans le mal*' – awareness in evil – and the first apparition of what Edgar Allan Poe described as 'the Imp of Perversity'.

Expelled in the morning, Charles was back home by the afternoon. From there, he wrote at once to the headmaster, stating that his mother's grief had revealed to him the full extent of his own affliction. The piece of paper he had refused to hand over was, he claimed, of virtually no importance and he apologised profusely for having laughed at the headmaster's suggestion that his classmate might thereby become an object of suspicion.[4]

The letter was never sent. Perhaps Colonel Aupick took it with him in person when he went to see the headmaster. An arrangement was reached by which Charles would enroll as a dayboy at the Collège Saint-Louis. There, according to the attestations of attendance attached to his *baccalauréat* certificate, he followed the philosophy course given by the school and maybe also had private lessons with the tutor he had mentioned to Aupick – Charles Lasègue.

On May 12, 1839, the insurrection organised by Barbès and Blanqui broke out in Paris. 'During those days of turmoil, Mamma was in a horrible state of anxiety,' Charles told Alphonse. 'It was all I could do to make her see things a little less bleakly ... Papa left on horseback with the officers and the general [Pajol], and then he was away for such a long time that there was a bit of commotion. He slept at the Carrousel' – probably the guard house at the Palais des Tuileries.

The rebellion was brought under control the following day. As in Lyons in 1832, the stamping out of insurrection brought promotion to Aupick and, a fortnight later, the Colonel and his wife were able to leave for Bourbonne-les-Bains in the Pyrenees – a thermal spa where the Colonel was hoping for some relief from his wounded leg.

Charles had been taken in by the parents of his tutor, the Lasègues. He was to take his meals at a nearby *pension* run by Mlle Céleste Théot on the north-west corner of the square in front of Saint-Sulpice. 'When I was introduced to Mlle Céleste,' Charles told his mother, 'the old spinster received me with lowered eyes, and a put-on conventual air, and an unctuous tone. I was quite surprised. A friend from Louis-le-Grand whom I found at the same table familiarised me with the ways of the house, and we had a good laugh about it. He told me that in that house, ideas of religion and legitimism are so strangely bound together that all you have to do is hate the Government for people to think you're a Catholic. It's all very entertaining. I told the story to M. Lasègue, and we both laughed about it.'

Charles seems to have adopted the house style to judge by a letter his friend Henri Hignard sent to his parents on July 31:

> I spent the day last Sunday with Baudelaire, whom I found to be as kind and generous as before. His parents are at Bourbonne-les-Bains, and he's staying here with a tutor. It seems his father has a good chance of becoming a general before long. We strolled about all evening on the boulevards and in the Tuileries ... he has turned out a very handsome chap, but what pleases me much more is that he's become studious, serious, and religious.[5]

Left to himself for a time, Charles thought of entering for the national competitive examination in philosophy, but failed to prepare for it. Perhaps he felt discouraged, perhaps also the outside world was interfering with his studies. Never before had he enjoyed so much freedom. In order to reach the Collège Saint-Louis from the *pension* under the towers of Saint-Sulpice, one had to pass through some rather shady districts. In particular, there was the huddle of one-night cheap hotels in the vicinity of the school, generally held to be places of debauchery. In July 1839, the headmaster sent the superintendent of the *quartier* 'to recall to decency a young man whose unbridled licentiousness knew no bounds'. According to the police report, the outrage had been committed in a boarding-house in the rue Monsieur-le-Prince, which looked onto the college quads. (The young man in question had been kissing his mistress in the window.)

On July 16, 1839, Charles wrote a mournful letter to his dear mother, wishing he could see her and telling her how uncomfortable he was living with 'strangers'. He claimed that M. Lasègue and his mother were 'constantly nagging' him, and complained about their 'triviality' and about the 'perpetual gaiety' that reigned in their house. The picture had obviously changed. Halfway through June, Charles had written of his complete satisfaction with the new arrangement, and of the warm and gracious welcome he had received from the Lasègues. But now, everything was going wrong: 'At school, I didn't bother much with classes, but at least I worked at something. When I was expelled, that shook me up, and I still kept busy some of the time at your house. Now there's *nothing, nothing*, and it's not a pleasant, poetic sort of indolence. No; it's a sullen, stupid indolence...' Here was confirmation of the anxiety that an attentive observer of the boy might have noticed fleetingly in the spring and summer of 1838. This was the crack that let in *ennui* and awareness of sin – the crack in which the first 'flowers of evil' were beginning to grow.

The remedy seemed to be to take the *baccalauréat* as soon as possible. Charles decided to start revising everything on July 16 – so as to be ready by the beginning of August ... From Bourbonne-les-Bains, Aupick gave permission for Charles to sit the examination. On August 13, the official newspaper printed the nomination of Aupick to the rank of brigadier-general. 'I've just seen a good piece of news,' wrote Charles, 'and I've a good one to announce. This morning, I read your nomination in the *Moniteur*, and I'm a *bachelier* as of yesterday afternoon at 4 o'clock. My papers were rather mediocre, except for Latin and Greek – very good – and that's what saved me.'

His results were mediocre indeed – even more so than he admitted, though one should note that examiners at the time had very high standards. His *baccalauréat* certificate shows the following marks:[6]

1st series	Greek authors	Pass
	Latin authors	Pass
	Rhetoric	Pass
	Composition	Quite good
2nd series	Ancient history	Pass
	Modern history	Weak
	Geography	Weak
3rd series	Philosophy	Pass
	Mathematics	Pass
	Physics	Pass

Comparing Baudelaire's marks with those of seven classmates, one discovers not a single 'Very good'. 'Quite goods' are rare and only one student managed a 'Good' in Rhetoric.

In one of his autobiographical notes, Baudelaire wrote: 'Expulsion from Louis-le-Grand and the story of the *baccalauréat*.' There does indeed seem to have been a little story connected with Baudelaire's examination, as Asselineau told Théophile Gautier after the poet's death:

> One detail you might not know about is that Baudelaire was given the *baccalauréat* as a special favour, and was treated as a simpleton. He was recommended as such to M. Patin by a Mlle Céleste who ran a boarding-house in the rue du Pot-de-Fer for devout Catholic students and who was apparently well in with the examiners.
>
> I was told about this by Baudelaire himself.

Like so many others, Asselineau may have fallen prey to the legend. Baudelaire was certainly not regarded as a 'simpleton', but it is not impossible that Mlle Céleste recommended her boarder – such a nice boy – to M. Patin, the Latin examiner, who, interestingly enough, lived nearby in the rue Cassette.[7]

When he congratulated the General on his promotion and announced that he was now a *bachelier*, Baudelaire was merely remarking on a coincidence. From the summer of 1839, Aupick's career and Baudelaire's life would follow divergent paths.

Baudelaire's school years appear to have been perfectly normal. Anyone familiar with the adult poet might have expected him to curse his loss of freedom, but the young Baudelaire made no stand against the education system. He seemed to be the loving son of pleasant parents. He tried hard to fit the mould his elders thought appropriate and, until the final step, mainly succeeded in doing so. The occasional irregularity in his work and results were apparently not uncommon either. With the exception of those who thrive on examinations, what child would not prefer to play? and how many schoolboys could do equally well in every subject?

One is struck nonetheless by the unpredictability of his effort. Whilst wishing all the time to please his parents, he seems to have suffered long periods of indifference. The boy had no ambition. His idea of taking the national examination in 1839 simply reveals a desire to make his mother happy. His own pride was not at stake; failure caused him no shame. Only a few traces of remorse are apparent and then only with regard to his parents.

All in all, one senses that the whole affair was of very little interest to him. He studied because his family required him to study. The education he received and absorbed was not the sort he would have chosen for himself. His dissatisfaction with other teachers becomes clear when he finds in M. Rinn someone to talk to instead of a trainer, or when he asks his stepfather for a tutor with whom he can really study – philosophy, religion, aesthetics, Greek – and not the sort of Greek that was learnt in school. There was in Baudelaire the pupil a man protesting at the goals and methods of the school system.

Baudelaire nevertheless accepted the system because the ties that bound him in youth provided comfort and security. The fear of leaving school and embarking on adult life reared its head early in 1838: it was not a pleasant thought that a career had to be chosen, that freedom was enjoyed only to be lost, that the certainties of clear obligations to family and school would vanish.

His various reports suggest that he must often have tried the patience of his masters and friends with his 'strange' behaviour. No doubt that was a way of expressing his sense of superiority and disdain for an order which he needed but considered artificial. Baudelaire sensed that once the constraints of school and legal infancy were removed, he would never be able to fit in with adult life.

The possibility that there was an element of unconscious motivation in the behaviour which led to his expulsion and the postponement of his first encounter with the adult world should not be discounted. The failure this represented also meant rebellion and rejection of the institution; but with that impulse which came so naturally to him, he immediately wiped the slate clean and returned to the narrow path – from Louis-le-Grand to Saint-Louis and the *baccalauréat* a few weeks later. Throughout his life, whenever he tried to shake off the humiliating shackles of the *conseil judiciaire*, he would act in a similar fashion – even on the day he vowed to beat up Ancelle in front of his wife and children.

The laugh with which he greeted the headmaster's insinuation – that nervous laugh, triggered off both by the deep unconscious and by the absurdity of the suggestion that he was exposing his friend to regrettable suspicions – seems to betray the sudden and unexpected presence of the abnormal. In that laugh, one might detect the opening of a crack and the severing of ties with the conventional world.

PART THREE

THE CHOICE OF A CAREER

CHAPTER 8

The Latin Quarter

August 1839–May 1841

With the departure of his landlord from Paris on August 15, 1839, Charles was left without a place to stay. He turned to his stepfather, and was probably advised to go home and await his mother's return from Bourbonne-les-Bains.

It was then that the question of a career was brought up for the second time. Earlier inquiries had met with evasive replies: 'You were kind enough,' he wrote to the General around June 18, 'to ask me what plans I have. Well, you're right, I am making plans; you know I'm always making plans, and that that's the way my mind is. Sometimes I dream up a future for myself, and then I'm full of things I want to discuss with those who love me. But let me put that off until another day.'

Ten days after obtaining his *baccalauréat*, Charles anxiously confided in Alphonse:

> So now my final year has ended, and I'm going to start a different sort of life. It seems a curious thing, and of all the worries that beset me, the greatest is the choice of my future career. It's already preying on my mind and tormenting me, especially since I don't seem to have a vocation for anything, just a lot of different inclinations that gain the upper hand at different times.

There must have been a few animated discussions in the family, with the stepfather advocating civil or military service, and the stepson not daring to divulge his passion for poetry, reluctant even to contemplate life in the diplomatic corps or in the army. Perhaps it was Alphonse who came up with the ideal solution: Charles would enroll in the School of Law – that gateway to so many careers in the public or private worlds. Why the family decided against the Faculty of Arts, which also led to various careers, is impossible to say. Maybe Charles would have been a more regular attender, though that too must remain in doubt.

Charles had been released from boarding school at the age of eighteen
and was already leading a 'carefree life', as he put it later in some autobiographical notes.[1] But this *vie libre* was also a *vie libertine* which left its
mark on the young man: even as early as November 1839, Baudelaire was
suffering from gonorrhoea.

This first mark of manhood may well have been a surprise gift from Sara
(or Sarah), the girl who was known as Louchette (from the verb, *loucher* – to
squint). Ernest Prarond remembered Sara when transcribing his memories
forty-five years later for Eugène Crépet:

> Jeanne was the woman he loved or favoured after India. Before India,
> there was the Jewish girl. I've forgotten her name (Sara, I think).
> Baudelaire called her Louchette. She lived in the rue Saint-Antoine. One
> day, Baudelaire took me along to the Eglise Saint-Louis on the pretext
> that he wanted to have another look at a *Pieta* by Delacroix. On the way,
> we asked a concierge, whose lodge gave onto a narrow passageway, if
> we could see Mlle Sara. She was not in. Baudelaire was quite keen on
> her at the time we knew him, but he was left with few fond memories
> of the girl [Prarond offers as proof of this the poem, 'Une nuit que j'étais
> près d'une affreuse Juive'*], and one should not do Jeanne the discourtesy
> of thinking that the poem . . . 'Tu mettrais l'univers entier dans ta ruelle'†
> was written for her.[2]

Charles informed his brother of the embarrassing accident. By a stroke
of good luck, Alphonse happened to have a pharmacist friend at Fontainebleau who specialised in the treatment of sores and secret diseases.
This friend, Denis-Alexandre Guérin, was entreated to offer advice to the
younger brother, and also to loan him the money he would need to procure
the appropriate medicine. Guérin obliged and may also have referred his
young patient to one of the hospital doctors he had worked with before
setting up shop. The prescription must have included Guérin's own patent
'balsamic opiate for recent and inveterate diseases'. This particular remedy
often produced stomach cramps, which might explain part of the following
letter, which Baudelaire sent to Alphonse on November 20, 1839:

> I'm so bored that I'm going to start working. I want some pleasure
> out of life, and I'm hoping that work will provide it. I want to become
> independent as soon as possible, by which I mean spending *my* money,
> the money that men will give me in exchange for a pleasure or service I

---

* 'One night as I lay next to a horrible Jewess'
† 'You'd set the whole world at your bedside'

shall provide them with, and I want to attain that goal in whatever way I can.

In the meantime, since it's your money I'm spending, accept my grateful thanks.

I've paid for my medicine. The aches and pains have disappeared, and so have most of the headaches. My sleep is much better, but I have ghastly digestion problems, and a small, continual discharge that causes no pain whatever. On top of that, I have such a wonderful complexion that no one suspects a thing...

I'm going to bury myself in science now. I shall take everything up again – law, history, mathematics, and literature – and forget all the world's pettiness and rubbish by reading Virgil. That at least is free and doesn't cause aches and pains. Farewell, and many thanks.

Charles

The first three subjects on the self-imposed syllabus were probably neglected in favour of the fourth. His one and only passion now was literature, a passion which inspired him, on February 25, 1840, to ask Victor Hugo for an audience:

Monsieur,

Some time ago, I saw a performance of *Marion de Lorme*.[3] The beauty of the play enchanted me so much and made me so happy that I keenly desire to make the author's acquaintance and thank him in person ... I feel (maybe this is pride) that I understand all your works...

I imagine, Monsieur, that with you I should learn a whole host of good and great things. I love you as one loves a hero or a book, or any fine thing, with pureness of heart and without self-interest ... I tremble at the thought that I shall make a fool of myself; and yet, Monsieur, since you yourself were young once, you surely understand the love a book inspires in us for its author ... At nineteen, would you not readily have said as much to a writer whom your soul held dear – M. de Chateaubriand, for example? All this is not sufficiently well expressed, and my letter fails to give the true measure of my thoughts; but I hope that, having been young like us, you will guess the rest, that my taking such a novel and uncommon step will not offend you too much, and that you will deign to honour me with a reply. I confess that I shall await it with extreme impatience.

Even in this early letter one can see a prefiguration of future relations between the two poets. Baudelaire's admiration hides a subtle threat: I shall be to you what you were to Chateaubriand. The latter – Hugo's childhood hero – was no longer at the height of his fame and seemed to be living on beyond his time. The *Mémoires d'outre-tombe*, read by a select few, was published only after the author's death.

Did Hugo answer the letter or receive his young admirer? Baudelaire's autobiographical notes mention as his 'first literary connections' Ourliac, Gérard de Nerval, Balzac, Le Vavasseur and Delatouche. Only after his 'Voyages to India' and 'Return to Paris' does the name of Hugo appear: 'Second literary connections: Sainte-Beuve, Hugo, Gautier, Esquiros.' Baudelaire was later to write that he occasionally met Hugo in the company of other writers, though Ernest Prarond remembered his friend making a few rare visits to Hugo's house between 1842 and 1846.

Some of these meetings with older writers may have been no more than chance encounters in the street or in the home of a friend. Hyacinthe de Latouche, a friend and adviser of Balzac and George Sand in their early days, was the author of a curious novel about a hermaphrodite – *Fragoletta* (1829); Gérard de Nerval could easily be found wandering the city streets or ensconced in cafés. As for Ourliac, he seems to have been quite close to Baudelaire, who may have been drawn to him by the fact that Ourliac had worked with Balzac; but little is known of their friendship, or even indeed about Ourliac himself who was a talented writer of farces, humorous articles and short stories.[4]

Baudelaire's first encounter with Honoré de Balzac was also recorded by Prarond, though he was unable to say whether it occurred before or after the voyage to the East: 'I can tell you how Baudelaire introduced himself to Balzac without a go-between. He told me about it himself the day after it happened. Balzac and Baudelaire were walking along in opposite directions on one of the quais on the Left Bank. Baudelaire stopped in front of Balzac and started to laugh as if he had known him for ten years. Balzac also stopped as if he had found a long-lost friend; and those two great minds, having recognised one another at a glance and exchanged greetings, went on their way together, talking and arguing, delighting one another, each trying in vain to astonish the other.'[5] This extraordinary meeting of minds may well have taken place before or after the voyage. It may also have been dreamt up by Baudelaire himself.

The other names on Baudelaire's list – Sainte-Beuve, Gautier and Esquiros – certainly belong to the period following the voyage. Le Vavasseur, on the other hand, was an earlier acquaintance.

When he first met Baudelaire, Gustave Le Vavasseur was, like him, studying law. (Unlike him, he soon obtained his degree.) Le Vavasseur was living at the time in a 'hall of higher studies' on the Place de l'Estrapade, in the heart of Bohemian Paris. Generally referred to as the Pension Bailly,[6] it was a tall, austere-looking building, which boasted its own amphitheatre and a large garden which stretched away towards the Eglise Sainte-Geneviève, where the townhall of the fifth arrondissement stands today.[7] It was, noted Eugène Crépet, 'a sort of middle-class boarding-house ... to which many provincial families were then sending their sons. Without causing any scandals, the boarders led the freest and most joyous life imaginable' – not, however, the sort of *vie libre* to which Baudelaire was referring, for this was freedom measured against the repressive life of the *collège*, where days began and ended with the drum. The master of the house was Emmanuel Bailly, co-editor of the Catholic newspaper, *L'Univers*, and founder of the first Saint-Vincent-de-Paul lectures. Bailly's numerous activities prevented him from devoting much time to the Pension, and he left the running of it to his wife and the educational side to his son's very young tutor, Marc Trapadoux – later to become a friend of Baudelaire.

Since Bailly and his wife hailed from the north of France, the majority of their boarders also came from that area. Other regions were represented too, Normandy and Brittany in particular, and there was also a small group of Belgians and Poles. The French students belonged for the most part to the landed gentry, fiercely Catholic and proud of their heritage. Discipline was fairly strict, but the boarders were always able to slip away from their supervisors to enjoy what Paris had to offer in the evening. To judge by the recollections of the *pensionnaires*, their escapades were nothing to be ashamed of and their lives in the big city were positively angelic by today's standards. Their behaviour was an understandable reaction to homesickness. A few days after arriving, Ernest Prarond sent this sorry message to his 'dear parents': 'I've been with M. Bailly for three days now, and that makes three days in which I haven't had much fun.' Further on, he asked his mother to tell him 'at what intervals I should get my hair cut. I'm not joking. I have to know when my hair gets too long.'[8] Baudelaire would very likely be able to provide him with a mirror, or the opinion of a lady-friend.

'Tall and strong, fair as a Barbarian and as hairy as a Merovingian, upstanding and honest beyond the call of duty, noble-hearted and passionate', Ernest Prarond had come to 'study law' at the Pension Bailly.[9] There, he became a friend of Le Vavasseur and of a younger man, also from Normandy – Philippe de Chennevières, a future *directeur* of the Beaux-Arts. Chennevières had the distinction of having already written a novel and several short stories, which he later published under the title, *Contes normands, par Jean de Falaise* (a pseudonym derived from the name of his birthplace). Baudelaire would write a very flattering review of this book in 1845.

Le Vavasseur, Prarond and Chennevières formed the nucleus of a group of friends which included 'the two volunteer day-boys of the Pension, always running from room to room in search of a friendly chat'. One of these unofficial *pensionnaires* was Baudelaire; the other was Jules Buisson. Born in Carcassonne in 1822, Buisson enrolled at the School of Law, but apparently never completed his studies. His real passion was painting and engraving: Buisson's works had appeared in the Paris Salon, and he later illustrated several books published by the three friends.[10]

Another regular visitor to the boarding house was a former classmate of Baudelaire's at Louis-le-Grand: Auguste Dozon, yet another 'law student' who never completed the course, though he was later admitted to the diplomatic corps and became a leading expert on Balkan languages. Dozon lived with his parents in a building which also housed a bookstore with a reading room. One of the bookseller's five children – Antony – received from Baudelaire, perhaps via Dozon, the sonnet which begins, 'Vous avez, compagnon, dont le coeur est poète...'. The same poem, with 'chère soeur' instead of 'compagnon' also appears in the album of Baudelaire's half-sister, Félicité.[11]

Le Vavasseur, Chennevières and another law student, Louis de La Genevraye, all came from Normandy, hence the name that was given to their little group – L'Ecole Normande. All the other members of the 'Norman School', living in or on the periphery of the Pension Bailly, came from different parts of France; but the group was united by its camaraderie and by that taste for technical virtuosity which was soon to find its most spectacular expression in Théodore de Banville's precocious poems, *Les Cariatides*, of 1842. In a poem to Prarond, Le Vavasseur described how the craze for poetry took hold of them:[12]

> Ce fut vers ce temps-là, que d'une amour fervente,
> Nous aimâmes aussi la Muse et sa servante;
> Nous nous mîmes à quatre à hanter la maison.
> Vous et moi, mon ami, Baudelaire et Dozon,
> Nous aimions follement la Rime; Baudelaire
> Cherchait à l'étonner, plus encor qu'à lui plaire.
> Avait-il peur de voir, par un soin puéril,
> L'originalité de sa Muse en péril
> Et son indépendance était-elle effrayée

De suivre en cette amour une route frayée?
– Peut-être, parmi ceux d'hier et d'aujourd'hui,
Nul ne fut moins banal ni moins naïf que lui.*

In the essay on Le Vavasseur published in 1861, Baudelaire remembered how, on more than one occasion, upon entering his friend's room, he caught him 'almost naked, standing perilously balanced on a pile of chairs' – a vivid illustration of his passion for *'tours de force'*. 'A difficulty for him has all the seductive charms of a nymph. Obstacles delight him. Witticisms and puns excite him. There is no music more pleasing to his ear than a double, triple, or multiple rhyme.' These were marvellous exercises for those who, like Baudelaire, practised their scales to perfect a higher art.

The two virtuosi wrote a little song together to the air of Béranger's *Roi d'Yvetot*, ridiculing Casimir Delavigne and the man he was supporting as a candidate to the Académie Française – Jacques Ancelot. Delavigne and Ancelot represented the *aurea mediocritas* in literature, and were therefore thoroughly despised by the young poets. The song was dropped in the letterbox of the satirical newspaper, *Le Corsaire*, and appeared on February 1, 1841. The Académie would not have been amused. It elected Ancelot to the vacant chair later that month.

Le Vavasseur left his own written portrait of his young collaborator and friend:

> He was dark, and I was fair, of medium height, and I quite short, thin as a hermit, and I as fat as a friar, sleek as an ermine, and I as scruffy as a poodle, dressed like an English embassy secretary, and I like a pedlar; he was reserved, and I was noisy, libertine out of curiosity, and I was good out of idleness, he was pagan by revolt, and I was Christian to conform; he was caustic, I indulgent; he racked his brains to poke fun at his emotions, and I let them both jog along together like a pair in hand.

While Baudelaire was making friends and acquiring undesirable habits, General Aupick had had little time to devote to his family. Having been appointed Commander of the Second Infantry Brigade in Paris, he was put

---

* ''Twas about that time that with fervent devotion, / We also loved the Muse and her maidservant; / The four of us started frequenting the place. / You and I, my friend, Baudelaire and Dozon, / Were madly in love with Rhyme; Baudelaire / Sought to amaze her more than to please her. / Was he childishly afeared to see / The originality of his Muse imperilled, / And was he, so independent, scared / Of pursuing in this passion a well-trodden path? / – Perhaps, among those of present and past, / There was none less banal or less naive than he.'

in charge of troops at Fontainebleau under the orders of the Duc d'Orléans. In September 1840, the General returned from manoeuvres to find that his stepson had decided to abandon his studies. Charles was eventually made to consent (with extreme reluctance) to return to Law School and to do his articles in the practice of a solicitor – probably Maître Jaquotot, a friend of the family.

Charles attended neither school nor practice. Come November, he was staying with Alphonse at Fontainebleau. This was probably meant to keep the boy out of bad company – and away from the General: in spite of her love for both husband and son, Mme Aupick was finding it more and more difficult to keep the peace. Baudelaire was seen during his stay in Fontainebleau by a guest of Alphonse; many years later, this guest recorded his first impressions of the poet: 'A tall young man with a distracted gaze, listless and seeking solitude. Even then, Charles Baudelaire was covering entire pages with easy, elegant verses on the first subject that came to his mind.[13]

On December 15, Charles and his friend Le Vavasseur witnessed the ceremony marking the return of Napoleon's ashes from St Helena 'We remained heroically perched on a grandstand in the freezing cold,' remembered Le Vavasseur. 'We saw the procession pass by – "The first light, the second light," etc.... but we felt that they had laid on the local colour a little too thick (retreat from Moscow, and all that). And we arrived that evening, frozen to the bone ... at the home of Mme Aupick who warmed us up at her fireside, and seemed to us to be kinder than ever.' Somewhere in the long procession of troops, the friends would have noticed the Second Infantry Brigade, led by General Aupick, who perhaps had given his stepson two free tickets. Le Vavasseur recounted the event in fourteen pages of stirring verse entitled 'Napoléon'. The poem, printed at Emmanuel Bailly's printing house, was not, however, a homage to the Emperor, but an attack on that 'remorseless tyrant'. Like Philippe de Chennevières, Le Vavasseur was a devout monarchist and, in 1848, the former members of the Ecole Normande, in the face of popular revolution, would show themselves to be fierce opponents of the new republic.

As usual, Charles took his time in writing to his brother and half-sister. He finally did so on 24 or, more likely, December 31, 1840. After thanking his hosts for their 'magnificent hospitality', he cynically told Alphonse: 'I think you might be rather glad to hear how I spend my days in Paris. Since you sent me back here, I've seen neither school nor solicitor, and as a result there have been complaints that I didn't turn up very often. But I'm postponing a general reform in my conduct until 1841.'

Charles went on to offer Félicité some music as a New Year's gift. Alphonse was given the following sonnet, 'which I've just composed and which might make you laugh':

> Il est de chastes mots que nous profanons tous;
> Les amoureux d'encens font un abus étrange.
> Je n'en connais pas un qui n'*adore* quelque *ange*
> Dont ceux du Paradis sont, je crois, peu jaloux.
>
> On ne doit accorder ce nom sublime et doux
> Qu'à de beaux coeurs bien purs, vierges et sans mélange.
> Regardez! il lui pend à l'aile quelque fange
> Quand votre *ange* en riant s'assied sur vos genoux.
>
> J'eus, quand j'étais enfant, ma naïve folie
> – Certaine fille aussi mauvaise que jolie –
> Je l'appelais *mon ange*. Elle avait cinq galants.
>
> Pauvres fous! nous avons tant soif qu'on nous caresse
> Que je voudrais encor tenir quelque drôlesse
> A qui dire: *mon ange* – entre deux draps bien blancs.*

After transcribing the sonnet, Charles added, 'Perhaps that might divert my sister.' 'Pervert my sister' would have been a more accurate expression of his intent. Doubtless Félicité was not allowed to see the poem, or if she was, both it and the letter would have been examined as curious artefacts which bore the telltale signs of mental derangement. These verses, so different from those that Charles had earlier sent to his 'dear sister', are remarkable in two ways. With their bizarre mixture of the sacred and the profane, and their casual, superior tone, they remind one of Pétrus Borel and the more eccentric members of the Petit Cénacle of the 1830s. Secondly, there is the fact that Charles very politely sent the poem to Alphonse, whereas it was obviously meant to be read by Félicité, who had a somewhat

---

* 'There are some sinless words we all profane; / Lovers indulge in strange excesses with their praise. / There is not one who does not *adore* an *angel* / Who, methinks, arouses little envy in those of Paradise.

That name, sublime and sweet, should be bestowed / On purest hearts, undefiled and free from stain. / Look there! some smut is hanging from her wing / When she, your *angel*, sits laughing on your knee.

When I was a child, I had my innocent fling / – Some girl as wicked as she was fair – / I called her *my angel*. Her boyfriends numbered five.

Poor fools! we thirst so much for their caresses / That even now I'd like to hold some hussy / Whom I might call *my angel* between the spotless sheets.'

restricted sense of humour. Charles was already the Poet, making wonderful use of the complex possibilities of juvenile civility, or incivility. The sonnet, of course, was to be viewed in the light of his venereal confessions, which Alphonse had perhaps mentioned to his wife. In any case, this provocative poem was not the sort of New Year's gift that would have found favour with Alphonse the magistrate.

At the beginning of 1841, 'painfully surprised' at his younger brother's renewed appeal for money, Alphonse asked him to place in his fraternal hands a full account of all his debts. Charles obliged with a detailed list of the sums he owed to tradesmen and friends. Once Alphonse had added his own advances, the debit column showed a frightening total of 3,270 francs. This prompted Alphonse to make the following annotation: '120 francs for 3 waistcoats. That's 40 francs a waistcoat. They only cost me between 18 and 20 francs and I'm colossal.' Alphonse was obviously unaware of his brother's taste in waistcoats, unlike Ernest Prarond, who remembered seeing him 'coming down the stairs in the Pension Bailly, slim, his collar open, a very long waistcoat, cuffs intact, holding a light cane with a small golden knob, and with a supple, slow and almost rhythmical step'.[14]

With cruel and cynical precision, Charles apprised his brother of the details concerning his debt to La Genevraye, one of the members of the Ecole Normande: '210 francs to Delagenevraye, one of my friends (an old debt), which went to clothe a girl, abducted in a house...' The sentence has two possible meanings. Either Charles had taken a prostitute (*fille* can denote a whore as well as a girl) from a house of ill repute in order to set her on the path of virtue, or else he had rescued a spotless maiden from the clutches of a heartless mother. The girl in question was probably Sara.

In answer to Charles, Alphonse went through the list debt by debt, and came to the conclusion that with a salary of 1,500 francs he was in no position to finance his younger brother's follies and mistresses. He accused Charles of ingratitude. Had not the General raised him as his own son? Charles should confess all his sins and pay off all his creditors. 'Think carefully about what you should do. You have already diminished the General's affection for you, and, in my eyes, that is very bad. You are causing your mother bitter grief, and you will make her future life very unhappy.'

On Monday, February 1, Charles was at the solicitor's office. He scratched a few lines on a piece of scrap paper:

> You wrote me a harsh and humiliating letter. – *I want to pay myself* what I owe my acquaintances.

As for the tradesmen, since I can't manage on my own, I *beg* you to pay off two of them – the two that are in a hurry – a shirtmaker and a former tailor of mine whom I still owe 200 francs and who *must* have the money by tomorrow, Tuesday. I owe the shirtmaker the same amount. – If you get me out of this, I'll manage the rest, without Mother and Father knowing about it. – If you don't bail me out, I'll really be in for it tomorrow.

Alphonse wrote back the same day. He was of course reluctant to anger the General by helping Charles out behind his back. He therefore offered to make a full confession for him, so as to draw the General's fire. He also promised to arrange a meeting of all his brother's creditors in order that some satisfactory way of paying the debts might be found.

For the following six weeks, no correspondence remains; but the epilogue of Baudelaire's first financial drama is contained in the minutes of the next meeting of the board of guardians. Three thousand francs' worth of debts were paid out of the boy's income. No doubt he also had to face the General's fire and fury, and his mother's tearful reproaches.

Calm seemed to settle on the household for a time. Aupick had been appointed Commander of the Officers' Training School on March 1, 1841. But on April 19, a letter from the General to Alphonse signalled the start of hostilities that would be the everlasting despair of Mme Aupick:[15]

My dear Monsieur Baudelaire,

The time has come when something must be done to prevent the complete and utter ruin of your brother. I am at last acquainted, or almost, with his situation, his ways and his habits . . .

In my opinion, and in that of Paul [Pérignon] and Labie, it is imperative that we save him from the slippery streets of Paris. There is talk of sending him on a long sea voyage to either of the Indies, in the hope that, with this change of scenery, removed from the bad company he keeps, and with all that he would have to study, he might hold fast again to the truth, and return to us a poet, perhaps, but one at least whose inspiration springs from better sources than the sewers of Paris.

The letter shows that Alphonse had failed to have a word with the General as promised. But someone had betrayed Charles: Aupick's friend, Edmond Blanc, who had connections in the Ministry of the Interior, may well have had the student tailed by a plain-clothes policeman.

Despite the General's desire to keep the scheme a secret, Charles got wind of the planned voyage. He told Alphonse, around April 27, of his imminent departure and received in reply a long-winded, pompous letter which took as its text the promises of childhood, the errors of the past and the glittering possibilities of the future: 'Think how proud your mother was of your achievements at school, and how your prizes displayed in the bookcase bore witness to your abilities. You scorned your achievements, and you sold your prizes. If I were you, I should hasten to renounce my past behaviour ... and impress upon others that, though I had experienced a few moments of waywardness, and though I was led astray by wicked people ... who sully the fair name of friend, I might still, by dint of work, good conduct, and a sincere desire to become a man of merit, bring happiness to my mother who has suffered so much, and to the General who loves you as his son, and to that brother who guided your first steps ...

This edifying sermon, of which the passage quoted is just a sample, produced a sarcastic sneer on the face of the heartless delinquent. On May 4, 1841, Aupick wrote once again to Alphonse:

My dear Monsieur Baudelaire,

The voyage overseas calls for an outlay of 4,000 francs (3,000 for the outward and homeward journeys as a passenger, and approximately 1,000 francs for essential minor expenses, the journey to Bordeaux and the return to Paris). The destination will be Calcutta. The duration of the voyage, about one year. The captain seems to be just the man we need.

Aupick considered that the sum in question should be borrowed from Charles' capital. It would therefore be necessary to convene the board of guardians. The ship would sail on the 15th. 'We shall summon Charles on the 7th or the 8th, so as to put him on the coach on the 11th. There's no time to lose.'

My wife is very keen that Charles should know nothing of this meeting of the board of guardians, so please do not mention it to him.

That is where we stand at the moment. Our temperaments clashed. Come as soon as you can.

Yours truly,
General Aupick

The ship was delayed and, probably after another altercation with the General, Charles was sent out to Creil, to the home of Aupick's friend, Dufour. In the neighbouring *château* lived 'a lady whose hands are white and who speaks French', as Charles informed his mother. This was the Mme Hainfray who had taken care of Caroline at the time of her miscarriage in 1828. The sixty-year-old widow had a room made up for Charles and served him his favourite dishes – onion soup and bacon omelette. Baudelaire's only other contacts in Creil were 'retired innkeepers, *nouveau riche* builders, and women who look like concierges'. These were probably people he met in the street or in one of the rare cafés of the little town.

Mme Hainfray was kind and Colonel Dufour full of concern, but Charles was brooding and thinking of his future. Only another eleven months and he would come of age – no more guardians and plenty of money. But there was no one to hear his plans and ambitions. Meanwhile, in Paris, stepfather and brother – the army man and the magistrate – were putting their heads together. In preparing the next meeting of the board of guardians, the Aupicks replaced friends from the first marriage (Naigeon, Julliot and Ramey were dead, and the Duc de Praslin was sick and dying) with friends of Alphonse: Paul Pérignon, counsel of the Conseil d'Etat, and Jean Labie, who had handed his solicitor's practice over to Ancelle in 1832. Pierre Zédé, first engineer in the navy, and Edmond Blanc, a top civil servant, were friends of the General. In order to ensure that six members were present at each meeting of the board, as required by law, Aupick would later call on two other friends, Louis Emon and Théodore Olivier, Ramey's son-in-law. These two former officers, both from the Ecole Polytechnique, were to play an important role in Baudelaire's life.

Aupick gave Captain Saliz the 5,000 francs for food and maintenance on board, and left Charles with 500 francs to prepare for the voyage and to meet any unforeseen expenses. On June 14, 1841 – the ship had sailed on the 9th – the guardians, 'confident of the eminent wisdom and prudence of M. and Mme Aupick', authorised a loan of 5,500 francs from the capital.

One of our regrets must be that we could not attend the meeting to which Charles was summoned in May, when the General, Alphonse and Paul Pérignon tried to force him to acknowledge his transgressions, to give undertakings and, in particular, to give his assent to a long and dangerous voyage.

These three years – 1839-1841 – were decisive in Baudelaire's life, as Jean-Paul Sartre and, after him, Marcel Ruff have pointed out. 'These were the years,' wrote the latter, 'of high spirits and light-hearted songs, of walks by the riverbank and first contacts with literary life.'[16] They were Baudelaire's brightest years, a period which he always remembered with delight, as he wrote much later in the essay on Le Vavasseur. But they were also the years in which the 'split' occurred to which Sartre attached so much importance in his essay on Baudelaire, basing his remarks on the following observation of the very conservative Jules Buisson: 'Baudelaire was a very delicate soul,

very refined, original, and tender, but his weak and feminine mind split at
its first encounter with life.'[17] With all due respect to Buisson, the 'split'
was a fortunate accident and the warning signs had begun to appear a little
earlier than that. One need only think of the schoolboy's mysterious
inertia and procrastination. Before leaving school, Baudelaire had dreamt of
following in the footsteps of Lamartine, Victor Hugo, or the Sainte-Beuve
of *Joseph Delorme*. As a poet, he practised above all the plaintive elegy and
the lyrical ode. After August 1839, he made a vital decision – a decision
that touched at once the realms of psychology, morality and poetry. He
saw that in the territories occupied by his predecessors the pickings were
poor and that rather than discover new horizons he would have to explore
a deeper vein. This he would find only within himself, at that point in the
psyche where Eros meets death, where evil germinates. That was the end
of the fine bourgeois ambitions other people had nurtured for him, as
Mme Aupick confessed to Asselineau in 1868: 'When Charles achieved his
successes at Louis-le-Grand, and when he completed his studies, [the
General] had glorious dreams of a brilliant future for him. He wanted to
see him reach a high position in society – it was by no means an impossibility,
since the General was a friend of the Duc d'Orléans. But how dumbfounded
we were when Charles declined all our offers of help, when he wanted to
strike out on his own and become a writer!' A writer! What a terrible waste!
Mme Aupick's confusion and distress make it possible to imagine the
atmosphere of those critical months. Baudelaire himself seemed to bear out
his mother's foreboding in one of the most beautiful poems of his youth –
a poem inspired by Sara:

> Je n'ai pas pour maîtresse une lionne illustre;
> La Gueuse de mon âme emprunte tout son lustre.
> Invisible aux regards de l'univers moqueur,
> Sa beauté ne fleurit que dans mon triste coeur –
>
> Pour avoir des souliers elle a vendu son âme;
> Mais le Bon Dieu rirait si près de cette infâme
> Je tranchais du Tartuffe, et singeais la hauteur,
> Moi qui vends ma pensée, et qui veux être auteur.*

His affair with Sara, his illness, the experience of evil, the will to incrimi-

---

* 'The mistress that's mine is no illustrious courtesan. / The wench takes all her lustre
from my soul. / Invisible to the eyes of the mocking world, / In my wretched heart alone
her beauty blooms –

Her shoes she got for the price of her soul; / But God would laugh if with that hussy / I
acted the Tartuffe and put on haughty airs, / I who sell my mind and would a writer be.'

nate himself and the desire to be a writer, the creation of a new artistic credo – all these were part of the same phenomenon. Baudelaire was not to be a mere writer, but a poet – one whose poetry would draw its very power from evil:

O fangeuse grandeur! sublime ignominie!*

As Sartre observed, the cliché 'He deserved a better life' could never be applied to Baudelaire. The poet deserved and was determined to deserve the life he had.

* 'Oh! sordid greatness! sublime disgrace!' (Last line of the poem, 'Tu mettrais l'univers entier dans ta ruelle')

CHAPTER 9

Voyage to the Indian Ocean

June 1841 – February 1842

'Voyages to India. My first adventure, a dismasted ship. Mauritius, the Ile Bourbon, Malabar, Ceylon, Hindustan, the Cape. Happy excursions.'[1]

Baudelaire's autobiographical notes are not entirely accurate. Whatever he said or wrote, and whatever he led other people to relate, Baudelaire was never in Malabar and never visited Ceylon or Hindustan. True, General Aupick and the board of guardians sent him down to Bordeaux so that he could board a ship bound for Calcutta with ports of call at Mauritius and the Ile Bourbon (Réunion); but the reluctant traveller refused to go further than the Ile Bourbon and sailed for Bordeaux on a different ship.

'It's time to put an end to the legend of Baudelaire touring India,' wrote Ernest Prarond. 'The truth is that, having been put on the ship against his will, Baudelaire jumped off as soon as he got to India ... Perhaps he obligingly let the general public believe those tales of lengthy peregrinations in fabulous lands because it gave him an air of mystery, and made him seem like a man who had returned from far-off places. He never spoke to us anyway about those trips. On his return, he said only a few words about calling at Mauritius or the Ile Bourbon. Did he go any further than that? I don't think so.'[2] Prarond had known Baudelaire before he sailed for the East and was not quite so easily deceived by the legend.

Here then is the true story. Having arrived in Bordeaux at the end of May or at the very beginning of June 1841, Charles probably had himself directed to the home of Captain Saliz. The Captain seems to have given him room and board until the embarkation. 'Captain Saliz is an admirable fellow,' he wrote to his mother. 'He's kind, imaginative and well-educated.'

On June 4, Saliz collected his mailbag from the post office at one o'clock, took the helm of the *Paquebot des Mers du Sud*, and began to steer his ship carefully up the estuary of the Garonne and Gironde rivers. On the 9th, the ship was anchored off Richard, under sail and ready to put to sea, and then at Royan, on the northern tip of the estuary. 'Today there is a moderate

74

breeze, east-north-easterly, weather is fine and seas are calm.' That same day, before the pilot left the ship and the ship weighed anchor, Charles scribbled a few lines to his mother: 'I don't want you to write me letters like your last one. They have to be gay. – I want you to eat well and be happy when you think that I am happy, since it's true, or almost. As soon as I can, I shall write to the General' – a far cry from the 'Papa' of happier years.

The tone of this letter makes it sound as though Baudelaire was setting off on a pleasure cruise, rather than on a disciplinary voyage. But was he being sincere? And what could he possibly find to say to the General when they were both still at loggerheads with each other? As far as we know, Charles wrote neither to his mother nor to his stepfather during the trip. Aupick himself was rather pleased: 'Finally,' he told a friend a few days after the embarkation, 'with willpower and effort, I achieved my goals. Charles is no longer exposed to ruin on the streets of Paris. He has come round to our way of thinking ... At the point of his departure, Charles wrote us a good letter. It's our first assurance of the beneficial effects we're hoping for from this great ordeal.'[3]

According to one of the local papers, Le Mémorial bordelais, the Paquebot des Mers du Sud was 'a fine ship with three masts and a poop', a capacity of 450 tonnes, 'lined, riveted and pegged with brass'. Captain Saliz had as his first mate his brother-in-law, Baron Charles Duranteau. The ship took on only a handful of passengers. 'It goes without saying,' wrote Charles Hérisson, 'that living conditions on board [for the passengers, at least] were not exactly comfortable, and that Baudelaire, with his refined tastes, must have suffered as a result. But the lack of privacy, and unavoidable contact with "other people" was, as we know, even more disagreeable to him.' The thought of Baudelaire sailing along in the muggy air of the African coast is indeed a little incongruous.

The voyage proceeded smoothly until the ship reached the waters off the Cape of Good Hope. Just as it rounded the Cape and sailed into the Indian Ocean on August 8 at midday, a whirlwind, a real hurricane in its variations, a tornado in its duration and violence, took the ship by surprise and broke off the masts. The storm continued all day and all night. The following day, an American sailing ship, the Thomas Perkins, offered the shipwrecked crew some replacement rigging.

'Baudelaire showed a good deal of sangfroid in those terrible circumstances,' according to an anonymous account published on September 13, 1867 by La Chronique de Paris. 'As it rounded the Cape in the open sea, the ship was lashed by a horrendous blast of wind. The hurricane and lightning tore off the sails and broke off the masts, and turned on its side, and completely *engagé*, as sailors say, the ship was saved only by a skilful manoeuvre in which Baudelaire took part. Amidst the waves pouring over the ship – now little more than a wreck – Baudelaire helped the first mate unfurl a *prélart* [a tar-coated sail] which, hurled by the violence of the wind against whatever taut shrouds remained, righted the ship as if by a miracle.' A document in the archives of the Quai d'Orsay indicates that the damage done to the ship – 'mainmast and mizzenmast broken, loss of rigging, sails blown off' – was indeed considerable. The repair bill ran to 17,640 francs.[4]

On September 1, 1841, the *Paquebot des Mers du Sud* dropped anchor in the harbour of Port-Louis, capital of Mauritius, its first scheduled port of call. The Captain ordered work to begin on the most urgent repairs. The ship put to sea again on the evening of the 18th, bound for Saint-Denis de la Réunion which it reached the following day. The *Chronique de Paris* takes up the story:

> On his arrival at Réunion, something happened that gives a good idea of Baudelaire's idiosyncrasies. At Saint-Denis de Bourbon, as everyone knows, due to the usual roughness of the sea and the difficulties experienced at the only point at which one can land, the disembarkation was effected in the past by means of a rope ladder hung, at the tip of a jetty constructed on piles, from a sort of gigantic scaffold. This ladder was maintained in a vertical position, taut and pulled down into the sea, by two enormous blocks of stone fastened to its lower end. In order to disembark, one had to grab hold of the rungs at the instant the rising wave had reached its highest point.
>
> Though informed of this necessary precaution, Baudelaire stubbornly insisted on climbing the ladder with books under his arm – an original method right enough, but also a little awkward. He scaled the ladder slowly and solemnly, pursued by the mounting wave. In a few moments, the wave had reached him. He was submerged and covered in twelve to fifteen feet of water. With great difficulty, they fished him out; but, incredibly, he still had the books under his arm. Only then did he consent to leave them in the boat which was holding steady at the foot of the ladder. Yet as he climbed back up, once again he allowed the wave to reach him, but this time held on, and reached the shore, setting off towards the town, calm and collected, seeming not to notice the excitement of the onlookers. His hat alone had fallen prey to the sharks.

It is tempting to imagine that the books Baudelaire clung to with such tenacity were the set of Balzac's published works which, according to Jules

Levallois, he had taken along with him[5] – though surely there had been no lack of opportunity to read them on the ship.

At Saint-Denis, Saliz completed the refurbishment of the vessel and set sail again on October 19 for Calcutta, leaving behind its eccentric young passenger, who had stubbornly refused to continue the voyage. Forced to give in, the Captain sent General Aupick a minute account of Baudelaire's conduct since leaving Bordeaux, explaining his decision and the arrangements he himself had made in order that Baudelaire's return voyage on the *Alcide* might be effected under the best conditions.[6]

Saint-Denis, Bourbon, October 14, 1841

General,

I have to inform you of my inability to make your stepson, M. Charles Beaudelaire [*sic*], complete the voyage you planned for him on the vessel I command ...

Since leaving France, all of us on board have been able to see that it was too late to hope that M. Beaudelaire might be brought to reconsider his exclusive taste for literature such as it is conceived of today, or his determination to adopt no other profession. This exclusive taste made him a stranger to any conversation that did not bear on that subject, and set him apart from those which most frequently arose among us sailors and the other passengers who were either army people or in business. I must also tell you, though I fear it may upset you, that his peremptory notions and expressed opinions on all social ties, contrary to the ideas we have been accustomed to respect since childhood, and painful to hear from the mouth of a young man of twenty years, dangerous, too, for the other young people on board – these, too, restricted his social intercourse ... despite his continued good health, he suffered bouts of melancholy from which, in spite of the work demanded by the steering of a dismasted ship, I tried to distract him in fear of the consequences. Contrary to my expectation, and to my great astonishment, our arrival at Mauritius merely increased this despondency ... Nothing in a land and society that were quite new to him attracted his attention or aroused his aptitude for observation. He conversed only with some men of letters who are unknown in a land in which they occupy a very inferior position, and his mind was set on his desire to return to Paris at the earliest possible opportunity....

I acknowledged that I had indeed no right to force him to follow me – and in any case I should not have accepted the task – but I pointed out to him that he was in no position to demand the money you had placed in my keeping. To that, he replied that he would try to do without it, that he would stay on in Mauritius, where he hoped before long to earn money enough to pay for his passage, all the while giving signs of his affection for me . . .

Therefore, when he alone was detaining me in Mauritius, I was obliged, in order to persuade him to embark, to hold out hope that I would consent to his wishes if he persisted in his request. . . .

Here, without going into any greater detail, I can tell you that he has simply persisted in his notion, that he has demanded the execution of the undertaking I gave him in Mauritius, and that I have been forced to consent to his embarkation on a ship from Bordeaux, which he found to his liking and which he chose himself – the *Alcide*, Captain Jude de Beauséjour. . . .

I do not doubt that M. Beaudelaire will confirm that our relations, apart from the differences of opinion I mentioned, were of the friendliest, and I can assure you that I have conceived a keen interest in him, and that I should be happy to learn that he has struck out on the path which in your affection for him you would wish to see him follow. . . .

I am, General,
            Your devoted servant,

                                                    P. Saliz

During his stay in Mauritius, Baudelaire was received by M. and Mme Autard de Bragard on their property in the Quartier des Pamplemousses – that idyllic part of the island which Bernardin de Saint-Pierre had used as the setting of *Paul et Virginie*. According to some accounts, Baudelaire met M. Autard de Bragard when out walking; Mme Javerzac-Saliz, the Captain's granddaughter, claims in her memoirs that he was introduced by Duranteau, the first mate.[7] Adolphe Autard de Bragard was a planter and magistrate born on Mauritius in 1808. Having taken his law degree in Paris, he married a woman 'renowned for her beauty', Emmeline de Carcenac. Baudelaire, too, was charmed by her grace and elegance.

From Réunion, the day after Saliz weighed anchor, Baudelaire wrote to his host:

My dear Monsieur Autard,
    You asked me on Mauritius to write some verses for your wife, and I have not forgotten your request. As it is only proper, decent, and fitting that verses addressed to a lady by a young man should pass through the hands of her husband before reaching her, it is to you that I send them, in order that you might show them to her only if it please you so to do.

Since leaving, I have often thought about you and your excellent friends. I shall certainly never forget the pleasant mornings that I spent with you, Mme Autard, and Monsieur B ...[8]

Did I not love Paris and miss it so much, I should remain with you as long as possible, and force you to like me and find me a little less *baroque* than I seem.

It is unlikely that I shall return to Mauritius, unless the ship on which I am sailing for Bordeaux (the *Alcide*) puts in there to pick up passengers.

Here is my sonnet:

Au pays parfumé que le soleil caresse,
J'ai vu dans un retrait de tamarins ambrés
Et de palmiers d'où pleut sur les yeux la paresse,
Une dame créole aux charmes ignorés.

Son teint est pâle et chaud; la brune enchanteresse
A dans le cou des airs noblement maniérés;
Grande et svelte en marchant comme une chasseresse,
Son sourire est tranquille et ses yeux assurés.

Si vous alliez, Madame, au vrai pays de Gloire,
Sur les bords de la Seine ou de la verte Loire,
Belle, digne d'orner les antiques manoirs,

Vous feriez, à l'abri des mousseuses retraites,
Germer mille sonnets dans le coeur des poètes,
Que vos regards rendraient plus soumis que des noirs.*

And so I shall expect to see you in France.
My very respectful regards to Mme Autard.

C. Baudelaire

The woman who inspired the sonnet died at sea on June 22, 1857, at the

---

* 'In that scented land caressed by the sun, / I saw, in a bower of amber tamarind trees / And palms from which indolence rains down on the eyes, / A creole lady whose charms are unknown.

Her skin is pale and warm; the dark enchantress / Carries her head with nobly mannered airs; / Tall and slender when she walks like a huntress, / Her smile is peaceful and her eyes are assured.

Were you to visit, Madame, the true land of Glory, / On the banks of the Seine or the verdant Loire, / You whose beauty might adorn ancient manors,

Would bring forth, in the shade of mossy retreats, / A thousand sonnets in the hearts of poets, / Whom your eyes would make more submissive than slaves.'

age of thirty-nine – the same week in which *Les Fleurs du Mal* appeared. Perhaps she read the sonnet, in a slightly different form, in *L'Artiste* on May 25, 1845. It was the first poem Baudelaire had published under his own name.

The embalmed body of the creole lady was interred in the Pamplemousses cemetery, where her husband, who died in Paris in 1876, later joined her. Emmeline's heart was enclosed in a casket of ebony encrusted with silver.

Despite the prediction of Captain Saliz, it was not until November 4 that the *Alcide* set sail. This three-master of 231 tonnes rarely took on passengers, and so it was thanks to good relations between the two captains that Baudelaire was able to board this ship which was carrying 4,088 bales of sugar, 397 bales of coffee and various merchandise, including a crate of family portraits.

On December 4, the *Alcide* reached the Cape. Perhaps Baudelaire took advantage of this call to compare the reality he discovered with memories of his great-uncle's book, the *Voyage de M. Levaillant*, published in 1790 – a remarkable description of the region. Did Baudelaire climb to the top of the Table Mountain, or descend on the other side to the famous vineyards of Groot and Klein Constantia? This might explain the reference in the poem 'Sed non satiata' to a 'vin de Constance', although many other writers who never visited the Cape allude to the same wine: it was a common sight on the tables of rich Frenchmen.

The *Alcide* entered the estuary on February 15, 1842. The following day, the passengers disembarked after a voyage of normal duration. On the 17th, the Bordeaux *Indicateur* published the Captain's report: 'I left Bourbon on November 4 . . . Having entered Table Bay (the Cape of Good Hope) on December 4, I was unable to leave before the 8th because of the bad weather. Until January 25, nothing noteworthy happened on the crossing. The Genoese brig-schooner, the *Mima*, sailing from Bahia to Genoa, gave me 100 kilos of biscuit which I needed. We were then abeam of the Azores . . . Shortly after this encounter, I had to ride out a storm so violent that we sprang a leak, and my vessel is still taking in about 54 centimetres of water an hour.' This report corroborates that part of Baudelaire's autobiographical notes in which he mentions his 'Voyages to India': 'My second adventure: return journey on a ship without provisions and running low in the water.'

The voyage to India was a poetic invention; but Baudelaire had been on a voyage nonetheless and a long one at that, with two real-life adventures.

The traveller may have resented the trip, but it left him with fragrant memories which, through poetry, he was able to reawaken and render without falling into facile exoticism.

> Quand, les deux yeux fermés en un soir chaud d'automne,
> Je respire l'odeur de ton sein chaleureux,
> Je vois se dérouler des rivages heureux
> Qu'éblouissent les feux d'un soleil monotone ...*

---

* 'When, with both eyes closed, on a warm autumn evening, / I breathe in the scent of your welcoming breast, / I see unfold a reach of happy shores / Dazzled by the fires of a monotonous sun ...' ('Parfum exotique')

CHAPTER 10

The *Conseil Judiciaire*

1842–1844

Back in France, the time had come for young men born in 1821 to register for military service. Aupick was to appear for Charles at the drawing of lots which would decide who would be called up; but before that day arrived, he received the long letter written by Captain Saliz on October 14, 1841, in which he learnt of his stepson's imminent and premature arrival.

One can easily imagine the General's rage. As for Caroline, she would have to conceal her happiness and relief at seeing her child return home safely. Without losing a minute, the General sent the Captain's letter on to Alphonse. After reading the news, Alphonse conveyed his condolences to Mme Aupick and spoke in his letter about the healthy effects of army life – a surprising theme for him, for when Alphonse was declared fit for service in 1826, he paid someone else to take his place. The General's letter to Alphonse has disappeared and so the brother's reply is the only document which allows us to picture the sort of welcome that awaited the prodigal son:

Let us try today to welcome Charles as the prodigal son returning to his family. Either he has recognised the full extent of his wrongdoing, and is held back and prevented from writing by his fear of owning up, or else he hasn't changed. In the latter case, we should examine his ideas to see whether their wrong-headedness is due to his failure to apply his knowledge correctly, or whether the cause is some abnormality in his system. He's going to draw lots for conscription, which gives us two possible courses of action. The first would be to let him experience life as a soldier if he doesn't show any gratitude for all that you and I have done for him. The second would be to put part of his fortune out of reach, since there would be nothing to stop him selling off Neuilly when he came of age in the hope of finding a replacement for himself ... Discuss this course of action with M. Ancelle. That might be enough to guarantee him a future, without our having recourse to other means that would be as distasteful to me as they would be to you.[1]

After leaving the ship at Bordeaux on February 16, 1842, Charles sent two letters to his parents. The one addressed to Mme Aupick was tender and loving, the other a little more casual:

My dear little Mamma, I shall give you a hug in two or three days . . .
I'm told by someone here that, apart from your worries, you're keeping well. That's good. – All I could think of at sea was your poor dear health. Now you can rest easy. – Carriages don't get lost quite as easily as ships.

C. Baudelaire

Here I am back from my long journey. I arrived yesterday evening, having left Bourbon on November 4. I haven't a penny left, *and I was often short of essentials.*
You know what happened to us on the voyage out. The return journey, though not quite as extraordinary, was far more tiring. Heavy seas and dead calms the whole time.
If I wrote down everything I thought about and dreamt of while I was away from you, the whole notebook would not suffice. So I'll tell you about it in person.
I think I've returned with good sense in the bag.
I shall probably leave tomorrow. So I'll give you a hug two or three days from now.

Such a rapid journey was impossible in those days, even if one had made an advance booking for one of the three seats in the mail coach. Charles would have found it difficult in any case to pay for the one-hundred-franc ticket. By taking the normal stagecoach leaving on the 17th he would arrive back in Paris on the 23rd, unless he decided to play truant and stopped off to explore one of the towns he had not visited with his parents in 1838 – Angoulême or Poitiers. There was also a strong temptation to put off meeting the General for a few days; but he was short of money and, more importantly, his 'dear little Mamma' was expecting him.

The prodigal's return was probably a joyful affair. The General decided that explanations could wait and managed not to rush into things. The drawing of lots for national service would take place on March 3 and the attitudes of both parties might change as a result.

On March 3, he went to the Palais de Justice and drew number 265. If the number was high enough, he would not be summoned by the recruiting

board the following May and might be able to avoid conscription ...
Deliverance came on April 20. The list of those to be called up was posted.
It stopped at number 211. Baudelaire had been exempted from military
service.

Intending now to live as he pleased, Baudelaire first had to loosen the
grip of his guardians. No sooner had he come of age than he was assuring
his parents once again of his intention and will to become 'a writer'. After
several discussions and probably a few angry outbursts, a compromise was
reached. Charles would leave home and find rooms of his own; the money
would be handed over to him. His parents honoured the agreement and by
the beginning of April, Charles had found a place to his liking on the Quai
de Béthune on the Ile Saint-Louis: it was the present-day number 22,
described here by Ernest Prarond:

> Ground floor, a single room with a very high ceiling. After passing
> through the main door, one entered the room by a door on the left.
> Facing this door was the fireplace. Between the fireplace and the window,
> a large trunk in which Baudelaire kept his books and locked away his
> money. He must have had secret cupboards for his clothes and linen ...
> Across from the trunk was a sofa. A very tall window (the only one in
> the room) looked out onto the street. The curtains were of heavy material
> and hung gracefully. Opposite the window, at the back of the room, a
> bed. – A few armchairs running about among the other things. Painted
> canvasses, mostly old, on the walls.[2]

Afraid that the rent of 225 francs a year might appear a little excessive,
he wrote to his mother to explain that no other lodging was available and
that he had a yearning for solitude: 'Don't worry about the cost. If I don't
have enough to live on, and I can't get any literary work, I've decided to
ask my former teachers to find me lessons to fill the holes in my purse.'
Baudelaire's yearning for solitude had taken him to the right spot – Prarond
and the other members of the Ecole Normande thought of the Ile Saint-
Louis as the back of beyond, a land more remote than Mauritius.

As far as we know, Baudelaire never gave any lessons. He would have
made a very unusual sort of teacher. Besides, nineteen days after coming
of age, on April 28, 1842, he came into possession of his own inheritance.
His parents had agreed to pay for the voyage, 'wishing once more to
indicate the affection they have for him', according to the memorandum
drawn up at the time. The final deed, signed by his parents on the 28th,
was approved by Baudelaire two days later. He declared himself to be
'sincerely grateful for the solicitude shown in the administering of his

person and property and for the care taken in all that concerned him' – words that obviously came from the pen of the family lawyer, Maître Ancelle. The sum of 18,055 francs was paid to him, as well as some shares and four pieces of land in the village of Neuilly – now part of the Quartier des Ternes in the seventeenth arrondissement. These would bring in a further 415 francs rent each year. His total annual income was estimated at 1,800 francs.

Though not quite as rich as he thought, Charles could nevertheless look forward to a comfortable existence provided he earned some money of his own. He must have been aware of the need to work, but did nothing at all to supplement his income. With 18,000 francs in ready cash, he began by paying off some of his debts. He bought furniture or paid for the pieces he had already acquired for his room on the Ile Saint-Louis – the trunk, sofa, bed, armchairs and paintings. To this he added some bedding, a mahogany table and a bedside table which his mother was to send him after it returned from the mender's.

It seems that Baudelaire may have settled down to study during May and June 1842, since, on July 12, he asked Mme Aupick to send his birth certificate and *baccalauréat* diploma, probably so that he could take the first-year law examination a second time, unless perhaps he was thinking of enrolling in the Faculty of Arts. It was just a passing whim. The registers of both Faculties for 1842 show no sign of any Baudelaire.

Relations with his mother were good. According to the few surviving letters from this period, he gave her a piece of antique material 'to dress up a washstand or a mantelpiece' and on another occasion made her a gift of 'some earrings with which to celebrate [her] new home' on the Place Vendôme. Mother and son were able to see each other alone fairly often. The General had been appointed Chief of Staff of the Observation Corps on the Marne – an important job, since the success of manoeuvres depended to a large extent on the competence of the person in that position.

For the General, the year was overshadowed by the death of the Duc d'Orléans. He had been with the Prince on the last day of his life, obtaining his signature on letters he had drawn up before the Prince left Paris. His death was a sad blow to Aupick, who loved his protector and chief. Some consolation came from the Duc de Nemours, who assumed command of manoeuvres and was as impressed as the Prince had been by his collaborator's efficiency. A few weeks later, the newspaper *Le National* made an ironic remark about the General's continuing good fortune: 'Even if something happens to the Duc de Nemours, you can be sure that Providence will take care of the orphan.'

On September 13, 1842, the Observation Corps was disbanded. Shortly thereafter, Aupick resumed his duties at the Officers' Training School, but not for long. On November 11, he succeeded General Pajol as 'Commandant du Département de la Seine et de la Place de Paris'. The Aupicks now took up residence in the Hôtel de Créqui, built in 1704, in the magnificent Place Vendôme. We described Baudelaire's relations with Mme Aupick as good, but money made them less than perfect. Baudelaire's short notes accuse her of making mountains out of molehills and mention her 'continual, cruel recriminations'. Mme Aupick suspected her son of living above his means. Her assumption was correct: on July 18, Baudelaire sold two shares in the Banque de France and 6,500 francs disappeared into the bottomless pit of the spendthrift's pocket. Three months later, he was asking Mme Aupick for another advance. She refused to give in to his pleas and, on November 6, Baudelaire borrowed 3,500 francs on his land at Neuilly, probably to satisfy the demands of an insistent creditor. By mid-November, he had no money left, or so he told his mother: 'My complete lack of trousers and hats are preventing me for the time being from attending the School.' It seems likely that Mme Aupick decided not to call his bluff and sent him a little money, since, on December 4, he was inviting her to come to 'a nice dinner at [his] place'.

The General was either unaware that these meetings were taking place or turned a blind eye. Stepfather and stepson continued to lead separate lives throughout the following year, to judge by a grim letter dated January 5, 1844. Temperamental differences between Charles and Aupick were still causing clashes:

> I spoke to you about leaving my card with the General, because I deemed it proper, and because I thought it would please you. Since you think he'd take offence, instead of understanding my true motive, there's nothing to be done ... Your dreams of reconciliation hurt me. As I told you, I can promise nothing more than a year of hard work and good sense – and that is all.
>
> There are forms of manly pride which you, as a woman and as his wife, cannot comprehend. Why do you force me to be so cruel, and why do you deceive yourself so?

One of the methods devised by Alphonse to prevent his half-brother from frittering the inheritance was the appointment of a *conseil judiciaire*. Baudelaire knew this to be a possibility if his 'prodigality' could be proved in court by his parents; and so, in order to prevent it, he had already made certain arrangements with his mother, assisted by Maître Ancelle. After putting his landed property up for sale on June 11, 1843, he left the proceeds of one of the lots – 31,000 francs – in the hands of his buyer, a friend of the family, and signed a loan contract at 5% interest, leaving him with an annual income of 1,550 francs. A few days later, on the 27th, he borrowed 5,000 francs and noted that he now owned 31,000 francs, plus 24,150 to be invested, giving a total of 55,150 francs and an estimated annual income of 3,300. The same day, he gave power of attorney to his mother and Ancelle. His mother would authorise spending, Ancelle would make the payments. It was up to them to decide which investments should be made and to pay the interest directly to him. His mother retained control of transferable securities, regulating the interest due to Charles, who was to provide her with his receipts. After the deduction of small sums intended to constitute a reserve, she had a moderate monthly income paid to her son by Ancelle. Charles, of course, undertook not to borrow money or create any debts.

The agreement was shortlived. At the end of October 1843, when moving to the Hôtel Pimodan, Baudelaire warned his mother not to say anything about *conseils judiciaires* to the landlord: 'If I realised you had done so behind my back, I'd clear out at once, and just for that, you'd never see me again, because I'd go and live with Jeanne.' (This is the first mention of Jeanne Duval in Baudelaire's correspondence. She and her mother had just moved into a neighbouring street on the Ile Saint-Louis – the rue de la Femme-sans-tête, now called the rue Le Regrattier.) Baudelaire's threat was worrying, but also rather unwise, for it would soon be used against him. His cohabitation with Jeanne was one more item to be added to the list of grievances.

A fresh crop of debts arose from Baudelaire's move to the Hôtel Pimodan, probably also from the equipping of Jeanne's new household. There was certainly no lack of opportunity to spend money. Each day, the young art lover was able to view the furniture, objects and, more especially, the paintings kept in sheds at the Hôtel by a secondhand dealer called Antoine Arondel, who described himself as a historical painter. In Arondel's curiosity shop, Baudelaire purchased several canvasses of dubious authenticity, gaily putting his name to promissory notes and bills: 300 francs on November 5, 1843; 1,500 francs on December 7; 1,100 on the 23rd – a total of 2,900 francs between February and April 1844.

Another major creditor at that time was the owner of the Tour d'Argent restaurant (which was not the splendid place it is today). The restaurant owner and Arondel were the poet's longest-standing creditors. Even after his death in 1867, they were still claiming payment from Baudelaire's executors.

Other debts were contracted in 1843 and 1844, and Mme Aupick was prevailed upon to lend him 8,000 francs during the first half of 1844. Baudelaire's correspondence sheds no further light on these various transactions. He seldom wrote to or saw his mother and steered well clear of Aupick: 'I couldn't possibly describe,' he told Mme Aupick on March 3, 1844; 'the depressing and brutal effect that great big empty house has on me; everyone there's a stranger but my Mother. I enter only with caution, and sneak out like a thief. I can't stand it any more. Forgive me, and leave me in my seclusion, until a book comes out of it.'

The General, whilst retaining his former position, became Chief of Staff of the Operations Corps on the Moselle on May 12, 1844. Despite the important duties that were keeping him away from Paris, it was decided in June that a *conseil judiciaire* should be appointed. Since the law said nothing about family relations, Charles' two relatives – his mother and half-brother – were empowered to petition the presiding judge. However, the petitioner was not allowed to be a member of the board of guardians, which would subsequently be called upon to give its opinion, and since Alphonse was on the board, it was Mme Aupick who had the unhappy privilege of presenting the following petition through her solicitor:

> ... that even before reaching his majority, this young man has displayed such a taste for spending money and such inclinations to idleness, that with a view of correcting them, the petitioners saw fit to make him undertake a long voyage, for which reason they obtained authority to borrow from the account of the said Baudelaire the sum of five thousand five hundred francs according to the terms of the decision reached by this court upon the opinion severally and jointly expressed by the board of guardians;
>
> That the said Beaudelaire [*sic*], instead of proceeding to Calcutta, the destination of his voyage, ended his journey at the Ile Bourbon where he spent the funds which had been placed at his disposal and returned to Paris without having derived any advantage whatsoever from this initial sacrifice;
>
> That having attained his majority around 1842, the said Beaudelaire received from his mother and stepfather the remaining balance of the monies in trust, which balance amounted to a sum of approximately one hundred thousand francs, made up as follows.

The petition gave a full account of the capital, which amounted to 99,568 francs, and then of Baudelaire's squandering of the same: the debit column showed a total of 20,500 francs. It went on to describe in detail Baudelaire's subsequent financial dealings with his mother 'who even now is being pestered with the most insistent demands for a further sum of five or six thousand francs'. The final clauses stated

That she has moreover every reason to fear that her son might sign promissory notes in favour of usurers, and that to give some idea of the disorder which reigns in the government of his life and fortune, it suffices to cite the claims of a restaurateur which amount to nine hundred francs and to note that two paintings purchased by him for four hundred francs produced, when auctioned, the sum of eighteen francs;

That in these circumstances, seeing one half of her son's fortune consumed, his expensive habits becoming more and more ingrained, and his stubborn refusal to adopt a useful profession, the petitioner feels that further waste in the near future and the utter ruin of her son can be averted only by having recourse to the intervention of the court, which should assign him a *conseil judiciaire*, without whose consent he might not henceforth engage in any act likely to involve his property...

Submitted in Paris this 31st day of July, 1844.

[signed] Legras

The legal wheels were set in motion. Aupick had already authorised his wife to deal with all the necessary formalities. The board of guardians was formed. It included four lawyers – Alphonse Baudelaire, Paul Pérignon, Jean Labie and Antoine Jaquotot – as well as two other friends of M. and Mme Aupick: Louis Emon – a former officer – and Emard Millot, a head clerk at the Ministry of Finance.

On August 20, Maître Corion, bailiff in Paris, served M. Baudelaire with notice to appear at the Law Courts for cross-examination on August 27.

Baudelaire had been warned many times that if he continued to run up debts he would soon find himself placed in the hands of a *conseil judiciaire* and thus condemned, perhaps for the rest of his life, to legal infancy; but all these threats had been taken with a pinch of salt: he believed that if the worst came to the worst, he could always appeal to his mother's compassion. The bailiff's visit dealt him such a blow that for some time he stayed in his room at the Hôtel Pimodan, fuming with rage. He wrote a letter to his mother and had it delivered 'under the seal of secrecy'. Angry in parts, calm in others, the letter was 'one last appeal' to Mme Aupick's 'common sense' and 'affection':

You told me that you consider my anger and grief to be a passing phase. You think you're giving me a little rap on the knuckles for my own good. But you should be convinced of one thing which apparently you still do not know, and that is that, for my sins, I am not like other men . . .

Look at your faulty reasoning and your illogical behaviour. You're inflicting a terrible punishment on me and doing something utterly humiliating perhaps the very day before the start of a successful career, on the eve of that day I've promised you for so long. And that's precisely the moment you choose to break my arms and legs. I told you that I wouldn't accept a *conseil judiciaire* as something anodyne and inoffensive – I can already feel the effect it will have. And while we're on the subject, you're under an even graver misapprehension in thinking that this will be an incentive. You can't imagine what I experienced yesterday, that feeling of despondency in the pit of my stomach when I realised the affair was turning serious. It was something like a sudden desire to send it all to the devil, to forget about everything, not to bother even going to fetch my letter from M. Ed. Blanc, telling myself with perfect equanimity: what's the point? I don't need it. All I have to do now is resign myself to taking whatever she feels like giving me . . .

To turn now to something else which will probably mean more to you than any sort of promise . . .

Recently, without knowing the first thing about law, I spoke to you off the top of my head about a donation worked out in such a way that it would revert to me in the event of death. I don't know if that's possible; but one thing is certain: you can't convince me that in the whole bag of notaries' tricks, there isn't some other way that would satisfy you . . . I would rather lose my fortune, and give myself entirely up to you than suffer some kind of imposition. One is an act of freedom; the other is an attack on my freedom.

To make an end of this, I beg you as humbly as can be to spare me this great affliction, and what for me is a terrible humiliation. But, for God's sake, let there be no judges, no strangers, and no meetings . . . I'm certain, absolutely certain, that after my first success, and with a little help from you, it will be easy for me to reach a good position *very quickly* . . .

M. Edmond Blanc gave me a very good letter which I'm going to use when I try to sort things out with the *Revue* this morning.[3] – One last time, don't forget that all I'm asking for is a commutation of means.

Charles

On August 24, M. Antoine Rouillon, magistrate of the former eleventh arrondissement, was presented with the final decision of the board of guardians:

> Whereas it is fully known to the members of the Board of Guardians that from the last years of his minority M. Charles Baudelaire has displayed tendencies of great prodigality;
>
> Whereas the Board of Guardians during this same minority saw fit to take steps with a view to protecting him against unfortunate impulses, and bringing him back to orderliness and regularity in his spending, but without these steps having had any effect whatsoever;
>
> Whereas M. Baudelaire, having attained his majority, and taken charge of his own fortune, gave himself up to the wildest extravagance, and, in the space of about eighteen months, squandered more than half his inheritance which amounted to a capital of about one hundred thousand francs ...
>
> The Board of Guardians is for these reasons in unanimous agreement with ourselves that there is every reason to provide M. Charles Baudelaire with a *conseil judiciaire,* without the assistance of which he might perform no action other than those demanded by the simple handling of affairs ...

On August 27, persisting in his refusal to appear before 'strangers', Baudelaire was absent; and so, two weeks later, on September 10, Maître Leroux, the bailiff, betook himself to the Hôtel Pimodan where, 'speaking with a woman in his service', he left the verdict of the court, the decision of the Board of Guardians, and the report of absence, to be transmitted to M. Baudelaire, along with a summons to appear before the Court of First Instance a week from then at ten in the morning.

The proceedings took their course and Ancelle was given the job of *conseil judiciaire.* Still silent, Baudelaire made no appeal. Why such resignation? 'A horrible state to be in,' he told his mother many years later: 'Resignation worse than rage.'[4] Had he finally admitted that he needed a mentor? Or was he loath to plead against his mother? On November 7, 1844, Ancelle signed an official acceptance of his role as '*conseil judiciaire* of Monsieur Charles Beaudelaire [*sic*], property-owner, living at No. 17, Quai d'Anjou'. He would remain in this post until the poet's death.

Thus, Baudelaire had done almost nothing to prevent this action being taken against him; and yet never at any time did he consider it to be anything but a disgrace. It was almost as if he had deliberately sought out the humiliation.

CHAPTER 11

Literary Beginnings

1842–1844

On his return from the Indian Ocean, Baudelaire had taken up again with his classmate from Louis-le-Grand, Auguste Dozon, and with his friends from the Ecole Normande who were still either staying at the Pension Bailly or using it as a place to meet. Henri de Saussine, the amateur artist, had turned his little room there into a studio in which the landscape painter Alexis Daligé gave free art lessons.[1] It was probably Daligé who introduced Baudelaire to the technical aspects of painting, before he met Emile Deroy and thereby gained admittance to the more prestigious studios, like that of Eugène Delacroix.

During the summer of 1842, Bailly's boarding school was transferred from the Place de l'Estrapade to the rue Madame. In its new location, its unofficial popularity declined; besides which, its young boarders, whose studies had suffered from the distractions of city life, were impatient to get their examinations over with and enjoy a little freedom before returning to their respective provinces.

Whereas this period sees the stabilisation (and stagnation) of the July Monarchy, the literary world, though it brought forth no great master-pieces, was in full swing. In 1841 and 1842, there was an extraordinary craze for humorous little monographs written by sarcastic chroniclers of Parisian life and illustrated by cartoonists like Daumier, Trimolet, or Gavarni. Subjects of these *Physiologies* ranged from the politician, the student, or the prostitute, to the Champs-Elysées, the Omnibus, or Paris dancehalls. Two of the most entertaining were Edouard Ourliac's *Physiology of the Schoolboy* and Balzac's *Physiology of the Office Clerk*. Baudelaire counted both these writers among his 'first literary connections',[2] though he may not have met them until after his voyage. The first literary event he witnessed in Paris, shortly after his return, was probably the stormy first night of Balzac's play, *Les Ressources de Quinola*, unpopular mainly because Balzac had bought up all the tickets and resold them at exorbitant prices.

This play, which Baudelaire was one of the very few to admire at the time, was performed at the Odéon on March 19, 1842 – one month before the appearance of the first volumes of a monumental work for which Balzac had only recently found a title: *La Comédie Humaine*. For Baudelaire, 1842 was also the year in which a posthumous collection of prose poems by Aloysius Bertrand appeared, with a preface by Sainte-Beuve. Baudelaire read the book as soon as it came out and was later to acknowledge his debt to Bertrand's *Gaspard de la Nuit* in the foreword to his own prose poems. And finally, Théodore de Banville, at the age of nineteen, made his dazzling début with a volume of poetry entitled *Les Cariatides*, as Baudelaire remembered in 1861: 'People were amazed when they leafed through that book in which so many treasures, a little confused and mingled, were piled up. Everyone talked about how young the author was, and most people refused to believe that such astonishing precocity was possible.' Baudelaire became a friend of the famous young poet, who lived in the rue Monsieur-le-Prince 'with his parents, but in a separate room with its own entrance'.[3] There, Banville sometimes entertained Prarond, Privat d'Anglemont and Pierre Dupont. Baudelaire's circle of acquaintances was rapidly increasing.

It would be hard to find two poets more dissimilar than Pierre Dupont and Théodore de Banville. Banville belonged to the great Classical tradition, which had discovered a new source of inspiration in the Renaissance poetry of the Pléiade – Ronsard's *Selected Works* had just been published in 1841. Pierre Dupont, on the other hand, came from a working-class background. He wrote songs for the common man and for the bourgeoisie and was on his way to becoming a second Béranger, but with more lyricism and pathos. In 1842, he was still an elegiac poet. *Dewdrops* was the innocuous title of a collection he advertised, but apparently never published, the proceeds of which were meant to allow him to buy his way out of military service.[4] The literary fervour of the time was such that a simple love of poetry could bring together very different writers like Banville and Dupont. When gleaning information about the period from Prarond, Eugène Crépet was made fully aware of what separated his own generation from Baudelaire's:

How lucky you were to awaken to literary life in that warm atmosphere, charged with an energy which we never knew, and which had a good, healthy effect on the sturdiest among you. I who came along nearly ten years later was nipped from the very beginning and frozen by the political chill ... Baudelaire, like you ..., arrived in time to receive the life-giving spark.[5]

This spark ignited and united temperaments which, at other times, would never have met or would have belonged to different camps. New coteries emerged, more flexible and eclectic than those of the first Romantics.

One such group, modelling itself on Victor Hugo's 'Grand Cénacle' of 1830, met at the home of Louis Ulbach, one of the future founders of the republican *Revue de Paris*. Its members were an odd assortment, including Banville, Eugène Manuel – a writer of intellectual poems about the poor – or the songwriter Pierre Dupont. One evening, Banville brought Baudelaire along with him:

> I can still see the intelligent smile and mocking look which accompanied his politeness ... Everyone recited their latest work. It must be said that we were pure of spirit, and that angels, diaphanous cherubs, ineffable feelings, musings in the blueberries, worshippings from afar or in obscurity, or, at the very most, the frolickings of the gods of Olympus with the goddesses – all these things found expression in our verses.
>
> Having withstood the crystalline flow of our poems, Baudelaire took his turn to recite. He began in a serious tone, with a slightly trembling timbre, an ascetic air about him, and recited the poem, *Gritty Manon*.
>
> The very first rhyme introduced Manon's 'soiled shirt', and the rest of the poem lived up to the first verse. The coarsest words, beautifully embedded in the text, and the boldest descriptions came one after the other. We listened, stupefied and blushing, folding away our seraphic poems, and feeling on our brows the beating of our guardian angels' frightened wings, shocked at the scandal.[6]

Baudelaire never returned to the little poetry group, but he certainly made his mark and made sure he was noticed. His cultivated originality and deliberate eccentricity, of which his interest in the theory and practice of painting was then an aspect, served to put new friends to the test, or to keep the unwanted at bay. No wonder then that one of Baudelaire's slightly older friends had a reputation himself for eccentricity. Alexandre Privat d'Anglemont, a very tall and handsome half-caste born in Guadeloupe in 1815, had arrived in Paris in 1825 and, after obtaining his *baccalauréat* eight years later, became one of the Latin Quarter's most colourful denizens, squandering his share of the family's sugar plantation on student friends and actresses. In 1843, he returned to Guadeloupe in order to settle affairs with his brother who had been appointed his legal guardian in 1834. Privat set sail again on the next ship for France, having stayed only twenty-four hours. With the family sugar bringing in less and less money, he was forced to spend more time producing articles, often anonymously, for reviews and newspapers. Some of these articles went to make up a curious book on *Unknown Paris* which paints a fascinating picture of all the little industries engaged in by people who, like Privat himself, lived on the edge of society: rag-pickers, maggot-breeders, human alarm-clocks, indoor shepherds, to name but a few.[7]

Baudelaire's closest friend was the person he referred to as 'his' painter – Emile Deroy.[8] Born in 1820, Deroy was the son of a lithographer, Isidore Deroy, who taught Emile the art of lithography and drawing. At seventeen, Emile became a student of Delaroche. His first encounter with Baudelaire was in April 1842, when they were near neighbours on the Ile Saint-Louis. They were soon inseparable; but the painter whom Baudelaire considered a genius died at the age of twenty-six, leaving only a few sketches and a few portraits – 'the work of a master', wrote Banville.[9] There is, of course, the 1844 portrait of Baudelaire, painted at the Hôtel Pimodan 'in four nighttime sittings';[10] then the portraits of Pierre Dupont, Privat d'Anglemont and the unfinished portrait of Banville's father; finally, his masterpiece, the picture of a little guitar-player known as 'The red-haired beggar-girl'. This girl, though an urchin, was evidently beautiful enough to make several conquests among those who saw her in the streets. 'A une mendiante rousse' is the title of a poem written by Baudelaire in the style of the Pléiade poets and later included in *Les Fleurs du Mal*; Banville, too, wrote an ode 'To a Little Street-Singer' and Deroy's portrait, described here by Banville, leaves little doubt as to the painter's own feelings: 'A child, a little girl with big eyes, refined features, charming and delicate, pink-skinned, with pearly flesh, lips as red as pomegranates, crowned with long hair, wild, tangled and curly, falling over her shoulders; she sings as she plays her guitar in a beautiful ray of sunlight.'[11] This painting, incidentally, also indicates Deroy's admiration for Delacroix, Frans Hals and the English portrait-painters. A more realistic portrait, however, emerges from Baudelaire's own description of the little guitarist: 'A rather pretty face with very clear, pronounced features and magnificent dark eyes; she's slightly pale and has grown tired.'[12]

Banville, Dupont, Privat, Deroy and Baudelaire would often meet on fine days in the Luxembourg Gardens – much larger than they are today. To the relief of people living in the *quartier* behind the park, an area of trees was later removed to make way for new roads, thus doing away with what at night became a danger-filled forest cutting them off from the rest of the city; but, lamented Banville, 'What a strange, savage, and delicious paradise it was they destroyed!'[13]

The friends would also visit the Bois de Boulogne or taverns on the edge

of Paris. 'At about five o'clock on a summer evening,' remembered Ernest
Prarond, 'we used to set off in search of a place that the bourgeois avoided
and that would be conducive to high-flown conversations of a literary,
artistic, or even moral variety. On certain days, the Chaussée du Maine and
the rue de la Tombe-Issoire heard propositions and declarations of principle
that would have shaken the Académie Française to its very foundations.'[14]
At the Bois de Boulogne, according to Jules Buisson, lying on the grass
under the trees, Baudelaire would recite poems which later appeared in
Les Fleurs du Mal. 'A tall, thin girl happened along, wearing an enormous
bustle ...' Baudelaire improvised a poem on the spot:

> A force d'empois et de serge
> Et d'aciers contournés en rond
> La crinoline en potiron,
> Avait transformé cette asperge.*[15]

In winter, they met in each other's apartments. Louis Ménard, for example,
had two rooms above the Place de la Sorbonne. It was there that Baudelaire
tried hashish for the first time. Whilst under the influence, he painted a
watercolour of himself, with top-hat, cigar and black coat, towering over
the column in the Place Vendôme.[16]

Baudelaire, as we saw, had his apartment on the Quai de Béthune. Louis
Ménard's friend, Charles Cousin, remembered it as containing chests, an
old table with turned feet, Venetian mirrors, books – notably the poets of
the Pléiade – some cats, and 'a bed of brown oak, without legs or posts –
a sort of sculptured coffin in which I suppose he sometimes slept'.

Dozon was another visitor to the Quai de Béthune. He sent Baudelaire
a poem in May 1842 entitled 'Le Livre', in which he enjoined his friend
to 'leave wine and flesh alone', and to come and read in his 'calm pages ...
what the wise man learnt in many long days of hardship and pain ...',
adding in a postscript, 'probably more than you'll learn from these lines
... but, you know, my Muse has completely abandoned me; it's very humiliating. Please pray for her return. I would willingly pray that *something else*
might disappear and leave you in peace, my friend. I shall come and see
you as soon as possible and hope to find you in slightly better shape.'[17]

'Le Livre', according to its author, was written as a sort of poetic
challenge with Baudelaire, who no doubt won the contest, perhaps by
writing the poem entitled 'Le Mauvais Moine'. Baudelaire nevertheless paid
homage to his friend's muse by reciting Dozon's 'The Wild Boar':[18]

---

*'With starch and serge/And twisted steel/The bustle turned the beanpole/Into a
pumpkin.'

Baudelaire, dwarfing the column in the Place Vendôme. A self-portrait, drawn
under the influence of hashish. See p. 96.

O triste sanglier, avec ton air farouche,
Tu désires les champs et les larges forêts,
Que bruyant et sans crainte, au soir tu parcourais,
Et la bauge boueuse où le jour on se couche.*

The 'something else' mentioned in Dozon's letter was probably the 'syphilitic affection' that Baudelaire told his mother he had caught 'when very young' and of which at one point he thought he was 'completely cured'. That happy delusion was soon destroyed.

The subject of syphilis demands a good deal of caution since very little was known about it at the time. It no longer inspired the same dread as during the Renaissance: cholera, plague and typhoid were considered greater evils. Fathers would warn their sons against it and suggest a few precautions, cracking broad jokes, but with a hint of anxiety. Baudelaire did not have the benefit of such paternal guidance. He probably would have contracted the disease in any case, but, with a more sympathetic ear, might have received better treatment. Syphilis, in fact, represented a sort of coming-of-age – an idea transmitted by Baudelaire in *My Heart Laid Bare*: 'The day a young writer corrects his first proofs, he's as proud as a schoolboy who's just caught the pox.'[19] Maupassant, too, in 1877, realising he had been infected for six or seven years, wrote to a friend: 'I've got the pox! Finally! the real thing!! ... The great pox that François I died of!'[20]

In Baudelaire's day, cures were still considered a possibility and this ill-founded belief did nothing to prevent the spread of the disease. Philippe Ricord, whose clinic on the rue de Tournon was always full, had managed to distinguish gonorrhoea from syphilis in his *Practical Treatise on Venereal Diseases* (1838), but he claimed that 'the latter, in its secondary lesions, was not contagious and that syphilis could be cured by the absorption of mercury and potassium iodide'. He countered the painful effect of mercury on the bowels by prescribing opium: 'Opium corrects the tendency of mercury to purge, and prevents the colics and "gripes" that some patients experience, particularly when using the sublimate.' In spite of Ricord, the virus, which was discovered and named only in 1905, continued to bring about general paralysis or hemiplegia. In Baudelaire's case, its undermining of the arteriosclerotic system was accelerated by alcohol.

In his book, *The Horror of Life*, Roger Williams claims that Baudelaire may have had nothing more than gonorrhoea; but Professor Marcel

*'Oh melancholy boar, with your savage air,/You long for the fields and the forests wide,/Which, in the evening, loud and fearless you ranged,/And the miry wallow where you slept in the day.'

Monnier, whose enquiry is the only serious study of the question based on the texts, comes to a different conclusion.[21] Baudelaire himself frequently refers to his ailment as syphilis, notably in letters to his friend and publisher Poulet-Malassis, written in February 1860. The poet describes the disease in detail whilst accepting the myth of a rejuvenating cure. The symptoms you mention, writes Baudelaire, are those 'I knew in the past ... mouth ulcers, painful constrictions in the throat which make it painful to eat, surprising bouts of weariness, loss of appetite ... [and] if you haven't experienced any weakness yet, any lack of flexibility in the knees or elbows, with tumours, even in the neck joints near the head, all that proves is that the beneficial treatment (sarsaparilla and potassium iodide) may have prevented those mishaps from occurring.' Though he was trying to convince his friend that he really had contracted syphilis, Baudelaire went on to say that it wasn't very serious, provided one did not allow oneself to be deceived 'by seeming recoveries'. In fact, 'there's no person healthier than one who has had syphilis and been fully cured, as army doctors and those who treat prostitutes know. It's a real rejuvenation.'

Baudelaire probably heard of this mythical rejuvenation from Ricord or from the homeopathist he visited in the early stages of the illness. One thinks again of Maupassant, writing to Frank Harris: 'Everyone gets it when they're young! But for ten years now, it's completely disappeared. I've been rid of it for a long time.'[22]

Not being quite such a braggart as Maupassant, Baudelaire eventually recognised the truth. The disease broke out again while he was in Dijon in 1849–50 and again in the spring of 1861, to the consternation of Mme Aupick. Baudelaire replied: 'You're probably thinking my bones will decay inside a week. Some people live sixty years with their blood infected. But it frightens me, if only because of the melancholy it breeds.' By this time, he knew that recovery was impossible. In February 1860, he was telling his friend that it wasn't serious; in May 1861, his dread was apparent. Even though the tertiary stage of syphilis had not then been identified, Baudelaire may well have guessed and then become convinced that his blood was 'infected'. Perhaps he had had some premonition of this when suffering his relapse in Dijon in 1849–50. It is interesting to note in any case that the poem he sent to Madame Sabatier in December 1852 – 'A une femme trop gaie' – ends with the poet's desire to inject the woman with his 'blood', whereas the 1857 version replaces 'blood' with 'venom'. The poem was condemned by the criminal court and reappeared only in the 1866 collection, Les Epaves, with a note rebuking the magistrates for their 'syphilitic interpretation'. In fact, the Deputy Public Prosecutor had merely requested that the judges consider the last three stanzas as a possible 'offense to public morals'. The 'syphilitic interpretation' was Baudelaire's.

Baudelaire contracted gonorrhoea before his voyage and was probably cured of it. Before, during, or after the voyage, he caught syphilis, thought he was cured, but then, in 1850, was forced to admit his mistake. One should be careful not to make too much of his fears and forebodings; but it is surely reasonable to suggest that he was haunted by a feeling of having signed away his life – and in particular his sex life – a feeling that was all the more frightening since it partly defied conscious expression.

Having left the Ile Saint-Louis to live for a short time on the ground floor of a house in the rue Vaneau, Baudelaire returned to the little island to occupy a flat on the Quai d'Anjou. Then, at the end of October 1843, he moved next door to the building which was known at that time as the Hôtel Pimodan.

The Ile Saint-Louis was and still is a place apart, 'a little provincial town' in the midst of Paris. 'In the evening more than at any other time the island takes on a special air. Cut off from the noise of Paris by two arms of the river which surround it like a belt, affording only rather intermittent bridges to the locals wishing to cross the water, this island has been inhabited for a long time by men of private means and *petits bourgeois*, peaceable, thrifty people who rarely step outside and who go to bed early. There was even a time, not very long ago ... when the inhabitant of the Ile Saint-Louis would go out as little as possible for the sake of economy; the one-sou toll on the bridge amounted to a lot of money for a modest budget ...'[23] The island, however, was not the exclusive property of the bourgeois. Artists went there in search of freedom and inexpensive lodgings. Jean-Jacques Feuchère, who was a talented sculptor before he sold out to commercial art; Auguste Préault, also a sculptor, but one who remained true to his genius; and painters: Emile Deroy and Meissonier, and Daumier, whom Baudelaire 'adored' even then.[24]

The Hôtel Pimodan was originally known, and is again today, as the Hôtel Lauzun, named after the adventurous courtier of Louis XIV who married the equally adventurous Duchesse de Montpensier, the 'Grande Mademoiselle'. The hotel had been built in 1656–57 by the Le Vau, father and son, for Charles Grüyn, a man who made his fortune as an army supplier, before being imprisoned for embezzlement. Neither he nor Lauzun enjoyed the hotel for very long. A century later it was bought by the Marquis de Pimodan, and finally, in August 1842, by Baron Jérôme Pichon, with whom Baudelaire was soon to have a brief altercation. Baudelaire stayed in the hotel for two years, from October 1843 to September 1845.

He would never find a better setting for himself, despite what the description of a fellow tenant, Roger de Beauvoir, might suggest: 'Thick, nauseating smoke used to drift up from the cellars with their large doors opened onto the Quai d'Anjou like so many vomitoria.'[25] Roger de Beauvoir's cabdriver told him: 'I pass by there quite often and I see streams of every colour flowing past the building.' The hotel was nicknamed 'The Dyers' Hotel' and the *Almanach du Commerce* does indeed indicate that a wholesale dyer occupied a large portion of the ground floor and *entresol* between 1839 and 1844.

Once the visitor had passed through the *porte-cochère* and taken a service staircase on the right, under the porch, with a wooden banister and tiled steps, he reached the third floor where Baudelaire 'was living in the attic'. Asselineau, a recent acquaintance in 1845, remembered an apartment costing 350 francs a year. It consisted of two rooms and a study. All the walls and ceilings were covered in red and black wallpaper, and the rooms were lit by a single window of which the panes, except for the top ones, were frosted, 'so I can only see the sky', claimed Baudelaire.[26]

This would suggest that Baudelaire's room looked down onto the inner courtyard. He lived, though, above Roger de Beauvoir, as Prarond discovered: 'One day when he had left a tap running he announced: "There's a torrent running through Roger de Beauvoir's place."'[27] Since Beauvoir occupied the grand apartment on the first floor, Baudelaire's room, too, must have looked out onto the banks of the Seine and his frosted panes were more likely to have been a deliberate act of eccentricity, intended to mystify his new friend, Asselineau.

Here is the rest of Asselineau's description: in the 'square, low-ceilinged room, hung entirely in red and black wallpaper ... there was a divan draped in a grey dustcover, the bed, and, in the middle, a square table'.[28] On the walls, Deroy's portrait of the master of the house, a copy of Delacroix's *Algiers Women* painted by the same and 'a head by Delacroix, with an extraordinary, intense, unearthly expression, representing Grief' (perhaps a sketch for *The Death of Sardanapalus*?).[29] In the adjoining study were 'various lithographs in black frames', including Aimé de Lemud's portrait of Hoffmann, and Delacroix's *Hamlet* series. On the mantelpiece, 'between two very ancient brass chandeliers with two branches, a terracotta group by the neighbouring sculptor, J.-J. Feuchère, depicting the nymph Callisto in the arms of Zeus, who has taken on the form of Artemis; it was dedicated by the artist to Baudelaire.'[30] Last of all, the room contained some cuckoo clocks – an essential item for the inveterate procrastinator.

Some time before July 1845, Baudelaire moved his mistress into a pied-à-terre in a nearby street on the island – the rue de la Femme-sans-tête. Surprisingly little is known about Jeanne Duval. When collecting material for his biography of Baudelaire, Eugène Crépet asked Ernest Prarond for any information he might have. Prarond remembered seeing her come to Baudelaire's previous home on the Quai de Béthune 'where she'd settle into an armchair by the fireside. Jeanne seemed a very passive girl ... She was a mulatto – not very black, or beautiful ... She was rather flat-chested, quite tall, and had an awkward gait.'[31] Curiously enough, Nadar, who knew her (in both senses of the word), found her most striking feature to be the 'exuberant and quite incredible development of her pectoral muscles' – a feature which is prominent too in Baudelaire's sketches of Jeanne. Banville confirms Nadar's observation and goes on to describe her in the following way: 'She was a coloured girl, very tall, and she carried her dark head with its wild waves of hair proudly and simply; her queenly step, full of savage grace, was that of a goddess, or a beast.'[32]

Baudelaire's first girlfriend had been a Jewess and now he had chosen a mulatto or a half-caste. These were hardly the sort of companions a respectable young man was supposed to adopt. Baudelaire's choice was another act of obvious eccentricity and also a symptom of his desire to be reprimanded.

Jeanne herself is a mystery; even her true surname is unknown. Baudelaire called her Mme or Mlle Lemer, Mlle or Mme Duval, or Jeanne Prosper. The only precise information we have is contained in the entry book of the hospital to which she was admitted in 1859. She gives her name as Jeanne Duval, her age as thirty-two and her place of birth as San Domingo. Her mother seems to have been a native of Nantes, but there is no trace of either mother or daughter in that city.

Jeanne had acted in a few minor roles at the small Porte Saint-Antoine theatre in the 1838–39 season and perhaps it was there that Nadar first came upon her. Baudelaire is unlikely to have met her until much later.

Jeanne was to be a part of Baudelaire's life for many years, at first an inspiration to the poet – Baudelaire dictated to her the poems he was afraid he might forget: 'Her spelling's simple,' he told Prarond, 'but she makes my rhymes so much richer.'[33] But in the end she weighed him down like a thankless though occasionally comforting responsibility. One has only to glance at the titles of the sadistic or masochistic poems she inspired – 'Une charogne' ('A Carcass'), 'Le Vampire', 'De profundis clamavi' – to see in Jeanne the accomplice of the poet who described himself as his own executioner.[34]

Baudelaire's social life at that time, like that of other young writers, centred in part on the cafés and taverns of the Latin Quarter. One of the liveliest of these was the Café Tabourey, situated next to the Odéon theatre opposite the entrance to the Luxembourg Gardens. Upstairs was the apartment of Jules Janin, the 'Prince of Critics', whose influential *feuilleton* appeared every Monday in the important newspaper, the *Journal des Débats*. In 1843, the Tabourey, already a 'literary centre', became one of the important scenes of a major battle in French theatrical history. In March of that year, Victor Hugo had suffered his first defeat on the stage: *Les Burgraves*, a long historical play – possibly his most original – was badly received at the Comédie Française, and this relative failure is considered even now as marking the demise of so-called Romantic drama. The *coup de grâce* was delivered at the Odéon in April when a 'Roman' tragedy, *Lucrèce*, was performed with some success. *Lucrèce* was the work of François Ponsard, a previously unknown playwright who had come up from the provinces, tragedy in hand. Ponsard was able to profit by the somewhat artificial Classical revival instigated on the Parisian stage by the actress, Rachel, who was enjoying considerable acclaim with her interpretations of Corneille and Racine. During the weeks in which *Lucrèce* occupied the stage of the Odéon, the Tabourey became 'the headquarters of Ponsard's supporters'.[35]

The new playwright had discovered a sponsor in Achille Ricourt, founder and director of the review, *L'Artiste*. Ricourt, who gave lessons in elocution, and liked to try his hand at 'discovering' writers and actors, would recite verses from *Lucrèce* in the Tabourey and then go upstairs to visit Jules Janin. Janin had almost stopped going to the theatre and depended on Ricourt to supply him with the information he needed for his weekly column. Ricourt seized the chance to promote his protégé and it was Janin who, convinced by Ricourt of the playwright's genius, was largely responsible for manufacturing Ponsard's reputation. This explains why one of the anonymous collaborators of the little book, *Les Mystères galants des théâtres de Paris*[36] – probably Baudelaire – referred the following year to 'Ricourt's *Lucrèce*' and described the promoter as a witty man who enjoys playing tricks on Parisian theatregoers.

Ten years later, Ernest Prarond described how the regulars of the Café Tabourey would recite snatches of Ponsard's play and poke fun at Hugo's *Burgraves*.[37] Baudelaire, on the other hand, saved his irony for *Lucrèce* and for other plays which, like Ponsard's, offered the ruling classes a flattering image of themselves. It was Baudelaire who lumped these playwrights together under the derisive name 'L'Ecole du Bon Sens' ('The Common-Sense School') and who, just a few days before the 1851 *coup d'état*, courageously denounced all these 'Decent Plays and Honest Novels'.

It was perhaps through Prarond that Baudelaire made the acquaintance at that time of the distinguished critic, Sainte-Beuve.[38] Though he cultivated this friendship, Baudelaire would not always have reason to be happy with his older friend: Sainte-Beuve often proved reluctant to use his influence as a critic in Baudelaire's favour. The young admirer sent him a letter from the Hôtel Pimodan, including a poem addressed to the author of the novel, *Volupté* – one of the first works of modern literature that Baudelaire had enjoyed – and of the *Life, Poems and Thoughts of Joseph Delorme*, a supposedly posthumous collection of prose and poetry which is in many ways a direct ancestor of *Les Fleurs du Mal*:

> Tous imberbes alors, sur les vieux bancs de chêne,
> Plus polis et luisants que des anneaux de chaîne,
> Que jour à jour la peau des hommes a fourbis,
> – Nous traînions tristement nos ennuis, accroupis
> Et voûtés sous le ciel carré des solitudes,
> Où l'enfant boit, dix ans, l'âpre lait des études.*

The astonishing fullness and beauty of these lines make it difficult to believe that this is the poem of an adolescent. Baudelaire was fully aware of his achievement, and so he signed his name, asking nonetheless for Sainte-Beuve's approval:

> These verses were written *for you*, and with such naivety that when they were finished, I wondered if they weren't a sort of impertinence, and whether the *person praised* might not have the right to be offended at the compliment. – I wait for you to deign to give me your opinion.[39]

Sainte-Beuve's reply has been lost, but it must have been positive since a relationship formed between the critic who mourned the loss of his poetic muse and the poet who drew from Sainte-Beuve's very modern work, *Joseph Delorme*, the poetic lessons it contained for the younger generation.

In his letter to Sainte-Beuve, Baudelaire revealed his identity; elsewhere, uncertain of the value of his work, he remained hidden. The mask was occasionally a playful device which allowed him to indulge his taste for blackmail or his talent for invective; at other times, disguise made it possible to play the role of art lover, connoisseur, aesthetician, or, more particularly, aesthete.

---

*'Beardless, every one of us then, on the old oak-wood benches,/More polished and shiny than the links of a chain,/Which the skin of men has burnished day by day,/We dragged around our boredom with us sadly, crouched/And stooping under the square sky of those lonely wastes/Where children drink for ten long years the bitter milk of learning.'

Under the July Monarchy, the aesthete was also the dandy, the elegant, disdainful and sophisticated man frequently depicted by Balzac. In the days of Louis XIV one could demonstrate one's inherent superiority and flout the established order by going into commerce just as well as by writing a book; but under Louis-Philippe, who governed France in the name of the bourgeoisie, to be a dandy was to stand apart from the world of money, to refuse to take things seriously. Since by vocation and temperament he belonged to the fringe, Baudelaire had joined for a time the ranks of Balzac's resourceful and cynical dandies.

The poet would often recite strange verses to his friends, who were not always sure whether they should be impressed or whether he was making fools of them. He chose his victims with sly discrimination: Charles Cousin and Louis Ménard, who did not remain on friendly terms with him for very long, were subjected to *Nightmare*, the 'lunatic poem' in which a lover witnesses the rape of his mistress by an entire army;[40] Charles Asselineau, who was somewhat gullible in the early days of his friendship with Baudelaire, was treated to the same piece; and Louis Ulbach was honoured with a recital of *Gritty Manon*, in which the prostitute's 'soiled shirt' makes a brutal appearance. Prarond, too, heard Baudelaire recite a great number of poems and it is thanks to his reliable memory that we know that even at the time he was a tenant at the Hôtel Pimodan Baudelaire already possessed an astonishingly large corpus of poems, all unpublished, and written in a curious new style. These were the poems which, modified and perfected over the years, would eventually go to make up a large part of *Les Fleurs du Mal*.[41]

It was because he was conscious of his own originality that Baudelaire changed his mind at the last minute and withdrew his contribution from a collective volume that Le Vavasseur, Prarond and Auguste Dozon were planning to publish. On February 11, 1843, Prarond received this short note:

On *Monday*, my friend, *you'll get my bits of paper*. Then you can show me how to do the pagination and lay out the pages. I'm still counting on you to do the proofreading.

Let me advise you once again to be very strict with any infantile writing.

By infantile writing, Baudelaire was probably referring to the sort of 'angelic' poetry recited by Banville's friends. Le Vavasseur explains what happened next:

He had left his manuscripts with me – the rough draft of some pieces which were later included in *Les Fleurs du Mal* (the *Spleen et Idéal* section). Without showing any repugnance, I made my comments and, like the foolish and indiscreet friend that I was, I even ventured to correct the poet. Baudelaire said nothing, didn't get angry, and withdrew his contribution to the volume. He did well to do so. His material was of a finer weave than our homespun cloth.[42]

One critic, Jules Mouquet, has claimed that some of Baudelaire's poems did actually appear in the book, under Prarond's name; but Le Vavasseur's account of the incident and the poems themselves are sufficient proof of the contrary.

Even without Baudelaire's contribution, the book was a respectable size. Modestly entitled *Vers*, it was published by Herman in May 1843. As it turns out, the reluctant contributor was discreetly present after all. There was the poem by Dozon, 'written for a friend', in which he encouraged the reveller to follow the straight and narrow, and then two poems by Prarond dedicated to Baudelaire. One, addressed 'To my friend C.B.', and dated October 5, 1842, began with this quatrain:

> Vous aviez l'esprit tendre et le coeur vertueux,
> Tous les biens convoités d'une amitié naïve,
> Lorsqu'une femme belle, et de naissance juive
> Vous conduisit au fond d'un couloir tortueux.*

The volume as a whole has a spiritualistic air about it that might have been to Baudelaire's liking around 1839 or 1840. But by 1843, his poetry had a more satanic gleam to it, and would have been out of place among these verses which were chaste enough for Le Vavasseur and Prarond to recite them at one of the lectures organised by Emmanuel Bailly.

Vers was not a success. At the end of December 1852, Dozon asked Prarond in a letter:[43] 'Are there any copies of our ill-fated volume left? I don't even have one for myself.' And in 1883, writing from Salonika, he remarked: 'I don't know if you kept up relations with Baudelaire; I hardly ever saw him after our famous three-person book. I sometimes ran into him by chance; but to him, I was a figure of scorn, a wretched little penpusher' – a far cry from the days when Baudelaire enjoyed reciting Dozon's poem, 'The Wild Boar'. After 1843, Prarond and Le Vavasseur

*'Your mind was tender and guiltless your heart,/You had every virtue pure friendship could desire,/When a beautiful woman of Jewish birth/Led you down to the end of a winding corridor.'

had very little direct contact with their old friend, though Baudelaire devoted a very flattering article to Le Vavasseur in 1861, and wrote to Prarond in 1866 from his sickbed in Brussels to thank him for a copy of his poems, *Airs de Flûte*: this book, he wrote (or rather, dictated, since by then he was incapable of writing), 'struck me as being what I would call the annals of friendship'. Baudelaire went so far as to point out three errors in versification in one of the poems, perhaps remembering the alterations that Le Vavasseur had wanted to make back in 1843. Before slipping into the long agony of death, the poet of *Les Fleurs du Mal* bade farewell in this way to his friends from the Ecole Normande and the old Latin Quarter. Dozon must have been mistaken: Baudelaire was a faithful friend and was never ashamed to acknowledge his former companions.

Prarond and Baudelaire, who were very close in 1843, also had the idea of concocting a verse drama – a fashionable ambition in the year that saw the battle of *Les Burgraves* and *Lucrèce*. Prarond fortunately kept among his papers a copy of the first and beginning of the second act of this play, *Idéolus*, which he later summed up for Eugène Crépet:[44]

> ... one of the main characters was going to be a drunkard. We were supposed to be writing this play together, without stooping to prose. – The drunkard, an old philosophical scholar, was given the working name of Socratès. The play was set in Italy in the 16th century. – Even before the outline was decided on, I had sketched out some scenes for the play in its embryonic form, and I've held onto a few rather feeble lines from those scenes.

The play was Baudelaire's idea, but the two friends worked on it together. The plot centres around a sculptor, Idéolus, who, like Baudelaire, knows all the birth pains of the creator. The sculptor is torn between the charms of Forniquette, the aptly-named courtesan, and his love for the more honourable Nubilis, whom he eventually marries. Socratès the drunkard is brought on to slow the action down and appears as an important character in his own right.

Idéolus had little dramatic interest and was really more the parody of a play than a true drama. Baudelaire's concepts for the stage were excellent, but neither the theatres nor the audiences of the time could adapt very easily to those ideas. Nevertheless, the theatre was a recurrent preoccupation for Baudelaire: he even tried at one point to obtain the directorship of a theatre in order to impose on the public his own subjects and style.

Baudelaire sometimes left the members of the Ecole Normande for a very different group of writers, more advanced politically and of a rather shady nature. Their meeting place was the home of Auguste Le Gallois (or Legallois), who had published the works of Alphonse-Louis Constant. A former abbé, Constant was following in the footsteps of another ex-abbé, Lamennais, and propounding a brand of socialist Christianity or Christian socialism which was frowned upon by the Catholic hierarchy and therefore, under the influence of the Church, by the political authorities too.[45] Constant brought to his expression of Lamennais's doctrines the respect or even worship of women, which brought him into contact with the courageous feminist, Flora Tristan.

Le Gallois himself, favourable to new ideas, was inclined to indulge in social criticism of a lighter variety. In October 1843, he advertised a work entitled *Les Actrices galantes de Paris*, which contained some defamatory statements concerning the classical actress, Rachel. Sued by the actress, Le Gallois apologised and escaped with a warning. The following year, however, using the name of a different publisher, he produced the *Mystères galants des théâtres de Paris*, the subtitle and contents of which indicate that it was a later version of its libellous predecessor – a hastily thrown-together potpourri of scandalous anecdotes on actresses, attacks on Rachel, Ponsard and even on one of the contributors, the abbé Constant. On March 3, Flora Tristan wrote to Constant, her 'Dear Boy': 'You probably know that Legallois has just brought out the *Mystères galants* ... your name's right there in black and white. It's good publicity, but awfully scandalous!'[46]

Constant was not the only one to suffer from the outrage. One of the anonymous writers took a swipe at Baron Pichon, the owner of the Hôtel Pimodan, and Arondel, who sold art objects on the ground floor of the building. Deploring the present-day commercialisation of love, the writer mentions 'Messieurs Hieronymus Pichon, Lord Arundell, and a fair few other lovers of vaguely Arabian nags, who skimp on their orgies, and fiddle the wages of the miser they keep. Today's debauchery is done from the fireside!'[47] Baudelaire anticipated the riposte by sending the following message to Baron Pichon. This, incidentally, is the letter which led Jacques Crépet to discover Baudelaire's involvement in the *Mystères galants*:

Monsieur,

I learnt yesterday that several people, on the word of Legallois the publisher, have been attributing to me some words of an article included in a book produced by that publisher, in which your name, or a name homonymous to yours is printed.

I declare that the allegations attached to this name are, to the best of my knowledge, completely untrue.

In any other circumstance, I would deem it futile, Monsieur, to contest these ridiculous accusations, against which your behaviour, your character, and public esteem are a sufficient defence.

Baron Pichon received this diplomatic letter at about the same time as this message from Arondel:

I hasten to inform you that I shall be inviting Baudelaire to lunch tomorrow and that you will probably be able to find him at my place between 11 o'clock and midday. As for Privat, he will be much harder to contact since he has no fixed abode. He's the trickiest customer I know; he uses all his wit and ability to malign and slander the friends of his friends. As for Baudelaire, I'm more than certain that he did not mean to insult either of us.

I shall assist you in whatever way I can to force him to apologise and to make a public retraction of the libellous statements they published.

You can count on me then for tomorrow. If he doesn't listen to reason and tries to leave, I'll force him to stay by using my stick, or, if need be, my fists.

I am, Sir, your very devoted servant.[48]

It seems likely that Privat d'Anglemont was indeed the guilty party; but other parts of the book are almost certainly by Baudelaire, notably the attack on Ponsard. In an article published in 1846 – 'Advice to Young Writers' – Baudelaire distinguished two sorts of critical attack: 'There's the curved line, and the straight line, which is the most direct route.' The first method might be that of the anonymous writer; the second is the one Baudelaire was apparently intending to use in the articles he offered to *Le Tintamarre* – a satirical newspaper he worked for in 1846–47. The *Tintamarre* turned down these articles for reasons it explained in its 'Petite Correspondance' column:

To M. Charles B***. His article on Mme L ... Co ... will not be printed. It includes details pertaining to private life and does not enter our field.

To M. Charles B***. The logical conclusion of his article is a 500 franc fine and three months in jail. We would prefer not to have to pay our writers quite so much.

The poetess Louise Colet had been an obvious target for satirists since 1840, being physically well-endowed and graced with numerous lovers. She was close enough to Victor Cousin, the patron saint of French philosophy, for Cousin to make sure she received the Academy's prize for occasional poetry once or twice. One journalist, Alphonse Karr, who had printed some scandalous gossip about her, received a surprise visit. She was brandishing a knife which the journalist managed to snatch away and which he later hung in his apartment with a sign saying: 'Given to me by Mme Louise Colet – in the back.' When, in the play sketched out by Baudelaire and Prarond, Idéolus wants to murder Forniquette and cannot find any poison, he 'settles for Mme Colet's knife' – a kitchen knife, according to a different version of the scenario. Baudelaire hated bluestockings, women writers and casual verse, and it is not surprising to see him offering articles on the subject of Louise Colet to *Le Tintamarre* as early as 1843. He had already submitted another such piece to the Fourierist periodical, *La Démocratie pacifique*, which refused it 'on grounds of *immorality*'. Baudelaire informed his mother of this and asked for her reaction to the article in question, adding proudly: 'The good thing is that the people there were sufficiently amazed by it to do me the honour of *asking hurriedly* for a second one, with much courtesy and compliment.'[49] It is not known whether the second article was accepted or even written, but it is interesting to note in Baudelaire's choice of a newspaper this strange association of what was usually a fairly virtuous form of democratic socialism with a lively taste for satirical attacks and lampooning, maybe even blackmail. He would later find better outlets for his anger or his 'voracious Irony' – in the *Salon de 1845*, for example, in which he attacks the 'painter of the bourgeoisie', Horace Vernet, or, later, in the words of vengeance that make up *Pauvre Belgique!*

Another lampoonist who contributed to the *Mystères galants* was Georges Mathieu, whose violent diatribes against the Jesuits or against Rothschild and Jews were published by his brother-in-law, Baudelaire's friend, Edmond Albert.[50] One should note that anti-Semitism and anticlericalism were dominant features at the time of one of the major forms of democratic socialism.

It was through Le Gallois that Baudelaire also met Alphonse Esquiros, a confirmed republican, who, after suffering much political persecution, eventually became a senator under the Third Republic.[51] Esquiros, the author of several articles on social conditions in Britain, where he lived from 1856 to 1869, met the other Alphonse – Constant – at the seminary he attended. With Le Gallois, he published in 1840 *The Mad Virgins*, first of a series of three short books defending women driven to prostitution by poverty, and, the same year, *The People's Gospel*, which earned him several months in prison. Baudelaire includes Esquiros in a list of his 'second literary connections'. His socialism was certainly not what attracted the poet: there is a passage in the *Salon de 1846* in which Baudelaire denounces 'Marion de Lorme-type literature [an allusion to Victor Hugo's play], which consists of preaching the virtues of murderers and streetwalkers'. The worthy cause of rehabilitating prostitutes was not one that Baudelaire would readily have espoused. Neither was he attracted by the feminism of Esquiros and Constant, but rather by their analogical conception of a universe ordered by *correspondances*. In 1845, Constant published a volume of poetry, *Les Trois Harmonies*, in which this idea is celebrated in a poem entitled 'Les Correspondances':

> Formé de visibles paroles,
> Ce monde est le songe de Dieu;
> Son verbe en choisit les symboles,
> L'esprit les remplit de son feu ...*

The language of flowers , the 'mystical' words which surge up from the 'living pillars' of nature's temple depicted by Baudelaire in his own poem entitled 'Correspondances,' lead by insidious paths to the passion and exhilaration of the 1848 Revolution. After all, it was, significantly enough, one of the leading figures of French socialism, Pierre Leroux, who is said to have invented the term '*symbolisme*'.

Baudelaire had all it took to be a success – and a failure in the eyes of his family and his family's friends: syphilis, a *conseil judiciaire*, a coloured concubine, debts and a keen desire never to adopt a career. Even to his own friends, he remained something of a mystery. They stood in awe of his originality, which in him took a particularly bizarre form, his awkward temperament, and the contrast between his youthful appearance and an intellectual brilliance which seemed to be that of a man ten years his senior. 'At the age at which one is usually just beginning to live, Baudelaire had already led a full life ... His mind, stimulated by his travels and by his precocious experience of the world, had already reached maturity. He had successfully dared what others scarcely dreamt of, and forced his audacity on those around him by the strength of his will, experienced and defying ridicule.'[52]

The Baudelaire his friends remembered was the figure in Deroy's portrait, described here by Asselineau:

> The face, painted straight from the palette, stands out, partly against a light background, and partly against darkened drapery. The expression

---

*'Composed of visible words,/This world is God's dream;/Its symbols by his word are chosen,/And the spirit fills them with his fire.'

is disturbed or rather, disturbing; the eyes are wide, the gaze direct, the eyebrows raised; a new beard, full and elegant, curls close around the chin and cheeks. The hair, very thick, gathers at the temples; the body, leaning on the left elbow, is gripped in a black suit from which there emerge the edge of a white cravat and cuffs of pleated muslin. Add to this ensemble a pair of leather boots, light-coloured gloves, and a dandy's hat, and you will have a complete picture of Baudelaire as he was when one might have met him in the streets surrounding 'his' Ile Saint-Louis, walking about in those impoverished and deserted areas with such uncommon luxury of dress.

This 'carefree life' that Baudelaire had been leading since the end of his schooldays was the result of his refusal to embrace a 'bourgeois' existence – a refusal which took different forms and which was itself the result of a deeper motivation which for the time being can only be guessed at: the 'split' brought about by the disturbing discovery of freedom presupposes an inherent weakness. Baudelaire had rejected a career (along with the economic laws that govern society) and a family, both his own and the one he might have started. His school years were supposed to integrate him into society, but as soon as they came to an end, he tried, successfully, to escape from restrictions his friends would adopt without complaint.

His desire 'to be a writer', though indicative of a vocation, meant nothing more to those around him, including his family, than a refusal to start on a career. During this period at least, Baudelaire had no desire to become a professional writer, a producer like Balzac; he wanted simply to be a *poietes*, a creator. On nearly every occasion, he avoided the sort of journalism to which Gautier and even Nerval sacrificed so much of their time. Baudelaire was much closer in this respect to his contemporary Gustave Flaubert. In order to avoid a career, Flaubert came up with an illness which enabled him to be declared unfit for active life. Baudelaire used a different stratagem for dropping out of society, since the illness he contracted was not one that was felt to constitute an excuse, though syphilis did prevent him from starting a family. Baudelaire's road to freedom lay through extravagance. Ignoring the limits imposed by a budget, and the relationship between assets and liabilities, he acquired furniture, clothes, books and works of art without counting the cost, as if he felt himself to be above practical considerations: he would not be held responsible for his own actions. This might explain why he accepted the imposition of the *conseil judiciaire*, even whilst cursing its existence.

Flaubert took refuge in his mother. Baudelaire could not do the same since that position was already taken. He made up for this by becoming economically dependent on her. Having cheerfully taken a large bite out of the paternal inheritance, Baudelaire, with his particular tastes, could never be content with the interest from the remaining capital. This led him on numerous occasions to ask his mother for loans which were intended to remind her of her maternal duty. Another dominant feature of his behaviour was the attempt to eliminate 'strangers' who stood in the way of a direct relationship with his mother. The father had already been eliminated: he was dead and died a second, symbolic death in the son's frittering away of the inheritance. The stepfather was more difficult to dispose of; but with the help of his debts – the earliest of which, moreover, represented disgrace, being a result of his gonorrhoea – Charles was able to break off relations with Aupick and perpetuate in his mind the years of childhood with his mother; but only in his mind. The role of guardian was taken, not by her, but by Ancelle, and this would be a continual source of reproach.

From our late twentieth-century viewpoint, it is perhaps too easy to pass harsh judgement on two people who belong to a period which we readily assume to be close to ours; historically, however, it belongs to a different stage of civilisation.

PART FOUR

THE DANDY AND THE SOCIALIST

CHAPTER 12

Monsieur Baudelaire-Dufaÿs

1844–1846

Having suffered the indignity of being assigned a *conseil judiciaire*, Baudelaire chose for himself a *nom de plume*, adding to his own surname his mother's maiden name. Since neither he nor Mme Aupick knew the correct spelling, it occurs in various forms: with the 'de' which the bourgeoisie liked to consider aristocratic (de Fayis), or a deliberately unusual diaeresis on the 'y' (Dufaÿs).[1] Generally, the 'Baudelaire' remains, probably to avoid confusion with a minor journalist called Alexandre Dufaï, who had been a supporter of the 'Common-Sense School' and who wrote for some of the newspapers in which Baudelaire's work was beginning to appear. When sending a copy of his *Salon de 1846* to his future literary agent, Julien Lemer, perhaps hoping for a review, Baudelaire asked him to note carefully the spelling of his name: 'I can't stand being confused with that rascal who has the nerve to call himself Dufaï.'

Baudelaire-Dufaÿs was not a poet, but an art lover – one might almost say a connoisseur – and a collector of prints, drawings, caricatures and old books. His bibliophily sets him apart from most other major writers of the period. Though his unsettled existence must have made things difficult, he managed to acquire rare editions and obtained excellent bindings for his own books, as well as for those he gave to friends. Baudelaire's choice of editions was governed by his often unusual literary tastes: Ernest Prarond reports having seen him in his rooms on the Quai de Béthune reading Ronsard in an edition which dates from 1623 and reciting an epigram by Ronsard's rival poet, Desportes.[2] Baudelaire's predilection for the love poetry of the Renaissance and especially for one of its most 'realistic' exponents, Mathurin Régnier, is indeed apparent in the aggressive beauty of the poem, 'Je n'ai pas pour maîtresse une lionne illustre . . .'

Baudelaire's active interest in painting dates from the same period. Prarond often found him 'sitting on a low stool, examining in minute detail a canvas he had purchased the day before and set up in front of him on a sort of easel'.[3] He bought paintings, grew tired of them and sold them again – probably at a loss.[4] In those days, there were many discoveries still waiting to be made; catalogues were incomplete and histories of art deficient.

Baudelaire was a daring, though rather unlucky collector. Living below him at the Hôtel Pimodan was Arondel, who had 'created a collection of paintings' and was planning to sell off part of this collection 'at cost-price'. This, at least, is what the dealer claimed in the Paris Appeals Court after Baudelaire's death, when trying to recover from Mme Aupick the sum of 14,900 francs which he said her son had owed him. This long-standing debt, which the Court reduced to 1,500 francs, was finally settled after Mme Aupick's death in 1872.[5]

The list of paintings sold to Baudelaire is, at first sight, extremely impressive: a *Madeleine* by Zuccari from the end of the sixteenth century for 1,200 francs; a *Saint Jerome* by Domenichino for 1,500 francs; a Poussin landscape for 1,000 francs; a Velasquez, a Tintoretto and a Corregio 'for just one hundred francs', in other words, about thirty-three francs for a Corregio – the equivalent today of approximately twenty pounds! These prices, especially when one compares them to Arondel's usurious rates of interest, say something about the authenticity of these paintings and explain why Baudelaire occasionally alludes in his art criticism to works that apparently never existed.[6]

Another result of Baudelaire's unfortunate errors of judgement was that he scarcely ever wrote about classical painting.[7] Certain allusions, as early as the 1845 *Salon*, indicate the broad extent of his artistic knowledge, but they betray at the same time a certain reticence and fear of repeating his mistakes, which he overcame only in his study of *Quelques caricaturistes étrangers*.

Furthermore, Baudelaire's taste in art often led him to explore uncharted territory. His admiration for recognised masters like Poussin and Velasquez lasted all his life, but he never once pretended to admire, for example, the Italian schools that might be called 'classical'. In the Louvre, 'which he seldom passed without a visit', he preferred to linger in the Spanish room, 'much better endowed than it is today, at least in violent torture scenes which King Louis-Philippe, their owner, withdrew in 1848'.[8] Baudelaire had sudden whims and would enter the Louvre just to see a couple of paintings by Theotocopulos (who was yet to achieve general recognition as El Greco). Prarond was not the only one to be struck by these infatuations. Champfleury remembered his own bemused irritation during walks through the Louvre with Baudelaire: 'He'd point out Bronzino to me – a rather affected artist – as the greatest painter of any school . . . On another occasion,

Van Eyck and the primitives had replaced that "rascal" Bronzino.'

Clearly, Baudelaire's tastes were often unconventional and entirely independent of academic opinion. Taking into account his desire to astonish
friends, one can detect in his surprising preferences a dominant interest in
works of the baroque period – an interest quite compatible with his
admiration for Delacroix, Daumier and the sculptor Préault, who, with
their impassioned styles, represent a sort of neo-Baroque.

Baudelaire's love of the arts – 'my great, unique and primal passion', the
'cult of images'[9] – was based on considerable experience. His father, and
his father's first wife, had both been painters, and the apartment in the rue
Hautefeuille in which Baudelaire was born was filled with their works and
those of their artist friends. A few steps away was an open-air museum of
sculpture – the Luxembourg Gardens. The Aupick household, though less
artistically inclined, was by no means hostile to the arts, as one can guess
from the confident tone of Baudelaire's letter describing the school trip to
the Versailles Palace museum. In his mother's salon, he was able to meet
the most celebrated miniaturist of the time, Mme de Mirbel, who would
later help Mme Aupick's young son gain admittance to certain artistic
circles. Before, and especially after his trip to the East, Baudelaire's friendship with Emile Deroy provided him with a rich source of information on
the technical aspects of painting. Baudelaire himself was something of an
artist, as his own sketches show, and even his literary activities during this
period indicate a strong predilection for the plastic arts. An early version
of *La Fanfarlo*, or perhaps some other short story, was to appear, he told
his mother, in the *Bulletin de l'Ami des Arts* – a review founded by Albert
de La Fizelière to defend artists rejected by the Salon jury; and during the
summer of 1844, he planned to offer to the more literary *Revue de Paris* his
'book on painting' – a work which suffered some delay when Baudelaire
spent a few days in the Hôtel des Haricots. (This was the prison in which
those who failed to do their compulsory day of service in the Garde
Nationale were confined.)[10]

Baudelaire therefore had every reason to believe that he was fully qualified
to be a collector of old paintings. His mistakes, in fact, are perfectly
understandable at a time when connoisseurs were rare.

In modern art, first-hand experience stood him in good stead. Deroy had
the makings of a great painter and, though a pupil of Paul Delaroche, he
was also an admirer of Delacroix. It was Deroy who painted for Baudelaire
the copy he possessed of his favourite Delacroix painting, *Algiers Women*.

At the Hôtel Pimodan, Baudelaire met one of Delacroix's friends, the
painter Boissard de Boisdenier, who, on April 1, 1845, moved into the

apartment which Roger de Beauvoir had just vacated. Boissard's mistress was one of the most beautiful models in Paris. Joséphine Bloch, known as Marix, had posed for Ary Scheffer and Delaroche, and had been living in a tiny apartment at the Hôtel Pimodan since the end of 1844. When Boissard moved in, he brought Marix down from her attic to the grand first-floor apartment, much to the horror of Baron Pichon's respectable and long-suffering tenants, who had only recently been relieved to see their riotous neighbour, Roger de Beauvoir, leave the Hôtel.[11] Baudelaire himself would derive some benefit from the extravagant lives led by the Hôtel's more illustrious inhabitants.

The annual exhibition of paintings at the Louvre had opened on March 15. The 1845 Salon included a work by Boissard – *Jesus on the Cross* – his other piece having been rejected by the jury. Arondel, who was an artist as well as a dealer, had had his picture of game birds accepted; no doubt one of the jury members owed him money. Baudelaire set to work on a review of the Salon – mainly to prove that he really was a writer. His true interests lay with the theoretical aspects of art, but in order to write his review, he nonetheless had to stroll through the Salon and examine the paintings. He praised the colour and texture of Boissard's work, and devoted a few ambiguous lines to Arondel.

Charles Asselineau had already heard about Baudelaire from Nadar, who considered him 'a man of much wit and talent, amusingly original', and also from Banville, who described his friend as 'a very superior poet'.[12] Baudelaire and Asselineau met face to face for the first time at the 1845 Salon, where they were introduced by Emile Deroy. Asselineau, who was busy writing his own *Salon* for the *Journal des Théâtres*,[13] later described his first meeting with the poet: 'We walked together through the galleries. He was wearing the black suit that he wore for so many years, a long waistcoat, narrow trousers and tails; on top of that, a straight, homespun overcoat that was a "secret" between him and his tailor. His head was completely shaved, and his face was very striking, not easily forgotten.' (Baudelaire changed his hairstyle almost as often as his shirt.)

We left the Salon, and went to a wineshop in the rue du Carrousel where some workers and a coachman of the King's household in livery were drinking. Baudelaire ordered white wine, biscuits, and *new* pipes ... I noticed him looking at me out of the corner of his eye to see how I'd take to the idea of going to the café to work ...

We parted company after spending an hour drawing up a list, with

Deroy's assistance, of the painters we'd mention. We arranged to meet again the following day . . .

After our second session . . . Baudelaire left to go and work at home – the notes he'd taken were all he needed – and he gave me his address. He told me his *Salon* would appear as a booklet, and I promised to give it a mention when it came out.

True to his word, Asselineau informed the readers of the *Journal des Théâtres* that his comments on Delacroix would be 'developed more freely and more expertly' by his friend Charles Baudelaire in his forthcoming *Salon*, as well as in his *History of Modern Painting*. This was the book that Baudelaire had been hoping to publish the previous year in the *Revue de Paris*.

Asselineau's flattering words are not the only hint of the strong ascendancy Baudelaire always had over his friend. Their two *Salons* reveal the same likes and dislikes, notably in the case of William Haussoullier's *The Fountain of Youth*, which receives 'violent praise' from Baudelaire and which Asselineau hails as 'the finest new arrival of the year'. The two friends may well have had similar tastes, but in view of their respective temperaments, it would probably be more accurate to ascribe these shared opinions to Baudelaire's hypnotic influence.

Baudelaire's own seventy-two-page *Salon*, of which 500 copies were printed, appeared in mid-May. On the inside cover, there was an advertisement for other works by the same author: the *History of Modern Painting* and two other books that were never published – *On Caricature* and *David, Guérin and Girodet*. Baudelaire nevertheless extracted material from these unfinished writings for use in other studies, including his next *Salon*.

Despite the provocative declarations of the *Salon de 1845*, and Baudelaire's aggressive praise of Delacroix and Haussoullier, the little book went almost unnoticed by the critics. A noteworthy exception was Champfleury, who had been briefed by Baudelaire himself: 'If you want to do me a favour, write something serious and talk about Diderot's *Salons*.' Champfleury, writing in the *Corsaire-Satan*, obliged his friend by comparing him to Diderot and also to Stendhal – the two writers whom Baudelaire most admired at that time. Diderot's neglected *Salon de 1759* had just appeared in *L'Artiste*, and it was perhaps his discovery of Diderot the art critic that prompted Baudelaire to adopt for his book on painting the more casual and fragmentary form of the traditional *Salon*. The theoretical part of his book was therefore rather short – 'A Few Words of Introduction' and a one-paragraph conclusion, which, however, contained the important notion that modernity is an essential ingredient of art. Apart from Haussoullier, wrote Baudelaire, there's nothing new this year: 'Nobody listens for tomorrow's wind; and yet on every side we're jostled by the heroism *of modern life* ... The true painter will be the one who is able to wrest from contemporary life its epic side, and make us see and comprehend how grand and poetic we are in our cravats and patent leather boots.' It is interesting to note that, for Baudelaire, despite his admiration, Delacroix was obviously not that long-awaited painter.

As for the main body of Baudelaire's work, it compares favourably with the other *Salons* published that year; but the author himself was unhappy with his work. Champfleury later recalled how Baudelaire, afraid that some of his ideas were too reminiscent of notions already expressed by Heine and Stendhal, destroyed all remaining copies of his first book: 'The ideal of that strange artist was to present himself to the public only once he had completely mastered his skills.'[14] Baudelaire was a severer critic than his friends: Gustave Le Vavasseur, in the local paper of Ernest Prarond's home town, Abbeville, wrote a good review which Baudelaire judged 'delightful';[15] and Auguste Vitu, a recent acquaintance, was equally positive in *La Silhouette*.

Baudelaire must have hoped for more critical reaction to his *Salon*, but could at least have derived some comfort from those friendly words as he lay recovering from a self-inflicted wound. On 30 June 1845, he had apparently tried to take his own life while sitting in a café with Jeanne Duval. In the opinion of Louis Ménard, Baudelaire stabbed himself with a knife simply in order to add another romantic touch to his image.[16] Ménard, however, fell out with Baudelaire early in 1846, and his version of the suicide attempt is almost certainly coloured by ill will. The letter Baudelaire sent on that same June 30 to his *conseil judiciaire* paints a much darker picture:

When Mlle Jeanne Lemer gives you this letter, I shall be dead. She does not know this. – You are familiar with my will. Except for the portion set aside for my Mother, Mlle *Lemer* is to inherit all that I leave, once you have settled certain debts of which I enclose a list ...

I am going to kill myself because I cannot continue to live, because I cannot bear the weariness of falling asleep and waking up. I am killing myself because I am useless to others, *and dangerous to myself*. – I am going to *kill* myself because I believe I am immortal and because I have *hope* ...

I give and bequeath all I possess to Mlle Lemer, including my few pieces of furniture and my portrait, because she is the only being with whom I have found any peace of mind. Can anyone blame me for wishing to pay for the few pleasures I have found on this terrible Earth?

I do *not* know my brother very well – he has not lived *within me nor with me*, and he doesn't need me.

My Mother, who has so often and always unwittingly poisoned my existence, doesn't need this money either. She has her *husband*; she possesses a *human being*, affection, and *friendship*.

I have only *Jeanne Lemer* ... I cannot bear the thought that anyone should wish to dispossess her of what I am leaving, on the pretext that I am not of sound mind. – You heard me talking with you these past few days. Was I mad then? ...

You can see now that this will is not some idle boast or a violation of society or family rules, but simply an expression of that which within me is still human – love, and the sincere desire to be of service to a creature who has been at times my delight and my repose.

There are several possible reasons for Baudelaire's drastic action: the relative failure of his *Salon*, a desire to bring pressure to bear on the family members who had humiliated him with the *conseil judiciaire*, or a deeper *ennui*, a feeling that life had lost its savour. Baudelaire's correspondence makes it clear in any case that his injury was real enough. Shortly after the attempt, he was unable to leave Jeanne Duval's apartment to see his mother: 'The Doctor,' he wrote, 'apparently doesn't want me to move.'

About Baudelaire's activities in the following weeks little is known, except that he stayed for a while in the Place Vendôme with Mme Aupick and the General. Perhaps this was an effort to make a new beginning, to accept a sort of discipline; but the undated letters from this period show Baudelaire apologising for his inability to return home at the proper hour: 'Please don't be angry with me for breaking the *Rule*, since this is the first time.' But the 'Rule' soon became too much:

I am leaving, and shall return only when my mind and money are in a better condition. I am leaving for several reasons. First, I've fallen into a terrible state of depression and torpor, and I need to spend a lot of time on my own in order to recover a little and get my strength back. – Secondly, I cannot be the person your husband would like me to be, and so to stay any longer in his house would be to cheat him; and finally, I do not think it *decent* that he treat me as he seems determined to do from now on.

Baudelaire gave Louis Ménard a rather different explanation of his desertion: 'Just imagine! The only wine they drink in that house is Burgundy, whereas *I* can't stand for anything but Bordeaux ... It was an impossible situation, and so I left. *Voilà!*'[17]

The Hôtel Corneille, opposite the Odéon theatre on the Left Bank, may have been the place in which Baudelaire first took refuge, having fled from his parents' home.[18] The 'Corneille' was known to Thackeray, who recommended it to impecunious visitors, adding that it was a place where, 'if by any strange chance you are desirous for a while to get rid of your countrymen, you will find that they scarcely ever penetrate'. George Du Maurier, who stayed there in 1855, described it as the haunt of students, 'and a noisy, rowdy crew they were, singing and shouting to their friends below from the open windows in warm weather'. It was a dilapidated, featureless building, 'dingy, mean-looking, and dirty, inside and out'. At the time Baudelaire moved in, Privat d'Anglemont was a frequent lodger, and Balzac had used it for the setting of his short story, *Z. Marcas*. The rooms, he said, contained nothing but a bed, a few chairs, a chest of drawers, a mirror and a table: 'What more do young people need ...?'

This was to be the new pattern of Baudelaire's life. Hounded by debt collectors and bailiffs from one cheap hotel to another, he nevertheless managed to complete his second *Salon* and his first short story. Clearly, the few pieces of furniture of Balzac's *Z. Marcas* could not satisfy Baudelaire's needs: 'You must send at once,' he wrote to his mother after leaving the Corneille, 'to M. *Baudelaire-Dufaÿs*, at the *Hôtel de Dunkerque, no. 32, rue Laffitte*, the small trunk which contains my linen – and some shoes and slippers – and the two black ties – *plus all my books*. I *must* have them immediately. Don't reproach me or press me to return, because I shan't.'[19]

Though true to his word, Baudelaire seems to have made a small effort to obey the aforementioned family 'Rule'. He enrolled, at the end of 1845 or beginning of 1846, in the section of one of the 'Grandes Ecoles' responsible for training librarians. His mother and stepfather probably imagined Charles engaging in this respectable career whilst indulging his interest in poetry as a hobby. No doubt they were disappointed that their son's name did not appear in December 1846 on the list of first-year examination candidates. Baudelaire preferred the editorial rooms of satirical newspapers, artists' studios, or cafés, which he visited in the company of Privat and other Bohemians, where he could forget his 'hovel', with its 'stupid, dusty, chipped furniture; the cold, empty fireplace soiled with spittle; the sad-looking windows, on which rain has traced furrows through the dust; manuscripts, scratched out or incomplete; the almanac, on which the sinister dates are marked!'[20]

With Privat, Baudelaire's relations were more than merely social, as Arsène Houssaye, who had become the director of the review *L'Artiste* in 1844, recalled in his *Confessions*: 'Baudelaire made his début in the literary world with an ingenious ploy. Some writers adopt a pseudonym, not wanting to make a public display of their name. Baudelaire went one better, and took as his mask a human being.' The mask was Privat d'Anglemont. 'Baudelaire dictated his first sonnets to his friend, who then signed them. D'Anglemont brought them to me, accompanied by the poet, who wanted to see what sort of impression they would make. D'Anglemont read me the sonnets, which were quite beautiful, though the distinctive mark of the French Edgar Allan Poe was not yet evident. "I, too, write poems," Baudelaire said; "but I'm not so stupid as to show them off! Poetry is the rarest of blooms; only in reverent and noble isolation may one enjoy its scent and pluck its petals. Nature did not make poets so that they could become comedians! ..." But, saying this, Baudelaire took d'Anglemont's sonnets – or rather, his own – and asked me to publish them in *L'Artiste*, which I did.'

On the strength of Houssaye's account, eleven poems printed between 1844 and 1847 in *L'Artiste, La Silhouette* and the *Corsaire-Satan*, signed by Privat or anonymous, have been attributed by various critics to Baudelaire,[21] who did in fact put his name to a sonnet in a similar 'Regency' style, which appeared in *L'Artiste* on May 25, 1845: 'A une dame créole.' Nine of these poems are included in the definitive Pléiade edition of Baudelaire's complete works. If the poems signed by Prarond in 1843 are almost certainly not by Baudelaire, as we have seen, Privat, on the other hand, was, by his own admission, an 'intellectual prostitute' and not averse to a little literary deception. Besides, his complicity is apparently confirmed by a note sent by Baudelaire to Banville in July 1845: 'I have every reason to be scared stiff of Privat. Try to shut him up. He'll know what I'm talking about.' Baudelaire was presumably afraid that his talkative friend would tell everyone that the poems he had published were actually the work of Baudelaire-Dufaÿs.

One reason for wanting Privat to keep their collaboration a secret can be found on the back cover of Baudelaire's *Salon de 1846*, as well as on certain books published by Pierre Dupont, Banville and Champfleury, between October 1845 and early 1847: 'To appear shortly: *Les Lesbiennes*, by Baudelaire-Dufaÿs.' This collection of poems, more serious than those signed by Privat, never appeared, though many of them, perhaps in a different form, went to make up, much later, *Les Fleurs du Mal*. One should note that the word '*Lesbiennes*' had not yet completely acquired its modern sense and signified primarily the female inhabitants of the island of Lesbos, the 'seekers of infinity' depicted by Baudelaire in his poem, 'Femmes damnées'.[22]

Baudelaire's '*Lesbiennes*' have little to do with the dancing girls celebrated in verse by Privat. One of these girls who danced at the Bal Mabille, an open-air cabaret frequented by students and artists, had a short affair with the poet:[23] she was Elise Sergent, known as Queen Pomaré – an allusion to the Tahitian queen who almost caused a conflict between France and Britain in 1843 by welcoming a little too warmly the Protestant missionary, Pritchard. After failing as an actress and spending two days in prison as a result of her liaison with a ruffian who passed himself off as a law student, she arrived one day in 1845 at the Hôtel Pimodan in search of a room. Baudelaire had left the Hôtel, but his furniture was still there, standing surety for his unpaid rent. Banville tells how Baudelaire returned to find 'Queen' Pomaré comfortably installed in his former home:

> Pomaré, all dressed up and looking for rooms, one day, led by the concierge, entered the pretty apartment occupied by the poet at the Hôtel Pimodan ... Enchanted by an artist's interior, the like of which she had never seen, Pomaré spent a long time admiring the wallpaper, with its thick red and black stripes, the head painted by Delacroix, the large walnut table, fashioned so artistically and with such subtle curves that when one sat down at it to read, each part of one's body fitted into it perfectly, the books, magnificently adorned with full bindings, the armchairs, broad enough to hold a priest or a dowager, and, in the cupboard, the bottles of Rhine wine surrounded by emerald-green glasses. In short, she didn't want to leave and adopted a little Turkish divan on which she slept at night and read Classical literature during the day; and I do believe she would still be there if the landlord's architect had not come one morning to direct repairs that would brook no resistance, since they began with the demolition of a large wall!

This brief encounter left a few traces in Baudelaire's work. Banville, a friend of both the poet and the dancer, recognised Pomaré in this phrase written by Baudelaire in 1846: 'Never slander Mother Nature, and if she has given you a flat-chested mistress, then say: "I have a boyfriend - with hips!" '[24] She was also the subject of this song – yet another that was probably written by Baudelaire but published under the name of Privat:

'Combien dureront nos amours?'
Dit la pucelle, au clair de lune.
L'amoureux répond: 'O ma brune,
  Toujours! toujours!'

Quand tout sommeille aux alentours,
Elise, se tortillant d'aise,
Dit qu'elle veut que je la baise
  Toujours! toujours!

Moi je dis: 'Pour charmer mes jours
Et le souvenir de mes peines,
Bouteilles, que n'êtes-vous pleines
  Toujours! toujours!

Mais le plus chaste des amours,
L'amoureux le plus intrépide,
Comme un flacon s'use et se vide
  Toujours! toujours!*

Elise was never to see this song in print: she died of a chest ailment on 10 April 1847, at the age of twenty-two.

Apart from Elise, a few other figures emerge from the Bacchic cohorts of young dancers who inspired the chivalrous poems written by Privat or Baudelaire. One should certainly include, for example, the young acrobat who bears a striking resemblance to the red-haired beggar-girl painted by Deroy:

A UNE JEUNE SALTIMBANQUE

Nous t'aimions bien jadis, quand sur ta triste harpe
Tu raclais la romance, et qu'en un carrefour,
Pour attirer la foule à voir tes sauts de carpe,
Un enfant scrofuleux tapait sur un *tambour*;

---

* ' "How long will our love last?"/Said the maiden by the light of the moon./Her lover replied: "Oh, my pretty brunette,/For ever and ever!"

When all is sleeping all around,/She, wriggling with pleasure,/Tells me she wants me to kiss her/For ever and ever!

And I say to her, "To lighten my days/And the memory of my grief,/Oh, bottles, why aren't you full/For ever and ever!"

But the purest of loves,/And most intrepid of lovers,/Are all used up and emptied like a flask/For ever and ever!'

Quand tu couvais de l'oeil, en tordant ton écharpe,
Quelque athlète en maillot, Alcide fait au tour,
Qu'admire le bourgeois, que la police écharpe,
Qui porte cent kilos et t'appelle *mamour*.

Ta guitare enrouée et ta jupe à paillettes
Etalaient à nos yeux le rêve des poètes,
La danseuse d'Hoffmann, Esmeralda, Mignon.

Mais déchue à présent, te voilà, ma pauvre ange,
Sultane du trottoir, ramassant dans la fange
L'argent qui doit soûler ton rude compagnon.*

Some of these ladies may have attended the 'Club des Hachichins', which held its meetings in the little boudoir adjoining Boissard's apartment in the Hôtel Pimodan. The name was invented by Théophile Gautier, who had written two articles on hashish, one of which was used by Dr Moreau de Tours in his work of 1845, *On Hashish and Mental Illness*. Moreau's 'Psychological Studies' are important in that they laid the foundations of neuro- and psychopharmacology by establishing an analogy between dreams and delirium.

Boissard gave the doctor an opportunity to widen his field of experiment by organising hashish 'fantasias'. One of the invitations he sent out has been found among Gautier's papers: 'My dear Théophile, We'll be taking some hashish at my place, *next Monday*, October 3rd [1845] under the auspices of Dr Moreau and d'Aubert Roche. Do you want to take part? If so, get here between 5 and 6 at the latest. You'll have your share of a modest dinner, and wait for the hallucination. You could even bring along the bourgeois you wanted to inject. Since people bring strangers to my inn, one more won't make any difference.'[25]

Visitors to these parties included Gérard de Nerval, Daumier, the painter Chenavard, the sculptor Pradier and his wife, Louise, who gave Flaubert

* 'We once loved you well, when, on your sorrowful harp/You would scrape out your lovesong, and, when on a corner,/To bring the crowd to watch your feats,/A scrofulous child would beat on a drum;

When, twisting your scarf, you longingly gazed/At some athlete in his vest, a well-turned Hercules,/Whom the citizen admires and the police beat up,/Who lifts a hundred kilos and calls you *my darlin'*.

Your raucous guitar and your spangled skirt/Revealed to us the poet's dream,/The dancing girl of Hoffmann, Esmeralda, Mignon.

But now there you are, my poor fallen angel,/Princess of the pavement, picking out of the mud/The money that will get your rough companion drunk.'

some ideas for his portrayal of Madame Bovary. At the 'fantasia' that took place on 22 December 1845, Honoré de Balzac was present. The next day, he wrote to his future wife: 'I stood up to the hashish and didn't experience all the phenomena; my brain is so resilient that I needed a stronger dose than the one I took. Nevertheless, I heard celestial voices and saw some heavenly paintings. I spent twenty years descending Lauzun's staircase, and beheld the pictures and gold decorations of the apartment in unbelievable splendour; but this morning, since rising, I've been asleep and have no will.'[26]

Baudelaire remembered things differently in his *Paradis artificiels*: 'He was presented with some hashish; he examined it, sniffed it, and handed it back without touching it.' This account was later confirmed by Gautier, who had moved into an annex of Boissard's apartment. Baudelaire may well have met Gautier at that time, shocking the other inhabitants with 'a monkey on his shoulder, a dog at his feet ... a book in his hand.' Despite his admiration for the poet, Baudelaire was put off by Gautier's vulgar joviality and described him in the *Corsaire-Satan*, but without naming him, as 'fat, lazy, and lethargic'. Their friendship dates only from the 1850s.

Baudelaire was an infrequent visitor to these 'fantasias'. Hashish scarcely satisfied his curiosity; but opium, in the form of laudanum, was soon to become 'an old and terrible friend, and, like all women, rich, alas! in caresses and betrayals'.

By 1 June 1846, Baudelaire-Dufaÿs, the art lover and collector, was also enough of an author to join the Society of Men of Letters. His literary baggage was light, but included two *Salons* and a handful of contributions to various organs of militant journalism, notably the *Corsaire-Satan*.

The *Corsaire*, which had joined forces with another satirical newspaper called *Satan*, was a nineteenth-century *Private Eye* or *Canard enchaîné*.[27] Its editor, Lepoitevin Saint-Alme, had been a friend of Balzac and, so he claimed, the 'author' of Balzac's earliest novels. Having made a living under the Restoration as a literary entrepreneur, the ageing Saint-Alme had managed to bring together at the *Corsaire-Satan* the promising young writers of Baudelaire's generation: Champfleury, Banville, Henry Murger, Auguste Vitu and many others. His paper thus acquired a certain amount of political influence. He allowed his journalists, whom he called his 'little cretins', to attack any personality they pleased. Theoretically, at least, there was no censorship – except for illustrations – but the strict laws on libel necessitated certain precautions: articles were anonymous and attacks were cleverly veiled. Saint-Alme himself was an expert at turning away with exquisite politeness the indignant celebrities who came to complain about defamatory articles. If the accusers (or victims) persisted, Saint-Alme would remove his hat to reveal, to their astonishment, the bald pate and wispy grey hair of an old man. Those who were not deterred even by this sudden transformation were offered 'a serious fight – a duel at four paces'.[28]

Baudelaire was naturally drawn to the paper, as Asselineau explained:

> Baudelaire was then seen on the boulevards in his fantastic black tail coat, which, cut by the tailor to the poet's design, was an insolent contradiction of contemporary fashion: long, buttoned down, flared at the top like a cornet, and ending in two narrow, pointed flaps ... Baudelaire actually wrote very little for the paper ... For one of his aristocratic nature, journalism was a public boxing match to be avoided, and he treated the offices of the *Corsaire* mostly as a literary salon.[29]

In 1846, *La Silhouette*, a rival newspaper, on which Baudelaire had several friends, described this 'salon' in some detail. In the following scene, Saint-Alme's young men arrive for work:

> Good morning, Monsieur Viard, good morning, Monsieur Vitu, good morning, Monsieur Baudelaire! – Three great men! So, Monsieur Viard, you're still not working?
>
> Your paper was so stupid yesterday. There was a disgraceful article in it ...
>
> Shut up, you over there, Vitu and Baudelaire. It's impossible to get any work done.
>
> *M. Baudelaire, continuing to speak*: You see, Vitu, creditors are like women ... You can't love them enough. As Eugène Delacroix said to me yesterday ...
>
> *Saint-Alme:* Hallo! that's good. Why don't you write it up?
>
> *M. Baudelaire:* You know perfectly well I don't write.
>
> *Saint-Alme:* Oh! that's right. Monsieur has too much genius. Monsieur is going to write us another book on painting, like last year. You've got no common sense, you know. Delacroix's gone to your head.
>
> *M. Baudelaire, in a serious tone:* I'm not talking to you, Monsieur. See, Champfleury, 'stylishness' and clichés will be the downfall of art. It's incredible how many new ideas I've introduced in my book ... I'm placing myself under the protection of the bourgeois and the artist.[30]

Baudelaire's first article appeared on November 4, 1845. It was a short, anonymous review of two books by Philippe de Chennevières, alias Jean de Falaise:

The article I wrote on you appeared in yesterday's paper. I hope you'll like it.

M. Le Poitevin Saint-Alme has read some of your stories ... and is delighted. He'd like you to do some for him.

Please see if you can write some *feuilletons* QUICKLY, at one and a half sous a line, which I believe comes to less than 20 francs for the 9 columns!!! But the real advantage is that when that fine fellow is keen on someone, he enjoys doing him all kinds of favours.

If the idea appeals to you, go and see him and tell him your name, *Chennevières*.

Did Labitte get his copies? ...

B. D.

Thanks to his resourceful young friend, Chennevières was able to extract a few sous from the *Corsaire*, and Jules Labitte, the publisher of the *Salon de 1845*, agreed to be the Paris distributor of the books Baudelaire had reviewed.

On November 24, the paper inserted an anonymous anecdote by Baudelaire, describing how Balzac had enlisted the help of three friends in producing the articles he had promised a publisher. The anecdote – 'How to pay your debts when you're a genius' – paints a very unflattering picture of Edouard Ourliac, Théophile Gautier and Gérard de Nerval. Balzac, the genius of the title, fares somewhat better, particularly in the revised version, printed eleven months later. This time, Baudelaire adds a postscript and signs his name. The customary retraction becomes a celebration of creative genius:

If some bright spark decided to take this as a journalistic joke, and an attack on the glory of the greatest man of this century, he would be shamefully mistaken. I wanted to prove that the great poet knows how to unravel his debts as easily as he unravels the plot of the most abstruse and complicated novel.

In the following months, in collaboration with three colleagues, Baudelaire produced a short pastiche of a *'drame antique'* by Arsène Houssaye, entitled *Sapho*, and, again anonymously, a four-line epigram ridiculing Paulin Limayrac, a collaborator of the respectable *Revue des Deux Mondes*.

Meanwhile, the art critic returned with an impressive study of *The Classical Museum of the Bonne-Nouvelle Bazaar*. The exhibition, held in a Paris department store, was the work of a society which raised money for impoverished artists. Among the seventy-one paintings on display were

eleven by David and thirteen by Ingres. In his review, Baudelaire devotes
most space to David – not so much the David of the Empire as the painter
of a tribute to one of the martyrs of the French Revolution – Marat: 'One
of the great curiosities of modern art,' writes Baudelaire, 'in which every
detail is historically accurate and true to life, like a Balzac novel.' Baudelaire's
own tribute to David and, indirectly, to Marat himself, was not purely
aesthetic in nature, but, interestingly enough, expressed strong sympathy
with the Revolution. It appeared on January 21, 1846, the anniversary of
the day on which Louis XVI was guillotined. The fact that Baudelaire was
well received at the *Corsaire* would seem to indicate that this was no mere
coincidence.

Before leaving the 'boxing ring' of the *Corsaire*, Baudelaire published
two more texts. First, a rather condescending review of *Prométhée délivré*, a
'philosophical poem' by his former schoolfriend, Louis Ménard, who retali-
ated more than eleven years later with an unpleasant review of *Les Fleurs
du Mal*. Secondly, on March 3, a *Choice of Consoling Maxims on Love*, in which
the author promises a more substantial work in a similar vein: the *Catechism
of the Loved Woman*. The same title is advertised on the cover of his 1846
Salon, as well as on two books by Champfleury, the following year, when
this *Catechism* is described as a collection of 'psychological novels on modern
love'. Baudelaire was in fact at that time an aspiring novelist. Even though
La Fanfarlo was the only short story he ever completed, Baudelaire managed
to obtain a loan of 200 francs from the Society of Men of Letters by assuring
them that two others were ready for printing: *The Man with the Ruysdaels*
and *The Malagasy Pretender*.

At this point, the world of journalism met that of Baudelaire's family
with rather amusing results. His *Choice of Consoling Maxims* was a sort of
indirect insult to his half-brother Alphonse, with whom Baudelaire was not
on the best of terms. He sent his work, as it appeared in the paper, to
Alphonse's wife, Félicité, who, in the accompanying letter, is addressed
with ironic reserve as 'Madame':

> You will perhaps be curious to know how Baudelaire-Dufaÿs treats a
> subject as difficult and as natural as Love. I am therefore sending you
> this opuscule, the latest product of my pen. I can choose no better judge
> than you, and submit to your judgement with complete confidence.
>
> How I wish my brother could see me pleading my cause, or rather
> that of the human race, before the *Court of Love*, to quote the article I
> am sending to you. Thus, he might be able to appreciate the vocation
> that attracts me to the Muses, as I can understand that enthusiasm with

which he tackles the hard and tedious labours of Themis. To each his own in this world. My lot is to instruct my fellow man in the ways that will lead him to happiness; and so, before long, I shall have the honour of sending you, Madame, in the hope of its being read and discussed, my *Catechism of the Loved Woman* ...

What will you think of my principles, and of the advice I give to that deceitful sex which often only feigns love? I wish the lover who is truly in love to be constant, and these words are proof of my desire: 'And yet love well the woman you love, *vigorously, boldly, orientally* and fiercely; let your love not disturb the love of another.'

This short passage will no doubt inspire you to read the whole article and the *Catechism* that is soon to appear.

Hoping, dear Madame, that you will be my Providence in the career that is opening up to me through the *channel of love* ... I almost said through the influence of women.

One can imagine the embarrassment of the magistrate's prudish wife when she received this insolent though apparently innocuous love-letter – she who did nothing to improve relations between Baudelaire and his half-brother.

There may be something of Félicité in Mme de Cosmelly, the more respectable of the two heroines of *La Fanfarlo*, which Baudelaire seems to have completed in 1846, since it appeared the following January in the *Bulletin* of the Society of Men of Letters. There is, however, no question of any amorous intent on the part of Baudelaire. His letter was an elegantly perverse little game and no more than that.

The other heroine of the story, La Fanfarlo herself, a provocative ballerina, is described by Baudelaire with such relish that it is impossible to believe she never existed. The poet may have been inspired by his unexpected visitor, 'Queen' Pomaré, or by other women whose relations with Jeanne Duval were perhaps somewhat dubious. A discovery made recently by Graham Robb suggests, however, that one woman more than any other was the model of the dancer courted in the story by the poet's alter ego, Samuel Cramer.

Lola Montès, Irish by birth and Spanish by reputation, was already famous when she returned to Paris in 1844.[31] Whilst in Berlin, she had ridden her horse through a royal parade and whipped the policeman who tried to arrest her. The *Corsaire* announced that she was to appear at the Opéra in a divertissement following a performance of *Der Freischütz*. Two days later, large notices were pasted on the opera bills informing the public that Lola had been removed from the programme, no doubt because pressure had been brought to bear on the management by defenders of classical ballet, who had not appreciated the spectacle of a ballerina dancing without underwear and throwing her shoe at the hostile audience.

She reappeared on the Parisian stage at the Porte-Saint-Martin theatre the following year in another divertissement, entitled *Dansomania*. The *Corsaire-Satan* announced her return with an enthusiasm not unconnected with the fact that she now included in her list of conquests the paper's music critic, Fiorentino.[32] A few days later, a tragic accident occurred. Roger de Beauvoir had invited some friends and actresses to a feast at the famous Frères-Provençaux restaurant. A quarrel arose between two important journalists, Dujarier and Beauvallon. Dujarier was killed in a duel at the Bois de Boulogne. Beauvallon fled to Spain, and Dujarier's bleeding body was carried back to Paris and into the arms of his anxious mistress – Lola Montès, who inherited the tidy sum of 20,000 francs.

Beauvallon was not immediately convicted of murder and the affair went to the Rouen Court of Appeal in March 1846. Lola turned up, ostensibly to testify against Dujarier's murderer, calling herself the fiancée of the deceased.

The real interest of the trial, however, lies in a phrase in the public prosecutor's speech. As the *Corsaire-Satan* reported, the prosecuting counsel denounced what he called 'the *favours of the feuilleton*', hinting strongly that certain journalists were in the habit of blackmailing the actresses who depended on them for favourable reviews. The *Corsaire* disagreed, rather hypocritically, since satirical newspapers were no strangers to blackmail. The same skulduggery plays an important role in Baudelaire's story, *La Fanfarlo*. Samuel Cramer, alias Charles Baudelaire, in his efforts to seduce the dancer called La Fanfarlo, is twice turned away at her door. Undismayed, he brings his journalistic expertise to bear:

> In those days, articles of praise or criticism carried much more weight than they do now. The *favours* of the *feuilleton*, as a respectable lawyer put it recently in an unfortunately famous trial, were much greater than today. A few actresses of talent had on occasion surrendered to journalists, and, from then on, the insolent behaviour of those thoughtless and daring young men knew no bounds. Samuel therefore decided to specialise in Opera – without knowing the first thing about music.

Samuel then launches a series of weekly attacks on La Fanfarlo in 'an important newspaper' – a flattering allusion to the *Corsaire*:

She was accused of being brutal, common, and lacking in taste, of trying to bring to the Parisian stage bad habits from beyond the Rhine or across the Pyrenees – castagnettes, spurs and boot-heels, not to mention the fact that she drank like a soldier, was overly fond of little dogs and the daughter of her concierge, and all the other dirty washing of private life that provides certain rags with their daily bread and titbits. Using that technique peculiar to journalists, which consists in the comparison of dissimilar things, Samuel contrasted her with an ethereal dancer, dressed always in white, whose innocent movements disturb no one's conscience. Sometimes La Fanfarlo would shout and laugh out loud towards the stalls as she leapt to the footlights; she dared to walk as she danced. Never would she wear any of those insipid gauze dresses that show everything and leave nothing to the imagination. She loved materials that make a noise, long, crackling, spangled, metallic skirts that must be lifted very high by a vigorous knee, or clowns' bodices. She danced, not with earrings, but with pendants, one might almost say with chandeliers.[33]

With her Germanic spurs and boot-heels, and Spanish *castagnettes*, La Fanfarlo is obviously closely related to this other dancer, enthusiastically acclaimed by the *Corsaire-Satan* in 1845:

As soon as the sound of the castagnettes marked the first steps of the *cachucha*, such an avalanche of bouquets covered the stage that the young ballerina could scarcely dance a step. We noticed in particular an enormous tub of greencry and flowers, a sort of explosive device, evidently directed against Mlle Montès' life by a malevolent hand. But the intrepid Spaniard continued to dance, undaunted, her light and agile steps amidst these floral pyramids, as if her life had not been seriously endangered.[34]

Théophile Gautier gave a more detailed description of the performance:

Mlle Lola Montès first appeared dressed as a Spanish woman: a Basque dress in black silk at the hip, and weighted at the hem to stretch out the folds; a black lace mantilla, a large comb in her chignon, a red carnation above her ear, and a fan, opening and closing like a butterfly's wing ... Then she returned ... in a fantastic dancing dress, teeming with spangles and glittering frills, and performed a cachucha which makes Dolorès Serral's look like a gavotte or a minuet ... Purists will say that Lola Montès lacks training, and that she breaks the rules. But who cares![35]

Lola's success as a ballerina was shortlived. Not to outstay her welcome, she left Paris in June 1846. Next December, her former lover at the *Corsaire*, Fiorentino, received a letter with a Munich postmark:

> No doubt you'll be amazed to get this letter from me, especially since you've probably forgotten that Lola exists? But I haven't forgotten that refined and witty Fiorentino who was always so good to me, especially in the last days ... I left Paris at the beginning of June, a lady wandering the highways and byways of the world, and now I'm about to be given the title of *Countess* – with a nice property, horses, servants, carriages, and everything that goes with being the official mistress of the King of Bavaria.[36]

The subjects of Ludwig I were not so pleased with the King's acquisition, and expressed their disgust by revolting and forcing his abdication.

Lola is one of several such women who appear in Baudelaire's work – in the poem 'Sisina', for example, where the loved one is compared to Diana, 'defying the finest horsemen', and to Théroigne de Méricourt, heroine of the French Revolution, mounting the staircase of the Tuileries palace, sabre in hand. Jeanne Duval, too, in her younger days at least, bears witness to what seems to have been, on Baudelaire's part, a deep-seated predilection for Amazonian women.

In the first months of 1846, several of Baudelaire's friends abandoned the *Corsaire-Satan*, partly as a result of disagreements with the editor and partly because a paper that attached little importance to serious literature could scarcely support the ambitions of so many young writers. Baudelaire's last article was his *Choice of Consoling Maxims*, though, like his colleagues, he must certainly have been responsible for several anonymous anecdotes or epigrams, written in the 'house' style and therefore unidentifiable.

There are tantalising traces of some more 'unknown Baudelaire' in the first – and last – issue of *Le Mouvement*, in May. The paper promises its prospective subscribers a work entitled *The Loves and Death of Lucan*, the title of which is evidence of Baudelaire's admiration for the unfortunate companion of Nero, whose *Pharsalia* he was later to think of translating. The fact that he had ties as early as 1846 with a paper of liberal leanings is also significant in the light of his activities during the Revolution of 1848.

Two other texts by Baudelaire did manage to get into print in 1846. In February, he published, in *L'Esprit public, Le Jeune Enchanteur*. This tale was considered for a long time to be an original work, until W. T. Bandy unearthed, in a Washington bookstore, the English original, *The Young Enchanter*, thus proving that Baudelaire's story was nothing more than a translation – and a rather faulty one at that. And, in April, the same paper published his lively *Advice to Young Writers*, which one might have expected to include a chapter on 'Successful Plagiary'.

The 1846 Paris Salon had opened at the Louvre on March 16. Baudelaire-Dufaÿs was hoping to make up for his relative failure of the year before and his wish would soon be granted. First, as a prelude to his second *Salon*, he composed, with the collaboration of Banville and Vitu, an anonymous *Caricatural Salon, A Critique in Verse and Adverse to Everyone, illustrated with sixty woodcut caricatures by Raimon Pelez* – an amusing parody of painters, public and jury members.

His own *Salon*, despite being larger than its predecessor, was already on sale at the beginning of May. That Baudelaire took so little time to produce what Auguste Vitu hailed as a work of '*haute esthétique*', can partly be explained by the fact that the chapters dealing with theory had already been written for the 'book on painting' previously advertised.

The *Salon* begins with a short dedication 'To the Bourgeois' which has caused much controversy among Baudelaire scholars. Was it a joke, a declaration of allegiance to the bourgeoisie, or the first sign of the poet's political involvement in the Revolution of 1848? The most reliable interpretation is surely that of his recent friend, Asselineau, who claimed that Baudelaire was addressing himself 'deliberately to the most public section of the public ... not, as one might believe, out of a love of paradox, but in order to exclude the semi-bourgeois and the bogus painters he hated and whom he refers to as "monopolisers" and "pharisees" '.[37]

The book is dominated by one important idea, summed up in a section bluntly entitled 'What is Romanticism?' Romanticism, says Baudelaire, is modern art, in other words, 'depth, spirituality, colour, aspiration toward the infinite, expressed by every means the arts possess'. This dynamic conception of Romanticism as a spiritual adventure is a far cry from the superficial declarations of Victor Hugo, who, when leading the French Romantics against the pillars of classical tragedy, claimed in 1830 that his movement stood for 'liberalism in the arts'.[38]

Delacroix is enthroned by Baudelaire as Romanticism's most eminent representative. But which Romanticism? Even he is absent from the *Salon*'s resounding *envoi*, in which Baudelaire illustrates his redefinition of Romanticism in terms of modernity and holds up instead a literary hero as an example to all would-be Romantic artists. Painting, he writes, lacks what Balzac has brought to the novel: 'Parisian life is rich in poetic and miraculous subjects. Miracles surround and nourish us like the air we breathe, but we fail to see them.'

One might assume that Delacroix, presented still as the unquestioned master, was touched by Baudelaire's praise, though slightly embarrassed to see himself so favourably compared to Hugo. Baudelaire was already one of the painter's regular visitors, or so he boasted to Lepoitevin Saint-Alme and his colleagues on the *Corsaire*. True, Delacroix's diary records four visits from Baudelaire-Dufaÿs between March and May 1847, and even indicates that Baudelaire was confident enough on one occasion to borrow 150 francs; but Delacroix did not consider himself a comrade of the young art critic: 'I'm wrong to express myself so freely with people who aren't my friends,' he writes on May 3.[39] With time, the distance between them increased and the artist, being of a law-abiding nature, was later reluctant to accept the praise of a poet convicted by the criminal court. The fact remains that their conversations were invaluable to Baudelaire as he elaborated his early theories of Supernaturalism in the arts.

We have no record of what Baudelaire's mother and stepfather thought of the *Salon*. One can, however, imagine the General discovering an allusion to himself in these derisive comments on Horace Vernet: 'I hate this art that is improvised to the roll of the drum ... just as I hate the army, or any armed force, and anything that drags noisy weapons into a peaceful place.'

The important newspapers and journals, with the exception of *L'Artiste*, carried no reviews of the book. His friends were more co-operative, in particular Henry Murger, who generously compared Baudelaire's criticism, in the *Moniteur de la Mode*, to that of Diderot, Hoffmann, Stendhal and Heine. Murger was not known for his erudition and it is more than likely that his review, like Champfleury's in 1845, was written under the guidance of the *Salon*-writer himself.

This book of only 140 pages succeeded in making a certain impression, not on the bourgeois public to whom it was dedicated, but on a circle of friends, colleagues and connoisseurs.

Whatever the critics or general public thought of his *Salon*, Baudelaire himself had every reason to be happy with his work. However, the spring of 1846 was overshadowed by an event which coincided with the appearance of the book. Emile Deroy, who had suffered the disappointment of seeing his portrait of the poet refused by the Salon jury, died on May 10.[40] The exact cause of death is unknown, but one can draw certain inferences from a letter sent by Baudelaire to Deroy, probably in April: 'I've been to see D'horozko [*sic*]. He says you're doing better and that your pustules aren't anything to worry about.' J.-A. D'Oroszko was the author of *Investigations in Homeopathy*, the title page of which reveals that he was a specialist in venereal disease. One suspects that Baudelaire had been to see him about his syphilis and Deroy's pustules can perhaps be attributed to the same disease. The two friends, finding no remedy, had turned to homeopathy and to the doctor who had written in his *Investigations*: 'Venereal disease, in its early stages, and in all its simplicity, when submitted to homeopathic treatment, can be cured quickly and with incredible ease.' One should not, however, discount the possibility that Deroy was suffering from tuberculosis. The address given on his death certificate – no. 3, rue des Fossés-Saint-Jacques – indicates that he was not living in comfortable surroundings. 'Poverty and isolation,' says Asselineau, 'had made him suspicious and caustic. He died sad and neglected, little missed by his colleagues, for whom he showed little respect, and who were afraid of him.' Baudelaire himself was to forget Deroy. Having dragged the portrait around with him for some time, he eventually grew tired of it and gave it away to Asselineau, saying, 'I don't like these daubings any more.'[41]

A few days after the death of Deroy, Ernest Prarond, who was preparing his law thesis, received a handwritten invitation from Messieurs Théodore de Banville and Auguste Vitu, requesting his presence in their rooms on June 1.[42] The invitation, which promised dancing, also included a list of names which gives some indication of Baudelaire's acquaintances in 1846: Champfleury and Pierre Dupont, whom we have already seen in Baudelaire's company, and some former colleagues from the *Corsaire*: Alfred Busquet, Hippolyte Castille and Jules Viard.

Baudelaire found himself once more in the company of Banville and Vitu, from September 1846 to April 1847, in the pages of the humorous weekly, *Le Tintamarre*. Under various pseudonyms – usually 'Joseph d'Estienne' – the three friends wrote a lively gossip column which, though of little factual importance, contains some interesting comment.[43] Lola Montès and the King of Bavaria appear alongside Alexandre Dumas, currently in Spain with his travelling team of ghostwriters. But who cares about Dumas? 'Every day, before our very eyes, dramas of much greater interest are being played out' by actors in black tail-coats – actors like the 'king of novelists', Honoré de Balzac, who 'may be a genius, but he isn't a fool'. Baudelaire indulged in these literary skirmishes with much amusement, but little seriousness.

The darkest months of the July Monarchy were soon to begin. For the young writers of Baudelaire's generation, who joined forces in their love of art, there was still hope for the future; but the Revolution of 1848 was to accentuate their differences. Banville, for example, would have almost nothing to do with it. Jules Viard, on the other hand, became fully involved, founding in February 1848 *Le Représentant du Peuple*, the mouthpiece of Proudhon. Baudelaire was somewhere between the two. For him, modernity had its political side, but the true cult of beauty was both contemporary and eternal.

In 1846, modernity, such as Baudelaire imagined it, still had a pleasant, even amusing appearance. Delacroix, in Baudelaire's *Salon*, rubs shoulders with Frédérick Lemaître, the famous actor of melodramas, and with William Macready, who had come to Paris at the end of 1844 to perform Shakespeare in English. Popular melodrama and Shakespeare are thus contrasted with the superficiality of French 'Romantic' drama. Similarly, English pantomime is contrasted with the pallid comedies and vaudevilles of the boulevard theatres. Baudelaire had perhaps experienced pantomime in 1842 and rediscovered it with delight at the Funambules Theatre in Champfleury's *Pierrot, the Servant of Death*. This is also the period in which Baudelaire began to write his essays on laughter and caricature, transformed by Daumier into a major art form. Classical dancing, too, had been revolutionised by the brilliant and unconventional Fanfarlo.

In a few months, Baudelaire's contemporaries would be trying to change the world by revolution. In 1846, the poet's ambition and that of his closest friends was to change art and to free it from its stifling conventions. If not immediately successful, they did at least lay the foundations of a new aesthetics which, to use Baudelaire's words, still surrounds and nourishes us, like the Parisian air.

CHAPTER 13

The Language of Flowers
and the Guns of the Barricades

1847–1848

These years of Baudelaire's life are still relatively mysterious. There are few documents to tell us of his day-to-day existence, and the task of describing a young man drawn to the various forms of philosophical and socio-political thought of the period is far from simple. This is especially true of Baudelaire, since his interests do not betoken any desire to support a particular party or group, but indicate instead the will to extract from each system its poetic substance. Furthermore, the life of a genius cannot be reconstructed in such straightforward terms as that of a normal person: in a month or a week, Baudelaire discovered whole areas of thought which others glimpse only after a long and arduous trek.

These varied systems of thought that were already bubbling up and about to reach boiling point in February 1848 also defy characterisation. Virtually anything in the political world was still possible. The bourgeois *coup d'état* of 1851 had yet to dampen down this revolutionary fervour and crush the aspirations of Baudelaire's contemporaries.

Though we possess very few details on Baudelaire's daily life in 1847, there is on the life of his mind a rich and somewhat confusing store of information.[1]

In order to gain an understanding of the period, one should first forget the modern, restricted sense of socialism, as applied to a political party. Socialism – or rather, socialisms – represent a series of different facets of Romanticism; and here again, Romanticism should be seen as something far broader than the name traditionally applied by literary historians to a period which, in France, began towards the end of the eighteenth century.

French Romanticism has in reality two faces: one of them is turned nostalgically toward the past; the other, more dynamically, looks to a utopian future, continuing the Age of Enlightenment's tendency towards progress. These two faces belong to the same being – a being which seeks to recreate that unity which, since the Renaissance and the advent of modern science, had been lost. This unity can be reconstructed only through forms of thought which are intuitive, symbolic and analogical, in contrast to the analytical, deterministic and logical thinking that is the basis of science. The structure imparted to the world by analogical thought is one that includes man by means of synaesthesia and correspondences. In Baudelaire's sonnet, 'Correspondances', for example, the intermingling of the different senses is a sign of the mysterious relations between the physical and spiritual worlds. Charles Fourier's utopian philosophy considers the world as unity and organises society in such a way as to render it harmonious. The word 'harmony' itself, in the years preceding the 1848 revolution and particularly before the *coup d'état* in 1851, has a much wider sense than usual, as is apparent in the works of Lamartine (his *Harmonies poétiques et religieuses* date from 1830) and in the poetry of Baudelaire.

When Baudelaire considers as a happy man the one 'Qui plane sur la vie, et comprend sans effort/Le langage des fleurs et des choses muettes!' * or when he evokes in 'Correspondances' the 'ténébreuse et profonde unité' of the world, he is adhering to a Romantic and socialist philosophy whose ambition is to reintegrate man into the cosmos.

This philosophy entails an awareness that society is devoid of harmony. The workers are exploited unmercifully by the bourgeoisie and rejected as soon as they are no longer fit for work. A Catholic writer and polemicist like Louis Veuillot, who could scarcely be considered a socialist in the modern sense and who belonged to none of the socialist parties of the time, could nevertheless describe his conversion to militant Catholicism by depicting the working class in the figure of his own father, 'a simple worker, humble and uneducated', who died of exhaustion at the age of fifty: 'It was then that I began to recognise and judge that society, that civilisation, those so-called men of wisdom who have renounced God and who, in renouncing God, have denied the Poor ... And I said to myself: this social edifice is unjust; it must fall and be destroyed. I was already a Christian, and had I not been, I would from that day have belonged to the secret societies.'[2]

Those who were not profoundly Catholic joined secret societies or called on the poor and the exploited to revolt – sometimes in the name of the class struggle. Marx, however, though he stayed for a time in Paris, had had no opportunity there to disseminate his ideas and denounced the French forms of socialism as varieties of utopian thought. For someone like Baudelaire, an incitement to revolution was really a form of protest against the disfigurement of the ideal world of harmony.

* 'Who soars high over life, and understands with ease/The language of flowers and silent things!' ('Elévation')

If, therefore, from a different perspective, one had made the same observation as Louis Veuillot at his father's graveside, the language of flowers
might lead one sooner or later to climb up onto the barricades. Thus, in
1846, Baudelaire was 'dazzled and moved' by Pierre Dupont's *Song of the
Workers*, 'that admirable cry of pain and affliction':

> Whatever party you adhere to, whatever prejudices you have fed upon,
> you cannot but feel compassion at the sight of that sickly throng breathing
> in the dust of workshops, swallowing cotton, absorbing white lead,
> mercury, and all the poisons called for in the creation of works of art,
> sleeping amongst the vermin in the depths of the city where the humblest
> and the greatest of virtues share a roof with the toughest vices and the
> filth of the gaols; that sighing, languishing host to whom the *Earth owes
> its wonders*, which feels, *flowing in its veins, its bright-red, fiery blood*, which
> casts a lingering glance, heavy with sadness, over the sunlight and
> shadows of the great parks, and which finds sufficient consolation and
> comfort in its deafening and redeeming refrain: *Let us love one another!*[3]

And yet this indignation at wretchedness and poverty does not necessarily
imply support for any political party. Baudelaire may have had a taste for
democracy, but he had none at all for demagogy. If at any time he loved
the Republic, he did so in opposition to republicans.

> Have you [Baudelaire asked the readers of his *Salon de 1846*] ever
> felt the joy that I do when I see a keeper of the public sleep ... beating
> up a republican? And, like me, you said to yourself in your heart of
> hearts, 'Strike, strike a little harder, strike again, guardsman of my heart;
> for in that supreme aggression I adore in thee the brother of Jupiter, the
> great dispenser of Justice. The man you are beating is an enemy of roses
> and perfumes, a utensil fanatic; enemy of Watteau, enemy of Raphael,
> the bitter enemy of luxury, of arts and letters, sworn iconoclast,
> executioner of Venus and Apollo! He doesn't want to toil away, the
> humble, nameless worker, on public roses and perfumes; he wants to be
> free, the ignorant fool, and hasn't the wit to found a workshop for new
> flowers and new perfumes. Batter religiously on the anarchist's back!'

The anarchist, identified here with the republican, is condemned, for
etymological reasons, as an enemy of harmony.

Baudelaire learned to decipher this harmony thanks to his very wide and
varied readings, from the neo-platonic philosopher, Plotinus, to Honoré
de Balzac. From these different sources, Baudelaire composed his own form
of 'mysticism' – a word which implies belief in the order and unity of the

world. This biography is not intended to be a history of Baudelaire's thought. One would have to try and determine what the poet owed to the utopian social reformer, Fourier, to Constant, or to Lammenais and Esquiros. His tastes were extremely eclectic: 'One day, Baudelaire would turn up with a volume of Swedenborg under his arm; no one in any literature, according to him, could compare with Swedenborg.'[4] In *La Fanfarlo*, Samuel Cramer, Baudelaire's double, sees springtime arrive from his window at the Hôtel Corneille: 'He resolutely blew out his two candles, one of which was still quivering over a volume of Swedenborg, and the other was guttering over one of those shameful books the reading of which is profitable only to minds possessed with an immoderate taste for truth.' This parallel reading could scarcely encourage the sort of concentration needed to understand Swedenborg, but Baudelaire's knowledge of the Swedish mystic may very well have come from Balzac's Swedenborgian novel, *Séraphîta*.

Swedenborg, Wronski, Lavater, the inventor of physiognomy – he, too, made more accessible by Balzac's novels – and Barbereau, 'a remarkable and little-known philosopher' – these are just a few of the thinkers whose works Baudelaire was exploring. Other obscure names appear in Baudelaire's introduction to his 1848 translation of Edgar Allan Poe's *Mesmeric Revelation*, published in *La Liberté de penser*. Baudelaire praises novelists who seek out their own systems, like Balzac, 'that great mind consumed by the legitimate pride of encyclopaedic knowledge, who attempted to combine in a unitary and definitive system different ideas drawn from Swedenborg, Mesmer, Marat, Goethe, and Geoffroy Saint-Hilaire. Edgar Allan Poe was also haunted by the idea of unity, and spent no less effort than Balzac in pursuit of this cherished ideal.' In writing these lines, Baudelaire was thinking about himself – that lover of systems he would later come to despise: 'Animal unity, fluid unity, the unity of raw materials, all these recent theories have occasionally fallen by some strange accident into the minds of poets, as well as scientists.'

It was Baudelaire's curiosity for this unorthodox, unitary thinking, in opposition to 'official' academic French philosophy, as much as his interest in the art of the storyteller, that led him to the works of Edgar Allan Poe, who, thanks to Baudelaire, has enjoyed such astonishing success in France.

Poe was not entirely unknown in France when Baudelaire discovered him. A few translations and adaptations, and even a plagiarised text, had appeared as early as 1844. Baudelaire owed his first encounter to the Fourierist newspaper, *La Démocratie pacifique*, which published a series of translations, beginning with *The Black Cat* at the end of January 1847. The translator was Isabelle Meunier, a woman of British extraction and the wife of an ardent Fourierist. The tale was presented by the paper as one of the 'strange arguments' to which 'the last remaining partisans of the doctrine of natural perversity [i.e. original sin] have been reduced' and Poe himself was thus seen as a reactionary – not something that would have attracted Baudelaire at the time. He saw in Poe, however, a mystic and a visionary, which explains why he first chose to translate the rather tedious *Mesmeric Revelation*. Baudelaire soon came to admire in Poe a creator of fantastic tales, superior even to Hoffmann, and finally, the writer who had forged a *method* for himself and who refused to be a slave to 'inspiration'. This is probably the aspect of Poe which most attracted Baudelaire, since he himself was in the process of becoming the first poet in French literature to construct his works with such precision that not even the smallest detail is left to chance. Baudelaire certainly recognised in Poe a quality he already possessed himself:

> In ... 1847, I came upon a few fragments of Edgar Allan Poe, and felt a strange sort of shock. Since his complete works were not collected in a single edition until after his death, I was patient enough to make the acquaintance of some Americans living in Paris so that I could borrow collections of newspapers which Poe had edited. And then I discovered, believe me if you will, poems and stories that I had already thought of, but of which I had only a vague, confused and disorganised idea, and which Poe had managed to put together and perfect. That was the start of my enthusiasm and of my long labour.

Long is the word: Baudelaire's translations did not begin to appear until the end of 1852; from then on, Poe came to represent the largest part of his literary activity until, thirteen years later in Brussels, he completed the volume of *Histoires grotesques et sérieuses*. Edgar Allan Poe died on October 7, 1849, and so Baudelaire and he could have corresponded with each other; but one wonders if Poe would have been able to answer the questions his French admirer might have asked.

Asselineau described the outward signs of this phenomenon of literary possession:

> No matter who he was with, and wherever he was – in the street, in a café, at the printer's, morning or evening, he always asked the same question: 'Do you know Edgar Allan Poe?' and, depending on the reply, Baudelaire would either give vent to his enthusiasm or plague his listener with further inquiries.

One evening, tired of hearing this new name crop up again and again in our conversations, buzzing in my ear like an angry fly, I, like everyone else, asked, 'Who is this Edgar Allan Poe?'

In answer to this direct inquiry, Baudelaire described or rather recited to me the tale of *The Black Cat*, which he knew almost by heart and which, in his improvised translation, made quite an impression on me.

From then on, he never stopped working on Poe ... Anyone who, rightly or wrongly, was supposed to know something about English or American literature, was literally *interrogated* by Baudelaire ...

One day I went with him to a hotel on the Boulevard des Capucines where someone had told him an American writer was staying – one who was said to have known Poe. We found him in shirtsleeves and underpants amidst a whole flotilla of shoes which he was trying on with the help of a cobbler. But Baudelaire showed no mercy. The man had to submit, willy-nilly, to the interrogation, between a pair of pumps and a pair of boots. Our host did not have a very charitable opinion of the author of *The Black Cat*. I particularly remember his telling us that Poe had a rather strange mind and that his conversation was not at all '*conséquioutive*'. On the way down the stairs, ramming his hat back onto his head, Baudelaire said to me: 'He's just a Yankee!'[5]

Baudelaire's preoccupation with mystics and visionaries also manifested itself in his choice of friends – notably Alphonse Esquiros, whom he had known since 1844 and his involvement with the scandalous *Mystères galants*, and the philosopher, Jean Wallon.

Wallon, who was the same age as Baudelaire, is one of the principal characters of Murger's *Scenes of Bohemian Life*, in which he appears under the name 'Colline' as a humorous crackpot with a penchant for puns and 'hyperphysical' philosophy. Wallon was in fact a true philosopher, the translator of Hegel's *Logik*, and, though he and Baudelaire did indeed suffer the hardships of Bohemia, they also profited by it, discussing ideas, establishing links between currents of mystical thought and the early existential philosophies, and pondering the curious personality of Hoëné Wronski, the Polish philosopher. Wallon had married the daughter of Wronski's French disciple, Lazare Augé.

Wallon belonged to a little group which included another Christian philosopher whom we have already seen at the Pension Bailly – Marc Trapadoux – as well as Baudelaire's former colleague from the *Corsaire*, Champfleury.

Champfleury was another inhabitant – and historian – of literary Bohemia, though his sense of personal discipline always kept him a good arm's length away from indigence and eventually from Baudelaire too. On November 14, 1847, Champfleury published a *feuilleton* in the *Corsaire* entitled 'Trott the Cat'. It was presented in the form of a writer's diary:

> We spent a pleasant evening with a friend of mine who shares my weakness for pantomime, painting, religion, and music ... He has in particular studied cats for many years; he stops them in the street, enters shops in which a cat is meditating, crouched on the counter, strokes them and mesmerises them with his gaze.
>
> It was cold that evening. Trott was sleeping on his mistress's shoulder, opening his eyes from time to time to watch the coal blaze up. For a few minutes, not a word was spoken, when, all of a sudden, Baudelaire exclaimed: 'You mustn't have him stuffed.' Those words made me shudder, and Trott himself, usually so calm, cast a sideways glance at the sinister giver of advice, who, scarcely troubled by his own premonition, said, 'Would you like to hear a sonnet I wrote tonight?'

Baudelaire proceeds to recite 'Les Chats': 'Les amoureux fervents et les savants austères/Aiment également, dans leur mûre saison,/Les chats puissants et doux, orgueil de la maison,/Qui comme eux sont frileux et comme eux sédentaires.' * This is the famous sonnet that provided Roman Jakobson and Lévi-Strauss with the subject of the first piece of structuralist literary criticism – an analysis which cast doubt on the seriousness of their intentions and which has itself been analysed much more than the poem itself. As for Trott the cat, he showed his appreciation by leaving the shoulder of his mistress for the lap of Baudelaire.

Having slaved away on the *Corsaire* at thirty sous a day, it was only right that the newspaper should reward Champfleury in some way for his labours. On January 18, 1848, Baudelaire published a flattering review of the three collections of tales Champfleury had brought out in 1847. One of these tales, *L'Automne*, was dedicated to Pierre de Fayis, alias Baudelaire. In 1887, Champfleury recorded that he spent twelve hours a day in the company of Baudelaire between 1848 and 1852 – a little excessive, perhaps, but, if one subtracts a few hours, true also for 1847.

Finally, another friend of Champfleury and a 'Bohemian' of Murger's *Scenes* deserves a brief mention. Charles Barbara, who jumped to his death from a window in 1866 after losing his mother, wife and child in a cholera epidemic, was a novelist originally from Orléans who shared Baudelaire's passion for Poe. His literary 'references' consist of a paragraph written by

---

* 'Fervent lovers and austere scholars/Both, in their riper years, love/Cats, powerful and soft, the pride of the home,/Who, like them, are prone to the cold and sedentary too.'

Baudelaire in 1857 in which he expresses admiration for Barbara's 'strict and logical mind'.[6]

With some of these friends, Baudelaire was by now a frequent visitor to the studio of Gustave Courbet. It was in 1847 that Courbet painted the second important picture of the poet. It is interesting to compare it with the 1844 portrait by Deroy, which shows Baudelaire with long hair, beard and moustache, looking casually at the spectator, with nothing about him to indicate a man of letters. Courbet's three-quarter portrait has Baudelaire reading a book which rests on the edge of a table; on the table is a goose quill in an inkpot, a blotter, some sheets of paper and another book. Baudelaire has neither beard nor moustache. His hair, 'close-cropped and of the finest black', forms 'irregular points on a forehead of dazzling white' and covers his head 'like a sort of Saracen helmet'.[7] A large, carelessly tied cravat and a white shirt emerge from the smock or shapeless overcoat which Baudelaire, indulging in a different form of dandyism, used to wear during those years in which he 'made a show of democratic sympathies'.[8] The same hairstyle appears in a series of self-portraits sketched by Baudelaire, along with other faces, including one that may be Jeanne Duval. Written portraits complete the picture: his eyes were keen and dark; the mouth 'quite large, very contractile, tightly twisted when he wished to express disdain for any man or thing'; the nose, 'well-formed' and 'nostrils always ready to puff out';[9] his 'wonderful resonant voice ... had a metallic and clear-cut quality to it'.[10] Baudelaire was of average height. His clothes may have been a little threadbare, but in spite of a life of poverty, his linen was always impeccably white.

From the beginning of 1847 until December 4, no correspondence remains, with the exception of a letter dated March 13, in which Baudelaire thanks his mother for lending him some money. Ever since her son's suicide attempt in 1845, and the ill-fated experiment of living together as a family, Mme Aupick had been forbidden to receive or even visit this Bohemian who kept such doubtful company. The only response open to Charles was to accentuate cynically the distance that already separated him from the establishment, as represented by the General. In an undated letter, Mme Aupick refers to a conversation her son had recently had with Ancelle:

... that supreme contempt for humanity, not to believe in virtue or in anything, it's all very frightening and overwhelming ... for it seems to me that when one does not believe in any human decency, there is but a short step between that and a criminal act, and that thought alone makes me tremble – I who took comfort in the thought that in spite of his chaotic life and extravagant notions, my son was full of honour and that I would never have to fear any ignoble act on his part. His pride was a further guarantee, and also a certain haughtiness of spirit, not to mention the fact that I felt he was still religious – not practising, but a believer at least ...

If I resigned myself to this separation, which has been so hard on me and which perhaps is the reason behind all the dissolute behaviour Charles has thrown himself into, it is because I thought I was doing the right thing and acting in his best interests. I did not want to inflict upon my husband the sight of a young man whose ideas and habits were so unlike his own.

As a woman, I see only emotion in all things.[11]

Baudelaire's behaviour with Ancelle, who symbolised for him 'the values of the Bourgeoisie',[12] probably was extreme. But Baudelaire saw more than just emotion; he also saw his work, partly written already, and needing to be organised and published: that was a task that would require a certain degree of affluence, or at the very least, stability. Hence a whole series of humiliating requests, most of which had to pass through Ancelle, and which Baudelaire reported to his mother with all the skill of a tragic actor:

This is my present situation. Delighted at having a place to live and some furniture, but no money, I had been trying to find some for two or three days, when, last Monday evening, worn out with irritation and hunger, I went to the nearest hotel, and since then I haven't moved, *and for a very good reason.* I gave the address of this hotel to a friend whom I lent some money four years ago, in the days when I still had some; but he's failed to keep his word. Also, I haven't spent very much – 30 or 35 francs in one week; but that's not the whole problem; for even if, out of your unfortunately ever-insufficient generosity, you were good enough to extract me from this unhappy mess, what should I do TOMORROW? For idleness is killing me, devouring me, eating away at me. I really don't know how I manage to muster the strength to cope with the disastrous effects of this idleness and still have absolute clarity of thought, and perpetual hopes of fortune, happiness, and peace. This, then, is what I *beseech* you to do, for I feel that I'm reaching the limits, not only of other people's patience, but also of my own. Send me, *no matter how difficult it might be for you, and even if you can't believe that this one last favour could be of any real use, not just the sum in question, but also enough to live on for 20 days or so.* Settle the matter as you see fit. I have such complete faith in timetables and my own will-power, that *I know for certain* that if I could just manage, for 15 or 20 days, to lead a regular life, *my mind would be saved*. This is a final attempt, a gamble. Bet on the unknown, my dear Mother, I beg you.

The last six disastrous years, he continued, can be summed up in the following way: blunders, procrastination, and, consequently, poverty, 'always poverty'. An example:

Sometimes I'd stay in bed for three days, either because I had no clothes, or because I had no wood. Frankly, laudanum and wine aren't much good against grief. They pass the time, but they don't mend one's life. And anyway, just to deaden one's mind takes money. The last time you were kind enough to give me 15 francs, I hadn't eaten for *two days* – forty-eight hours. – All the time, I was on the road to Neuilly. I didn't dare confess my sins to M. Ancelle, and the only thing that kept me awake and on my feet was some brandy I'd been given, I who hate liqueurs and get stomach cramps from drinking them. Let such confessions – for your sake or mine – never reach the ears of living men or posterity! For I still believe that posterity concerns me.

Baudelaire mentions the possibility of suicide and then the opportunity of returning to Mauritius where some people he knew would give him a job as a private tutor; and, finally, his literary plans:

About eight months ago, I was commissioned to write two important articles which are still on the drawing-board – one is a *history of caricature*, and the other a *history of sculpture*. They'll bring in 600 francs, and just meet some urgent needs. Those subjects are child's play for me.

On New Year's Day, I'm going to start on a new profession – the creation of purely imaginary works – the Novel. I don't have to point out to you the grandeur, the beauty and the infinite aspect of that art. Since we're talking about material things, suffice it to say that, *good or bad, everything sells*; all it takes is perseverance.[13]

Perseverance was the one thing that Baudelaire's temperament and way of life made it impossible for him to prove he had, though his work itself is a sufficient indication that he possessed this quality in abundance.

His long letter to Mme Aupick makes for confusing reading. Rational and irrational arguments are so inextricably interwoven, and his sincerity so easily becomes a disguise that the reader hesitates between painful surprise and admiration for a cleverly improvised scenario. His mother was moved. She had the money sent immediately and he wrote the next day to thank her. Eleven days later, on December 16, he asked her to meet him, rather surprisingly, at the Louvre, in the large 'Salon Carré' on the first floor: 'It's the best place in Paris for a chat; it's heated, and one can wait there without getting bored, besides which it's the most acceptable meeting place for a woman.'

Mme Aupick did not go to the Louvre. She and her husband, who had been promoted to the rank of Lieutenant-General, were moving out of their home in the Place Vendôme. Aupick was put in charge of the Ecole Polytechnique. He took up residence in the school, and was there at his post when the revolution of 1848 broke out.

On January 2, Charles turned down an invitation from his mother, mostly because he did not consider himself to be 'sufficiently well-dressed'. The tone of his letter is calm and affectionate. After that, the correspondence is silent again.

From the material point of view, 1847 was certainly one of the hardest years of Baudelaire's life. He was short of money and hounded by creditors. Often, when the rent came due, he was forced to take refuge at Jeanne Duval's apartment for a night.

But his work adapted well to this precarious existence:

> Le long du vieux faubourg, où pendent aux masures
> Les persiennes, abri des secrètes luxures ...
> Je vais m'exercer seul à ma fantasque escrime,
> Flairant dans tous les coins les hasards de la rime,
> Trébuchant sur les mots comme sur les pavés,
> Heurtant parfois des vers depuis longtemps rêvés.*

'Baudelaire wrote his poems in the café or in the street. At the café, he'd drink white wine and wouldn't let anyone offer him anything else.' Dinner was a different matter: ' "Tell me [he would say to a passing acquaintance], are you having anyone to dinner this evening?" "No, Baudelaire." "All right, then! I'll keep you company." ' Baudelaire repaid his victim, according to Charles Toubin, 'by the number of outstanding or famous men that he knew and to whom he'd introduce you, at their place, or in the street! Thanks to him, I more or less made the acquaintance of Préault, Th. Gautier, G. de Nerval, etc., and – my real claim to fame – I played dominos once or twice with Frédérick Lemaître at the Café de la Porte Saint-Martin, which he and the actor often visited.'

* 'Along the old *faubourg*, where on the hovels hang/Shutters, shields of secret lust ... / I shall practise alone my fantastic fencing, / Sniffing out in every corner the accidents of rhyme, / Stumbling over words as over paving stones, / Sometimes bumping into verses dreamt of long before.' ('Le Soleil')

The most important of the many cafés Baudelaire frequented at this time was the Café Momus, which plays a prominent role in Henry Murger's *Scenes of Bohemian Life* and where the real people depicted by Murger used to meet – around a single drink. There it was that Baudelaire had what almost became a fatal row with a second-rate poet of the pseudo-classical Ponsard School, called Armand Barthet. According to the reports compiled by the appointed seconds, Barthet had offended Baudelaire 'morally' and the poet replied with a 'physical insult'. Barthet, then, instead of proceeding according to the book and conducting matters through the seconds, slapped Baudelaire on the face. The poet, astonished that such a trivial quarrel could lead to a duel, 'consented to apologise for any causticity in his words, or aggressiveness in his tone'; but Barthet wanted blood – Baudelaire's blood, which, he said, had only ever been spilt in his poetry. The dispute finally fizzled out with the resignation of the seconds.[14]

Baudelaire's biting words and belligerent tone were noted by all his contemporaries, who, even in their irritation, admired the way in which a man who wasn't rich could nevertheless make his mark.

One of his greatest pleasures was arguing with restaurant-owners. He would interrogate them, and exasperate them with his comments, quibbles and demands, arguing every point until the man, pushed to the limit, made a scene.

'Monsieur, do you cook with butter or with fat? Is your butter very fresh? Is your wine *excellent*?'

'Are you hoping,' I'd say to him, 'that he'll reply, "No, Monsieur, my butter's rancid and my wine's been watered"?'

But this objection did not affect him.

Upon leaving the restaurant, if there had been a good argument, after eating a ratatouille, he would say to me with conviction:

'Well, we really had quite a good dinner, didn't we?'[15]

Aggressiveness, eccentricity, insolence and tyrannical kindness – Baudelaire had many of the traits of a spoilt child. And perhaps his companions – who rarely became his friends – imagined that this Parisian was a man of means. In a society based on law-of-the-jungle capitalism, this particular element certainly contributed to the fascination Baudelaire exerted over young men fresh up from the provinces, or who belonged to social milieux below his own.

These cafés, restaurants, editorial rooms, streets and boulevards were Baudelaire's stage; but there was also the real stage, on which he always dreamt of making a name for himself; and then of course there was the world behind the scenes.

Baudelaire perhaps admired Marie Daubrun for the first time at the Théâtre de la Porte-Saint-Martin in 1847. Marie Bruneau, to give her her real name, born in 1827, had already enjoyed success at the age of eighteen, just outside Paris at the Théâtre de Montmartre – 'Mary full of grace', one newspaper called her.[16] The 'marvel of Montmartre', having proved herself in the suburbs and at the Vaudeville theatre, came to the Porte-Saint-Martin on August 18, 1847, where she acted in the role of the Girl with the Golden Hair – a lavish adaptation of the fairy-tale. Baudelaire's poem, 'L'Irréparable', first appeared in 1855 under the title, 'To the Girl with the Golden Hair', and the allusions it contains can be understood only if one refers back to the play; and yet the first clear indication that Baudelaire and Marie Daubrun were on intimate terms dates from 1854.

This is not the only mystery connected with the actress. There is also the question of her possible presence in *La Fanfarlo* and a letter which has tantalised Baudelaire scholars since its first publication in 1894. The letter, addressed to 'Madame Marie', is undated, although the signature is one that Baudelaire does not seem to have used before the 1848 revolution, when he dropped the 'Dufaÿs'. Baudelaire sums up the letter at the end: 'You saw fit to throw me out, I see fit to worship you, and that's that.'

'When I heard that you were going to stop posing,' he wrote, 'and that I, unwittingly, was the cause, I felt a strange sadness come over me.' Albert Feuillerat, who devoted a book to the subject of Baudelaire and Marie Daubrun, concluded that Marie was posing for a portrait by Emile Deroy.[17] If this is true, then Baudelaire knew the actress as early as 1845 or 1846 and one might further conclude that the dancer, La Fanfarlo, who owes much to Lola Montès, might also have borrowed a few traits from Marie Daubrun, who had the figure, the energy and the touch of vulgarity that were appreciated in the suburban theatres. But one would then have to prove that 'Madame Marie' was indeed Marie Daubrun, and that the painter in question was Emile Deroy. Baudelaire, of course, was visiting several other artists' studios at the time.

That year, Baudelaire would have liked to write his third *Salon* and was hoping to have it published in the prestigious *Revue des Deux Mondes*. He appealed to Delacroix, who was in touch with the director of the review. Unfortunately for Baudelaire, Delacroix had just tried to help another out-of-work art critic gain access to the review and, without telling Baudelaire that he had been unsuccessful, used the fact that he was supporting someone else as an excuse for not writing a second letter of recommendation.[18]

Baudelaire nevertheless remained faithful to Delacroix and expressed his disappointment at this chilly reception only after the painter's death.

The next Salon, in 1848, would take place under a different regime.

CHAPTER 14

'We must go and shoot General Aupick!'

February 1848 – December 1851

France was growing tired of its government. In spite of popular support for electoral reform, the King made it clear in his speech at the opening of Parliament on December 28, 1847, that there was to be no change. A protest banquet which was meant to take place in Paris on February 22 was banned. In the ensuing demonstration, some cobblestones were torn up and a few shots were fired. Prime Minister Guizot called out the National Guard for the following day; but on the 23rd, the guardsmen turned against the government, crying 'Long live Reform!' Guizot resigned. That evening, on the Boulevard des Capucines, a clash with soldiers sparked off the revolution, which continued throughout the night. On the 24th, Louis-Philippe abdicated and a provisional government was formed.

Baudelaire and Champfleury were regular visitors at that time to the Rotonde, a café located in a former chancel in the rue Hautefeuille, not far from Baudelaire's birthplace. Also known as the Café Turlot, the Rotonde was the meeting place of a group of friends centred around Gustave Courbet, who soon after moved in above the café. It was there that Baudelaire met Charles Toubin, a compatriot of the painter, and an accredited journalist on the *Corsaire*. Toubin was introduced to the poet by his friend and colleague, Champfleury, as he later recalled: 'Unlike the other Bohemians, Baudelaire was always very clean in his linen, shoes, and clothes. Though he was not a republican, he wore a red cravat with a rather loose knot, and one of those shapeless overcoats which had been in fashion some time back, and which he liked to wear in order to hide the gracility of his body.' Toubin's importance lies in the fact that his *Souvenirs d'un sept-uagénaire* – from which this description is taken – make it possible to retrace Baudelaire's steps during the three days of the February revolution.[1]

On February 22, 1848, I, like a whole crowd of other people, went to see what was going on over by the Champs-Elysées. I was with Promayet, the musician,[2] Courbet, and Baudelaire. A detachment of mounted guardsmen was riding forward slowly in order to prevent crowds from gathering. They forced us back onto the parapet of the little gardens which in those days lined the Place de la Concorde. It was just before nightfall. There we were, surrounded by soldiers, watching for our chance to get away, when some firemen went by, headed for the Avenue de Beaujon, where we were told a handful of rioters had taken a small guardhouse by surprise and set fire to it. A few moments later, the firemen passed us again, going in the opposite direction, forced to turn back by the insurgents who were pursuing them with stones. Suddenly, the scene changed. From the end of the Champs-Elysées some foot-soldiers appeared, bayonets fixed, and now it was the rioters' turn to flee. One of them, chased by two soldiers – though he was unarmed – ducked around a tree, tripped up, and there, right in front of us, one of the guardsmen stuck his bayonet into the man's chest. We all cried out in horror, and a worker who had taken refuge with us on the parapet had a violent fit of hysterics. Promayet and myself had to lead him back to his home in the rue Godot-de-Maury, whilst Courbet and Baudelaire went off to *La Presse* to denounce this terrible act of savagery to Emile de Girardin. That was the first blood spilt in the revolution. Whether or not the article appeared the next day in *La Presse*, I couldn't say. One thing followed another so quickly that I never had the chance to find out.[3]

The next day, about one in the afternoon, Champfleury, Baudelaire, Promayet and myself set off from the Café de la Rotonde in search of news. We met D'Abrantès,[4] who told us there was fighting in the Saint-Denis quartier ... From the Place du Châtelet, we heard the shouting. We moved on. All the shops were shut and every door was closed. Without knowing where we were going, turning back when we saw a barricade, which happened two or three times, we walked from street to street for more than half an hour, trying to reach the boulevard at some point between the Porte Saint-Denis and the Bastille. Suddenly, in a street at right angles to ours, less than 100 metres away, we heard the sound of running feet, like soldiers attacking, then a violent burst of gunfire, people shouting, 'Oh my God!' – the piercing cries of wounded and dying, then silence. It was a company of the 17th Light Infantry, the Duc d'Aumale's regiment, which had just removed a barricade – not without spilling some of their blood on the cobblestones of that street which afterwards I tried to find again. Hearing no further sound, we moved towards the place all that noise had been coming from and walked straight into that poor group of soldiers who were picking up three or four dead or dying comrades. What a heart-rending business those civil wars are! You should have heard those valiant soldiers voicing their fury at those who had decimated their ranks. 'Good God! We fought the Bedouins for seven years just to get slaughtered here by Frenchmen!' They were livid, but not one of them thought of shouting at us. Three months later, the rebels would have forced us to stand behind their barricades and the soldiers would have shot us as accomplices of the insurgents ...

At last we came to the Boulevard du Temple. Just then, the resignation of Guizot's government was announced. The civil war had ended almost before it began! What joy! What an indescribable scene! The shops, all at the same time, opened up again, and as night began to fall, windows lit up and flags were hung, again, all in the same instant. Here and there on the boulevard, some companies of infantry and all the armed forces were fraternising with the citizens. Promayet recognised a sergeant-major from his home town and went over to shake his hand. 'It's all over, and not a minute too soon,' said the sergeant-major. 'That bloody Guizot was beginning to get on our nerves ...'

All at once, a huge column, densely packed, taking up the whole breadth of the boulevard, with drums and flags in front, came from the direction of the Porte Saint-Martin. National guards in uniform, workers in their smocks and students from the Polytechnique, all arm in arm, singing [the *Marseillaise* and the *Girondins*], with the drums marking the beat and everyone – all except a few drunken hooligans – rejoicing and forgetting to curse Guizot ...

Never in my whole life have I seen such an outburst of enthusiasm, or anything at all comparable to that exhilarating demonstration – wonderful sunshine born of the storm, but which, that same evening, would end with an awesome unleashing of the elements.

It was nearly 9 o'clock when we returned to the Right Bank. Baudelaire offered to keep me company during dinner, as he liked to put it. He was delighted with what he'd seen in the last two days. The opening scenes of the drama had kept him on the edge of his seat, but he didn't think much of the dénouement and felt that the curtain had fallen too soon. I had never seen him looking so happy, bright and tireless – he who was not at all used to walking. There was a gleam in his eye. After dinner, we went to the Rotonde, and there in the café that had been so lively the past few evenings, we found Courbet sitting all alone in front of a beer, with only his pipe to keep him company. The night was horribly black

and a lugubrious silence enveloped the whole *quartier*. Suddenly, the
tocsin began to sound at Saint-Séverin, and then at Saint-Etienne-du-
Mont and Saint-Sulpice. A man ran past, crying in a voice that made our
blood run cold: 'To arms! They're slaughtering our brothers ...' We
rushed into the street; no one was there to tell us what was going on,
but the bells of Saint-Sulpice continued to ring out and we ran in that
direction at the risk of falling over and breaking our necks in the dark.
The ringing stopped, and just as we came out onto the church square, a
hail of bullets hit the wall of a house above our heads. We retreated, faster
than we had come. Hearing the tocsin sound so close, the guardsmen in
the rue de Tournon had come running, bayonetted the bell-ringers and
then, stationing themselves in the doorway of the church, were firing
whenever they heard footsteps approach. More than one of them, apparently, the next day, paid for this act of insanity with his life ...

Turned back on that side, we went down to the Pont-Neuf which we
found to be occupied by an army battalion which was letting people pass
from the Right Bank to the Left, but not in the opposite direction. Every
now and then, frightened people would arrive from the Right Bank,
telling us about the awful business on the Boulevard des Capucines –
corpses carried about by torch light and the barricades rising everywhere.
Poor Paris! Poor France!

Overcome with fatigue, and exhausted by so much excitement, I
decided to go home. It was almost 3 in the morning.

At the Ecole Polytechnique, General Aupick had had his hands full. The
students observed by Toubin on the boulevard singing patriotic songs had
been asked by the General not to leave the school, but the *polytechniciens*
had left-wing sympathies and the revolutionary fever was infectious. One
first-year student described what happened on the 24th:[5]

A company of some regiment or other was patrolling the *quartier*. A
troop of common people attacked the soldiers in front of the school. The
company opened fire and killed one or two of the men. The General
came up and had the soldiers brought inside the school. One man aimed
a gun at the General, but he was stopped by some students and his friends
who shouted to him, 'It's the General of the school!' Nevertheless, the
crowd was demanding that the soldiers be disarmed, which, of course,
was not at all a part of the General's plan; and so the crowd remained
on the Place de l'Ecole, still shouting, still threatening to invade the
school. The General summoned the students who were present, and it
was decided that we would confiscate those poor soldiers' guns and lead

them back as prisoners to their barracks ... We left by a back gate ... and our expedition went off successfully, to cries of 'Long live the Ecole! Long live the Infantry! Long live the Republic!'

Most of the students under General Aupick's command were hoping to find a peaceful solution to the troubles by interposing themselves between the government forces and the people. Another student – a future politician – described how his comrades decided to go to the nearest townhall by the Panthéon in order to organise themselves into squads.[6] 'A normal head would have sent us back to our studies, perhaps even refused to give us a hearing; but General Aupick was no ordinary head. Along with a good deal of firmness, he possessed benevolence and uncommon sagacity.' Aware of the possibly explosive results of stubborn refusal, Aupick allowed the students to carry out their plan, requesting only that they remain within the bounds of the humanitarian mission they had described to him. 'During the day, an armed band took hold of the school's guard post and would have killed the General if two students had not come running just in time to shield him with their bodies.'

Aupick's attitude in the face of unrest was both prudent and effective. Though bound by gratitude and loyalty to the House of Orléans, he realised that an age had ended and, on March 1, the official newspaper, the *Moniteur universel*, listed his name among those who had rallied to the provisional government. On March 3, his renewed appointment as Commander of the school was confirmed.

In the meantime, Aupick's stepson was treating this revolutionary outburst as an excellent opportunity to create that more harmonious world and to settle at the same time a domestic quarrel. Baudelaire threw himself into the revolution partly out of admiration for the great Revolution of 1789 – 'it was the love of an artist, more than that of a citizen'. But he also revelled in the literary side-effects of insurrection: 'Though his verses were always so clear and precise, he was not averse to a certain vigour and grandiloquence in poetry or prose' – notably verses from the great Revolution, which he used to declaim, 'with his arms wide apart, eyes shining with delight'.[7]

On the morning of the 24th, Charles Toubin woke up late, dressed and hurried down to the street. The whole *quartier* was strewn with barricades. At the Buci crossroads, he found Baudelaire and Barthet, 'armed with hunting rifles and ready to fire, behind a barricade which covered them only to the waist'. Jules Buisson remembered meeting Baudelaire in the same place, 'in the midst of a mob which had just looted a gunsmith's':

He was carrying a handsome double-barrelled shotgun, all shiny and new, and a superb leather cartridge pouch which was just as immaculate. I waved to him, and he came over, making a show of great excitement: 'I've just fired a shot!' he said. Smiling, and looking at his brand-new, gleaming weaponry, I asked: 'Not for the Republic, surely?' He didn't answer and kept shouting out the same refrain: 'We must go and shoot General Aupick!'[8]

Baudelaire later described his own feelings at the time in *My Heart Laid Bare*: 'My exhilaration in 1848. What sort of exhilaration was it? A taste for vengeance. The *natural* pleasure of demolition. A literary exhilaration. Remembered readings.'

Since encouraging the guardsmen to beat up the 'enemy of roses and perfumes' in the *Salon de 1846*, Baudelaire had not changed his mind. He was fighting neither for the Republic, nor for the revolution, but satisfying a deeper instinct for revolt. His anger transcended politics. True, it almost provided him with an opportunity to take revenge on Aupick, who was loyally protected by the Polytechnic students; but, for Baudelaire, his stepfather was more than anything else the representative of a conservative order to which he knew he would never belong.

A more concrete example of 'literary exhilaration', related by Charles Toubin:

Almost as soon as it was formed, the provisional government decreed the unconditional freedom of the Press . . . 'What about starting a newspaper?' Baudelaire and Champfleury said almost at once . . . In order to create a newspaper in normal circumstances, four things were needed: a title, an editorial room, money, and some coherence in the views and opinions of the principal contributors. The editorial room was quickly found. We all agreed to use the room on the second floor of the Café Turlot where hardly anyone ever went, and which had the advantage of costing us nothing. Once the paper had flourished and grown, we would find a new home for it. Why not the Boulevard des Italiens? The title was chosen just as quickly. Baudelaire suggested *Le Salut public*, which seemed to me a little too strong, but my two colleagues pointed out that in times of revolution one had to talk loudly in order to be heard, and I bowed to their opinion. The question of money was a little trickier. It was the end of February, and wages weren't due from the *Corsaire* for another two or three days. Champfleury had only 40 sous in his pocket, and that was supposed to last until March 1. Baudelaire confessed that his first instalment of the year had already been spent by January 6 . . .

My brother and I, by turning out our pockets, were able to come up with 80 or 90 francs, and it was with this impressive capital that the *Salut public* was founded. As for the coherent views and opinions, we didn't even think about them. All of Champfleury's political views came down to the same thing – hating policemen. Baudelaire loved the revolution as something violent and abnormal, and for that reason I feared him more than I liked him. But I gave in to what was already a *fait accompli*.

The title chosen by Baudelaire, recalling as it does the infamous Committee of Public Safety formed under the Terror, bespeaks his admiration for the first Revolution and for Robespierre himself, whose style he appreciated, at least in his youth – 'burning ice, rebaked and frozen like abstraction' was how he described it.[9] The first issue of the *Salut public*, printed in a run of 400 copies, cost the editors no more than thirty francs.

Since most of the workshops were closed, it was not very difficult to find vendors; but like the raven that Noah sent out at the end of the Flood, our birds did not return. This first number had been written in less than two hours on three tables on the second floor of the Café Turlot. The next issue was more carefully prepared, and the third, because of our diminishing capital, never appeared.

The first issue of the *Salut public* was ready on February 27 and the second probably on March 1. The latter boasted an illustration by Gustave Courbet. It depicted a man wearing a smock and a top hat,[10] standing on top of a barricade, with a rifle in one hand and a banner in the other, bearing the words, 'Voice of the People, Voice of God'.

Baudelaire, in whose mind nothing was incompatible, piously gave a complimentary copy to the Archbishop, and democratically took another to Raspail, who was living [nearby] on the Place de l'Ecole de Médecine. (Ever since reading *L'Ami du peuple*, Baudelaire had been professing boundless admiration and affection for Raspail.) Since he attached more importance than Champfleury to the success of this second issue, he donned one of his white smocks, and, thus attired, bravely sold our product to passers-by in the rue Saint-André-des-Arts, whilst a young widow disguised as a worker did the same in the rue des Saints-Pères. Between the two of them, they brought back about 12 to 15 francs, and it was decided, first, that the Republic would just have to do as best it could in the future without our enlightened advice; secondly, that a magnificent banquet commemorating the birth and death of our newspaper would be held, limiting the number of guests, however, to five:

the three founders, my brother who had backed us, and the young widow, who, having returned to the ark, seemed to us to be a real dove.

It is difficult to determine which of the short articles in the *Salut public* were written by Baudelaire. The three friends all seem to have been fired with the same revolutionary enthusiasm. A section entitled 'The Beauty of the People', however, with its vision of humanity revived by the sun of freedom, recalls a poem of *Les Fleurs du Mal* ('J'aime le souvenir de ces époques nues') and an attack on classical tragedy calls to mind the conclusions of Baudelaire's first two *Salons*: 'Intellects have grown. No more tragedies, no more Roman history. Aren't we bigger today than *Brutus*, etc.?' These, and other attributions must remain hypothetical. The important thing to note is the revolutionary, even messianic fervour of the *Salut public*, in which the people are praised, both for their virtue and for their 'eminent reason', in which the writers declare their love of the Republic and hail a socialist Christ. Though the past is always hard to understand, however close it may appear, May 1968 provides a useful analogy with 1848 – a certain style which, for a few days, was the common property of an enthusiastic group of friends. Baudelaire later assessed this enthusiasm without much leniency: '1848 was entertaining only because everyone was building utopias like castles in the air. 1848 was delightful only because it reached the very height of Absurdity.'

In 1848, Baudelaire's enthusiasm was such that he joined the Central Republican Party formed by Auguste Blanqui at the end of one of his many terms in prison. The *Courrier français*, having printed Blanqui's invitation to 'men of intelligence and devotion to start a club', published the names of the officers and a list of several affiliated members two days later on February 28: Baudelaire, Alphonse Constant, Jean Wallon and Pierre Dupont. Baudelaire's name does not appear in the definitive list published on March 10.[11]

By the integrity and intransigence of his republicanism, and by his revolutionary spirit, Blanqui was for Baudelaire a sort of nineteenth-century Robespierre. There exists an ink drawing of Blanqui, sketched by the poet on a sheet of paper along with the verses by Gray and Longfellow which are the basis of the poem, 'Le Guignon'. The drawing dates from 1849 or 1850 and, as his future publisher Poulet-Malassis pointed out, it must have been drawn from memory: Blanqui was tried by the provisional government a few months later and, having once known the dungeons of Mont-Saint-Michel, was imprisoned in May 1848 on Belle-Ile, off the Breton coast.

On May 4, elections took place. Provincials living in Paris rather arrogantly formed committees in order to choose candidates for their respective regions. Charles Toubin remembered attending the meeting for the Aisne *département*, presided over by Jean Wallon, with Champfleury as assessor. Baudelaire, who was there with Toubin, listened to the first candidate – Alphonse Esquiros – denounce the 'infamous' Guizot and Louis-Philippe, and then paint a 'powerful and gloomy picture of the sad conditions of the workers'. Some of the listeners had tears in their eyes, when, taking advantage of a pause during which the speaker mopped his brow, Baudelaire asked him whether he did not consider the interests of small tradespeople to be as sacred as those of the working class. Esquiros managed to find a diplomatic reply and prepared to return to his theme, when Baudelaire stood up again: 'Since we're on the subject,' he continued, 'what is your opinion on free trade – that vital question which one might regard as the keystone of the social edifice?' This 'vital question', according to Toubin, was one with which the general public was entirely unfamiliar at the time. Esquiros became flustered and was forced to admit that he had not yet been able to study that particular problem. Arsène Houssaye, who was next up to speak, also suffered from Baudelaire's talent for awkward questions. Like Esquiros, Houssaye began by indicting the Government, in particular for its 'undignified' policy towards England, and quoted a phrase attributed to Lord Palmerston: 'I shall make France pass through the eye of a needle.' Interrupting, Baudelaire asked for his opinion on the right of access and the treaties of 1815. Houssaye fared little better than Esquiros: 'He apologised for having failed as yet to direct his attention toward those questions which he would examine in detail as well as all other historical and social problems if the meeting were kind enough to choose him as candidate.'

After the demise of the *Salut public*, Baudelaire may have worked for another newspaper in April 1848. A pilot issue of *La Tribune nationale* ('Organ of the Interests of All Citizens') gives the name of the 'editorial secretary' as Baudelaire.[12] If this is indeed Charles Baudelaire, it seems likely that he confined himself to his secretarial duties: the newspaper was sensibly democratic, in favour of reform, a defender of law and order, and somewhat boring.

Baudelaire had already entered a different world. He was no longer so close to his friends from the Ecole Normande, who in any case were leaving Paris for their home towns, having sown their wild oats – a middle-class expression perfectly applicable to those cultivated, bourgeois young men. Unlike them, Baudelaire remained on the fringe – a fringe which was growing ever wider.

*

Alphonse de Lamartine had become Minister of Foreign Affairs and was making changes in the diplomatic corps. General Aupick was appointed Ambassador to Constantinople. 'He had been attached for a long time to the royal family, but members of the Government and the Minister of the Interior himself [Ledru-Rollin] were confident in designating Aupick as the man to represent the Republic in a place ... where diplomatic problems might easily arise.'[13]

Before the Aupicks' departure in May, Baudelaire tried to arrange a meeting with his mother, hoping at least to make her aware of some financial difficulties which might become more serious in her absence. On May 15, the provisional government was nearly toppled: 'Still the taste for destruction,' Baudelaire reflected. 'A legitimate taste, if everything natural is also legitimate.' These weeks were full of uncertainty for Baudelaire. The despised General had gone, but so had his mother, leaving him with no resources against the ever-inflexible Ancelle.

His vitality returned with the June Days, an insurrection caused by the sacking of workers from the National Workshops. It was brutally suppressed by government troops. Baudelaire took part in the revolt, as Le Vavasseur recalled. While walking through the Gardens of the Palais-Royal, he and Chennevières met a national guardsman from their native Normandy, and offered to buy him a drink at the Café Foy.

> Then, coming towards us, we saw two people of quite different appearance: one of them was nervous, excited, feverish, and agitated; the other man was calm and almost cheery. It was Baudelaire and Pierre Dupont. We entered the café. I had never seen Baudelaire in such a state before. He was holding forth, declaiming, boasting, frantic to run off and become a martyr. 'They've just arrested De Flotte,' he said. 'Is it because his hands smelt of gunpowder? Smell mine!' Then he launched into some socialist slogans, the apotheosis of social bankruptcy, and such like. Dupont could do nothing to stop him. How we cautious Normans got him out of that tight spot, I can hardly remember; but I believe the cockade of my friend the guardsman played a silent, evident and beneficial role in the rescue we performed.
>
> Whatever people might have thought about Baudelaire's courage, he was brave that day, and would have got himself killed.[14]

Baudelaire's own comments, written much later on, are undeniably accurate: 'The horrors of June. Madness of the people, madness of the bourgeoisie. A natural love of crime.'

From Constantinople, General Aupick judged things from a different point of view: 'I have read the details of that terrible struggle in which civilisation and true liberty did battle with anarchy and barbarity.' He added that the recent events in Paris had not been well received in Constantinople: 'My position will suffer as a result; relations will still be excellent ... but recognition of the Republic might be delayed.' Aupick was right. The Sultan refused to recognise the French Government until August 25, partly, however, because he was concerned about the reactions of Russia and Austria. The following day, Aupick was finally able to present his credentials to the Sublime Porte.

Back in Paris, Baudelaire was employing his own curious form of diplomacy in trying to establish relations with one of the great writers and thinkers of the 1848 revolution – Pierre-Joseph Proudhon. Proudhon's 'daily newspaper for the workers', *Le Représentant du peuple*, was suspended for the second time in its short existence on August 21. The same day, Baudelaire wrote a letter expressing a wish to see Citizen Proudhon '*whatever the cost*', in order to apprise him of matters urgently concerning his safety: 'Admiration and sympathy are sufficient justification of my action.' The letter-writer added that he would wait for a reply at the corner café, and, before signing his name and reiterating his devotion, set down this phrase worthy of a member of the Convention in the great days of the 1789 Revolution:

> Now that turmoil reigns in every mind, all men of heart must not be slow to speak.

Proudhon must have scribbled a quick note, asking for an explanation, since Baudelaire wrote back that day or the day after: 'At the next demonstration, even if it's directed against the people, in other words, the next time there's any excuse, you might be *assassinated*.' Baudelaire went on to justify his presentiment and then expressed the hope that he might be given a chance to speak to Proudhon about possible changes to his newspaper. He also suggested producing a vast quantity of very large notices, signed by Proudhon himself as well as by other representatives and writers from the newspaper, 'ORDERING the people not to move'.

> These days you are more famous and influential than you think. An uprising that starts out being legitimist can eventually turn into a socialist revolt; but the opposite can also occur ...
>
> Thus, at the next sign of any commotion, however slight it may be, *make sure you're not at home*. If possible, get a secret bodyguard, or demand police protection. In any case, *the government would probably be very glad to*

accept a gift like that from the wild animals of ownership; so perhaps it would be better if you took your own precautions.

Charles Baudelaire

'The wild animals of ownership' was certainly a fitting phrase to set before the editor of the periodical described by the *Grand Dictionnaire* of Pierre Larousse as 'the terror of the bourgeoisie'.

Baudelaire and Proudhon did eventually meet, but it was a few days later, in September, as the poet told Poulet-Malassis shortly after Proudhon's death:[15]

I went one evening to look for Citizen Jules Viard in the offices of the *Représentant du peuple*.

Proudhon was there, surrounded by his staff, handing out instructions and giving advice on next day's paper. One by one they all departed, until he and I were there alone. He told me that Viard had left some time ago, and we began to talk. As we talked, we discovered that we had some friends in common ... and so he said, 'Citizen, it's time for dinner. Would you like to dine with me?'

We went to a little *traiteur* which had recently opened in the rue Neuve-Vivienne. Proudhon held forth, forcefully and at length, telling me, whom he knew not at all, about his plans and projects, and, involuntarily, so to speak, coming out with a whole host of witty remarks.

I noticed that the polemicist was devouring vast quantities of food and hardly drinking anything, whilst my abstemiousness and thirst contrasted with his appetite. 'For a man of letters,' I said, 'you eat an astonishing amount.'

'It's because I have great things to do,' he answered in such a straightforward manner that it was impossible to tell whether he was serious or joking.

I should add ... that once the meal was over and I had rung for the waiter in order to pay for what we both had eaten, Proudhon objected so strongly that I let him pull out his purse; but, somewhat to my surprise, he paid only for his own dinner. Perhaps you might infer from this that he had a very definite taste for equality and an exaggerated love of justice?

This encounter was of no further consequence. Baudelaire must have appeared to Proudhon to be no more than an intelligent amateur; but in his courageous article on 'Les Drames et les Romans honnêtes' in November 1851, the poet expressed his admiration for the economist and polemicist by describing him as 'a writer who will always be the envy of Europe'. Proudhon had nothing new to learn from Baudelaire's warning letters: he was already well aware that his life was in danger. In March 1849, he was tried and found guilty, fled to Belgium and returned to Paris incognito, only to be arrested again in June.

Shortly before or after his memorable dinner with Proudhon, Baudelaire's own career as a political journalist took him to Châteauroux in the Indre region, 157 miles south of Paris. Arthur Ponroy was a young poet and dramatist whom Baudelaire had met on the *Corsaire-Satan*. His father was planning to start a newspaper, *Le Représentant de l'Indre*, which, though describing itself as 'moderate', was in fact quite clearly conservative. Ponroy gave the following account of this episode to a journalist, Firmin Boissin:

The position of chief editor came open. Ponroy offered it to Baudelaire who accepted and left for Châteauroux.

As soon as he arrived, a large banquet was held in honour of the chief editor. The principal shareholders of the paper were present – rich and worthy bourgeois, all a little pompous. Baudelaire said not a word. Over dessert, one of the guests remarked on his silence:

'But Monsieur Baudelaire, you aren't saying anything.'

The joker replied:

'Messieurs, I have nothing to say. Have I not come here to be the servant of your intellects?'

The next day, he horrified the lady who printed the paper – she was an old widow – by asking her where the staff brandy was kept.

The day after, the good readers of the *Journal de Châteauroux* were even more appalled. Baudelaire's first article began like this: 'When Marat, that gentle soul, asked for 300,000 heads, and when Robespierre, that decent fellow, requested that the guillotine be set up permanently, they were simply obeying the ineluctable logic of their system.' Although the conclusion was as authoritarian as Joseph de Maistre, everyone was scandalised, and poor old Baudelaire didn't last very long at Châteauroux.

Besides, his irregular lifestyle was hardly likely to arouse the sympathy of the family men who directed the paper. Baudelaire had brought an actress with him from Paris whom he passed off as his wife.

He was found out, and when he was fired, Baudelaire received the following rebuke from the President of the administrative committee – a solicitor who had read some Casimir Delavigne:

'Monsieur, you deceived us. Mme Baudelaire is not your wife, she's your "favourite".'

To which Baudelaire retorted:

'Monsieur, a poet's "favourite" can sometimes be the equal of a solicitor's wife.'

That was his parting shot. The very same evening, he left for Paris.[16]

The *Journal de Châteauroux* mentioned in this account is surely an inaccurate reference to Ponroy's *Représentant de l'Indre*, especially in view of the article which appeared in the first issue on October 20, 1848. The writer reproaches a member of the Government for having claimed that British money was at the root of the June riots:

> No! one should have the courage to admit the truth. Proudhon was the first and the only one to say it: *Revolt is socialist by nature*. He, at least, is no liar. He is brutal and unambiguous ... The insurrection cost nothing; the criminal acts were free. For every promise, a gunshot. You decreed complete emancipation and instant happiness. Come on then, quick, to work, before I kill you! The insurrection was legitimate, and so was the killing.

This admiration for Proudhon and the bold assertions seem to indicate the hand of Baudelaire. The temporary chief editor apparently took his job seriously, at least until he became exasperated with the conservative owners of the paper. It was probably in his official capacity as editor that Baudelaire wrote to Philippe de Chennevières asking him to deliver copies of all his work to Jeanne Duval. Baudelaire told him he needed three *feuilletons* and promised to have them published – no doubt in the Châteauroux newspaper. His visit there is further confirmed by a note sent to Mme Aupick on 8 December 1848: 'M. Ancelle told me that you paid for my trip to the Indre without my knowing it.'

These two letters are the only information we have on Baudelaire's life between August 1848 and July 1849. They tell us that he was living then in Neuilly, not far from Ancelle, and that Jeanne was staying with him.

The next letter to have survived merely adds another mystery. On July 13, 1849, Baudelaire wrote to an unknown correspondent on behalf of a certain M. Schoman, a musician who had been forced to leave Dresden after the revolution and who wanted to publish a study on *Tannhäuser*. Wagner's opera had only recently been introduced to the readers of the *Journal des Débats* by Franz Liszt in an article prefaced by a few words from Hector Berlioz. Nothing at all is known about the mysterious M. Schoman, but the letter is revealing in that it shows that Baudelaire even then was an admirer of Wagner's music. He also talks of Théophile Gautier in terms that suggest the two writers were already well acquainted in July 1849.

At the end of that year, or in the first days of 1850, Baudelaire was once again away from Paris, this time in Dijon. It was a visit which left him with 'bitter memories': 'He never mentioned that city without grinding his teeth,' wrote Asselineau.[17] His reasons for going there are still unclear, though journalism may once again have been the motive.

The city of Dijon, though rather sleepy and conservative, nevertheless had its own socialist newspaper, *Le Travail, journal des intérêts populaires*, which boasted on its staff Jules Viard, a friend of Baudelaire since his days on the *Corsaire* and one of the founders of Proudhon's *Représentant du peuple*. After a series of prosecutions, *Le Travail* was eventually forced out of existence, 'despite Madier de Montjau's admirable defence speech', as the newspaper told its readers in its last issue on March 20. Montjau was a lawyer who specialised at the time in defending left-wing papers. Baudelaire met him during his visit to Dijon, as he told Ancelle:

Madier de Montjau, who was returning from some legal triumph or other ... passed through here, and came to see us. As you know, that young man is thought to be extremely talented – a real democratic genius. I found him pathetic! He was playing the ardent revolutionary. So I talked to him about the socialism of peasants, an unavoidable, savage, stupid and bestial form of socialism, like socialism of the torch and the scythe. That scared him and cooled him off a bit. He couldn't stand up to logic. He's an idiot, or rather a very vulgar man with ambitions.[18]

Madier de Montjau was later elected to Parliament in the Saône-et-Loire region. Baudelaire's deflation of his opponent (perhaps he was remembering Balzac's all-out attack on grass-roots socialism in his novel *Les Paysans*) recalls his provocative questioning of Esquiros in 1848. A radical himself, he had little time for the simplistic thinking of democratic socialism.

One can only guess that Baudelaire went to Dijon in order to prepare Jules Viard's arrival at the newspaper. Perhaps his duties on *Le Travail* were merely editorial? No article in the paper seems to bear his distinctive mark.

With the exception of his short term on the 'moderate' newspaper at Châteauroux, which seems to have been an act of provocation and an attempt to earn some money, Baudelaire had remained faithful since February 1848 to what might loosely be termed his 'left-wing' convictions, or at least to his taste for rebellion.

What of Baudelaire's literary activity during this period? In December 1849, two newspapers – *La Presse* and *L'Evénement* – announced a work in prose: 'The Last Drinkers, by M. Charles Baudelaire',[19] to appear in a collective volume about which, unfortunately, almost nothing is known. His poetry, on the other hand, was beginning to emerge from the shadows. We know that on departing from Paris at the end of 1849, he left his poems in manuscript form with a professional calligrapher. Ancelle, who was then beginning to volunteer his inexpert services to Baudelaire the writer, went to fetch the completed work. Baudelaire was far from pleased: there were ridiculous spelling mistakes in the table of contents, the binding was cheap and the gold lettering was poorly done – 'He took advantage of my absence ... to rob me of my money.' Writing to Ancelle, Baudelaire mentioned only one volume; Asselineau, however, who was very close to him from 1850 on, remembered seeing two: 'He showed me ... the manuscript of his poems, magnificently copied down by a calligrapher, and forming two in-quarto volumes bound in boards and gilded. This is the manuscript that was used in the printing of *Les Fleurs du Mal*.'

Baudelaire had found a new title for his collection of poems, abandoning *Les Lesbiennes* for *Les Limbes*. In November 1848, *L'Echo des marchands de vins*, curiously enough, announced that *Les Limbes* was to be published by Michel Lévy on February 24, 1849. This was the first anniversary of the revolution and must surely have been a deliberate choice. Jean Wallon, who came across the title when reviewing newspapers published during the revolution, concluded rather hastily that *Les Limbes* were socialist verses 'and therefore not very good'. He went on to bemoan the fact that his friend had become a disciple of Proudhon. Wallon's fears were clearly unjustified. The title might, however, be taken as an allusion, not to Proudhon, but to Charles Fourier, whose philosophy of history includes '*périodes limbiques*', otherwise defined as an 'age of social beginnings and industrial hardship', which heralds the creation of a harmonious society. Along with the socialist connotation, there is also the theological sense of limbo as the place inhabited by the souls of children who die before baptism. More generally, though, the word was supposed to evoke that abyss of melancholy and 'spleen' in which the poet and his generation of *déclassés* were struggling. This was obviously the sense it had in a further announcement in June 1850: 'The book ... which will appear very shortly ... is intended to represent the unrest and melancholy of modern youth': and, finally, a similar description introduced eleven sonnets published on April 9, 1851 in *Le Messager de l'Assemblée* – a paper which had recently printed Baudelaire's essay on wine and hashish, the first version of *Les Paradis artificiels*.

The eleven sonnets from *Les Limbes* thus appeared on an anniversary of a different sort – Baudelaire's thirtieth birthday. Again, this was no mere coincidence. He had friends on the paper – Champfleury in particular – and must have enjoyed considerable esteem for the editors to insert eleven sonnets in the part of the paper where the reader usually expected to find light reading.

Though Michel Lévy had apparently agreed to publish *Les Limbes*, Baudelaire did not eventually choose him as the publisher of *Les Fleurs du Mal*. That honour fell to a young man who was as unconventional in many ways as Baudelaire himself. Born in Alençon in 1825 of a long line of printers, Auguste Poulet-Malassis had come to Paris in 1847 to study at one of the Grandes Ecoles. He was soon completely taken up with the February revolution and in June 1848 he founded his own newspaper – *L'Aimable Faubourien, journal de la canaille*. It was a title worthy of that kind and cynical man, whose works are few, but whose wonderful letters express the most subversive views with exquisite courtesy and apparent indifference.

As a revolutionary, Malassis was not quite as lucky as Baudelaire. During the June Days, he was arrested with a gun in his hand. 'Saved from summary execution by a friend from Alençon ... he was cast into the dungeons of the fort at Ivry, and then transferred to the prison ships at Brest.' Freed in December 1848 and granted permission to continue his studies the following year, he spent most of his time in the literary cafés of Paris. This turned out to be a very useful experience. His father died in March 1850 and left him with the family printing business. He took as his partner his brother-in-law, Eugène De Broise, a pale and timorous character who made a strange associate for the exuberant Malassis.

Baudelaire met his future publisher in the company of Champfleury at a restaurant in the rue du Petit-Lion-Saint-Sulpice in 1850. The poet was apparently a regular customer, enjoying discussions with unsuspecting victims like Bermudez de Castro, a great admirer of Balzac. 'Know this, Monsieur,' said Baudelaire. 'People who admire Balzac sniff each other out like dogs.' [20] Baudelaire was not averse to taking the opposite side for the sake of argument. In fact, Balzac's death that August affected him deeply and shortly afterwards he developed a lively interest in the novelist's much maligned plays which he saw as a truly new form of theatre.

From May 10, 1850, Malassis begins to appear in Baudelaire's correspondence. From the tone of his letters, one can tell that the poet was trying to enlist him as another disciple: the procedure had succeeded with Asselineau, but with Malassis, it failed, for the good of both writer and publisher.

In Constantinople, General Aupick had enjoyed a successful two and a half years in his first post as Ambassador. In the Winter and Summer Palaces at Pera and Therapia, he and his wife received foreign representatives, members of the French community, important visitors (Lamartine in the summer of 1850), or less illustrious travellers like Maxime Du Camp and Gustave Flaubert. A letter Flaubert wrote to his mother on December 4, 1850 testifies to the Aupicks' generous hospitality: 'We're dining the day after tomorrow at the Embassy with the General. The good General doesn't go in much for diplomatic niceties. In private, he gives Maxime hearty slaps on the back, and calls him an old devil.'[21] But Maxime himself lacked diplomacy. After dinner one evening, Aupick asked him if any noteworthy new names had appeared in the literary world since he and his wife left Paris:

> I told the General about Henry Murger's play *La Vie de Bohème*, which had been a great success at the Théâtre des Variétés, and added: 'A few days ago, I received a letter from Louis de Cormenin in which he told me, "At Théophile Gautier's recently I saw a Charles Baudelaire who's going to make a name for himself; his originality is a little too contrived, but his verses are good and solid; he's got the temperament of a poet, and that's a rare thing these days."' As soon as I uttered the name Baudelaire, Mme Aupick lowered her eyes, and the General glared at me, as if to accept a challenge. Colonel Margadel touched my foot to warn me that I was on dangerous ground. It left me quite crestfallen; I realised that I had committed a *faux pas*, but had no idea what it was. Ten minutes later, the General and Flaubert were arguing about some book by Proudhon. Mme Aupick came up to me, and, very quietly, said, 'He *is* talented, isn't he?' 'Who?' 'The young man M. Louis de Cormenin spoke highly of.' I nodded without replying, for I understood less and less what was going on.
>
> Colonel Margadel withdrew at the same time as we, and led us to his apartment in the embassy palace in order to show us his fine collection of lepidoptera. 'Good God!' he said. 'You almost hit the powder keg when you brought up Charles Baudelaire-Dufaïs [*sic*]. That's Mme Aupick's son. He and the General have often come to blows. The General won't let anyone speak his name in his presence. Let that be a warning to you. Don't do it again.'[22]

The General's new job was no sinecure: many problems had arisen as a result of the recent revolutions in Central Europe. There was also the impossible financial situation of the Sublime Porte and its consequences for other countries – a situation which bears comparison with that of South

American countries today and which forced the General to become something of an economist.

Promotion was not long in coming. On February 20, 1851, General Aupick was appointed Ambassador to Her Britannic Majesty Queen Victoria. Two months later, the Aupicks set sail from Constantinople, the General hoping for a period of rest, Mme Aupick sorry to leave the city and the luxurious Summer Palace.[23]

The return voyage took them through Athens, Naples, Rome, then onto Lyons and back to Paris on the night of June 3. As Aupick explained to his friend, Thouvenel, the future Minister for Foreign Affairs, he had already reached a decision concerning his new appointment. The day after his return, Aupick was granted an audience with the President, Louis Napoleon, soon to become Emperor Napoleon III:

> An hour later I left him, relieved of the immense honour he had been kind enough to bestow on me ... they should have realised that I could not possibly accept ... I had said nothing at Pera, nor at Athens, not even to my wife, who was dreaming of going to England ... You know why I refused to go to London. I could not accept the role that my position would have forced me to play in front of the Orléans [King Louis-Philippe had fled to England after the 1848 revolution]. People may say what they will, but that job will always be a form of superior espionage. I cannot accept it ... I am the last of my race, and shall go to my grave a soldier and a man of honour ...

One should note that it was the honourable soldier more than the loyal servant of the Orléans who turned down the appointment.

On June 18, 1851, Aupick was posted instead to Madrid. The Orléans family was also present in Spain, but they were not pretenders to the French throne and Aupick probably viewed them as Spaniards. He neither sought nor refused to have contact with them. When they were stripped of their fortune by the decree confiscating the property of the House of Orléans, he had the courage to inform the Ministry of the bad impression this had created in Spain. The Orléans, in fact, in no way resented Aupick's rallying to the Republic and then to the Empire when it was created in 1852. After the death of Ancelle in 1889, the Comte de Paris, son of the Duc d'Orléans and grandson of Louis-Philippe, sent his condolences to the family: 'I am very familiar with the name of General Aupick. My mother mentioned him quite often, and told me how much my father liked and admired him. That is one of my earliest childhood memories.'[24]

Madrid was a far cry from the palaces of Constantinople. The previous ambassador had sold his residence and the Aupicks were forced to accept temporary housing. Mme Aupick prepared for visitors, but the diplomatic corps showed little sign of life and social events were rare. The General himself had few important matters to attend to; efficiency, he found, was not much in evidence: 'I thought the East had taught me all there is to know about the force of inertia. I was wrong. Madrid's the place to study that.'

The Aupicks were in Spain for less time than they had been in Constantinople. Aupick was made a senator on March 8, 1853, having turned down another term as ambassador to the Sublime Porte.

The General did not leave Spain with fond memories, but during his ambassadorship he made an excellent impression on the French community in Madrid and on his visitors. Emile Bégin, who later worked with Aupick on the team responsible for the publication of Napoleon's correspondence, described the welcome he received in his *Voyage pittoresque en Espagne et au Portugal*:

> It was not without real pleasure that on our arrival in Madrid, we saw once again that honourable General ... his lady wife is a charming woman, such a gifted speaker, and, what is more unusual, a good listener. The General appeared more serious than before, without having lost any of his expressiveness. The unfortunate events he had to suffer in '48 seemed to have left a few wrinkles on his brow, but his mouth shows the expression of calm hopes which time no doubt will realise.
>
> In Spain, everyone is unanimous in praising our ambassador.

It was during Aupick's term in Madrid that the *coup d'état* took place in Paris. The President had dissolved Parliament on 2 December 1851 and suppressed the uprising that was threatening to develop. The following year, he was proclaimed Emperor Napoleon III. Being a man of law and order, Aupick saw the *coup d'état* as a good thing.

Relations between Mme Aupick and her son had improved somewhat, though Charles complained about his mother's silence – 'that concerns your conscience, and maybe your husband's too' – and his own letters were few and far between. Mother and son were nevertheless able to meet in Paris before the Aupicks set off for Madrid. Baudelaire wrote, almost affectionately, on June 7:

> I wish I could express myself in a way that would not insult you in your affections, but you can easily guess why my dignity forbids me to set foot in your home.

Moreover, the respect I owe you does not permit me to receive you in the home of a person whom you detest. Thus, I would hope that your affection will permit you to be kind enough to come to *Neuilly*, to a place *where I'm alone*. For those two days, Sunday and Monday, I shall remain indoors. If, in spite of myself, some unsatisfactory word has managed to creep into this letter, don't be cross with me. You know what a clumsy writer I am.

The meeting was a success, to judge by the letter Baudelaire wrote to his mother on July 9, before her departure.

You probably noticed the infinite pleasure it gave me to see you again. I must confess I would not have believed it myself. I expected a cold and inquisitorial reception, and was bracing myself for it. You quite disarmed me, and gave me complete confidence in the future . . .

I promise you that I shall work unceasingly, not only to pay off the debts which are placing me in a painful and ambiguous position, but also to create for myself a daily regulator which will diminish the influence of all the stupidity and passion that are always bubbling up within us. I promise not to contract any more debts. As for the old ones, it will be hard to pay them off; but it's not entirely a lost cause.

In 1868, after her son's death, Mme Aupick told Asselineau: 'When I came to spend two months in Paris in between our two embassies . . . what a terrible state I found him in! What destitution! And I, his mother, with so much love in my heart, with so much good will towards him, could do nothing to extricate him from that situation!' Baudelaire and his mother were closer to each other during those few weeks in June and July 1851 than at any other time before the General's death.

Baudelaire promised his mother to write twice a month, but it was August 30 before he sat down to tell her about his new financial problems:

I'm very worried and very unhappy. It must be said that Man is a very weak-willed creature, since virtue can't survive without habit. *I had no end of a job settling down to work again.* And even then, I shouldn't be saying 'again', since I don't think I ever really started. What an extraordinary thing! A few days ago, I had in my hands some manuscripts from Balzac's youth. Nobody could possibly ever imagine how clumsy, foolish and *stupid* that great man was in his youth. And yet he managed to get, *to obtain for himself*, so to speak, not only grandiose ideas, but also a tremendous amount of wit. But then he worked *the whole time*. No doubt it's a rather consoling thought that by work alone one can acquire not only money, but also unquestionable talent. But by the age of thirty, Balzac had already been in the habit for several years of working non-stop, and until now the only things I have in common with him are debts and projects.

Accompanying this letter was a little brochure which Baudelaire claimed was important only in that it had been very well paid. It was a preface to the *Chants et Chansons* of his friend Pierre Dupont, interesting and important first because of Baudelaire's description of the working conditions of the poor, and secondly because the text he was sending to his mother, apparently in all innocence, contained allusions to his own upbringing:

> The infancy and youth of Pierre Dupont resemble those of all men destined to achieve fame. They are very simple, and explain the age to come. The fresh experience of family life, love, constraints, and the spirit of rebellion combine in sufficient quantities to create a poet ... Each of us, at least once in his life, should experience the pressure of odious tyranny. One learns to hate it ... How many rebellious souls have grown up under a cruel and punctilious soldier of the Empire! O nourishing discipline, how many songs of freedom we owe you! A poor, generous soul breaks out one fine morning, the Satanic charm is shattered, and only the essential remains, a memory of grief – yeast for the dough.

Mme Aupick certainly knew who this 'cruel and punctilious soldier' was supposed to be. The General himself would not have read the article: he and his stepson had nothing more to do with one another.

At the end of 1851, a group of friends formed a small review, the *Semaine théâtrale*. No more than two or three hundred copies were printed, and there were only nine issues, from November 6 to February 1, 1852. The force behind it was an ambitious young man who had only recently come up from Bordeaux, Charles Monselet. Among his recruits were Banville, Asselineau, Vitu, Champfleury and Baudelaire.

Just before the *coup d'état*, Baudelaire contributed to this little review a daring article entitled 'Les Drames et les Romans honnêtes'. In it, he condemned the sort of moralising literature that was being encouraged in the theatre by government subsidies and, negatively, by a virtual ban on serialised novels, which were held responsible for the demoralisation of the working classes. The main object of Baudelaire's attack was the 'Common-Sense School', which he ridiculed in the person of Emile Augier, whose play, *Gabrielle*, had been performed at the Comédie Française. Gabrielle's husband is a man who has all the qualities called for in a spouse. Quite understandably, she wants to go off with her lover; but finally she realises that this lover is not a serious man and that her husband, a solicitor, is not only serious, but also a 'poet' ... Baudelaire comments:

A solicitor! You can just imagine that 'decent' woman billing and cooing lovingly over her man's shoulder, and giving him languid looks, like those she's read about in novels! And all the solicitors in the theatre cheering the author who treats them as equals, and who avenges them of all those rogues who have debts and who think the poet's job consists of rendering the lyrical impulses of the soul in a rhythm regulated by tradition!

One of those solicitors was obviously meant to be Ancelle, who had just become Mayor of Neuilly. But he was still the *conseil judiciaire* of Charles Baudelaire, slow to hand out money and quick to give advice.

Baudelaire sent this article on to Madrid, along with his other contributions to the *Semaine théâtrale*: 'I should be pleased if you read them, when you have the time. I doubt very much you'll understand them completely. I don't mean to be impertinent when I say this.' The real impertinence was not in the letter, but in the article itself.

The only record of Baudelaire's reaction to the *coup d'état* is a few notes in *My Heart Laid Bare*, which betray the later influence of Joseph de Maistre's political philosophy:

My fury at the *coup d'état*. How many times I was shot at. Another Bonaparte! What a disgrace!

And yet everything calmed down. Doesn't the President have to justify himself?

What Emperor Napoleon III is. What he's worth. Discover the explanation of his nature, and his providentiality.

After the *coup d'état*, Baudelaire lost interest in politics and returned to it only on rare occasions. Besides, politics had become a dangerous business. He even failed to vote in the elections which, on February 29, 1852, gave France a legislative body prepared to accept an imperial regime. Five days after the election, he told Ancelle: 'DECEMBER 2 physically depoliticised me ... All of Paris is Orléanist now, it's a fact, but it doesn't concern me. Had I voted, I could only have voted for myself. Maybe the future belongs to the *déclassés*?' Baudelaire was looking a long way ahead.

Since 1977, in the wake of Walter Benjamin, German critics of Baudelaire have attempted to view the poet as an authentic revolutionary – overt or covert, depending on the circumstances – and to read a revolutionary message into his work.[25] Their studies have shown at least that Baudelaire was indeed openly hostile to the overwhelmingly bourgeois society of his time which stifled his aspirations and tried to destroy his work.

When one has a deep sense of individuality, however, and when egalitarianism appears to be the most pernicious of all utopias, one has no choice but to hate society and be a rebel. Baudelaire's only political characteristic is his resolutely anarchic philosophy. Having been a left-wing anarchist, he was about to become a right-wing anarchist. Baudelaire belonged to that race of 'good haters', to use the words he attributed to a poet very similar to him in many respects – Byron. There was nothing Marxist about Baudelaire and it would be unreasonable to interpret his work as one might interpret the work of Balzac who, though his explicit declarations are those of a monarchist, was in fact protesting just as effectively against the state of the society he described and against the restoration of the old order.

If Baudelaire drew any conclusion from those years of turmoil, it surely is contained in these lines from 'Le Reniement de Saint Pierre', written at the end of 1851 and published by the *Revue de Paris* in October 1852:

> – Certes, je sortirai, quant à moi, satisfait
> D'un monde où l'action n'est pas la soeur du rêve ...*

*'– I, for one, shall be happy to leave/A world in which action is not the sister of dream ...'

Didier-François Foyot,
Baudelaire's maternal
great-grandfather,
by J. L. Reinold
(*Private collection*)

François Baudelaire, the
poet's father, by Regnault
(*Private collection*)

Baudelaire as a schoolboy (*Private collection*)

The banks of the Rhône in Lyons (*Private collection*)

Jacques Rinn, Baudelaire's
favourite teacher at
Louis-le-Grand
(*Bibliothèque Nationale*)

The Lycée Louis-le-Grand (*Roger-Viollet*)

Caricatures by Baudelaire: (*right*) the headmaster of
Louis-le-Grand. (*Private collection*)

General Aupick in 1852 (*Private collection*)

Baudelaire in 1844, by his close friend, Emile Deroy. This painting, reproduced on the cover, shows Baudelaire as he was when living in the Hôtel Pimodan. It is one of the few surviving works by Deroy, who died in 1846. (*Musée de Versailles*)

Henri de Saussine
(*Private collection*)

Auguste Dozon
(*Private collection*)

Ernest Prarond
(*Private collection*)

Alphonse Baudelaire, the poet's
stepbrother (*Private collection*)

Félicité Baudelaire, Alphonse's wife
(*Pascal Soalhat*)

Désiré-Narcisse Ancelle
(*Private collection*)

Philoxène Boyer (*Bibliothèque Nationale*)

Pierre Dupont, by Emile Deroy
(*Pascal Soalhat*)

Baudelaire in 1847, by Gustave Courbet (*Pascal Soalhat*)

Edgar Allan Poe
(*Bibliothèque Nationale*)

Charles Asselineau (*Archives Photographiques*)

Mme Autard de Bragard, recipient of Baudelaire's poem, 'A une dame créole' (*Pascal Soalhat*)

The red-haired beggar-girl of Baudelaire's poem, 'A une mendiante rousse', by Emile Deroy (*Pascal Soalhat*)

'La Fanfarlo', drawing by Baudelaire (*Private collection*)

Lola Montès, by Charlet (*Bulloz*)

Mme Sabatier, by Meissonnier
(*Musées Nationaux*)

Marie Daubrun (*Pascal Soalhat*)

Jeanne Duval, drawing by Baudelaire
(*Pascal Soalhat*)

Baudelaire in 1855, by Nadar (*Archives Photographiques*)

Baudelaire, caricatured by
Nadar (*Roger-Viollet*)

Félix Nadar (*Bibliothèque Nationale*)

Baudelaire in a Louis XIII armchair, by Paul Nadar
(*Archives Photographiques Paris- SPADEM*)

Baudelaire in 1860, by Nadar (*Archives Photographiques*)

The Place d'Armes in Alençon, home of Poulet-Malassis' printing house (*Bibliothèque Nationale*)

Poulet-Malassis
(*Bibliothèque Nationale*)

Baudelaire in 1860. This photograph, reproduced on the back cover, was taken by the journalist and caricaturist, Étienne Carjat, in whose review, *Le Boulevard*, Baudelaire later published several poems and articles. (*Pascal Soalhat*)

Baudelaire with engravings, by Etienne Carjat (*Pascal Soalhat*)

Seated woman in profile, by Constantin Guys (*Bulloz*)

Berthe (*Bibliothèque Nationale*)

A page from Baudelaire's notebook (*Private collection*)

Baudelaire in 1862, by Nadar (*Archives Photographiques*)

Laure Dulong (*Private collection*)

Mme Manet, detail from 'La Pêche'
(*Rights reserved*)

Dr Marcq, by Félicien Rops (*Speltdoorn*)

Baudelaire, by Charles Neyt.
Baudelaire wrote to Poulet-
Malassis: 'The only being whose
laughter lightened my sadness in
Belgium'. (*Pascal Soalhat*)

Mme Paul Meurice
(*Rights reserved*)

'L'Atelier', by Alfred Stevens
(*Pascal Soalhat*)

Baudelaire with cigar, by Charles Neyt in 1864 (*Pascal Soalhat*)

PART FIVE

THE POE TRANSLATIONS
AND
LES FLEURS DU MAL

CHAPTER 15

Literary Life and Family Relations

1852–1856

February 1848 had been a time of dreams and expectations, but the hopes it raised were dashed in December 1851, when the *coup d'état* announced the return to power of the bourgeoisie and instituted an authoritarian regime. Confidence was restored and the economy was able to develop. Publishers and booksellers began to flourish (although the same was not necessarily true of writers), and it was under the Second Empire that the publishing houses, Hachette, Lévy and Larousse, became important commercial enterprises.

The 1848 revolution, 'which gave so much business to lawyers', 'dealt a lethal blow to writers and artists'. Creative literature was now considered to be a luxury item and the industry that produced it was immediately put out of action.[1] Those responsible for the *coup d'état* could certainly claim to have given a new lease of life to the sort of literature that painted a flattering picture of the propertied classes, but they had also succeeded in confirming the divorce between the general public and writers of originality – a divorce already apparent under the July Monarchy. New and unusual authors could now expect to enjoy the limelight only when passing through the criminal courts.

The proliferation of little reviews which vanished after only a few issues was a characteristic phenomenon of those years in which access to the larger, more important journals was denied to young writers. These little reviews were unable to attract enough subscribers and sometimes their only readers were the collaborators themselves. The *Semaine théâtrale* was an early example. Baudelaire published in it his courageous attack on 'Les Drames et les Romans honnêtes' and a matching article on 'The Pagan School', aimed at poets who refused to venture beyond the realms of classical mythology. In addition, the two 'Crépuscule' poems of *Les Fleurs du Mal* appeared in the last issue on February 1, 1852. When the *Semaine théâtrale* folded, Baudelaire decided to create his own review, intending to retain editorial control. He enlisted the help of the more experienced Champfleury and took on three other writers from the previous team. The format and typography were discussed, lists of possible subjects were drawn up and distributed, and a sleeping partner was found. Unfortunately, but not surprisingly, the sponsor withdrew just as the project was getting off the ground and *Le Hibou philosophe* (*The Philosopher Owl*) never saw the light of day.

Among the books to be reviewed in Baudelaire's paper were the *Unpublished Letters and Opuscules* of Joseph de Maistre, the theoretician of Catholic counter-revolution. Baudelaire would certainly have reserved this job for himself. The book in question, published in 1851, had as its frontispiece a portrait of de Maistre which inspired Baudelaire to write a brief physiognomic description in his first major study of Poe, that same spring of 1852:

> It is a very pleasureable and worthwhile exercise to compare the features of a great man with his works ... Who has not sometimes tried to distinguish the acuteness of Erasmus' style and his clarity of thought in the sharp edge of his profile ... the power of command and prophecy in the distant gaze and solid features of Joseph de Maistre, the eagle and the ox?

Baudelaire's reference to de Maistre was, of course, a piece of propaganda. De Maistre was his latest discovery. The following exchange took place in 1850 or 1851, at the home of Nadar:

> The conversation was long and amusing. Nadar and Baudelaire launched into politics and J. de Maistre (whom Nadar, incidentally, admitted he had not read). 'But,' he added, 'in my world, people know exactly what de Maistre is all about!'
> Baudelaire, who was reclining on the couch ... rose up on his fists, and paralysed Nadar with this terrible question:
> 'Have you read the refutation of Locke's system?'
> 'No,' said Nadar, embarrassed.
> 'Well then!'[2]

The discovery of Joseph de Maistre may well have had some influence on Baudelaire's image of Edgar Allan Poe. Whilst still being portrayed as a visionary, Poe was beginning to appear above all as the man of constitutional bad luck or *guignon* and as the inventor of skilfully engineered tales. Perhaps not very long after writing the 1852 study, Baudelaire indicated what for him was the vital connection between the two writers: 'De Maistre and Edgar Allan Poe taught me to think.'[3]

His first major study of Poe appeared in March and April 1852 in the *Revue de Paris*, to which Baudelaire had sent twelve poems, two of which were printed. The *Revue de Paris* was slightly to the left and, as is often the case, its progressive tendencies – republicanism at the time – made it moderately supportive of new writers. Baudelaire was received with a degree of reticence, as was Flaubert when, a few years later, he submitted to the same review a novel entitled *Madame Bovary*. Baudelaire the presenter of Poe was given a warmer welcome than Baudelaire the poet; and yet, in presenting Poe, Baudelaire was also projecting a poetic image of himself:

> Some lives are marked by fate. There exist in the literature of every nation men who bear the word *guignon* inscribed in mysterious characters in the sinuous folds of their brow. Some time ago, an unhappy wretch was brought before the courts, and on his brow was a strange tattoo: *bad luck*. Thus, he carried with him wherever he went the label of his life, as a book does its title, and the cross-examination proved that his existence had been in keeping with his sign. In the history of literature, there are similar destinies. It is as if the blind Angel of Expiation had taken hold of certain men, and whipped them with all its might for the edification of others.

Again, at the end of the study, Poe was also Baudelaire:

> One could write on his tombstone: 'All you who have ardently sought to discover the laws that govern your being, who have aspired to the infinite, and whose repressed emotions have had to seek a terrible relief in the wine of debauchery, pray for him. Now his bodily being, purified, floats amid the beings whose existence he glimpsed. Pray for him who sees and knows, he will intercede for you.'

In the body of the text, Baudelaire was thinking once again of himself when he emphasised 'what an immense part adolescence plays in forming the definitive genius of a man': 'Then it is that objects deeply sink their imprint into the tender, yielding mind. Then it is that colours are loud, and sounds speak a mysterious tongue.' Elsewhere, the evocation of 'the sombre years of confinement' at school, as described in *William Wilson*, or the story of Poe's first book of poetry – the 'eternal story of the first book' – were once again personal reminiscences. These intimate passages were removed when Baudelaire revised his study to turn it into the 1856 preface of the *Histoires extraordinaires*.

Arsène Houssaye, who had been a famous figure in Paris since 1840, was one of the directors of the *Revue de Paris*, as well as being the owner of *L'Artiste*. When in 1849 he became Director of the Comédie Française, he handed *L'Artiste* over to his brother, Edouard. Like Gérard de Nerval, Baudelaire would often have to reckon with this influential man of fashion, whose prose was flabby and whose poetry was weak.

Houssaye was ably assisted in his duties at the Comédie Française by his secretary, Jules Verteuil, who dealt with requests for complimentary tickets. This 'kind and gentle man' was teased by Baudelaire to the point of persecution. On one occasion, says Asselineau, Verteuil almost fainted when the poet described to him 'slowly, in minute detail, and with the patience of a inquisitor, the torture scenes I had taken him to see at the Salle des Missions in the rue du Bac!'

> Poor old Verteuil, whose usual sustenance was the smile of an actress, squirmed about behind his desk, gasping for breath. But that dreadful Baudelaire would not release his prey, and piled on the details: 'They pull the skin off their heads, hair and all. They root out their fingernails and toenails.' 'Oh, God!' breathed Verteuil. 'Is it not a fine thing, Monsieur Verteuil, to suffer for one's faith?' 'I suppose so, yes, it's a very fine thing, but I must confess, Monsieur Baudelaire, that such faith is quite beyond me! . . .' 'What! Monsieur Verteuil, would you not willingly die for your convictions?' From time to time, a simpering, cuddly little actress would slip into the office, to ask for a box or a few days off, Verteuil would cling to her as if to his saviour, grabbing her breasts or buttocks as if to regain his footing in the real world. 'One of those Chinese soldiers,' continued Baudelaire pitilessly as soon as the actress had left, 'opens up his victim's chest with his dagger, snatches out the bleeding heart, and swallows it! A pun in action! Do you see, Monsieur Verteuil? – To take heart!' Verteuil finally begged for mercy, and, in his state of distraction, gave us tickets for a box in the grand circle. Baudelaire left the theatre, beaming. It was such a wonderful spectacle for him that he didn't even use the ticket. The real triumph would have been for Verteuil to die of a heart attack during the night.[4]

The theatre (not only the stage itself but also the world behind the scenes) was a constant temptation. In 1843, he had worked with Prarond on *Idéolus* and then abandoned the project. In 1853, his thoughts turned to the Opera and on March 26 he told his mother that the Opera director had asked him for a libretto of a new sort to be set to music by an up-and-coming musician of some renown – perhaps Meyerbeer himself:

It was a stroke of good luck, and might have meant a perpetual source of income. – But poverty and disorder create such weariness and melancholy that I missed all the meetings. – *Fortunately*, I had not received any money for it!

That's not all. – The associate of a director of the Théâtre du Boulevard is asking me for a play. It was supposed to be read this month. – *I haven't written it.* – Out of consideration for my relations with this gentleman, one of the heads of the *claque* lent me 300 francs which were supposed to ward off another catastrophe last month. If the play was finished, it wouldn't matter. I'd have the debt paid by the director's partner, or have it taken out of future profits from the play or from the sale of tickets. But the play's not written …

Baudelaire's plans, which sometimes never got further than the title, are so numerous that it is impossible to determine which one was intended for the Opera. Perhaps it was *La Fin de Don Juan*, in which the eternal seducer was to meet the shade of Catilina. Asselineau felt that this particular project was an excuse 'to spend whole days lounging about *chez* Roqueplan', the Opera director. Baudelaire would apparently hold everything up while he had a drawing made of a certain exotic tree for the scenery, or tried to obtain the services of a particular musician. In any case, Baudelaire's opera eventually turned into a ballet.

As for the play commissioned by the Théâtre du Boulevard, it too is difficult to identify, although, in January 1854, Baudelaire presented the outline of a play entitled *The Drunkard* to Hippolyte Tisserant, one of the most popular actors at the Odéon. Tisserant had heard Baudelaire recite his poem, 'Le Vin de l'assassin', and suggested that he turn it into a two-act drama. In addition to the outline itself, we also have Asselineau's description of the play:

One of the backdrops was to be a seaport, with a sailors' inn in front, all cluttered up with curios brought back from the islands – parrots, monkeys, etc. It was to be a scene of military and maritime debauchery. I vaguely remember that in its final metamorphosis, the play had become a sort of tableau of cosmopolitan drunkenness. Rouvière was to play the drunkard. One day when Baudelaire was telling him about one of the main scenes for that role – a scene in which the drunkard, after killing his wife, had a resurgence of affection and a desire to ravish her – Rouvière's mistress cried out in indignation at the atrocity of the scene. 'Eh! Madame,' Baudelaire said. 'Anyone would do the same; and those who wouldn't are cranks!'[5]

Baudelaire toyed with the idea of *The Drunkard* for many years (until 1860 at least) and embellished the plot each time he described it to his friends. Asselineau was probably wrong in saying that most of those projects were just an excuse to spend time chatting with people he liked, but it would be difficult to prove that Baudelaire had any real feeling for the stage, or that he had the patience to see a scenario through to the end. His theatrical experiments bore fruit in other fields – in the prose poem, 'Portraits de maîtresses', for example. For Baudelaire, the theatre was associated with dreams of riches, glory and romance, such dreams are not always productive.

It was the theatre that gave Philoxène Boyer some fleeting fame shortly after his arrival in Paris.[6] Born in Cahors in 1829, and therefore much younger than Baudelaire, he wrote admiring letters to Houssaye and sent Victor Hugo a panegyric in honour of *Les Burgraves* and his book on the Rhine. When he came up to Paris, he brought with him a one-act verse play entitled *Sapho*, which found favour with Banville and the Hugo clan. It was performed at the Odéon on November 13, 1850 and published a few days later by Michel Lévy, with a dedication to Banville, who had attended rehearsals in the absence of the author. Philoxène had hurried home in the meantime to collect a large inheritance from his mother – 80,000 or 100,000 francs – much more than Baudelaire had spent in two years. Boyer managed to dispose of the sum in almost half that time, simply in satisfying the demands of his particular ailment – logorrhea. 'For two or three years, all the papers talked about were the dinners he gave in the best restaurants in Paris ... One sumptuous winter, people remember seeing a whole fortune being thrown out of the windows of the Café de Paris.'[7] By the age of twenty, Boyer was already an old man with white hair and when he died at the age of thirty-seven he showed 'all the characteristic signs of old age – the collapse of biological functions, mental deficiency, etc.'.

The extent of Boyer's circle is apparent from the album in which his friends inscribed verses, thoughts, or pieces of music. Baudelaire copied out his poem, 'Les Litanies de Satan', wrote a maxim on the right to contradict oneself and sketched amusing caricatures of Pierrot, the head-master who expelled him from Louis-le-Grand, Saint-Alme, the chief editor of the *Corsaire*, Champfleury and himself.[8]

Boyer's extravagant spending had only one aim:

Philoxène was a voice. He could have done without arms and legs, since he was used to having other people fetch and carry for him. A mouth was all he needed; he lived only for talking. Baudelaire admired the way he could cheer himself up no matter what the circumstances just by speaking. He would mimic Philoxène saying, 'I'm very unhappy, I don't have any money; but *I shall speak* on such and such a day in such and such a hall, or at so and so's place.' It is quite true that for a long time he refused to publish his poems, because, as he said, once they were published, he wouldn't have any excuse to recite them ... To shut him up was impossible, besides which, it would have been the worst insult. Baudelaire told him one day, 'Philoxène, in the next revolution, you'll be up on the scaffold.' 'Yes, but I'll speak, too,' said Philoxène in ecstasy. 'No! they won't let you. There'll be the drums.' And Philoxène lowered his head and looked devastated.

This little exchange left its mark on the prose poem, 'La Solitude':

> There are among our chattering peoples individuals who would bow with less repugnance to their execution, if they were allowed to hold forth copiously from the top of the scaffold, without the fear that the drums might, at an untimely moment, cut them off.

Boyer would by now have been forgotten had he not had friends like Banville, Baudelaire and Asselineau. His poetry is second rate and his only interesting work is an end-of-the-year review, *Aristophanes' Feuilleton*, written in collaboration with Banville, in which Balzac is hailed as 'the Homer of today', and in which Courbet and Realism are attacked, along with Berlioz and Dumas's *Lady of the Camellias.*

These friends would often meet, after the *coup d'état*, in a café just a few steps away from the Opera, called the Divan Le Peletier.[9] Around the red velvet divan in the centre of the room, dozens of writers regularly met, some of them already famous – Pétrus Borel, Nerval, Théophile Gautier, critics and publishers. It was a wonderful audience for those who wished to recite their verses. Baudelaire gave a rendering at the Divan of his poem, 'Le Reniement de Saint Pierre'. Among the other regulars were the painter Chenavard, the sculptor and wit, Auguste Préault, and the Fourierist, Alphonse Toussenel, who presented Baudelaire with a copy of his book, *The Spirit of Beasts.* This gave Baudelaire an opportunity to express his rejection of the analogical systems of thought he had favoured before 1850. The influence of De Maistre was inclining him now towards a form of pessimism based on a firm belief in original sin. Also present at the Divan were Gustave Planche, the formidable literary critic of the *Revue des Deux Mondes*, and two brothers from the Vaucluse, Henry and Jules de La Madelène. Henry, the younger of the two, 'signed up with a little band of volunteers commanded by Charles Baudelaire and Théodore de Banville, who, having ten years' service under their belts, were beginning to be seen now as members of the old guard'. In a review called *Paris*, Henry published an article on the Divan, in which he described Baudelaire reciting 'Les Chats', and, later in 1853, he invented a continuation of Baudelaire's *La Fanfarlo*, which he entitled *The Story of Samuel's Boots*.[10]

Henry de La Madelène was one of the regulars at the Divan celebrated by Banville in a light-hearted poem which devotes a stanza to Baudelaire and Asselineau:

> On voit le doux Asselineau
> Près du farouche Baudelaire.
> Comme un Moscovite en traîneau,
> On voit le doux Asselineau.
> Plus aigre qu'un jeune cerneau,
> L'autre est comme un Goethe en colère
> On voit le doux Asselineau
> Près du farouche Baudelaire.*

The writers and artists mentioned above give some idea of Baudelaire's circle of acquaintances around 1855. Another list is provided by a notebook in which Asselineau recorded twenty-four 'friends of Baudelaire'.[11] Even though the list is long, there are gaps. Very few people in any case could claim to be true friends of the poet – perhaps only Champfleury, Asselineau and Poulet-Malassis ever had that honour.

Asselineau's list is interesting, however, in that it includes the name of Gustave Mathieu.[12] Mathieu belonged to a very different milieu – the branch of literary Bohemia that was characterised by its taste for wine and song. It was closely related to Courbet's group and, in spite of its favourite drink, to Henry Murger's impoverished 'Water-Drinkers'. A socialist and republican poet, Mathieu triumphed over difficult circumstances to launch a periodical entitled *Jean Raisin, revue joyeuse et vinicole*, with a wine-coloured cover and a Gustave Doré illustration showing the wine-harvest in Burgundy. The subtitle ran as follows: 'For the use and recreation of Wine-Growers, Waiters, Bottlers, Coopers, Wood-cutters, and all other workers living on, by, and for the vine, including winesellers, wholesale and retail, under the direction of Gustave Mathieu.' *Jean Raisin* was the title of a song

* 'You can see gentle Asselineau / Next to the forbidding Baudelaire. / Like a Muscovite in his sleigh, / You can see gentle Asselineau. / More bitter than an unripe walnut, / The other is like an angry Goethe. / You can see gentle Asselineau / Next to the forbidding Baudelaire.'

by Mathieu that was popular at the time. The review lasted only from 15 October, 1854 to 10 March, 1855, and included in its 15 November issue a poem by Baudelaire, 'Le Vin des chiffonniers', previously unpublished but no doubt recited several times in cafés by its author.

From 1848 on, Baudelaire would occasionally meet Mathieu in a large, smoky, German-style beer hall, the Brasserie des Martyrs,[13] in the company of his friends, Pierre Dupont, Antonio Watripon, Fernand Desnoyers and others. Because of his political songs, which expressed opposition to the counter-revolution, Pierre Dupont was hunted by the police and lay low for six months after the *coup d'état*. In 1852, he was arrested and sentenced to be deported for seven years to Lambessa; it was an extraordinarily severe punishment. Since there was really nothing terribly dangerous about Dupont he was released through the intervention of friends; but his talent seems to have suffered as a result. Baudelaire's 1861 article on the song-writer was somewhat cooler than the 1851 preface to the *Chants et Chansons* of his friend. By then, Baudelaire no longer had any sympathy for the socialist tendencies which Dupont represented, and which he himself had enthusiastically supported in his youth.

Antonio Watripon was 'the archetypal modern journalist always short of copy'. Thus it was that he asked Baudelaire for some details about himself and his work for a biographical index.[14] Baudelaire offered the following information: 'You might like to say that I was born in Paris in 1821, and that while still quite young, I went on several voyages in the Indian Seas. I don't think that sort of thing should be mentioned.' Once again, Baudelaire was taking advantage of an opportunity to embellish his own legend. He was so successful that he eventually believed it himself. When complaining to Ancelle in 1864 about the awful weather in Brussels, he wrote: 'I who first became familiar with the sea and the sky at Bordeaux, the Ile Bourbon, Mauritius, and Calcutta.' The other details Baudelaire gave Watripon concerned his works – 'there's scarcely anything but articles'; and finally:

> To that, you can add: *Physiology of Laughter*, which will soon be appearing, probably in the *Revue de Paris*, and also the *Salon des caricaturistes*, and poems, *Les Limbes*, to be published by *Michel Lévy*. It won't be a lie, since it's going to appear very soon, probably before your biographical index. But this all seems very conceited to me. Put it in order *or leave things out*; do what you will. If there's anything I've forgotten, then that's just too bad.

Watripon's note did not appear. Baudelaire was nevertheless sufficiently well-known (and well-connected) by now to be included in a little

'pantheon' of contemporary writers. Nadar's caricature of the poet in the
Journal pour rire was published with the following caption:

> Charles Baudelaire – a nervous, testy, irritable, and irritating young
> poet, often utterly unpleasant in private. Very much a realist under his
> paradoxical airs. His poetic form has all the style and austerity of antiquity,
> and of the few minds marching along these days in the solitude of the
> *self*, he is, I think, the best, and the one who is most sure of the path he
> is following. Very difficult to publish, since in his poems he calls God
> an 'imbecile', Baudelaire has also produced a book on the 1846 Salon
> which is every bit as remarkable as Diderot's finest articles. A contributor
> of the new *Revue de Paris*.[15]

Nadar's caricature matches the description given by Du Camp after a
meeting he had with Baudelaire during the summer of 1852. His dress,
however, was quite different. Nadar shows him very soberly attired, but
the translator of Edgar Allan Poe had probably dressed up with the intention
of shocking the bourgeois director of the *Revue de Paris*:

> His suit was immaculately clean, and coarse in its style and material.
> A madras scarf was wrapped around the collar of a shirt of such strong
> cloth that it looked like the untreated fibre. Large, bronze-plated buttons
> closed a greyish overcoat which was cut like a sack. Blue stockings
> appeared above hunting shoes that were gleaming with polish. His hands
> ... moved in a slow, pretentious fashion. The head was like that of a
> young devil turned hermit. His hair was cut very short, his face was
> clean-shaven, his eyes were small, sharp and anxious, more reddish than
> brown; the nose was sensual, and bulbous at the tip; the mouth was thin
> and rarely showed a smile, the lips were almost always pursed. He had a
> square chin and prominent ears. These features made him unpleasant to
> look at at first, but one very soon got used to it. His voice was steady,
> like the voice of a man who chooses his words carefully and who enjoys
> speaking. His middling height and solid build revealed his muscular
> strength, and yet there was something harrowed and limp about him
> which indicated weakness and neglect.[16]

Evidence of Baudelaire's reputation at this time can be found in Ernest
Prarond's book *On Some New Writers*. The introduction mentions those
who have 'lapsed into silence' and whom the author hopes are not 'lost for
good'. Prarond refers in particular to 'a poet who, by occasionally giving
recitals for himself or for a few friends of great poetry, has had the rare
good fortune to become almost famous without publishing a single verse'.

Prarond goes on to say that 'on the occasion of an exhibition at the Louvre [the 1846 Salon], Baudelaire has also written a whole catechism of modern painting'. Prarond was mistaken in only one respect – since the appearance of eleven sonnets from *Les Limbes*, Baudelaire was no longer such a clandestine poet.

Another two poems appeared in the spring of 1855 in a *Festschrift* co-edited by one of Gustave Mathieu's friends from the beer hall. Fernand Desnoyers, who would now have been forgotten were it not for this *Festschrift*, considered himself to be one of the period's truly creative poets – a distinction he more perceptively awarded at the same time to Pierre Dupont, Banville and Baudelaire. The volume in question – *Fontainebleau, paysages, légendes, souvenirs, fantaisies* – was a 'Homage to C. F. Denecourt', an unassuming man whose passion in life was the forest of Fontainebleau. Denecourt had tried to enhance the beauty of Fontainebleau by opening up paths, creating avenues and had written several books on the subject. Contributors to the *Festschrift* included many of Baudelaire's friends, as well as some of the leading lights of the previous generation – Lamartine, Hugo, Musset, Gautier and Nerval. Desnoyers wrote to Baudelaire asking for a few verses. He received the following reply:

My dear Desnoyers, you wanted some poetry from me for your little book – poetry on *Nature*, isn't that it? On woods, the lofty oaks, greenery and insects, and the sun, I suppose. But you know perfectly well I'm incapable of getting sentimental about plant-life, and that my soul protests at that strange new Religion which, it seems to me, will always be slightly *shocking*** to any spiritual being. I shall never believe that 'the soul of the Gods resides in plants', and even if it did, it would be a matter of little concern to me, and I should consider mine to be of far greater worth than that of sanctified vegetables. What's more, I have always thought that there was in *Nature*, rampant and rejuvenated, something offensive, harsh and cruel – something verging on impudence. Since I cannot satisfy you entirely according to the strict terms of your programme, I am sending you two pieces of poetry which more or less sum up the reveries that assail me in the twilight hours. In the depths of forests, closed in underneath those vaults which resemble those of sacristies and cathedrals, I think of our astonishing cities, and the miraculous music that rolls out over the heights comes to my ears as a rendition of human lamentation.

This letter was printed in the volume, followed by Baudelaire's two

* In English in the original.

'Crépuscule' poems. By declaring war in this way on the love of nature, Baudelaire was keeping his distance from that 'strange new Religion' of so-called Romantics and presenting himself as a poet of the city. City-dwellers dream of the radiant or melancholy charms of nature; Baudelaire, in the forest, dreams of the city. These are the origins of the section of poems later to appear in the second edition of *Les Fleurs du Mal* – the 'Tableaux parisiens'.

In the table of contents of the homage volume appeared the name of another friend of Gustave Mathieu – Charles Vincent.[17] Vincent was responsible for one of the more peculiar incidents of Baudelaire's publishing career. In July 1850, a certain A. Z. Pannélier had founded a newspaper for bootmakers called *L'Innovateur*. Three years later, he took on Charles Vincent as a partner, hoping that 'many other well-known and high-ranking writers' would follow in Vincent's footsteps. Sure enough, on November 15, 1853, the paper announced the forthcoming collaboration of Pierre Dupont, Fernand Desnoyers and Charles Baudelaire. According to the December 1 issue, Baudelaire's contribution was to be a piece entitled *Cobbling for Ladies*. The title reappeared in several later issues, until March 31, 1854, by which time it had changed its title to *The Ladies' Cobbler*. The work itself was never published.

Baudelaire's unusual title is an indication of what seems to have been a fetish. One thinks, for example, of a page in his notebook in which he dreams of dressing a prostitute called Agathe in 'Very fine, openwork silk stockings – black if the dress is black or brown, pink if the dress is light. Very open shoes. Flirtatious garters.' And the following detail: 'A bath. Very well-groomed feet and hands. Perfume all over.'

Baudelaire's brief appearances in *The Innovator* can be put down in part to his desire to stand out from the crowd. For the same reason, he once expressed a wish to write for Louis Veuillot's Catholic newspaper, *L'Univers*, and at the same time for the *Moniteur de l'Epicerie*.[18] But it is also indicative of the state of the press under the Second Republic, and, even more so, under the Second Empire, that Baudelaire advertised *Les Limbes* in *L'Echo des marchands de vins*, offered his poem, 'Le Vin des chiffonniers' to *Jean Raisin* and promised the bootmakers' *Innovateur* a piece entitled *The Ladies' Cobbler*.

From the early 1850s until the end of his conscious life, Baudelaire's letters to his mother are our main source of information. Mme Aupick's replies have yet to be found. They may still be hidden away somewhere, although there is also a possibility that they were destroyed by Mme Aupick herself or by her inheritors.

Relations between mother and son gradually improved from 1851 on, although upsets continued to occur. Even much later, the bothersome question of money frequently cropped up. When it did, Baudelaire would try to play his mother off against Ancelle and rarely lacked opportunities to do so.

On their return from Madrid at the end of April or the beginning of May 1853, the Aupicks rented a pied-à-terre in Paris. The General took his seat in the Senate and on September 7, 1854 became a member of the commission formed 'to collect, co-ordinate, and publish' the *Correspondence of Napoleon I*. Each summer, the couple probably left to take the waters at Barèges in the Pyrenees or Bourbonne in the Haute-Marne: the General's old war wound was still troubling him.

On March 7, 1855, Aupick bought a house on the clifftop overlooking the port of Honfleur on the Normandy coast. The view across the estuary of the Seine towards Le Havre reminded him of the estuary of the Bosphoros at Therapia. This little house, nicknamed the *maison-joujou* (the 'toy house') by Baudelaire, and the garden which separated it from the cliff edge became the General's favourite retreat during the last years of his life.[19] The overhanging terrace was christened the Bosphorus and, at the other end of the garden, a raised pavilion of rustic appearance was built, with coloured glass, topped with a signal mast. The house itself had two floors looking onto the street. Another floor gave onto the garden, which was at a lower level; it housed the kitchen, pantry, cellar and laundry. At street level were the dining room, two bedrooms (for the General and his wife), toilets, Aupick's study, the living room and an adjoining veranda facing north towards the estuary; Aupick named this the Mirador. From the veranda, stairs led down to the garden. A corridor with windows gave onto the courtyard, which was reached by a granite staircase. On the west side of the courtyard were the sheds and stables; to the north, the circular winter garden laid out to the General's orders; and to the south was the rue du Neubourg. On the second floor there were three attic rooms, one of which later became Charles' room; the others were intended for guests.

This was the 'modest retreat' chosen by the General for his old age. He had little time left in which to enjoy it. He stayed there when he was not sitting in the Senate, in which he played a fairly discreet role, or attending the Regional Council for the Département du Nord.

Aupick's letters from this period to his friend Thouvenel are full of scenes and anecdotes, all of which bear witness to his skill as a letter-writer. They also contain bad news about his own health and that of his wife. On

October 9, 1856, writing from Honfleur, he told Thouvenel about his trip
to take the waters at Bourbonne:

> I found there nothing but pain, and suffered also from the sight of the
> glorious wounded from the Crimea who were there in great numbers.
> In general, however, they benefited from the effect of the waters, and,
> apart from the unpleasant feeling I experienced when I saw their deform-
> ities, I felt sincere admiration at the sight of their virile, warlike faces ...
> As for myself, the crippled soldier from Ancient History, I dragged
> myself among them as best I could. It doesn't seem to have been a very
> fruitful experiment. Back in Paris after what they call a season, my wife
> and I returned to our hermitage in a sorry state. I was scarcely able to
> walk and so we go out only in the carriage ... So far, it's nothing to
> worry about, but being unable to move is a bitter blow for an old soldier
> like myself.

Charles had been showing much concern for his mother: 'As a reward
for your perpetual favours, I should like just for once to give you great
satisfaction,' but, 'for the time being, that is scarcely possible. – Who
knows? Maybe next month?' These words were written at the end of March
1854, shortly before his thirty-third birthday. Mme Aupick, torn between
husband and son, was hoping for the impossible reconciliation. Charles
wrote back on July 28: 'Yes, yes, everything will be settled; yes, the
reconciliation will take place, and honourably, if your husband will just
have a little wit; yes, I know how much you've had to put up with because
of me.' The General certainly had wit, but not enough to understand his
stepson.

Writing to his mother on December 20, 1855, Charles realised that she
had been refusing to see him for more than a year, and that before anything
else, there would have to be a 'reconciliation' between them: 'I'm not
exactly an old man, but I might be before long. I can't imagine your wanting
things to go on like this. I've had my fill of every kind of humiliation.'
While setting his papers in order, Baudelaire had found a great many letters
from his mother.

> I tried rereading several of them. They were all full of deep concern,
> purely material, it's true, as if debts were all that mattered, and as if
> spiritual pleasure and happiness meant nothing. But since they were
> maternal more than anything else, they set me on the most painful train
> of thought. All those letters stood for the years that have passed – years
> of unhappiness. Soon I couldn't bear to read on. In certain situations,

nothing is more odious than the past. And as thought followed thought, it occurred to me that this situation is not only monstrous and shocking, but even dangerous. Just because my mind is a certain way, which you clearly find eccentric, you shouldn't conclude that I derive some sick pleasure from this utter isolation and estrangement from my Mother.

But the General continued to prevent any real reconciliation. After writing to his mother, Baudelaire learnt that Delacroix was about to be made a senator and wrote to Ancelle: 'Now M. Aupick will be forced to sit near a very lowly person.' Only the death of one of the antagonists could solve the conflict. Would it be the son or the stepfather?

The first of the family to die was the son of Alphonse and Félicité – Edmond Baudelaire. He died at Fontainebleau on December 26, 1854, at the age of twenty-one. Three days later, Charles sent a letter to his half-brother. He had heard about 'the tragic event' too late and had been unable to attend the funeral.

> I am unaware of the full extent of the misfortune that has befallen you. I can only guess that it is immense. I have absolutely no idea what consolation might be offered. – We have not seen one another for many years now, and I don't know why the thought of the misfortune that befalls you and the thought of our estrangement should strike me at the same time.

He promised him a visit 'in a few days', finding himself for the time being 'overburdened with business', and added a word of sympathy for the mother.

Baudelaire's note should be compared to the letter written on the same occasion by the General:

> It was only yesterday evening at 10 o'clock that I was given the terrible message in which you inform me of the dreadful blow you have just suffered. My wife, having been a happy mother herself in days gone by, thought at once of Mme Baudelaire. – Poor mother, she said, she whom I saw so proud and happy to have such a charming infant! How I pity her, to whom no consolation can be given! and tears were in her eyes. – And you, my poor Monsieur Baudelaire, we pity you too; and yet I find that I must tell you that the moment has come for you to be courageous for two, more for your wife than for yourself, for who could claim to know how much love there is in a mother's heart?[20]

Alphonse was obviously a man the General liked, a man he might have been pleased to have as his stepson. Charles, on the other hand, was seen as the cause of Caroline's unhappiness.

It seems unlikely that Baudelaire went to Fontainebleau. On January 9, 1856, he explained to his mother that Alphonse had offended him on two different occasions. One was the imposition of the *conseil judiciaire*; the other, the bitter reproaches resulting from Baudelaire's sending letters and poems to Félicité, or from the elder brother's settling of Charles' debts:

> The name for my brother's crime is stupidity . . . I prefer *wicked* people who know what they're doing, to *good people who are idiots* . . . Nothing in the world is more precious than a *poetic mind*, and *chivalry*. His political and scientific incompetence, his cynical opinions on women, to whom one should at least show gallantry, if not passion – everything, in short, makes him a stranger to me.

There is little doubt that Alphonse was no great mind. In many ways he was the archetypal bourgeois, dull and sententious. Despite his excellent connections, he remained all his life a mere magistrate at Fontainebleau.

In 1851, the prefect of the Seine-et-Marne region called for an inquest into the strange behaviour of Judge Baudelaire who had given a political prisoner a pair of compasses and told him that 'if I were a judge, I would acquit you'. The Public Prosecutor's report contained the following description of Alphonse:

> He is a good man, a scrupulous and hard-working magistrate, but disorganised and unmethodical, lacking discrimination and strength of character. His investigations bear the mark of this lack of sense and discernment, and certain persons have thought, incorrectly, I believe, that his decisions were a sign of undesirable political opinions. He is, moreover, too often inclined to exercise extreme and inappropriate leniency towards certain defendants.

Furthermore, as a member of the Municipal Council, 'M. Baudelaire has an exaggerated idea of his role and of his own importance, and brings to this sort of work, too, a zeal that is more vigorous than effective'. The Prosecutor added that M. Baudelaire's financial situation, weakened by the support he gave in 1848 to one of his brother-in-laws [Ducessois, the printer], was not one likely to inspire respect for his magisterial authority. Finally, in the words of another magistrate, 'Nobody takes him seriously.'

As a result of this damning report, the case in question was taken away from Alphonse. He remained a magistrate until his death and never became president of the tribunal.

The abyss that separated the two brothers becomes even more apparent in the following account. On January 12, 1856, Ernest Prarond was leaving the Black Eagle hotel in Fontainebleau:

I heard someone shout to the driver of the omnibus, 'To the home of Monsieur Baudelaire'. The carriage pulled up in front of a fine-looking house. A man flew into the vehicle like a whirlwind. It was Monsieur Baudelaire, physically enlarged, taller and stronger, brusque, impetuous and jerky in his motions – a Baudelaire with convulsive gestures. Unlike his brother's, Baudelaire's agitation was concealed under a very calm and deliberate exterior. The immoderate Baudelaire and the calm Baudelaire looked very much alike. There was something more square about him, a bigger frame and bigger cheekbones.[21]

Alphonse was a caricature of Charles and his personality was probably an exaggerated version of their father's; and the sight of one's own caricature is not necessarily something that would inspire affection.

CHAPTER 16

Jeanne Duval, Mme Sabatier, Marie Daubrun

1852–1856

At the end of 1855, Baudelaire had decided to settle down 'once and for all'. Writing to his mother on December 20 he submitted his current situation to the sort of general review he often indulged in. This moral inventory usually indicated a desire to make a fresh start, to be rid of the *conseil judiciaire* and to reach a state of equilibrium in his life. None of those dreams was ever likely to come true, but perhaps their continual frustration was also a condition of creativity.

> I'm sick and tired of this life of cheap restaurants and furnished rooms. It's killing me and driving me up the wall. I don't know how I've managed to put up with it.
>
> I'm tired of having colds, migraines and fevers, and especially of having to go out twice a day, and of the snow, the mud and the rain . . .
>
> There is a condition more serious than physical pain, and that's the fear of witnessing the gradual deterioration, collapse, and disappearance of that wonderful poetic vision, clarity of thought, and power of hope which make up my true capital.
>
> My dear Mother, you have so little idea of what a poet's life is, that you probably won't be able to understand that particular argument very well; and yet that's the root of my principal fear. I don't want to die in obscurity; I don't want to see old age draw near without my having a regular existence. I shall NEVER resign myself to that; and I believe my person to be very precious – I won't say more precious than others, but precious enough to me.

When he wrote to his mother in Madrid, Baudelaire was living in the rue des Marais-du-Temple. On 27 March 1852, he told her he would soon be moving. His aim: to escape from Jeanne Duval. As a substitute wife, Jeanne had provided some means of escape from this sordid way of life, but the poet would always be a long way from the domestic situation described in *Fusées*: 'Passionate cohabitation can offer a glimpse of the joys of a young household.' On December 8, 1848, Baudelaire wrote that his love for that 'poor woman' had long been sustained only by a sense of duty. Honour alone made him persevere in 'this curious relationship, in which I have nothing to gain, and in which atonement and a desire to reward devotion play the largest part'.

However many times a woman has been unfaithful, however hard-hearted she may be, once she has shown a few glimmerings of good will and devotion, that should be enough to make an unselfish man, and particularly a poet, feel compelled to repay her.

By March 27, 1852, the situation had become intolerable:

Jeanne has become an obstacle, not only to my happiness – that would be of little importance; I, too, am capable of giving up my pleasures, and I've proved it – but also to the perfecting of my mind. The past nine months have been a decisive experiment. Given such conditions, I shall never be able to accomplish the great goals I had set myself – the payment of my debts, the conquest of financial security, the acquisition of fame, the alleviation of the grief I have caused you. *There was a time when she had some merits*, but she's *lost* them, and I have become more lucid. TO LIVE WITH A CREATURE who shows no gratitude for your labours, who frustrates every effort with her continual negligence or malevolence, who sees you only as her servant and her piece of property, with whom it is impossible to talk politics or literature, a creature who *wishes to learn nothing*, though you yourself have offered to teach her, a creature WHO DOES NOT ADMIRE ME, who even shows no interest in my studies, who would throw my manuscripts on the fire if that would bring her more money than allowing them to be published, who sends my cat away – my only distraction in the home – and introduces dogs, precisely *because* the sight of a dog makes me ill, who doesn't know, or doesn't want to understand *that to scrimp and save, just for* ONE *month*, would provide the momentary respite needed to complete an important work. Is all that possible? Is it possible? Tears of shame and anger are in my eyes as I write these words; and, in truth, I'm glad I have no weapon with me. I think of times when I can't listen to reason, of that terrible night when I opened her head on a sideboard.* This is what I now have found where ten months ago, I thought to find relief and rest.

* There is no other trace of this incident in Baudelaire's correspondence.

It was then that Baudelaire left Jeanne and took a room in a hydro-therapeutic establishment run by a doctor he knew – 'a nice room, an attractive garden, excellent meals, a cold bath and two showers every day'. A dream come true. But Jeanne still had to be taken care of. Giving her a large sum of money was obviously out of the question and so Baudelaire continued to provide her with small amounts – hardly the ideal solution for someone who had apparently decided to break up once and for all.

From May to July 1852, Baudelaire lived on the Boulevard Bonne-Nouvelle. The following letter to Mme Aupick, in which he claims to have been separated from Jeanne for a year, refers to that address. The letter is dated March 26, 1853:

> I paid off the year's deficit, and lived on my own. – This is when the trouble started up again. I was living in a house where the landlady caused me so much grief with her slyness, her bickering, and her deceitfulness, and I was in such poor health that I left, as I usually do, without saying a word. *I owed her nothing*, but I was stupid enough to let the rent mount up, even though I wasn't living there, and so now the money I owe her is payment for a place I didn't occupy ... Meanwhile, a publisher – a kind and wealthy publisher – took a liking to me and asked me for a book. Some of the manuscripts I needed were over at *that place*. – I tried to start again from scratch. I redeemed some books, and was determined not to write to you. On January 10, my contract forced me to deliver the book. I received my money, and gave the printer such a messy manuscript that after the *composition* of the first sheets, I realised that there were so many *corrections* and *revisions* to be made, that it would be better just to dismantle the *formes*, and *reset* the whole thing. You're not familiar with all this terminology. What it means is that the part composed by the workers was virtually useless, and since it was my fault, honour forced me to pay for the damage.

The publisher was Victor Lecou, and the book, the translation of Poe's tales for which Baudelaire later negotiated a contract with Michel Lévy in August 1855.

The same letter, written from the flat he occupied for a year and a half in the rue Pigalle,[1] indicates that although he was separated from Jeanne, she was still an important part of his life. Two or three times a month, he took her small sums of money. She was now seriously ill and extremely poor: 'I never talk to M. *Ancelle* about this,' Baudelaire continued. 'It would give the wretched man too much pleasure. – Obviously a small part of what you send me will go to her.'

She's really made me suffer, hasn't she? ... But faced with such ruin, with such profound sadness, I feel tears well up in my eyes, and, if the truth be told, my heart fills with remorse. Twice now I've squandered her jewelry and furniture, I've made her go into debt for me, I've hit her, and, finally, instead of showing her how a man like myself should behave, the only example I've set her is debauchery and an unstable existence. She suffers, and is silent. – Isn't that reason enough to feel remorse? And am I not guilty in that respect as in all others?

The letter needs no further comment and is itself a form of commentary on several poems of *Les Fleurs du Mal*.

Baudelaire nevertheless went on to express his hatred of 'the values of the Bourgeoisie' and begged his mother to send as much money as possible, 'but without putting yourself out, since, all in all, it's only right that I should suffer'. The money he received from Mme Aupick allowed him to salvage the books and manuscripts left with the tyrannical landlady on the Boulevard Bonne-Nouvelle, and to 'bring some relief to that unhappy woman'. This man who was so cruelly ironical had more true charity than those who debarred him from their society.

An examination of Baudelaire's legal and financial situation at the time shows that he was still contracting debts or renewing them without his creditors being aware that he was not legally responsible. The *conseil judiciaire* was too much of a humiliation to be used as a safety net; and so, at a time when debtors could still be threatened with imprisonment, he was often hunted from dawn to dusk. One can well understand why the poet was as attentive to the coming of dawn or the onset of evening as a Moslem during Ramadan.

> Voici le soir charmant, ami du criminel,
> Il vient comme un complice, à pas de loup; le ciel
> Se ferme lentement comme une grande alcôve,
> Et l'homme impatient se change en bête fauve.*

A wild animal, but also a free man.

Around April 1853, a letter addressed to Mme Aupick:

I had to leave my home tonight, and am forced to sleep – probably for two days, until someone settles the matter for me – *in a shady little hotel where no one can find me*, because I was surrounded and spied on so

---

* 'Here is the enchanting evening, friend of the criminal, / It comes like an accomplice, softly; the sky / Closes slowly like a great alcove, / And the restless man becomes a savage beast.'

much at home that I couldn't go anywhere. I left my room without money for the simple reason that there wasn't any there. This letter is to ask you for 10 francs to get me through these two days until the 15th. I'm still in bed, and anxiously await your reply.

This sort of existence was not doing Baudelaire's health any good. In Dijon, in 1849–1850, his syphilis 'erupted again'.[2] Laudanum and alcohol conspired with the disease to eat away at his system. In March 1852, he was in an 'inflamed state'. A year later, his 'abominable life style and brandy' had 'ruined [his] stomach'. He decided to do away with alcohol, but it was alcohol, even more than the syphilis, that eventually did away with him.[3] He was experiencing 'unbearable nervous attacks – just like women'; but this pain and misery was also the price to pay for his poetry.

These reports on his health are drawn from Baudelaire's letters to his mother, in which cruelty goes hand in hand with contrition, unkindness with sorrow, and in which strategy and cunning (which Mme Aupick occasionally brought upon herself) certainly play an important part. A great poet is also a great manipulator; not even Racine or Claudel could deny that simple truth.

Lugubrious news in a letter dated November 18, 1853:

My dear Mother, the day before yesterday, I had to bury someone. I gave all that I had, but the total cost came to 140 francs, 60 of which I still owe and which I promised to pay in two days' time, in other words this morning. You realise of course that I thought of everyone else before turning to you ... Please don't write me sentences like this one: 'Really, Charles, you distress me,' etc., or: 'When one is a member of the establishment, one always has enough money at home to pay for such things.' EITHER REFUSE COMPLETELY OR SEND ME THE MONEY.

The money was sent and, the following day, Baudelaire told his mother that the burial had taken place at Belleville cemetery.

On December 26 his letter unfolded another emotional drama. This time, money was needed for 'the exhumation and reburial of a woman who gave me her last savings without a murmur, without a sigh, *and especially without giving any advice*':

I have to write to a mayor, and then to the Prefect of Police. The plot is going to cost me 86 francs, and there will obviously be another tip to pay – some grave-digger's swindle. THAT will come before my new shoes, and in any case, I'm so used to physical discomfort, and so good at arranging two shirts underneath a pair of torn trousers and a coat which let the wind through, and I'm so adept at fitting straw or even paper soles into shoes with holes in them that it's practically only the mental pain that I feel – although I must confess it's reached the point where I don't dare make any sudden movement or even walk too much for fear of collecting still more rips and tears.

What woman of sensitivity could possibly resist such a worthy cause – the reburial of a human being? The shoes and clothes would come later. The same day, Baudelaire wrote again to thank his mother, but then he added, 'I'm convinced you took my sad story to be a fabrication ... yet I was very careful to tell you that this cemetery business would precede the satisfaction of my most urgent needs.' The reality of the woman to be buried is not what counts here, but the argument itself.

Having received the money twice, Baudelaire sent a rather casual reply which must have frozen the smile on Mme Aupick's face that New Year's Eve:

> You wrote me a very sad and charming letter, but it still bore the mark of your incurable tendency to exaggerate. The dead woman was someone I almost hated. But I let her die in the most genuine poverty. And was I the one who invented prejudices and respect for the dead? It is, in short, a simple matter of propriety.

This was written at half-past seven in the morning. At midday, another letter followed, concerning once again the poet's wardrobe – a wardrobe the Belleville corpse was probably instrumental in equipping. The whole complicated procedure could be summed up in the following phrase from that same letter:

> Good grief! What diplomacy and effort it takes to clothe oneself!

The buried woman did actually exist. She was the mother of Jeanne Duval. Jacques Crépet discovered her death certificate in the Seine Archives.[4] Jeanne Lemaire (or Mme Duval according to Baudelaire) died at Belleville on November 15, 1853. The certificate gives her birthplace as Nantes, her age as sixty-three (the register of burials says seventy-three) and describes her as a widow of private means. The interment took place on the 17th. She was given a temporary burial or perhaps even placed in the common grave. At the end of December, the body was exhumed and reburied, probably in a plot with a five-year lease.

Jeanne Duval's mother had been seen by Louis Ménard some time between 1842 and 1846. Even in those days, she was 'an old, respectable-looking negress, with thick, greasy hair which tried in vain to twirl over her cheeks and ears'. Baudelaire's letters to Mme Aupick are probably all we shall ever know of his relations with his 'mother-in-law'.

Whilst Jeanne was still young and attractive, her fidelity had never been entirely above suspicion. Baudelaire himself hinted or did nothing to prevent others from hinting that she was unfaithful. A certain Rioux de Maillou suggests as much, but his memoirs are little more than gossip.[5] Charles Toubin's testimony, which dates back to the 1848 revolution, is more difficult to refute:

> His mistress, as everyone knows, was a coloured girl called Jeanne Duval whom he caught one day in flagrante delicto with her hairdresser ... Baudelaire ... was furious. 'With anyone else,' he told us, 'I wouldn't have minded, but with a barber!' Two days later, we ran into her at the Cheval-Rouge crossroads. He went straight up to her and, in front of all the passers-by, gave her a severe talking-to. He took her back a few days later.[6]

Jeanne's lover, of course, was not entirely above reproach himself. When living in the rue Pigalle in 1848, Baudelaire had a package sent to him care of Mademoiselle Caroline Dardart[7] – probably a friendly prostitute who helped him to forget Jeanne's betrayals and recriminations.

On December 9 or 10, 1852, shortly after the ratification by plebiscite of the Second Empire, Mme Sabatier received the following anonymous message. Its passionate, even respectful, sadism was well calculated to astonish a *demi-mondaine*:

> The person for whom these verses were written, whether or not she like them, and even if they seem to her entirely ridiculous, is very humbly *beseeched* not to show them to *anyone*. Deep feelings have a modesty that will not be violated. Is not the absence of a signature a mark of this invincible modesty? The man who wrote these lines in one of those states of reverie into which the image of she who is their object often casts him, has loved her deeply, without ever telling her so, and he will always have for her the most tender affection.

The verses in question were the stanzas of 'A une femme trop gaie' – the original title of a poem which was later included in *Les Fleurs du Mal*. The conclusion is well known:

> Ainsi je voudrais, une nuit,
> Quand l'heure des voluptés sonne,

Vers les trésors de ta personne,
Comme un lâche, ramper sans bruit.

Pour châtier ta chair joyeuse,
Pour meurtrir ton sein pardonné,
Et faire à ton flanc étonné
Une blessure large et creuse,

Et, délicieuse douceur,
A travers ces lèvres nouvelles,
Plus éclatantes et plus belles,
T'infuser mon sang, ô ma Soeur.*

What did the recipient think of the poem? Mme Sabatier was not a critic capable of perceiving different levels of meaning. Perhaps she read it as a madrigal, a chivalrous compliment. As for the writer himself, the 'syphilitic interpretation' should not be excluded. Baudelaire's curious form of Petrarchism was not without its bold streak of sadism and it bore the mark of his attitude towards women – more precisely, towards women who were not prostitutes.[8]

Aglaé-Joséphine Savatier, who took the less vulgar-sounding name Sabatier at the start of her Parisian career, was born at Mézières in the Ardennes on April 7, 1822. She was the creation of a laundry woman and the local prefect. Fortunately for the father, who was rich, married and in a position of some importance, a surrogate father was found. A soldier stationed in Mézières – André Savatier – agreed to recognise the child before a notary public. André and the mother were joined in marriage, and later had three children of their own. The youngest of the three – Adèle – was the 'crazy little girl' who, upon meeting Baudelaire, asked him, '*Are you still in love with my sister, and are you still writing her superb letters?*'

The mother was widowed in 1832 and moved to Batignolles village, which was then just outside Paris. Aglaé had a pretty voice. She studied singing and the piano, first at school and then with a special teacher. Shortly after 1840, she seems to have travelled to Italy with the painter Meissonier. In 1844 or even earlier, she became the mistress of an Englishman, Richard

---

* 'Thus, one night, I'd like, / When the hour of pleasure sounds, / To crawl, like a coward, silently / Toward the treasures of your person.

To punish your joyful flesh, / To bruise your pardoned breast, / And carve in your astonished flank / A wide and hollow wound,

And, delicious sweetness, / Through those lips, new-formed, / Brighter and more lovely, / To inject you, my Sister, with my blood.'

Jackson. On the death of his father, Jackson inherited an immense fortune and took the name Richard Wallace. In Paris, he is known to this day for the drinking-water fountains he gave to the city and, in Britain, as the founder of the Wallace Collection. He never forgot his young girlfriend, and after she was abandoned by her official protector he took her on several journeys and later arranged for her to be paid an annual pension of 50,000 francs.

In 1844, Aglaé was still looking after herself. Since she had a body to match the beauty of her voice, she was able to become a professional model: this is how she came to be the mistress of the sculptor Clésinger. She shared his wayward life until 1846. At the beginning of 1847, Clésinger began to take a lively interest in Solange Dudevant, the daughter of George Sand, and married her the following May. In the meantime, Aglaé may have been bestowing her favours on other artists – Vincent Vidal, Jules Dupré and Théodore Rousseau – all of whom had studios close to Clésinger's in the Bréda *quartier*.

In 1846, she became the mistress of Alfred Mosselman, who belonged to a wealthy Belgian family. Mme Sabatier, as she now called herself, was installed in an apartment in the rue Frochot, where she stayed until 1860. Théophile Gautier's daughter, Judith, remembered her at the height of her beauty while she was still living in that apartment:

> She was quite tall and well-proportioned ... Her hair was very silky and golden-brown, and seemed to arrange itself of its own accord in rich waves full of sparkle. She had a clear and smooth complexion, with regular features, and there was something mischievous and *spirituel* about her ... Her triumphant air seemed to surround her with happiness and light.
>
> She dressed very tastefully and her clothes were full of fancy. She scarcely kept to current fashions, and created styles of her own. The great artists who came to her Sunday gatherings used to advise her and draw patterns for her.[9]

When Mme Sabatier sold off some of her possessions in 1860 after breaking up with Mosselman, the sale included the life-size bust of herself in white marble by Clésinger which had been exhibited in the 1847 Paris Salon under the title, *Bust of Mme ****. At the same Salon, the sculptor had presented another piece in marble displaying a young woman, unclothed and apparently suffering a rather pleasant fainting fit. The title – *Woman Stung by a Serpent* – was meant to veil the cause of her convulsions. This statuette was the result of Mosselman's desire to see the perfections of his mistress immortalised. Mme Sabatier agreed to submit to the painful process of being cast in plaster. Several casts were made and the finished marble – which differs in pose and facial features from the plaster original, indicating the use of different models – was sent to the Salon entitled simply *Woman*. A small bronze serpent was added before the opening to disguise the sexual aspect of the subject, but the public was not to be fooled, and flocked to see the delicious scandal of the *Woman Stung by a Serpent*. The piece was reproduced many times and has been hailed by Luc Benoist as one of 'the most successful experiments of French sculpture under the Second Empire'.

Baudelaire may well have met the model herself before 1852: Mme Sabatier was a visitor to Boissard's apartment at the Hôtel Pimodan from 1845 to 1849, where she spent 'the richest, the happiest and most carefree hours of her artistic life'.

From the end of 1852, she presided gracefully over the dining room and drawing room at the rue Frochot. She was a 'good-hearted girl' – a welcome change from dull wives and prostitutes. She managed to create an atmosphere of freedom without restraint, but also without excess.

It was Théophile Gautier who christened her Apollonie and referred to her as the 'Présidente'. Gautier was also responsible for the motto she used on her book-plates: '*Vis superba formae*' – 'the irresistible strength of beauty', or 'the sovereign power of beauty'. And it was Gautier, too, who sent her the infamous 'Lettre à la Présidente' which could reasonably be described as pornographic and which is probably untypical of the usual tone of her Sunday *soirées* (although these were by no means genteel). Most of her guests were friends of Gautier – Maxime Du Camp and Gustave Flaubert, who used Mme Sabatier in his depiction of Rosanette in *L'Education sentimentale*. Other visitors included Flaubert's faithful companion, Louis Bouilhet, Ernest Feydeau, the caricaturist Henri Monnier and Apollonie's former lover, Meissonier. Baudelaire, who was apparently introduced by Gautier in 1851,[10] enjoyed visiting this salon in which he could practise his irony, despite the fact that there were never any bourgeois at the rue Frochot to be scandalised.

Flaubert's Rosanette, the lovable hussy, has little in common with the Angel, the Muse and the Madonna worshipped by Baudelaire in the poems he began writing in December 1852; but Rosanette had other models too and Flaubert was little inclined to portray his women in an idealised light. In Baudelaire's eyes, she was a pretext for poems of pure love – not the least of his paradoxes, since Mme Sabatier was far from being an ethereal creature.

There is in any case nothing to prove that the poems Baudelaire sent her anonymously were originally intended for her. Felix Leakey, who rightly believes that Baudelaire wrote much of his poetry early on in his career, has pointed out that in the short story, *La Fanfarlo*, Mme de Cosmelly describes Samuel Cramer's verses in terms that clearly recall the Mme Sabatier poems:[11] 'By the strangest of contrasts ... you keep your most mystical incense for bizarre creatures ... and you swoon platonically at the feet of queens from the brothel.' Professor Leakey goes so far as to imagine 'L'Aube spirituelle' being written on a living desk – the body of one of those brothel queens. This was a method invented by Valmont in Laclos's *Liaisons dangereuses* when writing to *his* 'Présidente'. Valmont's passionate letter, so he claims, is so respectful as to threaten not even the strictest virtue. The episode described below does indeed suggest that Baudelaire's poem was composed in similar circumstances.

The poems of the Mme Sabatier cycle in *Les Fleurs du Mal* are certainly reminiscent in some ways of a literary exercise, as are the accompanying letters. Like Gérard de Nerval writing to a mythical woman, whom he lightly identified with a comic-opera singer, Baudelaire was creating a sort of epistolary novel. The women themselves are not essential. When he sends Mme Sabatier some 'anonymous bits of idiotic rhyming which sound horribly childish', the poet seems to be poking fun at himself; but the poems in question survive any derision on the part of writer or reader. The poet's only sincerity lies in the words which accompany the last poem on May 8, 1854: 'I'm an egoist; I'm using you'; but then, catching himself, he writes, 'Here's my unhappy piece of drivel.'

The most beautiful poems of the mid-nineteenth century rose from the plump flesh of Jenny Colon and Aglaé Sabatier. But neither Laura, nor Aglaé, nor Jenny Colon were responsible for Petrarch, Baudelaire or Nerval. 'Poetry is what is most real; it is that which is completely true only in *another world*.'[12]

'Réversibilité,' 'Confession' and perhaps 'L'Aube spirituelle' were sent to Mme Sabatier in May 1853 from Versailles. Proof of Baudelaire's stay there is contained in a note to his mother and a letter to Asselineau. The letter has disappeared, but a description of it appeared in a catalogue: 'too curious to be printed in its entirety'. Fortunately, we also have the memoirs of one Emile Geidan, a provincial who came up to Paris to study law.[13] Towards the end of 1852, one of Emile's flatmates brought the irrepressible Philoxène Boyer to their lodgings and in his wake came Banville, Baudelaire, Henry Murger and others. One day, 'Philo' turned up to speak to Emile about an important affair. He and Baudelaire had apparently decided to go to Versailles in order to prepare a history of Louis XIV, based on the lives of the various figures whose portraits adorned the palace galleries. Emile Geidan remembers only that 'Philo' took advantage of his visit to borrow a shirt, 'which he put on, leaving me in exchange a revolting old smock'. Two weeks later, 'Philo' reappeared at the door in a state of considerable agitation:

> 'We've done something very foolish!' he said. 'We put up in a grand hotel in Versailles, and our funds were soon exhausted. We left the hotel the evening before last, kicked out by the owner, our pockets empty, and leaving our few pieces of luggage behind as a guarantee of payment.'
>
> 'Baudelaire then advised,' Boyer went on, 'that we take refuge in a brothel; and he's still there as security. I've come to plead with all our friends to help us out of this sticky situation.'
>
> Disgusted by the story, we were more than a little reluctant to loosen our purse-strings.
>
> Philo went away. To our great astonishment, he reappeared three days later.
>
> 'I went back to Versailles,' he told us, 'taking with me an insufficient sum of money. Baudelaire received me rather coolly, and said, "Wait here. I'll be back this evening." He never returned, and my hosts threw me out like a common criminal.'
>
> 'I've just come from Versailles on foot. I'm exhausted and dying of hunger.'
>
> We gave him a bit of pocket-money, and from that day on we never heard of the two Bohemians again.

No wonder, then, that the letter to Asselineau could not be printed in its entirety. Asselineau himself gave only a vague indication of its contents: Philoxène 'once left him as a hostage for a whole month in Versailles, in an inn where they had been given credit. He went off to try and find some money in Paris, but always returned empty-handed. I still have two or three sorry-sounding letters which Baudelaire wrote at that time asking me to go and deliver him.'[14]

One can also see why Baudelaire, having written 'L'Aube spirituelle' in an establishment which required its customers to consume, prefaced it with the following remark (in English): 'After a night of pleasure and desolation, all my soul belongs to you.' One might even understand how, by the law of contrast, such beautiful poems of pure love took wing in such a place.

Mme Sabatier probably knew nothing of this escapade; but she must have realised who the author was. Her younger sister had been laughing at the 'superb letters' Baudelaire was sending, long before the poet mentioned this to Mme Sabatier herself: 'I saw, first, that when I was trying to hide, I was not being very successful, and then that your charming face conceals an unkind heart.' Furthermore, one of the poems – 'Que diras-tu ce soir, pauvre âme solitaire ...' – had already appeared in a novel by Charles Barbara in the *Revue de Paris* on January 15, 1855. The poet, still anonymous, was described however as one 'whose clear aptitude for the most arduous speculations does not prevent him from creating warm, colourful, essentially human and original poetry'. His identity was finally revealed in June of the same year when 'Réversibilité', 'Confession' and 'L'Aube spirituelle' were published in the *Revue des Deux Mondes*, signed by Charles Baudelaire.

The poem-letters to Mme Sabatier seem to have been written in fits and starts – December 1852, May 1853, February and May 1854. According to Albert Feuillerat, these dates correspond to the times when Marie Daubrun was away from Paris ('out of sight, out of mind...');[15] but a close investigation of the dates in question fails to provide any such tidy conclusion.

Marie Daubrun's successful débuts in Montmartre and Paris have already been mentioned. Her first appearance at the Odéon did not come until September 11, 1852, with the end-of-year review written by Philoxène Boyer and Théodore de Banville, *Aristophanes' Feuilleton*. Marie may already have become Banville's mistress: he did her the favour of including parodies of two of her rivals in the review. Baudelaire must surely have been introduced to her by then and would soon get to know her quite well. When describing the plot of *The Drunkard* to Tisserant on January 28, 1854, was he thinking of Marie? 'The woman must be pretty. – A model of sweetness, patience and *reason*.' Perhaps his desire corresponded to the image he had of Marie, but it bore little relation to reality: her dealings with theatres in 1853 and 1854 show her to have been a self-willed and cantankerous sort of person.

In February 1854, Baudelaire escaped from the rue Pigalle and took a room in the Hôtel d'York on the rue Sainte-Anne, near the Bibliothèque Nationale. The hotel, later known as the Etna, recently changed its name to the Baudelaire-Opéra and used to welcome guests by presenting them with a photograph of the poet. Baudelaire then returned for a time to the rue Pigalle, before moving to the Hôtel du Maroc in the rue de Seine, not far from the river on the Left Bank. Jeanne was not with him; but he wrote to his mother and asked for some money to send her: 'I forbade her to come and visit me here; it was my odious pride that made me do it. – I don't want people to see a woman of mine looking poor, sick, and scruffy, when they knew her as a beautiful, healthy, and elegant woman.'

Whether he was acting out of a sense of pride or out of charity, Baudelaire was trying to keep Jeanne at a distance, perhaps so that he would have more time to spend with Marie.

On June 25, 1854, he wrote:

> My dear Mother, I am FORCED, *really forced* to take a person to dinner THIS EVENING. Since the food here is unbearable, thanks to my landlord's extreme indigence – *about which I knew nothing* – I am having to take this person to the *traiteur*. Even if I sent her a note to stop her coming – a lie, like being away or indisposed – I'd still be rather glad myself of the opportunity to eat out a little...

The person in question could only be Marie Daubrun. Subsequent letters to Mme Aupick show Baudelaire taking advantage of Marie's engagement at the Gaîté Theatre to promote his own play, *The Drunkard*. On August 22, 1854, he was hoping to have it produced at the Porte-Saint-Martin, in collaboration with the director, Marc Fournier, and trying at the same time to obtain a role for Marie – this in spite of the fact that (as he told his mother) the actress was 'detested by the director's wife'. One might assume that Marie had had a brief affair with Fournier   a director's charms are often hard to resist. Baudelaire's love for Marie was more than matched by the perverse pleasure he took in these tricky negotiations. His schemes were devised with the same passionate care that informs his subtlest verse. Baudelaire knew the art of putting his correspondents in difficult positions.

Marie continued to play at the Gaîté. Before her appearance as the Duchesse de Guérande in a melodrama, *The Birds of Prey*, on 16 October Baudelaire wrote to Théophile Gautier and to another drama critic, Paul de Saint-Victor, recommending Mlle Daubrun: she is 'one of those people who are sometimes good and sometimes bad depending on the circumstances, her nerves, and the encouragement or discouragement she receives'. Saint-Victor praised the actress in a sentence.

Since Marc Fournier was showing no sign of interest in *The Drunkard*, and since Marie was still at the Gaîté, Baudelaire turned to the director of that theatre and, on November 8, offered Hippolyte Hostein his 'play about *drunkenness*'. The play was just another pipe-dream, but Marie herself was a more tangible reality. Baudelaire obviously felt that they were on very intimate terms: he told his mother that if he had not moved in with Jeanne by the date on which he was to vacate his room at the hotel, then he would go and stay with 'the *other* woman ... I need *a family* at all costs. It's the only way to get any work done and reduce expenses.' The 'other' woman was almost certainly Marie. In fact, Baudelaire neither returned to Jeanne nor went to live with Marie. January 1855 found him still a lodger at the

Hôtel du Maroc. Neither was there any correspondence between him and Mme Sabatier from May 1854 until the publication of *Les Fleurs du Mal*, though he probably attended some of her Sunday *soirées*.

At certain points in 1854, Baudelaire might have seemed to be the man with too many lovers. By the end of the year, he was not only without a woman, but also practically homeless.

Baudelaire must have remained at the Hôtel du Maroc until the beginning of March 1855. On April 5 he wrote: 'In the last MONTH, I've been forced to move SIX times, living in plaster, sleeping in fleas, my letters (the most important ones) refused, shifted around from one hotel to the next. I made a great decision. I lived and worked at the printer's since I couldn't work at home any more.' This was the printer of the newspaper, *Le Pays*, in which Baudelaire's Poe translations were being serialised. Other addresses appear in his correspondence during this period, and the contract signed with Michel Lévy on August 3 for the publication of the *Histoires extraordinaires* and the *Nouvelles Histoires extraordinaires* shows that he was living once again in the rue de Seine, probably in a furnished room.

In the meantime, Marie Daubrun had broken off her engagement with the Gaîté, thereby arousing the wrath of the director, Hippolyte Hostein, who swore to sue any theatre that dared to employ the renegade actress. As a result, she was forced to sign up with a troupe that was about to leave Paris on a tour of Italy.

Deprived for the time being of his 'impetuous madonna', Baudelaire asked his friend, the actor Philibert Rouvière, to intervene on Marie's behalf with one of the directors of the Odéon. But Marie was stuck in Nice; the director of the troupe had gone bankrupt in Italy. Hostein, the disgruntled director of the Gaîté, agreed to exempt the Odéon from his ban. Rouvière was given a role in that theatre's production of George Sand's *Maître Favilla*. As for Marie, she was already known to the author of the play, who thought well of her.

On August 14, Baudelaire picked up his finest quill to plead Marie's case. He informed George Sand that the actress's request for a slight increase in pay had prevented an agreement being reached with the theatre and that now only she could help. Sand wrote from Nohant on the 16th, promising to do what she could. Baudelaire sent a ceremonious letter of thanks. The director, however, felt that Marie was too plump for the role. George Sand protested that she had seen the actress the year before 'and as for her figure, there was not an inch too much; her beauty was unmistakable'.

Marie Daubrun was not included in the cast of *Maître Favilla*. Baudelaire decided that Sand had either failed to put in a word, or even tried to dissuade the director from signing her up. He took the letter he had received on the 17th and added a few uncharitable annotations: 'Note her faulty French: *"De suite"* instead of *"tout de suite"*'; and, 'Madame Sand deceived me and did not keep her word.' Sand critics and others have taken this incident to be the origin of Baudelaire's insulting remarks in *My Heart Laid Bare*: 'She has that famous *flowing style* so dear to the bourgeois. She's stupid, she's clumsy, and she prattles. Her moral precepts have the same profundity and emotional subtlety as those of concierges and kept women.' '*De suite*' instead of '*tout de suite*' is a serious mistake – one which Baudelaire himself had made at least once;[16] but the true explanation of his violent aversion to George Sand lies in his rejection of facile moralising with its refusal to acknowledge the fundamental perversity of man. The episode involving Marie Daubrun exacerbated this irritation but was not the cause of it. The virtuous might regret the fact that Baudelaire appealed to the novelist for help; but one should remember that the poet had his own code of conduct, and that his morals were those of a person who lived on the edge of society and felt no obligation to respect its conventions.

After the summer of 1855 and the misadventure with the Odéon, Marie Daubrun drifted away from Baudelaire and drew close again to Banville. The latter gave a poetic version of his affair in *Story of an Actress, Ninette*, published that autumn with the following dedication: 'To Mademoiselle Marie Daubrun, this short story written at her hospitable table by her friend, Th. de Banville, 1855.' He could hardly have been more indiscreet. Baudelaire's affection did not wane. Four years later, he tried again to lure Marie away from Banville and gave her a copy of the first edition of *Les Fleurs du Mal*, inscribed 'To my dear Marie'. Relations with Banville probably cooled off a little, though in 1856 and 1857, Baudelaire presented him with copies of his first two volumes of Poe translations, both bearing the inscription, 'To Théodore de Banville, Souvenir d'amitié, Ch. Baudelaire'. The message accompanying the first edition of *Les Fleurs du Mal* was a little more terse – 'To Théodore de Banville, Ch. Baudelaire' – but the fact that Baudelaire gave him one of the rare copies on *papier de Hollande* proves that he still had great regard for his fellow poet.

When Baudelaire moved again at the very end of 1855, it was to a flat in the rue d'Angoulême-du-Temple which he intended sharing with Jeanne. It was not an easy move, since they had almost no possessions – no furniture, no mattress, no linen, no pots or pans. Mme Aupick helped out and Baudelaire settled in, but it was not long before he was drifting once again from hotel to hotel. Eventually, in June 1856, he found a room to his liking in the Hôtel Voltaire, across the river from the Louvre. There he stayed until mid-November 1858. Just a few doors away was the printing shop of the official newspaper, the *Moniteur universel*, which, from February to April 1857, would be publishing Baudelaire's translation of *The Adventures of Arthur Gordon Pym*.

In his letters, Baudelaire had been referring to Jeanne as his 'wife'; but she never joined him at the Hôtel Voltaire. On September 11, 1856, he sent the following letter to Mme Aupick, hoping that she would not be too delighted about the bad news:

> My affair with Jeanne, an affair that lasted fourteen years, has ended. I did all that was humanly possible to prevent this separation ... Jeanne kept telling me ... that one day I'd thank her for this decision. That's the guileless, bourgeois wisdom of women for you ... I put my every last hope on her, like a gambler. That woman was my only distraction, my only pleasure, my only friend, and despite all the anguish of a stormy relationship, the idea of breaking up altogether never really occurred to me. Even now, though I'm quite calm, when I see some beautiful thing, a beautiful landscape or anything pleasing to the eye, I catch myself thinking, 'Why is she not here to admire it with me, or buy it with me?' You can see I'm not trying to hide my wounds. It took me a long time, I can tell you, so violent a shock was it, to realise that work might give me some pleasure, and that, after all, I did have duties to fulfil ... I saw before me a never-ending stream of years, without a family, without friends, without a companion, years filled only with isolation and uncertainty, and nothing for the heart. I couldn't even derive any comfort from my pride, since everything that happened was my own fault. I used and abused. I amused myself with torture and was tortured in my turn.

Baudelaire never deserted Jeanne and kept trying to help her out with small sums of money. On November 4, 1856, after the separation, he confessed to his mother:

> I never once stopped thinking of that girl, but I'm such an old hand at the business of life, which never amounts to anything more than lies and vain assurances, that I cannot imagine myself getting caught up in the same inextricable emotional web as before. The poor child is sick now, and I refused to go and see her. She's been avoiding me like the plague for a long time, because she knows my dreadful character – all cunning and violence. I know she's leaving Paris, and I'm quite glad that she is, though I must confess that sadness overcomes me whenever I think of her going off and dying far away.

As Jacques Crépet pointed out, the letter written on September 11 seems to echo the one Charles sent to his mother on July 16, 1839, when he was missing her and when she was away with the Colonel at Bourbonne-les-Bains. Perhaps Mme Aupick noticed the similarity and perhaps she was hurt by it . . .

> Mère des souvenirs, maîtresse des maîtresses,
> O toi, tous mes plaisirs! O toi, tous mes devoirs!
> Tu te rappelleras la beauté des caresses,
> La douceur du foyer et le charme des soirs,
> Mère des souvenirs, maîtresse des maîtresses!*

Baudelaire never knew the sweetness of home. 'When will I ever have a manservant and a cook – and a household?' he asked his mother. It was a rhetorical question. At the end of 1848, he informed her that with his 'immense poetic ambition' he was 'cut off forever from *the world of decent people* by [his] tastes and principles'. His mother despaired of ever seeing him behave 'like everyone else'. Would she ever be able to present him to her friends? 'Alas!' he replied. 'You know full well I'm not like that, and that *my* destiny will be different. Why don't you talk to me a bit about marriage like everyone else's mamma?'[17]

Nonetheless, this 'world of decent people' has 'rehabilitated' Baudelaire and one is bound to ask oneself whether, in recounting his life, one is not trying to extract virtuous tears from those who would have rejected him. Nothing is easier than giving hypocrisy a clear conscience. One should always bear in mind the letter of December 20, 1855, in which Baudelaire contrasted the 'wonderful poetic vision, clarity of thought, and power of hope which make up [his] true capital' (an image drawn from economics!), with the ephemeral capital he lacked – the sort of capital that would have made it possible for him to settle down and work in peace, far from that 'filthy cow of a landlady'[18] who intimidated him so much that for several nights he refused to go home for fear of running into her in the building.

It was Baudelaire's intellectual integrity and consequent refusal to draw a clear line between creation and criticism that led *Le Pays* to turn down one of the three articles he had prepared on the Universal Exhibition of 1855. 'Méthode de critique' and 'Eugène Delacroix' were accepted, but the paper rejected 'M. Ingres', probably because they deemed it insulting to an Academician. *Le Pays* did however agree to add a postscript to 'Méthode

* 'Mother of memories, mistress of mistresses, / You, my every pleasure! You, my every duty! / You will remember the beauty of caresses, / The sweetness of home and the charm of evening, / Mother of memories, mistress of mistresses!'

de critique' which revealed remarkable assurance, even in such apparently casual remarks:

The Exhibition of English painters is quite beautiful – beautiful in a most curious way, and it deserves a long and patient study. I wanted to begin by singing the praises of our neighbours, that race so marvellously rich in poets and novelists, the race of Shakespeare, Crabbe, and Byron, of Maturin and Godwin, the fellow citizens of Reynolds, Hogarth, and Gainsborough. But I would first want to pursue my study a little further. My excuse is excellent: out of extreme politeness, I shall postpone this pleasurable duty. I shall delay in order to improve.

I shall begin therefore with a simpler task, and swiftly examine the principal masters of the French school, and analyse the elements of progress and the seeds of destruction it bears within itself.

The year 1855, the year of Nerval's suicide, was the year in which Baudelaire gained full confidence in his own genius. The translations which went to make up the *Histoires extraordinaires* and the *Nouvelles Histoires extraordinaires* appeared in *Le Pays* from July 1854 to April 1855. The prestigious *Revue des Deux Mondes* published eighteen of his finest poems under the previously unknown title of *Les Fleurs du Mal*. An editorial note pointed out the review's openness to the latest trends and held up as a feature of particular interest 'the vivid expression, curious even in its violence, of some deficiencies, some mental sufferings which, without sharing or discussing them, one should endeavour to recognise as a sign of our times'. In short, the poems were printed for their psychiatric value.

Baudelaire was mistaken in thinking he was on good terms with François Buloz and his worthy review. When on June 13 he offered him some short stories, Buloz did not reply. Baudelaire's name never appeared again in the *Revue des Deux Mondes*. That possibility was ruled out once and for all by the prosecution of *Les Fleurs du Mal*; but the fact that the future title of the collection first appeared in that review has an air of poetic justice.

On August 3, 1855, Baudelaire signed a contract with Michel Lévy Frères for the two-volume edition of the *Histoires extraordinaires*. The first volume came out in March 1856, while the *Aventures d'Arthur Gordon Pym* were appearing in the *Moniteur*. The *Histoires extraordinaires* were an immediate success and were reprinted the same year.

This was one of Baudelaire's most productive periods: poems, trans-lations and also literary criticism in the preface to the *Histoires extraor-*

dinaires, in which Baudelaire recalled with some affection the death of Gérard de Nerval. The art critic and theoretician was also present in the articles on the Universal Exhibition, and in a small review called *Le Portefeuille*, which published the piece on Ingres which had been rejected by *Le Pays*, as well as the essay on laughter: *De l'essence du rire et généralement du comique dans les arts plastiques*. This remarkably original study was, according to the review, an extract from a book entitled *Peintres, statuaires et caricaturistes* soon to be published by Michel Lévy. Baudelaire had first thought of writing the book ten years before, but it was never completed.

Baudelaire had been well advised to choose Michel Lévy as his publisher. Lévy had published the *Salon de 1846* as well as the Poe translations and was clearly in the forefront of commercial publishing. Poetry, however, appealed to a smaller audience. It found its own guardian angel in a publisher who was making interesting innovations in typography and artwork. Poulet-Malassis was a great discovery for Baudelaire, as he was for Banville and for Asselineau: 'Do you remember, my dear friend,' runs the latter's dedication to Banville in a book published in 1862, 'that year of grace, 1856? ... At last we had found a publisher after our own heart – a young, courageous, liberal-minded man in love with beauty, and very happy to espouse our literary fortunes.'

On October 4, 1855, Baudelaire told his mother: '*Michel Lévy* will also be publishing (but when?) my book of Poetry, and my critical studies.' But the poet was afraid that quality might be sacrificed to commerciality and, at the beginning of December 1856, it was Poulet-Malassis who drew up a publication contract for *Les Fleurs du Mal*. On December 9 Baudelaire wrote to his new publisher: 'Those are almost the same conditions Michel was offering before he started bringing out his one-franc books in runs of six thousand; but with you, I shall have it produced decently and elegantly.' On December 30, 1856, Poulet-Malassis and De Broise, printers at Alençon, and Charles Baudelaire signed a contract for the publication of *Les Fleurs du Mal* and for a collection of articles bearing the title, *Bric-à-brac esthétique*, some of which can be found in the *Curiosités esthétiques* of the posthumous *Œuvres complètes*. The print run for each volume was set at 1,000 – quite a normal figure for a poet who was virtually unknown to the general public, then as now.

CHAPTER 17

The Publication and Trial of *Les Fleurs du Mal*

1857

Baudelaire, on the eve of publishing *Les Fleurs du Mal*, was no longer the dandy, art-lover and collector, nor the clandestine poet of earlier years. This 'brittle, bony man with small, sharp, restless eyes, his lips pursed ironically as he made some cutting remark, this man whose incipient baldness made him look like a monk consumed by the burning desires of the flesh',[1] had made a name for himself as the translator of Edgar Allan Poe. The *Histoires extraordinaires* appeared in March 1856; the *Nouvelles Histoires extraordinaires* went on sale in March 1857; and between February 25 and April 18, 1857, the *Moniteur universel*, 'official organ of the Empire', devoted its literary *feuilleton* to the *Aventures d'Arthur Gordon Pym* – Poe's fantastic sea story which was giving its translator 'a lot of bother'. In order to keep a close eye on the printing and make final changes to the text, Baudelaire had taken a room in the Grand Hôtel Voltaire, close to the newspaper offices.[2] Similarly, in the spring of 1858, he travelled to Corbeil to supervise the printing of the volume to be published that May by Michel Lévy. Baudelaire's uncommon professional integrity would soon be giving Poulet-Malassis more than his fair share of headaches. Baudelaire insisted on complete command of the material he was translating. Asselineau described his friend scouring the inns and eating places of Paris in his attempt to find an English seaman who would be able to give him the precise meaning of certain navigational terms.[3]

One day when I found him racking his brains over a detail concerning compass bearings, I had the misfortune to tease him about his meticulous attention to detail.

'Well?' he said, looking up. 'What about the people who read with their finger on the map?'

I can still feel his eyes on me, full of scorn and fury, as if to say, 'You mean you don't realise that everything I write must be above reproach, and that I mustn't expose myself to the censure of a sailor any more than to the criticism of another writer?'

I must confess that I had to laugh that day when I thought of a *Moniteur* reader perusing his paper with a finger on the atlas.

And yet I was wrong, and Baudelaire was right. Only by taking such scrupulous and uncompromising care can one manage to give a work its lasting value. It is because of that unremitting application that his translation of Edgar Allan Poe achieved the highest goal a work of that sort can hope to attain – to naturalise a writer in the literature of another country with the approval of that writer's compatriots.

During the first six months of 1857, unsure of what each new day would bring, translating *Pym* and overseeing its publication in the *Moniteur*, Baudelaire was working at the same time on the proofs of *Les Fleurs du Mal*. The manuscript had been delivered at the beginning of February, and the two hundred and forty-eight pages of the book might have been printed in the space of a few weeks; but Baudelaire was full of misgivings. He besieged both printer and publisher with his incessant inquiries. The work was delayed even more by his translation of *Pym* and by the postal service: the printing shop was at Alençon and Poulet-Malassis rarely came up to Paris.

The title of *Les Fleurs du Mal* had already been found. It was invented in 1855 by the talented critic and novelist, Hippolyte Babou.[4] The oxymoronic title renders perfectly the antithesis of beauty and evil, though it did not prevent a journalist on the *Gazette de Paris* from declaring that the title 'isn't French' and adding: 'I defy anyone to tell me what it means.'[5] The dedication, which was quite long in its original form, was submitted to Théophile Gautier on March 8 in the offices of the *Moniteur*. Gautier, addressed with the familiar '*tu*,' was astonished to read the following lines:

> I know that in the ethereal realms of true Poetry, Evil does not exist any more than Good, and that this wretched dictionary of despondency and crime may justify the reactions of morality as the blasphemer confirms religion.[6]

Gautier explained to his avowed disciple 'that a dedication should not be a profession of faith', and that he was also 'making the mistake of drawing attention to the scabrous aspects of the book and denouncing them'.[7] These 'scabrous aspects' had not escaped the attention of Poulet-Malassis and when he saw Baudelaire's eighteen 'Fleurs du Mal' in the *Revue des Deux Mondes* in 1855, he asked Asselineau to congratulate Baudelaire on his 'horrors'.[8] Baudelaire himself, with all the good faith of a poet, was less aware of such things. He realised of course that some risk was involved, but thought only of a possible charge of blasphemy. When 'Le Reniement de Saint Pierre' appeared in the *Revue de Paris* in October 1852, he had narrowly escaped prosecution. For this reason he inserted a precautionary note above the title of the 'Révolte' section. He claimed to have been forced, 'as a consummate actor, to mould his mind to every specious argument and every form of corruption'. Baudelaire failed to notice, however, the dangerous implications of other poems – poems that might well be construed as an 'offence against public morality', especially since the reigning standards had all the severity of principles that are rarely observed in private.

Baudelaire nonetheless had every opportunity to reread the poems and assess the risk he was taking. Like Balzac and like Marcel Proust, he treated the proofs as a sort of fair copy. Some poems were excised;[9] others were added. He complained about the typeface Malassis was using and asked him not to make the book appear too old-fashioned by using red lettering. (Malassis had recently reintroduced this on his title pages.) He requested that particular care be taken to observe the punctuation, for it indicates '*not only the sense, but also* how the poems should be RECITED'. His greatest fear was that the book might appear too small and insignificant.

The work, which had begun in February, went on into June. Malassis found himself caught between friendship and professional responsibility, between Baudelaire's flattering remarks and insolent observations; but by now he was resigned to his fate: the *Fleurs* would appear 'when it pleases God and Baudelaire', he told Asselineau. His brother-in-law, De Broise, was not so blessed with patience. His exasperation at receiving proofs plastered with corrections was met by Baudelaire's own righteous indignation. He accused De Broise of falling behind with his work(!) and advised him: 'If you don't want any corrections, Monsieur, then don't send me proofs as *messy* as those you sent whilst *M. Malassis was in Paris.*' One brother-in-law was skilfully played off against the other.

On June 13 Baudelaire sent De Broise a list of review and presentation copies to be distributed, starting with Gautier, and including, notably, Sainte-Beuve, Barbey d'Aurevilly, Philarète Chasles, Asselineau and Buloz. Longfellow was to receive a copy and, in Britain, Tennyson, Browning, Thomas De Quincey and Victor Hugo, who was in voluntary exile on Guernsey. Baudelaire asked for and obtained just over twenty copies specially printed on *papier de Hollande*.[10] These he presented to friends and patrons, as well as to his mother and Mme Sabatier. The copies intended for

Mme Aupick, Mme Sabatier and Achille Fould, Minister of the Emperor's Household, along with five others on ordinary paper, were entrusted to Lortic, the binder. Like no other writer, Baudelaire was a master of the art – full or half-bindings in plain morocco leather with spines enhanced by very prominent cords, masterpieces with all the discreet perfection of the dandy. This is something that clearly distinguishes Baudelaire from a writer like Gérard de Nerval. Both suffered the same privation, but whilst Baudelaire took the greatest care of his own books, it is impossible to point to a single instance of a book by Nerval being bound at his own request. Even Baudelaire's inscriptions are excellent examples of concision and style, from the flamboyant declaration, '*A Eugène Delacroix, témoignage d'éternelle admiration*' to the simpler '*A mon très cher Ch. Asselineau*'.

Poulet-Malassis printed approximately 1,100 copies. The book went on sale in Alençon on June 28, 1857 and, on the same day, or even a little earlier, *Les Fleurs du Mal* arrived in Paris.

Baudelaire's relations with his mother were entering a different phase. Even as *Les Fleurs du Mal* was being printed, the great obstructor disappeared. General Aupick died at his Paris home on April 27, 1857, at the age of sixty-eight. The death was declared by his colleague, Baron Lacrosse – who went to the Senate to deliver a speech in praise of the deceased – and by Louis Emon, his neighbour at Honfleur, a former member of Baudelaire's board of guardians. Baudelaire attended the funeral, but came away with bitter memories of Emon's insulting behaviour: 'Do you think,' he asked his mother on July 9, 'that I can forget his vulgarity, his brutality, and the boorish way in which he accepted my handshake on that painful day when, in order to please you, and for no other reason, I humiliated myself even more than you yourself have humiliated me for so many long years?'

Emon would now replace the General in Caroline's life as the representative of the offended bourgeoisie, although, at the time of the funeral, that respectable class had yet to suffer the insult of *Les Fleurs du Mal*. One can imagine how the General would have reacted to the trial.

Things had certainly improved between mother and son since 1851; but it was only after the General's death that Charles was able to draw close again to his mother. Until then, and from the moment he truly became aware of himself, Baudelaire had continually striven to accentuate in his mother's eyes his own eccentricity, to exaggerate his faults, to vilify himself and convince her of his guilt. Since he could never recreate himself in the image of Aupick – the man his mother loved and, so he thought, preferred to him – he would try to be the very opposite. He could thus be certain of keeping her in a state of suspense and confusion; he would be a cause of anxiety and remorse. The General stood for order, respect and the social hierarchy. Baudelaire would stand for chaos, insolence and promiscuity. But with Aupick in the grave, Mme Aupick became his mother once again, chided only for her trivial and pernickety attachment to bourgeois protocol.

Mme Aupick decided to make Honfleur her permanent home. Charles was very attentive to her needs; he sent her a prayerbook bound for a person in mourning, worried about the proceeds of the auction of her belongings in Paris – furniture, horses and carriages – and made sure that her pension as a Senator's widow would be adequate. There was really no cause for concern. Mme Aupick was to receive an annual income of about 11,000 francs – enough to provide a comfortable existence in 1857. Baudelaire's own income from his capital amounted to only 2,200 francs. Emotionally, he took her under his wing. The following letter is dated 3 June, 1859:

> I have at times been very cruel and uncouth with you my poor Mother; but at least I had the knowledge that someone was looking after your happiness, and the first thought that struck me when this death occurred was that from now on that duty would naturally fall to me. Everything that I allowed myself to get away with – negligence, selfishness, and violent language – all that is now forbidden. Everything it is humanly possible to do in order to create a new and special happiness for the last part of your life *shall be done*. – Besides, it won't be as difficult as all that, since you attach so much importance to the success of all my plans. In working for myself, I shall be working for you.

Baudelaire had at first resolved not to show her his volume of poetry, but since she would hear about it anyway, he decided to send it after all. He informed her of this on July 9, adding that her copy was still at the binder's. Having expressed satisfaction with this book 'of cold and sinister beauty', and his conviction that 'this volume, with its virtues and faults, will make its way in the memory of the reading public, along with the finest poetry of V. Hugo, Th. Gautier, and even Byron', he went on to issue the following warning:

> Just one piece of advice: since you're living with the Emon family, don't let the book get into the hands of Mlle Emon. As for the priest, whom you probably invite over, you can show it to him. He'll think I'm a lost soul, and won't dare tell you. – People have been spreading the rumour that I'm going to be prosecuted, but it won't happen. A

government with the terrible Paris elections on its hands won't have time to prosecute a lunatic.

He ended this affectionate and fairly optimistic letter by telling his mother about his visit to the cemetery. The General's remains had been transferred to their final resting place in the vault: 'Your wreaths, withered by the heavy rains, had been carefully placed on the new grave. I added some more.'

Unfortunately for Baudelaire, prosecuting a lunatic was a matter of some importance to an authoritarian government wishing to reassure its supporters. In contrast to the Restoration and the Second Empire, the July Monarchy (1830–1848) had shown a fair degree of tolerance to writers. The scandalous scenes daringly portrayed by Balzac in *La Fille aux yeux d'or* (one of Baudelaire's favourite novels), in *Illusions perdues*, or in *Splendeurs et Misères des courtisanes* had given rise to no legal recriminations. However, despite the fact that Napoleon III had gained full control of the country more quickly than Louis-Philippe, obscenity trials were on the increase. In February 1856, Xavier de Montépin was sentenced to three months in prison and a 500-franc fine for his supposedly obscene book, *Les Filles de plâtre*. True, *Madame Bovary* had escaped the censor, but Flaubert benefited by a discreet and effective intervention from Princess Mathilde, the Emperor's cousin. In fact, Flaubert's acquittal merely increased the likelihood of a successful prosecution: the next writer accused of immorality would have to face a criminal court which had been cheated of its prey. It may well be (though it would be impossible to prove) that the Government prepared its victim for the slaughter by first creating a suitable climate in public opinion. On July 5, Gustave Bourdin published in his father-in-law's paper, the *Figaro*, a short article in which he drew the Courts' attention to four poems from *Les Fleurs du Mal*: 'Le Reniement de Saint Pierre', 'Lesbos' and the two poems entitled 'Femmes damnées' – 'four masterpieces of passion, art, and poetry; but one could say – in fact it is one's duty to do so – that whilst one might be able to understand a twenty-year-old poet allowing his imagination to run away with him and exploiting these themes, nothing can be said in defence of a man of over thirty who advertises such monstrosities'. Similar compliments followed. Asselineau later agreed with Baudelaire that the pointing finger was attached to the long arm of the Ministry of the Interior.[11] Another attack on the poet appeared in the *Figaro* on July 12. Baudelaire cut out the article and added his own remarks: 'M. J. Habans is a young man protected by M. Billault [Minister of the Interior]. But the *Figaro*'s journalists probably felt that M. Gustave Bourdin's denunciation wasn't enough.'[12] The writer in question, who had already had some unpleasant things to say about Baudelaire's poem, 'Le Flacon', published in the *Revue française*, no doubt had a personal grudge against the poet. The satirical newspaper he worked on was not well-thought-of in high places and, by twice attacking Baudelaire, it was probably trying to curry favour with the Government. It is therefore extremely likely that the *Figaro* was at least partially responsible for the charges brought against the author of *Les Fleurs du Mal*.

The second attack was really just an attempt to add insult to injury. As early as July 4 – the day before Bourdin's article appeared – Malassis received the following letter from Lanier, his Paris distributor:

> My dear Monsieur Auguste, there is a rumour very much abroad, especially in high society, that the *Fleurs du Mal* are going to be seized. I convey this information to you as a friend. I do not know what basis in fact these rumours have. Today, a copy of *Les Fleurs du Mal* was delivered to Baron d'Ideville who wanted to obtain one for himself, claiming that the book was about to be confiscated. I believe you told me before your departure that that would never happen, but I prefer to warn you about these developments rather than keeping quiet.[13]

Malassis had been strangely inspired in choosing, or rather, retaining as his Paris distributor the 'Religious Printers and Publishers, Julien, Lanier, Cosnard and Co.'. Shortly after his warning letter, 'Father Lanier' told Malassis that the 'nature of the books' he published forbade him from putting his staff at Malassis' disposal for the retailing of *Les Fleurs du Mal*.[14] Baudelaire was already complaining about the poor distribution of the book and, on July 11, accused Malassis of failing to advertise it 'seriously'. The same day, he heard that proceedings were under way.[15] A report had been drawn up for the 'Sûreté Publique' section of the Ministry of the Interior, declaring that *Les Fleurs du Mal* constituted 'an act of defiance in contempt of the laws which safeguard religion and morality'. 'Le Reniement de Saint Pierre', 'Abel et Caïn', 'Les Litanies de Satan' and 'Le Vin de l'assassin', it said, 'are a tissue of blasphemies'. 'Along with these poems and a few others in which the immortality of the soul and the most cherished beliefs of Christianity are repudiated, there are others which express the most repugnant lubricity: "Les Femmes Damnées" is a paean of praise for the shameful love of women for other women; "Les Métamorphoses du Vampire" and "Les Bijoux" offer in every line the most licentious images rendered with the utmost brutality.' The conclusion declared M. Baudelaire's book to be 'one of those unhealthy and profoundly immoral works destined to have a *succès de scandale*' and urged that the matter be referred to the Public Prosecutor. The Minister of the Interior accordingly apprised the Public Prosecutor of his official opinion. The book was a clear outrage to 'public morality'.[16]

Baudelaire lost no time in writing to Malassis:

Quick, hide the whole edition, and hide it well. You should have 900 copies in sheets. There were still 100 at Lanier's. Those gentlemen seemed very surprised that I wanted to rescue 50 of them. I put them in a safe place and signed a receipt; and so there remain 50 with which to feed the Cerberus of the lawcourts.

That's what you get for sending copies to the *FIGARO*!!!!

In a postscript, he added:

I told Lanier that since the fifty copies I was leaving with him could be given up for lost, he should at least send them out as quickly as possible to the various dealers who had not yet received any; but he refused. He thinks that the Inspector, when buying his copy, checked the number of remaining copies with his eagle eye.

Baudelaire's optimism was flagging. On July 11, he appealed for advice to Théophile Gautier, who was well-thought-of in official circles, and, on the 12th, he asked the critic of the *Moniteur*, Edouard Thierry, to write an article on the *Fleurs* as soon as possible. With a good review in the Empire's official organ, he surely would not be dragged before the courts. Thierry responded with a favourable notice which appeared on July 14: 'The poet does not delight in the spectacle of evil'; he writes under 'the severe patronage of Dante'. Nothing was said of what the authorities were calling immorality – a marked contrast to the invective of the Catholic *Journal de Bruxelles*, in which 'Z.Z.Z.' described *Madame Bovary* ('that hideous novel') as 'a work of piety compared to *Les Fleurs du Mal*': 'common decency does not permit one even to quote from the book.'

Despite the article in the *Moniteur*, the Public Prosecutor directed that a preliminary investigation of Baudelaire and his publishers be conducted. All copies of the book were to be confiscated. The order was carried out immediately in Alençon, but perhaps not in Paris, where friends of the author (Asselineau in particular) were hiding some of the copies. Probably only a handful were ever found by the police.

On July 20, Baudelaire wrote to Achille Fould, Minister of the Emperor's Household. He reminded him of his work for the *Moniteur* (the paper was answerable to Fould's Ministry) and cited Thierry's excellent article: 'He

showed clearly that the book is meant only for a small number of readers
... and his marvellous conclusion was that despair and melancholy are the
single but sufficient moral of the book in question!' Thierry had as a matter
of fact expressed regret that the *Fleurs du Mal* lacked any sort of storyline
which might enable readers to perceive the overall meaning. Baudelaire was
playing the morality game, despite having told his mother on July 9: 'You
know that I have only ever considered literature and the arts as pursuing a
goal unrelated to morality, and that the beauty of conception and style
alone are enough for me.'

The poet thanked the minister for the opportunity he had been given to
publish his work in the *Moniteur* and the son of Mme Aupick – she whose
husband (so he told the minister) 'left her without any fortune' – declared
himself grateful for the minister's part in obtaining her pension. He concluded by asking for the minister's protection as a patron of the arts,
claiming to have abandoned the idea of sending a written defence to the
Minister of Justice, Abbatucci, since this might appear to be a confession
of guilt. Baudelaire was hoping that Fould's apparent sanction of the
favourable review in the *Moniteur* would create some disagreement between
him and the Ministers of Justice and the Interior. Baudelaire did in fact tell
his mother that Abbatucci had complained to Fould about the article,
saying, 'Why do you praise a work I'm trying to prosecute?' Was he really
the cause, as he claimed, 'of an argument between three ministers'? It is
clear in any case that the affair was taking on a considerable degree of
importance. Barbey d'Aurevilly – a friend of Baudelaire since the early years
of the Second Empire – arrived at the offices of the daily newspaper, *Le
Pays*, only to find 'official instructions' that Baudelaire was not to be
mentioned in the paper.[17] Writing to his mother on the 27th, Baudelaire
remarked: '*That is absolutely illegal*, since I haven't been convicted, only
accused.' By then, he had been cross-examined by the judge assigned to the
case and knew which poems had been singled out as a breach of religious
or public morality. There were thirteen in all: on the first count, 'Le
Reniement de Saint Pierre', 'Abel et Caïn', 'Les Litanies de Satan' and 'Le
Vin de l'assassin'; on the second, 'Les Bijoux', 'Sed non satiata', 'Lethe',
'A celle qui est trop gaie', 'Le Beau Navire', 'A une mendiante rousse',
'Lesbos', the two 'Femmes damnées', counted as one poem, and 'Les
Métamorphoses du Vampire'.

Baudelaire had yet to choose a defence counsel. He had been recommended 'a famous lawyer' who was 'well in with the Ministry of State'.
This description fits Chaix d'Est-Ange senior, but Chaix d'Est-Ange was
about to be made Imperial Public Prosecutor and would have been unwilling

to take on the case. He referred Baudelaire instead to his son, Gustave. On the 27th, Baudelaire summed up the situation as it appeared to him:

> I have on my side M. *Fould*, M. *Sainte-Beuve*, and *M. Mérimée* (who is not only a famous writer, but also the only man who represents literature in the Senate), M. *Pietri*, who is extremely powerful, and who, like M. *Mérimée*, is a close friend of the Emperor.
>
> *What I need now is a woman.* There might be some way to get Princess Mathilde involved in the affair, but no matter how hard I try, I can't work out how to do it.

Fould was given the copy of *Les Fleurs du Mal* Baudelaire had had bound for his mother. The minister may have been well-disposed towards him, but Mérimée, who also received a copy on *papier de Hollande*, was not as supportive as Baudelaire thought. Mérimée told Mme de La Rochejaquelein on August 29 that he had done nothing to prevent Baudelaire's being burnt at the stake, except to suggest to a minister that he might care to burn some other poets first. He considered the book to be 'mediocre, but in no way a threat'. It contained 'a few sparks of poetry', but 'only those you might expect to find in a poor boy who knows nothing of life and who is tired of living because he's been jilted by a harlot'. Mérimée was not acquainted with the author, but would wager he was 'silly and respectable'. The man Baudelaire described as 'extremely powerful' – Pierre-Marie Pietri – was Prefect of Police. He too received a copy of *Les Fleurs du Mal*. There is no record of his opinion. As for Sainte-Beuve, his attitude was unwaveringly ambiguous. He merely provided the younger man with a few 'little means of defence as I see them', of which the essential argument ran as follows: 'Everything was taken in the realm of poetry ... What Baudelaire took. He was virtually forced into it.'[18] In other words, only the subject of evil remained. This was an old argument, one that had already been used by the satirical poet, Auguste Barthélemy, in *Syphilis, a poem in two cantos*, after the Latin poem by Frascator: 'I told myself,' he wrote in the preface, 'that since all genres have now been deflowered, there now exists none so virginal as SYPHILIS.'[19]

Another possible argument lay in contrasting Baudelaire's prosecution with the state funeral granted to Béranger by the Emperor. The ceremony had been hurriedly arranged in order to prevent the opposition from turning the popular songwriter into a revolutionary hero. Baudelaire attended the event out of curiosity. Roger de Beauvoir ran into him and congratulated him on his large black hatband. 'Don't get me wrong,' Baudelaire retorted, 'I'm in mourning for my *Fleurs du Mal* which have just been seized at

Malassis' place yesterday evening at five o'clock.'[20] In his 'little means of defence', Sainte-Beuve rather coyly suggested that Baudelaire compare himself to the national bard. Some of his refrains, wrote the critic, 'are a *hundred times* more dangerous than what you are producing. And yet they aren't dangerous: there is also a certain gaiety which removes and dissipates the danger.' The branch Sainte-Beuve was holding out was not exactly solid. The logical conclusion was surely that Baudelaire's poems *were* dangerous because of their melancholy. Musset, who had passed away on May 2 was also invoked. His more indelicate verses had not prevented him from entering the Académie Française. This shaky line of defence was in fact the one adopted by Baudelaire's lawyer, even though it appears to point to its own refutation: the fact that certain pornographic poets had not been brought to trial in the past was no proof of Baudelaire's innocence.

In the notes he drew up for Chaix d'Est-Ange, Baudelaire developed the argument: 'Which do you prefer – the sorry poet or the gay and shameless one; the horror of evil, or frivolity; remorse, or impudence?' Though realising that 'it might be unsound to put too much weight on this argument', he nevertheless encouraged Chaix d'Est-Ange to quote '(with disgust and horror) some good bits of filth from Béranger' which contained obvious attacks on religion and morality. Veuillot, too, the Catholic writer who was then on cordial terms with Baudelaire, advised him to use Béranger as proof of the Government's hypocrisy.[21] And Gustave Flaubert, denouncing 'that smutty bourgeois who sang of casual love and threadbare coats', urged him to make the same comparison.[22]

Whilst preparing notes and documents for his lawyer, and asking that the book be 'judged *as a whole*, and then a terrifying moral emerges', Baudelaire was having four favourable reviews of the book published together in a small, in-quarto brochure entitled, *Justificatory Articles for Charles Baudelaire, Author of* Les Fleurs du Mal.[23] The one hundred copies printed were intended first of all for the Public Prosecutor's department and the judges of the criminal court. Two of the articles have already been mentioned – those of Edouard Thierry and Barbey d'Aurevilly. Baudelaire added a piece by Frédéric Dulamon, published by a small review called *Le Présent*, which had recently accepted some of the poet's own work, and an excellent article by Charles Asselineau, which the *Revue française* was too wary to print until after the trial. Asselineau left aside the accusations of immorality and considered *Les Fleurs du Mal*, not as a piece of didactic or moralising literature, but as the fulfilment of the expectations Baudelaire's contemporaries had of him. The poet had breathed new life into poetry, he wrote, thanks to 'this tightly-knit form in which the image sometimes explodes with the sudden brilliance of the aloe flower'.

Baudelaire's preparations for the trial were not confined to the realms of literature. In the early days of August, he was still searching for someone to intercede on his behalf. Barbey d'Aurevilly offered to have a friend of his place a copy of the *Justificatory Articles* under the eyes of Ernest Pinard, the prosecuting counsel; but Baudelaire, remembering Flaubert's acquittal, had in mind a woman – a woman seductive and influential enough to put pressure on the judges. He decided that Mme Sabatier, the recipient of his anonymous poems from 1852 to 1854, might fit the bill. Two days before the trial, on August 18 he sent her one of those letters that only he could write, in which a declaration of love accompanied a request for intercession and a precise indication of what the enclosed volume, beautifully bound by Lortic, owed to the woman who inspired him: 'All the verses between pages 84 and 105 belong to you.'

> Can you believe it? Those wretched men (by which I mean the examining judge, the prosecutor, etc.) have dared to incriminate, amongst other pieces, two of the poems written for my darling Idol ('Tout entière' and 'A celle qui est trop gaie')? The latter poem is the one that the venerable Sainte-Beuve declared to be the best in the book.
>
> This is the first time I have written to you in my true handwriting. If I wasn't so taken up with business and letters (the hearing is the day after tomorrow), I'd take this opportunity to beg your pardon for so many acts of folly and childishness.

But the Muse and Madonna had already taken her revenge, having told her sister, Bébé, that she was receiving those 'superb' letters and poems. Baudelaire went on then, at the risk of arousing her mirth, to confess once more his undying love: 'Indeed, I believe (though I have too much personal interest in the matter), *that fidelity is one of the signs of genius.*'

> You are more than an image dreamt of and cherished – you are my *superstition*. Whenever I make some awful blunder, I say to myself: '*My God! What if she knew?*' And when I do something good, I say: '*There's something that will bring me closer to her in spirit.*'
>
> And the last time I had the good fortune to meet you (quite in spite of myself)! – for you can't imagine how careful I am to avoid you! – I said to myself: 'How strange if that carriage were waiting for her; perhaps I ought to go a different way.' – And then, '*Bonsoir, Monsieur!*' in that beloved voice whose accents enchant and torment. I walked off, repeating

to myself as I went along, '*Bonsoir, Monsieur!*' trying to recapture your voice.

I saw my judges last Thursday. I won't say they're unattractive. They're horrendously ugly; and their souls must resemble their faces.

Flaubert had the Empress on his side. I need a woman; and the peculiar thought that maybe you, by perhaps rather complicated channels and connections, might have a sensible word or two conveyed to those fatheads, entered my mind a few days ago.

After listing the names of the judges and the prosecuting counsel, Baudelaire begged her once again to say nothing about his private thoughts. 'Farewell, dear Madame. I kiss your hands with all my Devotion.'

A society lady would have failed to understand the letter and dismissed it out of hand. After all, it was saying in effect: 'Because I love you, you ought to intercede on my behalf.' Baudelaire was certainly offering Apollonie an important role by placing her on a footing with the Empress; but why had he waited until two days before the trial? Perhaps he was anticipating some delay in the proceedings, or waiting for her copy of the poems to return from the binder. The second possibility might explain the very elaborate style of Baudelaire's declaration of love, recalling as it does the formal and rarefied tone of the 1846 letter to his half-brother's wife and that of the letter of Mme Marie.

Mme Sabatier asked no such questions and made no attempt to distinguish real emotion from artistic sentiment. Accustomed to broad humour and lewd remarks, she was finding out, as her correspondent wrote, that 'pests are *idolatrous*'. Despite the passionate feelings she would soon be expressing, it was difficult for her to help. Mme Sabatier apparently had herself introduced to Louis-Marie de Belleyme, a respected judge who had recently been promoted to the Court of Appeal.[24] But even if Belleyme had been willing, it was already too late to take any effective action.

On Thursday, August 20, 1857, Baudelaire appeared before the Sixth Criminal Court, which usually heard the cases of petty crooks, pimps and prostitutes. Among the four judges were Raymond Nacquart, the son of the doctor of Balzac and François Baudelaire. It was Doctor Nacquart who had played an 'abominable trick' on the poet in 1851: Baudelaire had been visiting Balzac's widow, attempting to gain access to the great writer's manuscripts. He was prevented from doing so by the doctor. 'What got into that wicked man,' he asked his mother at the time, 'that man I haven't seen for more than twenty years, and whom I knew only from the predictions he made of my death and the threat of the tortures he wanted to put me through?' In the end, it was left to Raymond, the son, to put the poet to torture.

The Deputy Imperial Prosecutor was Ernest Pinard, a future Minister of the Interior. Pinard, described by Baudelaire in his letter to Mme Sabatier as 'formidable', was to give a more successful speech for the prosecution than at the beginning of the year when Gustave Flaubert had been standing in the dock. Before the hearing, the accused paid a visit to the lawyer's chambers and, 'with perfect good faith, expressed his astonishment, and candidly expounded an artistic theory which M. Pinard was unable to share with him'. Pinard was at least 'convinced of the absolute sincerity of the man whose indictment he was about to request, and his opinion of [Baudelaire's] literary integrity explains the tone of his speech which, for the time, was very moderate'.[25]

Pinard quoted lines from 'Les Bijoux', 'Lethe' and 'A celle qui est trop gaie', and told the judges that they would find depicted in 'Lesbos' and in 'Femmes damnées' 'the most intimate habits of lesbian women'. Along with 'Les Métamorphoses du Vampire', these poems were held up as a breach of public morality. As for religious morality, Pinard opined that the guilty poems were 'Le Reniement de Saint Pierre', 'Abel et Caïn', 'Les Litanies de Satan' and 'Le Vin de l'assassin', but, without pressing the point, he left the judges to decide 'whether Baudelaire, that tormented mind, had been aware that he was committing that particular offence'. The judges were not convinced and the charge of blasphemy was dropped.

Returning to the question of public morality, Pinard brushed aside two objections. First, that the melancholy tone of the collection constituted a moral lesson. Pinard had drawn up a catalogue of the sensual passages, proving that he had read the *Fleurs* with an expert eye. Secondly, that other works every bit as offensive to public morality had escaped the courts' attention. Pinard replied that the prosecution could not allow itself to be bound by such precedents. He concluded with the following words:

> Be lenient with Baudelaire, who is of a highly-strung and volatile nature. Be lenient too with the printers who hide behind the author. But, in condemning at least some of the poems in the book, issue a warning that has become necessary.

This appeal for indulgence – even though the accompanying words are scarcely flattering to the poet – betrays the predicament of the Deputy Prosecutor, as Barbey d'Aurevilly noted: 'You could tell he was caught between the Minister's instruction and his own conscience.'

The ensuing speech for the defence by Maître Chaix d'Est-Ange was far from brilliant. Gustave was but the son of a famous man. He failed to take Baudelaire's case to heart and allowed himself to be guided by his client.

Comparing the poet to Dante, as Edouard Thierry had done, as well as to Christian preachers, moralists and Molière, he observed that Baudelaire depicted vice in such a way as to render it odious to the reader: 'The affirmation of evil is not the criminal approbation of evil.' The poems, he said, using the argument of Barbey d'Aurevilly's article, should not be considered in isolation. Poetically, as well as morally, they lose a great deal if not read in the order in which they are arranged. Thus, the three poems attacked on the ground of religious morality can be understood only if restored to their proper place in the section entitled 'Révolte'. (One of the three poems, 'Le Vin de l'assassin', actually comes from a different section.) The poet's true feelings, according to Chaix d'Est-Ange, are expressed in the poem 'Bénédiction' and even a piece like 'Femmes damnées' contains a message which exonerates it from the charge of indecency: 'Descendez, descendez, lamentables victimes,/Descendez le chemin de l'enfer éternel . . .' Once again, the lawyer fell back on Baudelaire's predecessors – the very argument that Pinard had rightly dismissed: Musset, Béranger, Gautier (for *Mademoiselle de Maupin*), Balzac (for *La Fille aux yeux d'or*), George Sand (for *Lélia*) and several others, including La Fontaine and Lamartine.

Whereas Flaubert's defence counsel, Maître Sénard, had shown the novelist to be, so to speak, 'a member of the club', by invoking his well-respected father and brother, Chaix d'Est-Ange said nothing at all about his client's family. Had Baudelaire instructed him not to mention his mother (the trial would be a bitter enough blow to her without that), or his illustrious stepfather, the former ambassador and senator who had recently passed away? The lawyer's silence on this point is in any case rather curious.

The trials of Flaubert and Baudelaire could be summed up in the following way: Flaubert was well defended by a former Minister of the Interior; Baudelaire was badly defended against a future Minister of the Interior. Whereas Flaubert's sentence was postponed, allowing time for political influence to take effect, Baudelaire's court reached a verdict the same day. It decided that with respect to the offence against religious morality an insufficient case had been made out; but with respect to public morality and accepted standards, it ruled that there were grounds for conviction as the book contained 'obscene and immoral passages or expressions'.

Baudelaire was sentenced to a 300-franc fine. Poulet-Malassis and De Broise each received a 100-franc fine. In addition, the court ordered the deletion of the following poems: 'Les Bijoux', 'Lethe', 'A celle qui est trop gaie', one of the 'Femmes damnées' ('By the pale light of the languishing lamps ...'), 'Lesbos' and 'Les Métamorphoses du Vampire'.

On leaving the courtroom, Asselineau asked his friend if he had expected to be acquitted. 'Acquitted! I was expecting them to make amends.'[26] Baudelaire was also anticipating a polite gesture from the Deputy Prosecutor and an invitation to dinner.[27]

The verdict was published the following day in the *Gazette des Tribunaux* and in *L'Audience*. It stated that whatever mitigating comments the volume might contain, nothing 'could dissipate the harmful effect of the images he presents to the reader, and which, in the incriminated poems, inevitably lead to the arousal of the senses by crude and indecent realism'. The key word in the verdict and the mark of the poet's infamy was the word 'realism'. Though Pinard had not actually used the term, it was clearly implicit in his exhortation to the judges to react 'against this unhealthy fever which induces writers to portray everything, to describe everything, to say everything'.

Significantly, this undiscriminating form of Realism, such as it existed in the mind of the layman, had just been described and denounced by Count Montalembert in a discourse delivered at the annual public meeting of the Institut de France.[28] His words were printed in at least three of the great Paris dailies. Speaking before the five Académies of the Institut, Montalembert attacked those modern young men who are devoid of any 'passion for elevated things' and corrupted by crude empiricism: 'Under the name of *Realism*,' he added, 'a word less barbaric yet than the thing itself, this fatal influence is already contaminating literature, art, and even philosophy.' A few days later, the Count, who was taking the waters at Evian, asked a friend in Geneva to find him a copy of *Les Fleurs du Mal*, 'that latest product of *Realism*, which, according to *Le Siècle*, one cannot condemn without being an enemy of France and French youth'.[29] Montalembert had therefore not read the book when denouncing the evil influence of Realism; but the poems were tacitly included in the attack through their overall context and the criminal court had presumably acted from a similar perspective.

The word Realism, of course, was originally an insult, applied to the work of Gustave Courbet and then to the works of his defenders, the foremost of whom was Champfleury. During the Second Republic, Baudelaire had been in the vanguard of Realism, because of his friendship with the leaders of the movement, but he abandoned it after discovering the work of Edgar Allan Poe and Joseph de Maistre. There are some notes for an article he probably intended to write in 1855 – 'Since Realism Exists' – which would have been a highly amusing defrocking of Courbet and co. 1855 was the year in which Courbet responded to rejection by the Salon jury by setting up his own exhibition, which included *L'Atelier*. Baudelaire is featured in the painting, on the far right-hand side, but his face was drawn from the portrait painted back in 1847. In addition, Baudelaire managed to persuade his friend to obfuscate the coloured woman (who must be Jeanne Duval) standing behind the allegorical poet as the personification of inspiration.

This reluctance to adhere to a particular school made no difference. Baudelaire had spent time in Realist circles; and, in any case, all works which lay beyond the bounds of conventional art were taxed with Realism. Flaubert's new novel was '*réaliste*' and Baudelaire's new poetry must be too. This is in fact what the disparaging *Journal de Bruxelles* had claimed on July 15; and Champfleury himself had been right to warn Baudelaire before the trial: 'You'll certainly be accused of Realism.'[30]

The difference between the trials of Flaubert and Baudelaire was that, although both writers were reproached for their '*réalisme*', the accusation achieved official status only on August 17, 1857, when Montalembert fulminated against the movement in front of the assembled Académies. By 20 August, Realism had become a synonym for immorality and a Realist was obviously someone who should be treated as a public enemy.

This is certainly how the situation was interpreted in Honfleur – not by Mme Aupick but by her entourage: the priest, a few local worthies and M. Emon in particular. Between July 27, 1857 and Christmas Day, Charles sent no letter to his mother; she received the book only at the end of December. Baudelaire reminded her of the humiliation he had had to suffer at the funeral in April.

> But later, when, after writing me letters which contained nothing but scolding and bitterness, after upbraiding me for that accursed book, which, after all, is but a very defensible *work of art*, you invited me to come and see you, whilst explaining that M. Emon's absence would make it possible for me to stay at Honfleur, *as if M. Emon were in a position to open or close my Mother's door to me*, and being very careful to advise me not to run up any debts in Honfleur, – well, after all that, I was so confused and so surprised that I very likely became unjust. See how vividly I remember that letter? I didn't know what to do or how to reply. After reading it, I fell into a state of indescribable agitation, and finally, after a fortnight, not knowing what to do, I decided to do nothing.
>
> I truly believe, my dear Mother, that you have never quite understood how unbearably sensitive I am.

The letter to Mme Aupick on July 27 ended with the following words: 'I embrace you, and ask you to consider this scandal (which is causing quite a stir in Paris) only as the start of my fame and fortune.' After signing the letter, he added: 'I don't need to tell you that the book is still selling, but secretly, and at twice the normal price.' One might suspect Baudelaire of wanting to derive some bourgeois approval from the inflated price. Mme Aupick would have noticed only the word 'scandal' with its close association to 'Realism'. Even after the death of her son, she suggested to Asselineau that he might want to leave 'Le Reniement de Saint Pierre' out of the posthumous edition of *Les Fleurs du Mal* – despite the fact that the poem was not one of those condemned by the court.

The contrast with Flaubert's family is striking. At the time of Gustave's trial, the Flauberts rallied round. 'They have to realise at the Ministry of the Interior,' Gustave wrote to his brother, Achille, 'that in Rouen, we are what is known as "a family", in other words that we have deep roots in the region, and that by attacking me, especially on grounds of immorality, they will also be offending a great number of people.'[31] Flaubert's mother, his 'poor, dear, adored old woman', was obviously not of the same breed as Mme Aupick, who yearned more than anything else for respectability and an easy conscience. It is, however, difficult to imagine Charles writing *Les Fleurs du Mal* whilst living in perfect harmony with his mother.

In Baudelaire's mind the trial was the result of a 'misunderstanding'[32] caused by the fact that for him literature and art could be considered only as 'pursuing a goal that is unrelated to morality – unrelated, but not opposed.[33] For his defence, he allowed himself to be drawn into legal arguments. After the trial, he realised that the judges could not be made to understand his views and gave up the idea of an appeal.

Now the consequences had to be faced – the fine and the censored poems. Malassis subjected the book to what Baudelaire termed a 'surgical operation'.[34] The censored pages were torn out, along with the other poems which happened to be on the same leaf. Next, he agreed to compose some inserts by resetting the uncensored poems affected by the operation. Other copies yet to be bound were left intact and some even reappeared in their complete form, dated 1858.

The ban on the censored poems was not lifted until May 31, 1949. The Appeals Court declared that year that the poems contained no word that might be considered obscene or even vulgar and that 'though certain descriptions may, by their originality, have alarmed certain minds at the time – and appeared to the first judges as an offence to moral standards, this assessment, based only on a *réaliste* interpretation of the poems, which ignored their symbolic sense, has shown itself to be quite arbitrary. It has been ratified neither by public opinion, nor by the opinion of the literary world.' Baudelaire, accused of Realism, would have rejoiced to see his judges condemned of the same crime.

The 300-franc fine was a hefty punishment for an impoverished poet. Having decided against an appeal, Baudelaire wrote to the Empress on November 6, 1857, asking for the fine to be reduced:

Madame,

It takes all the prodigious presumption of a poet to dare to occupy the attention of Your Majesty with a case as small as mine.* I have had the misfortune to be convicted for a collection of poems entitled *Les Fleurs du Mal*, the awful candour of my title having failed to protect me. I had thought to create a fine and noble work, above all, a work of great clarity. It has been judged obscure enough for me to be ordered to reorganise the book and to excise some of the poems (*six* out of *one hundred*). I must say that I was treated by the Courts with admirable courtesy, and that the very terms in which the sentence is expressed imply acknowledgement of my pure and lofty intentions. But the fine, enlarged by costs I fail to comprehend, exceeds the capacity of the proverbial indigence of poets, and, encouraged by so many marks of esteem which I received from such highly-placed friends, convinced at the same time that the Empress's Heart is ever ready to commiserate with all tribulations, be they spiritual or material, I decided, after ten days' indecision and trepidation, to solicit the very gracious kindness of Your Majesty and to beg you to intervene on my behalf with the Minister of Justice.

Please accept, Madame, the homage of the sentiments of deep respect with which I have the honour to be the very devoted and very obedient servant and subject of Your Majesty.

Charles Baudelaire
19, Quai Voltaire

The letter seems to have had some effect, since the fine was reduced in January from 300 to fifty francs, 'the offender having evinced regret' or so says a note in the files of the Criminal Division. Two days before, the Ministre de l'Instruction Publique had paid a grant of 100 francs to the translator of Edgar Allan Poe and the author of various pieces of art

---

*Not being a native speaker, the Empress would have missed the possible *double entendre* in the word '*cas*' (case), which, at the time, could also designate the penis. Baudelaire, who perhaps had not intended the pun, must have noticed it with a sarcastic smile when he reread the letter.

criticism. It was a mere coincidence, but one that says much about the inconsistency of the Government. Despite these windfalls, Baudelaire was very slow in paying the fine. After two warnings, he eventually sent in the sum of 53.70 francs (including 3.70 to cover the cost of the summons).

His publishers, fearing that an appeal would only serve to increase the fine, also paid up. Both parties were deprived of their civic rights. Baudelaire and Malassis probably could not have cared less, but De Broise, who later blamed the poet for this disgrace, waited until his brother-in-law went into exile and then tried to regain his right to vote. Asking for the Emperor's pardon in 1863, he pointed to his good standing in the local community and explained that 'more especially occupied with the printing shop in Alençon than with the Paris bookshop, [he] had not even read the censored book'. His platitudes were appreciated in high places and his rights were restored.

Though she had been unable to offer any help, Mme Sabatier at least provided the persecuted poet with some consolation. The following letter was written on either August 22 or 29:

> ... I can tell you, without your being able to accuse me of exaggeration, that I'm the happiest of all women, that I have never felt more clearly that I love you, that, quite simply, I have never seen you look more handsome and more adorable, my divine friend ... Now, whatever happens, I shall always see you in that way; that is the Charles I love. You can purse your lips as much as you like and knit your brows without my getting scared. I shall close my eyes and see the other man.[35]

On August 31, Charles replied, using Apollonie's real name, Aglaé. The protector, Mosselman, was invoked, allowing the reluctant lover to withdraw:

> ... You will forget me; you will betray me; you will tire of the one who amuses you. And today, I say in addition: he alone will suffer who, like a fool, takes affairs of the heart seriously. – As you can see, my very beautiful darling, I have *hateful* prejudices concerning women. – In short, I don't have *faith*. – You have a beautiful soul, but all in all, it's still a female soul.
>
> See how our situation has been turned upside down in just a few days. First, we are both afraid of hurting a decent man who is lucky enough still to be in love.
>
> Secondly, we are afraid of our own confusion, for we both know (I, especially) that some knots are difficult to untie.[36]

And finally, a few days ago, you were a deity, which is so convenient, so fine, and so inviolable. Now you're a woman. – And what if by some misfortune I should acquire the right to be jealous! Ah! how terrible just to think of it! But with a person such as you, whose eyes are full of smiles and favours for all, one would have to suffer agonies.

... Well, come what may, I'm something of a fatalist. But of one thing I'm certain: I abhor passion, because I know it, with all its humiliations; and now the beloved image which dominated all my life's adventures is becoming too seductive.

I don't dare reread this letter too much; I might be forced to change it, for I fear I shall be hurting you. I feel I must have let something of the nasty side of my character show through.

... Farewell, dearly beloved. I'm a little cross with you for being too enchanting. Consider then that when I leave with the perfume of your arms and hair, I take with me too the desire to return. And then, what an unbearable obsession that is!

Charles

Baudelaire seems not to have been expecting such a passionate reception from Mme Sabatier and was apparently worried that she would become a burden to him. Might she not be rash enough to break up with Mosselman and complicate things for the poet? The forlorn lover replied at once:

Look here, my darling, would you like me to speak my mind, and tell you the cruel thought that gives me so much pain? It is that you do not love me ... Does not one sentence of your letter give me proof of that – a sentence so explicit that it makes my blood run cold? – 'In short, I don't have faith.' – You don't have faith! but then you can't have any love. What can I say to that? Isn't that as clear as can be? Oh my God! how that thought makes me suffer, and how I should love to weep on your breast! I feel that that would comfort me. However it may be, I shall leave arrangements as they are for our meeting tomorrow. I want to see you, if only to try out my new role as friend. Oh! why did you try to see me again?

Your very unhappy friend

In those early days of September 1857, Baudelaire was sending Aglaé short notes apologising for being unable to come to dinner. He sent her theatre tickets, with letters that Mosselman could safely have read. In mid-September, she wrote to him again:

Your letter has arrived. As you can probably guess, I was expecting it to say what it did. So, we shall have the pleasure of your company for only a few moments! Very well, as you wish. I'm not in the habit of disapproving of my friends' behaviour. You seem to be terribly afraid of finding yourself alone with me, yet that's exactly what we need! Make of it what you will. When this whim of yours has passed, write to me or come and see me. I am merciful, and shall forgive the harm you have done.

... What am I to think when I see you flee from my caresses, if not that the other woman is on your mind – she whose black face and black soul have come between us? In fact, I feel humiliated and degraded. If I had no self-respect, I'd insult you. I should like to see you suffer. Jealousy consumes me, and reason is impossible at such times. Ah! dear friend, may you never suffer the same emotion. What a night I spent, and how often I cursed this cruel love!

... Good day, my Charles. How is what remains of your heart? Mine is calmer now. I scold it harshly so that I won't bore you too much with its failings. You'll see! I shall manage to force it down to your ideal temperature. I shall suffer beyond a doubt, but, just to please you, I shall resign myself to bearing every imaginable sorrow.

Mid-September saw the last of these passionate letters. From then on, Baudelaire appeared in the Présidente's salon only as one of the regular guests. The first of Mme Sabatier's letters in August shows that there had been no 'fiasco' in the Stendhalian sense of the word. Nonetheless, Charles was probably unable to see himself in the lover's role and, besides, the opulent charms of Mme Sabatier were not to his taste. Baudelaire preferred whores – a class to which his passing mistress had never belonged. Trying to comprehend her curious lover's loss of affection, Mme Sabatier inserted in her own copy of *Les Fleurs du Mal* a picture of Jeanne Duval drawn by the poet. Underneath, she wrote the words, 'His ideal';[37] but the ideal in question belonged to Baudelaire's younger days: by 1857, it was just a sad reality.

Baudelaire had sought a protector and intercessor, and found a lover. On top of all the worries connected with the trial came the need to extricate himself from a relationship which he himself had prepared with great care, even with love.

The trial of *Les Fleurs du Mal* – the scandal that was to be 'the start of [his] fame and fortune' – was not entirely the fault of other people. Baudelaire must have had at least some inkling of the risks involved, especially after the action taken against Flaubert and other writers. Even if it was only the result of an unconscious desire, he brought the trial upon himself. He did so partly because of the reputation if would bring him (in this, his wish was granted), but also because prosecution satisfied those masochistic tendencies which allowed him to feel different from other men and which were therefore one of the marks of the dandy. Baudelaire did not wish to be spared the trial any more than he had hoped to elude the *conseil judiciaire*.

PART SIX

CONDEMNATION
AND
RECOGNITION

CHAPTER 18

'As resistant as marble'

1857–1860

There is a portrait of the convicted poet by the Goncourt brothers, who met him in October 1857 at the Café Riche – the haunt of publishers, writers and journalists:

> Baudelaire was dining at the next table, wearing neither tie nor collar, his head shaved, dressed just like a man about to face the guillotine. His only concession to elegance: small hands, washed, scrubbed, and tawed. The head of a lunatic, and a voice as sharp as a knife. A pedantic delivery. He tries to sound like Saint-Just and succeeds. Rather stubbornly, and with a certain obdurate passion, he denies having outraged moral standards in his poetry.[1]

The trial put Baudelaire in the public eye: from then on, his daily life became a matter of general interest and he acquired a reputation that could at times be described as dubious, even loathsome. The side effects of prosecution were aggravated by the legend that was growing up around the poet and which seemed to have been officially corroborated by the legal ban. It would be a mistake to dismiss this legend as purely anecdotal, for it actually constitutes a particular aspect of Baudelaire's work: his poetic achievements were not confined to *Les Fleurs du Mal* and *Le Spleen de Paris*.

In February 1860, when giving advice to Poulet-Malassis about syphilis, Baudelaire encouraged him to follow a strict course of treatment, adding optimistically: 'There's no person healthier than one who has had syphilis and been cured ... It's a real rejuvenation.' For Baudelaire, rejuvenation came in the form of the trial. Never before had he known such creative euphoria, or been more self-assured, not only in day-to-day life, but also in the creation of works of art. The physical rejuvenation was unfortunately an illusion. On January 13, 1860, he experienced 'a strange attack' – 'a sort of stroke' – which was followed almost immediately by another attack: 'Bouts of nausea and such weakness, with dizzy spells, that I couldn't climb a step without thinking I was going to faint.' After the attacks came a feeling of immense fatigue. The symptoms described by Baudelaire seem to indicate arterial spasms brought on by an attack of the virus on the cerebral arteries.[2] After the end of 1860, depression was once again his daily lot. His creative mind was losing much of its vigour and relative fertility, though his sureness of touch never deserted him.

The Courts of the Second Empire are to be congratulated for having made Baudelaire fully aware of his own originality. By excising six of the most beautiful poems in the French language from the first edition of *Les Fleurs du Mal*, they were also partly responsible for the composition of a second edition which was published early in 1861.

It was only to be expected: despite the mitigating terms of the verdict, the trial had repercussions on Baudelaire's family life. Mme Aupick expressed her disapproval, influenced as she was by Alphonse and by the neighbour who had been so unpleasant to Baudelaire at his stepfather's funeral – Louis Emon. If she refrained from further protests, it was probably because she felt that she and the son she had failed to understand were at last beginning to draw closer to one another. Nevertheless, when Poulet-Malassis found himself convicted of the same crime eighteen months later for having published Louis Lacour's edition of Lauzun's *Mémoires*, Baudelaire told him: 'You're very lucky to have a Roman mother. Mine, on similar occasions, went over onto the side of the persecutors.' The plural 'occasions' surely refers not only to the recent trial, but also to the enforced voyage and the *conseil judiciaire*.

Baudelaire made no subsequent attempt to hide the hostile reviews of his book that appeared. Emon and other charitable souls would have shown the cuttings to Mme Aupick with ingratiating smiles, and besides, her irritation soon gave way to kinder feelings. Shortly after the trial, she invited, and then urged him to come and live with her in Honfleur. Baudelaire addressed her as '*vous*' until the end of January 1858. On February 19, he was using the familiar '*tu*' as he thanked her for her kind remarks on *Les Fleurs du Mal* and told her of 'another horrific article' on the book – an article by J.-J. Weiss which he later sent on to her. This more trusting relationship was disturbed now only by a few outbreaks of respectability on the part of the mother and some impatient outbursts from the son.

By the beginning of 1858, Baudelaire had many reasons to be happy. Emile Deschamps, one of the founding fathers of 1830s Romanticism, published a long and laudatory poem in *Le Présent* describing his reaction to *Les Fleurs du Mal*. Gustave Flaubert, writing to Baudelaire on July 13, declared: 'You've found a way to inject new life into Romanticism ...

You're as resistant as marble and as penetrating as fog.' Victor Hugo added his own resonant phrases: 'Your "flowers of evil" are as radiant and as dazzling as stars ... You have just received one of the few decorations the present regime can bestow. What it refers to as its justice has condemned you in the name of what it likes to call its morality.' Sainte-Beuve lacked conviction when he thanked his 'dear friend' for the 'nice book'.[3] One senses the critic's embarrassment; he must have realised that his own poetry left him far behind and he seemed almost ready to accuse Baudelaire of having gone too far:

> You tried to wrest their secrets from the demons of the night. By doing so with subtlety, refinement, curious skill and an almost 'precious' abandon of expression, by working away at the detail, with your Petrarchism of horrible things, you give the impression of pretending; and yet you have suffered, and were eaten away by the sorrows, nightmares, and mental torments you bore within you. You must have suffered greatly, my dear boy. That special sadness your pages exude, in which I recognise the final symptom of a sick generation whose older members we both know well, that too will count in your favour.

Sainte-Beuve hoped that his 'dear boy' would be less wary in future of passionate feelings: 'If I were walking with you by the seaside along a clifftop, without trying to act the teacher, I'd try to trip you up ... and cast you quickly into the waves so that you who can swim would thenceforth be moving in the light of the sun and the pull of the current' – or perhaps drowning in the sea?

Those who criticised the book were generally not the sort of writers who reach the happy shores of posterity. Louis Ménard had not forgotten Baudelaire's sarcastic remarks on his *Prométhée délivré* in 1846 and, in the *Revue philosophique et religieuse* in September 1857, he refused to take the poet's experience of evil seriously: 'He must be a tall and rather clumsy boy, with a long, black frock coat, a sallow complexion, myopic eyes, and the haircut of a seminarist. He talks incessantly of the vermin and scorpions he has in his soul, and considers himself to be the living image of every vice, but it's clear to see that his greatest fault is an overly lascivious mind – a fault one often finds in scholars who spent their youth in monastic retreat.' Ménard expressed the hope that Baudelaire would enter 'normal life', become a family man and publish 'books that he can have read to his children'. He could hardly have been more impertinent. J.-J. Weiss was just as unpleasant, accusing Baudelaire of having soiled 'grace, beauty, love, youth, freshness and springtime . . . and M. Baudelaire has people who read him . . . who admire him! and extol him! and we're all supposed to discuss him as we would some great event!' At the end of 1858, Baudelaire told Malassis that he had not seen the *Figaro* (which had printed a few snide remarks about him): 'I don't give a damn, and the same goes for the *Gaulois*, and all the other smutty rags which seem all the more repulsive to me since I'm busy with sadder or more serious things.'

Criticism also came from friends – Louis Veuillot and Barbey d'Aurevilly. As Catholic writers, they should have understood, as Huysmans did after them, that the lifeblood of *Les Fleurs du Mal* was profoundly Christian. Nevertheless, Veuillot attacked the poet in the extreme right-wing Catholic weekly, *Le Réveil*, on May 15, 1858, and went so far as to compare him to Béranger – the 'secret' Béranger[4] whose pornographic *chansons* were sold on the black market. Veuillot's mention of 'ears caressed by Béranger' inspired Baudelaire with the following marginal note: 'This Veuillot makes me want to have another taste of the *criminal courts* by caressing HIS with something other than my verses.'[5] Veuillot's attack scarcely gives a true measure of his worth, especially if one bears in mind the advice he gave to Baudelaire before the trial. As for Barbey, his criticism, in the same issue of *Le Réveil* was directed against the drunkenness of Poe, whom he dubbed the 'King of Bohemians'. Baudelaire was amazed: 'I've been very violently attacked,' he told his mother, 'by a writer of whom I never would have expected such a thing.' In the end, he kept up relations with both Veuillot and Barbey, albeit with less regularity than before. On July 9, 1860, Baudelaire told Barbey about two evenings he had spent with Veuillot: 'His stupidity disarmed me . . . I wanted to take him to some dancehalls, but he worries about the slightest threat to his virginity.' What he and Veuillot had in common was their rejection of the idea of 'Progress' preached by democrats. Barbey – the only writer Baudelaire ever forgave for criticising Poe – was appreciated for that unorthodox form of Catholicism which he shared with the poet.

The small storm produced by the trial died down only at the end of 1858. The controversial debate gave rise to several caricatures[6] – Baudelaire sniffing a bouquet of flowers of evil; a dainty little girl in a crinoline skirt and big wide hat, with an angry father spluttering: 'Who can have put that awful Mister Baudelaire's *Fleurs du Mal* into the hands of my daughter! . . .'; or a picture of two feet belonging to a man thrown back in his bed by what he has just read in that infamous book.

There was little in any of this to bring a smile to the face of a man who was anxious to keep control of his own legend. Hence Baudelaire's reaction to a colour caricature drawn by his friend, Nadar. It showed the green-gloved poet contemplating a carcass beset by a swarm of flies – an allusion to the poem, 'Une charogne'. Baudelaire scolded his friend in a letter dated May 14, 1859: 'It grieves me to be taken for the Prince of Carcasses. You probably haven't read a whole host of things I've written which are nothing but musk and roses. That aside, you're so crazy that I suppose you might have thought, "He's going to like this." '

Baudelaire himself was indirectly responsible for the parodies and cartoons perpetrated by friends and by those who would otherwise have remained indifferent.[7] It would be difficult to distinguish his genuine acts of eccentricity from those that were ascribed to him, whether they had their basis in fact or in poems in *Les Fleurs du Mal*. As Asselineau observed, people thought that Baudelaire was guilty of 'the vices and crimes he described and analysed'. An unsuspicious reader accused the poet of having 'mistreated a poor glazier who didn't have any coloured glass to sell him' – a rather literal interpretation of the prose poem, 'Le Mauvais Vitrier'. As for his acquaintances (if they were the least bit gullible – or even if they weren't), Baudelaire enjoyed telling them tall stories. While talking to Nestor Roqueplan, the director of the Opera, Baudelaire pulled from his pocket a book 'supposedly bound in human skin': 'Human skin, and that surprises you! ... but, my dear fellow, at the Gobelins that's the only material they work with these days, and when you come over to my place, I'll show you some riding breeches I had cut out of my father's hide.' The director merely smiled, unlike the young mother Baudelaire ran into one day in the Jardins des Tuileries:

'Is that your child who's playing over there?'
'Yes, it is, Monsieur,' the poor woman answered with the pride one usually expects to find in a mother.
'Good God! Madame, he's horrible!'

Or the restaurant-owner who served him a fillet steak cooked to perfection:

'That's just the *filet* I wanted ... it's as tender as the brain of a little child.'

A different version of the same anecdote has Baudelaire eating fresh walnuts in a wineshop and exclaiming in ecstasy: 'It's as if one were eating a young child's brain.' His provocative behaviour recalls the eccentricities of the Jeune-France of the 1830s and prefigures the insolent acts of the Surrealists. One of Théophile Gautier's daughters, Judith, remembered seeing Baudelaire knocked over in the mud by a dog on whose tail he had just deliberately stepped. He who was a great lover of cats was described by one journalist as having picked a cat up by the tail: holding it aloft, he plucked out its whiskers with a glee that bordered on frenzy. This particular act certainly has more to do with hysteria than affectation. Whatever the truth of it, Baudelaire would certainly have agreed with W. C. Fields that anyone who doesn't like children or animals can't be all bad.

Impertinent questions and incongruous propositions were also a way of trying out new friends. When Asselineau first met him in a café in 1845, Baudelaire begged him 'with the most studied politeness for *permission* to offer [him] a glass of what [he] was drinking'. Extreme courtesy, noted Asselineau, was one way he had of shocking people.[8] After chatting for a while in the street with Banville, the poet inquired, 'Would you not find it agreeable, dear friend, to take a bath with me?' 'What!' cried Banville, not wishing to show astonishment, 'I was just about to suggest it myself.'

Other reactions were not quite so friendly. When Maxime Du Camp first met Baudelaire – shortly after the founding of the *Revue de Paris* – he offered him 'some beer, some tea, or a grog'. Answer: 'Monsieur, I thank you, but I only drink wine.' Bordeaux or Burgundy? 'Monsieur, if you allow, I shall drink both.'

> Two bottles were brought, with a glass and a carafe. 'Monsieur,' he said, 'please have this carafe removed. I find the sight of water most unpleasant.' During the hour our conversation lasted, he drank down both bottles of wine, in large gulps, slowly, like a peasant. I remained impassive – especially when I noticed that each time he emptied his glass, he tried to see what impression this was making on me.

Not surprisingly, Du Camp never became one of Baudelaire's friends. He was, however, one of the regulars at Mme Sabatier's Sunday gatherings, along with another second-rate writer, the pretentious Ernest Feydeau. In 1858, Feydeau achieved fame with a novel entitled *Fanny*. Baudelaire wrote a fulsome letter of praise and received in return a stilted letter written in that pompous, epic style so dear to Hugo: 'Pass the book around. Write books yourself. Let us defend one another. We are not great in number. We are under attack. Let us take each other by the hand. Let's face up to the hypocrites, and, by God! close ranks,' etc.[9] Feydeau's exhortations, 'written in the first flush of success', were allegedly found many years later in a box on the quais, serving as a bookmark in a work by Thomas Hood. The letter was printed, with this introductory explanation, in the *Petite Revue* – director, Poulet-Malassis. Typically, Baudelaire's attitude to Feydeau's novel was contradictory. On December 11, 1858, he described *Fanny* to his mother as '*a huge success*, a repugnant, really repugnant book'. In 1860, he felt obliged to write once again to Feydeau on the publication of the latter's *Catherine d'Overmeire*. 'I shall find time to read *Catherine*. I consider it indecent ... not to read what our friends are producing.'[10] A few days later, on March 6, he wrote to Mme Sabatier, apologising for having failed to attend her *soirée*. He had been prevented from going by 'a terrible fear of having to talk to Feydeau about his latest novel'. After finishing Baudelaire's *Paradis artificiels*, Feydeau sent the poet a condescending letter in June 1860 in which he invited him to come and see the annotations he had made in the book. Baudelaire in turn annotated Feydeau's letter: 'An autograph made all the more curious by the fact that I never asked M. Feydeau for his opinion.' Along with the pompous letter concerning *Fanny*, Feydeau's notes on *Les Paradis artificiels* were offered by the recipient to Poulet-Malassis: 'Feydeau's corrections and reflections are horribly numerous and very amusing. I must admit that some of them are useful, and I shall transcribe them onto my own copy.'[11] The poet responded to other people's conceit or impertinence with modesty.

Baudelaire was constantly in search of originality, or, to use a word he favoured, singularity. He had a marked taste for the artificial, which makes him a forerunner of Des Esseintes, the hypersensitive aesthete of Huysmans' novel, *A Rebours* (*Against Nature*). From the moment he first contended that nature and original sin were closely linked, his aesthetics and theology hung together marvellously well, as can be seen in the section of *The Painter of Modern Life* entitled, 'In Praise of Cosmetics'. 'M. Baudelaire is artificial in all things. He powders himself, say his closest friends, and even puts on make-up.' One of these friends was told by the poet: 'I've just seen an adorable woman. She has the most beautiful eyebrows in the world – which she draws with a matchstick – the most provocative eyes – the brilliance of which is due solely to the khol on her eyelid – a voluptuous mouth – drawn with cochineal – and, on top of all that, not a hair of her own' – in short, 'a great artist!' Baudelaire himself dyed his hair green without managing to shock Maxime Du Camp:

'Don't you see anything out of the ordinary in me?' 'No, I don't.' 'But I have green hair, and that's not very common.' 'Everyone's hair is more or less green,' I replied. 'Now if yours were sky-blue, that might surprise me, but as for green hair, there's many a hat in Paris hiding that!'

Most of the anecdotes connected with the Baudelaire legend were later used by Jules Vallès in an extremely acrimonious obituary article. Vallès was unable to see the man behind the mask. Henry de La Madelène's article provides a more reasonable conclusion:

Baudelaire has often come under attack because of his great fondness for affectation, and, for many people, he's still the *poseur par excellence*. Far be it from me to deny the furtive pleasure he took in saying monstrous things as naturally as could be, but I pity those who judge him on appearances alone.

The feeling of superiority that went with the creation of a legend, which was itself inseparable from an artistic credo of strangeness and surprise, was particularly evident in the years following the publication of *Les Fleurs du Mal*.

Acts of provocation that were more or less acceptable in Paris would have been out of place in Honfleur. That, however, was not what prevented Baudelaire from leaving the capital: 'To think that a charming room is waiting for me at home, and that I'm prevented from reaching that Promised Land because of a few miserable debts!' When writing these words to Poulet-Malassis on December 10, 1858, Baudelaire had been trying for over a year to leave 'that cursed city where I've suffered so much, and where I've wasted so much time'. His dreams of happiness and repose were inspired in part by the example of the 'Hermit of Croisset', Gustave Flaubert, 'who found sufficient peace of mind' in his monastic retreat 'to finish a very beautiful work and become famous at one go'.

Debts were certainly the main cause of delay. Baudelaire felt obliged to pay off one person by borrowing from another. The old debts – those that were eventually settled after his death – were less of a problem. Men like Cousinet, the owner of the Tour d'Argent restaurant, were perfectly happy to offer usurious rates of interest and, as Baudelaire told his mother, 'Only one or two of those old tigers at the very most wakes up once a year.'[12] Recent debts were more of a worry, since he had had no legal right to contract them. These were incurred mostly in satisfying his various tastes – engravings, books, bindings, *objets d'art*, meals, wines and spirits, and prostitutes. With the equivalent of a deputy chief clerk's salary, Baudelaire was obviously living above his means. One is tempted to ask, however, whether he was not deliberately trying to lock himself into a vicious circle, constantly reminding himself that he was dependent on Mme Aupick and the *conseil judiciaire*. This dependency was something Baudelaire needed, if only because it had to be there for him to inveigh against it. It is also rather strange that his letters never refer to protests from his mother or Ancelle, who must have pointed out to him that he was legally incompetent. Needless to say, this incompetence was a closely-guarded secret and Baudelaire felt it his duty to reimburse creditors who had lent him money in good faith.

In 1857, his financial situation was catastrophic. After the General's death, Mme Aupick paid out the huge sum of 7,313 francs. Little is known of the details, except that money loaned by Poulet-Malassis accounted for 800 francs of it. In January 1858, Baudelaire's perseverance brought some temporary relief: his fine was reduced to 50 francs and 100 francs was paid to him at the request of Armand du Mesnil at the Ministry of Education. But his letters to Du Mesnil – one of which concerns a secondhand clothes dealer[13] – show that his general situation remained as desperate as ever.

Baudelaire's financial affairs were not always quite so sordid and depressing. In January 1859, he was being harried by a banker who wanted immediate payment of a debt – this despite the fact that the banker was an old school friend of Baudelaire's. The poet turned to one Polydore Millaud, who, besides being a banker, was also a press agent. Baudelaire offered him the promissory note in question, as well as 'some *novellas* of a new sort' for *La Presse*. He also asked – incredibly enough – for advice on investing money. Millaud had his colleague pass Baudelaire off onto someone else, who was unknown to the poet. Baudelaire replied:

Monsieur,
    I had the displeasure of concluding, without your assistance, the affair I came to propose . . .
    Do not be surprised, Monsieur, next time I think I have something worthy of being offered you, if I simply have a message conveyed to YOUR money that it is to conduct a deal with MINE.

Baudelaire's rare insolence depended on his perfect mastery of the French language, thanks to which Polydore Millaud has not entirely sunk into oblivion. (This was presumably not the poet's intention.)

Debts, however, were not the only thing keeping Baudelaire in Paris. There was also the *conseil judiciaire* and the consequent need for regular visits to Ancelle in Neuilly. The walk from Paris was arduous enough as it was and would of course be impossible from Honfleur.

In 1858, Baudelaire was finding it more and more difficult to put up with Ancelle's good-natured and punctilious supervision. On February 25, Ancelle took it upon himself to visit the Hôtel Voltaire in order to ask Baudelaire's landlord a series of indiscreet questions. Baudelaire later found out about this from the landlord himself. 'Does M. Baudelaire receive women?' Ancelle had inquired. 'Does he come home late?' And don't believe M. Baudelaire if he says he'll pay you, because he won't. Ancelle's secret investigation was the cause of one of Baudelaire's most spectacular outbursts – five letters written to his mother from midday until the evening of the 27th. Here are the main points:

Ancelle is a scoundrel whom I shall SLAP IN THE FACE IN FRONT OF HIS WIFE AND CHILDREN. I SHALL HIT HIM[14] *at 4 o'clock* (it's half-past 2 now), and if I don't find him in, I shall wait for him. I swear that there will be an end to this, a terrible end.

If he doesn't make *dramatic amends* for this, I shall strike Ancelle, I shall strike his son, and a *conseil judiciaire* will be seen attacking M. Ch. Baudelaire before the courts for assault and battery.

I'm absolutely heart-broken about the grief I'm causing you. I have to work, and now I've got to look for seconds in case there's a real fight between myself and Ancelle, or between me and his son. The little chap's big enough for that.

I have already consulted two people on what I ought to do. Striking an old man in his family home is a dastardly thing to do. But I want retribution . . . I must – *at the very least* – go and tell him, in front of his wife and family, what I think of his conduct.

By the following day, his anger had abated and, on March 5, he summed up the whole affair after a conversation with Mme Aupick's lawyer, Jaquo-tot – the man Baudelaire was hoping would take over from Ancelle as *conseil judiciaire*: Ancelle had apparently tried to prevent Mme Aupick from lending Baudelaire the money he needed to leave for Honfleur. He then refused to sell the deed that would provide the cash and went instead to Baudelaire's hotel in order to conduct his surreptitious enquiry. A title deed was in fact sold on March 11, 1858, producing enough money – 3,000 francs – to pay off the most urgent debts.

Baudelaire was also detained in Paris by his literary activities. *Arthur Gordon Pym* was at the printers and Baudelaire, as we know, liked to keep a close eye on every stage of a book's production. Then there were the studies on hashish and opium, printed in the *Revue contemporaine* and afterwards published by Poulet-Malassis as a book – *Les Paradis artificiels*. Malassis also brought out the essay on Théophile Gautier which was about to appear in *L'Artiste*.

The attempted assassination of Napoleon III by Orsini on January 14, 1858 had allowed the Government to rid itself of the newspapers and reviews which formed an unofficial opposition. Among these was the *Revue de Paris*, which had published poems by Baudelaire as well as Flaubert's *Madame Bovary*. Maxime Du Camp was one of its directors. Baudelaire sent him a letter of condolence, though, as he reminded him, he was not exactly a friend of his friends – in other words, of those who believed in the possibility of progress through science and democracy. Baudelaire's real reason for writing was that Du Camp had twice lent him 200 francs, which were eventually reimbursed by Ancelle in 1871. Baudelaire promised to pay him back in newspaper articles.

He turned then – or had done so already – to the *Revue contemporaine*. This review was directed by Alphonse de Calonne, who made it toe the official line. The Empire had many newspapers at its disposal, or even in its pay, but it lacked an important review. Having decided that Calonne was not subservient enough, it transferred its financial backing to the rival *Revue européenne*. When the new ministerial review approached Baudelaire in January 1859 about a possible contribution, probably hoping for some Poe translations, the poet allowed himself the luxury of an insolent letter to the Minister of Education. He thanked him for the grant, which had been awarded because of the intervention of friends from the *Européenne*, explaining, however, 'I was forced to reply that I would remain with M. de Calonne, until the moment he founders in the struggle he wishes to support, and that I was bound to him more by his kindness than by our agreement.' Baudelaire added that he was certain these sentiments would please the minister(!). Nevertheless, it was to the *Revue européenne* that Baudelaire gave his important study on Wagner in 1861.

Calonne's *Revue contemporaine* had been responsible for the attack by J.-J. Weiss on *Les Fleurs du Mal*. This gave Baudelaire an opportunity to play a trick on the review, as he boasted to his mother on February 19:

> The *Revue contemporaine*, an official journal, committed a serious offence by thus dissenting from the eulogies of the *Moniteur*. I went to complain to the Minister of State, and to complete my vengeance, borrowed a few hundred francs from the *Revue contemporaine* on the strength of a study I'm in the process of writing. I sense that my conscience is not entirely clear. This is the first time I've ever asked a favour of people I wanted to discredit. But my excuse lies in my terrible financial difficulties.

This subtle contrivance is Baudelaire all over. Poetic devices could be used to manipulate people as well as words. No doubt he managed to use the negative review by Weiss to inject a sense of guilt into Calonne, hence the loan of a considerable sum of money, although the promised study on hashish did not appear until the end of September.

Baudelaire also drew up a long list of 'articles I can write for M. de Calonne'. The list included a study of philosopher painters – 'in other words painters who subordinate art to reasoning and thought' or didacticism. (Baudelaire wrote only a few notes and paragraphs for this piece.) There were also others, on English painters, on museums that have disappeared (a reference to the Spanish paintings withdrawn from the Louvre by Louis-Philippe before he went into exile) and museums to be created. These titles recur in plans and notes up until 1866. Another study was to deal with the subject of dandyism in literature. It would be centred on Chateaubriand and include sections on Joseph de Maistre, Barbey d'Aurevilly and others. Baudelaire also offered Calonne the fourth volume of his Poe translations – *Eureka*. But in the end, apart from a few poems, the only works of Baudelaire to appear in the *Revue contemporaine* were two studies on hashish and opium, soon to become *Les Paradis artificiels*.

CHAPTER 19

Honfleur and Paris

1858–1860

Baudelaire was very active in October 1858, as Philippe de Chennevières discovered, when he ran into him in Alençon with Poulet-Malassis:

> Guess who I found there, drinking cider brandy? [he asked Prarond] – the author of *Les Fleurs du Mal*, Baudelaire himself, like a fish out of water in Lower Normandy, though he was already preparing to get back on the train to Paris. Poulet told me that the wily old fox had found a way to get an incredibly huge advance from the *Revue contemporaine*, which has been slinging mud at his *Fleurs du Mal* – all on the strength of the advertising power of his name and some articles he promised to write. That Baudelaire is one of the great hypnotisers of our time.[1]

On October 12, having already received a first advance, Baudelaire signed his contract with Calonne, agreeing, apparently, to deliver 192 printed pages a year for 3,000 francs. Some of the fee would of course end up with Poulet-Malassis: Baudelaire was heavily in debt to his friend. Nonetheless, it was a considerable sum and exceeded the poet's annual income by several hundred francs. One can imagine how pleased he must have been. On the 19th, he told his mother that he would leave for Honfleur the following day for a quick visit. 'I've been to see the place,' he told Malassis on November 3. 'It's perched above the sea, and the garden itself is like a little stage set. Everything there,' he added, 'is made to astonish the eye.' For Baudelaire, there could be no higher praise.

After a second visit to Alençon, a temporary move from the Hôtel Voltaire to Jeanne's apartment in the rue Beautreillis, and setting his literary and financial affairs more or less in order, Baudelaire left for Honfleur at the end of January 1859. Mme Aupick had prepared two attic rooms for him in the '*maison-joujou*'. The bedroom looked out over the town of Honfleur. From the adjoining study could be seen the 'fullness of the sky, the mobile architecture of the clouds, the changing colorations of the sea, the twinkling of the beacons' and the 'slender forms of the ships, with their complicated rigging set swaying harmoniously by the swell'.[2] By March 4, he was back in Paris, intending to stay perhaps only for 'two or three days, maybe a little longer'. He stayed for six weeks, with Jeanne Duval. Literary affairs detained him in the capital and then there was the Paris Salon, which opened on April 15. Baudelaire visited it only once and, in order to write his *Salon de 1859*, trusted to his 'old memory, stimulated by the catalogue', for, by April 21 at the latest, he was back in Honfleur. There he stayed until the middle of June. From the end of the month, he was in Paris again, making only one short trip to Alençon to see Poulet-Malassis. He took a room in the Hôtel de Dieppe, in a street which runs alongside the Gare Saint-Lazare.

Except for a few weeks during which he lived with Jeanne in Neuilly, the Hôtel de Dieppe was Baudelaire's home until he left for Brussels in 1864. He had a spacious room on the fifth floor, now divided, as the plaster mouldings show, into three small bedrooms. The fact that Baudelaire chose a hotel from which one could watch the trains leaving for Le Havre (from there, boats crossed the estuary to Honfleur) proves that he had not forgotten the '*maison-joujou*', though all his future trips to the coast were very brief. Honfleur never left his mind: it stood for sanctuary, peace and security. But Paris always claimed him, whether or not he had a good reason to return there, and in the end, Baudelaire spent far more time in the unfriendly city of Brussels than he ever did in Honfleur. As he told his mother on March 5, 1866, a few days before collapsing from the stroke which left him paralysed: 'My move to Honfleur has always been my dearest dream.'

Nevertheless, for a few weeks in 1859, the dream twice became a reality. Baudelaire's visits to Honfleur in the winter and spring coincide with an amazing outburst of creative energy and with a relatively satisfactory state of health. Most of the letters from this period exude optimism and happiness. This was the second peak of his creative life, the first having occurred between 1842 and 1846. He strolled around the harbour or went to visit painter friends at the Ferme Saint-Siméon. Evenings he spent with his mother practising English.[3] He was also hard at work on an adaptation of Thomas De Quincey's *Confessions of an English Opium-Eater* and then on the *Salon de 1859*. The loss of six poems from *Les Fleurs du Mal* and the consequent need to reorganise the collection forced Baudelaire to compose several new poems – notably 'Le Voyage' which, as a faithful debtor, he dedicated to Maxime Du Camp – not without a certain ironic smile: this poem, the last and longest in the 1861 edition, sets out to demolish the progressive ideas that were dear to Du Camp. Baudelaire also wrote or rewrote 'L'Albatros' and then, in the spring, 'Les Sept Vieillards', which begins in Paris – 'Fourmillante cité, cité pleine de rêves!' – and ends with the 'untameable, shoreless sea'. This was the poem in which Baudelaire believed he had 'merely managed to exceed the limits assigned to poetry'. 'Les Petites Vieilles', 'La Chevelure' and a few other poems were probably also composed in Honfleur. 'You can tell that the *Sea Muse* suits me well,' he told Calonne.

A different muse was to keep him in Paris – Marie Daubrun – and Baudelaire was not entirely a free man in Honfleur either: his reputation had gone before him. In 1900, a local scholar still remembered that extraordinary 'Beaudelaire' and his 'eccentric behaviour'. It seems, though, that the poet's strangeness manifested itself only in his wearing of a red tie[4] and one suspects that he was careful not to cause his mother any embarrassment. Unfortunately, whilst in Honfleur, he signed some promissory notes and, when her son was back in Paris, Mme Aupick was left to face the creditors. And then there was the added difficulty of obtaining opium. Though he used it at first as a potion to ease stomach pains caused by syphilis, laudanum had become a daily need. The wife of the local chemist later remembered the poet as a frequent visitor to her husband's shop: 'He looked old, but was very pleasant and very distinguished in his manner ... He had got into the habit of taking opium, and used to beg my husband to give him some; but M. Allais only ever gave him as much as a conscientious chemist would.'[5] Baudelaire's contacts with other Honfleurais must have been few and far between, which explains the warm welcome he gave to friends from Paris. Alexandre Schanne (the Schaunard of Murger's *Scenes of Bohemian Life*) claimed to have run into Baudelaire when visiting Honfleur with Gustave Courbet.[6] The story seems to be inaccurate in some respects, but Courbet himself certainly went there to visit Eugène Boudin, whose studio, filled with paintings of seas and clouds is described in Baudelaire's *Salon de 1859*. Baudelaire's friendship with Courbet had survived their ideological differences and the *Bouquet of Asters* in the Basel museum, dedicated 'to my friend Baudelaire, 1859', is perhaps a token of their meeting in Normandy.

Honfleur breathed new life into the poet, but the inveterate lover of Paris streets was incapable of leading a life of blessed retirement. When he decided, in May 1860, that he wanted to see his mother again, he first tried to organise a visit for her to Paris.

Jeanne was fighting a losing battle with paralysis and was admitted early in 1859 to a municipal clinic in the Faubourg-Saint-Denis. Baudelaire continued to support her financially. Then Marie Daubrun reappeared in his life. Baudelaire tried once again to adopt the role of impresario, but the actress left for Nice at the end of November with a theatrical troupe and a very sick poet – Théodore de Banville. Baudelaire never saw her again. This short-lived resurgence of affection produced the poem, 'Chant d'automne', and the ensuing jealous rage inspired the verses 'A une Madone'. Both affairs had been brief, but Baudelaire never forgot her. There exists a copy of the 1861 edition of *Les Fleurs du Mal* inscribed 'To Marie Daubrun, A token of old affection'. It was bound for the actress by a modest craftsman who also bound her copy of Banville's *Poésies* published by Poulet-Malassis in 1857.[7] Banville and Baudelaire remained on good terms, though Marie was Banville's mistress until 1863 – the year in which the poet met his future wife, a widow, Mme Rochegrosse.

Marie Daubrun, literary editors and debts kept Baudelaire in Paris; perhaps, more perversely, he was also bound by the hate he felt for his native city – Baudelaire was occasionally Parisian in this respect, too.

Relations with Calonne at the *Revue contemporaine* were quite satisfactory in 1858 and 1859, especially since Baudelaire seems to have developed quite a liking for the charming Mme de Calonne, who was one year older than he. She encouraged him to write more poetry for the review. Her husband, however, frequently objected to Baudelaire's style and one senses from a letter written on April 28, 1860, that things were becoming a little strained: 'I am very sorry to have to point out to you for the tenth time that *one does not make alterations to* MY *verses*. Kindly do not print them.' The following conversation, reported by Asselineau, may well have taken place between Calonne and Baudelaire:

'Do you not find, Monsieur, that this verse is a little weak?' 'Yes, Monsieur,' the poet replied, biting his lip; 'and the following verse is also weak, but they are there to introduce the next one, which isn't weak at all.' 'I quite agree, Monsieur; but it would be much better if all three were of equal strength.' 'No, Monsieur,' answered the poet, this time in anger, 'for then where would be the gradation? It's an art, Monsieur, an art that I've taken twenty years to learn and ...' (he dared not add) 'about which you know absolutely nothing.'[8]

Having assigned to Malassis whatever fees were paid to him by the *Revue contemporaine*, Baudelaire was chained to Calonne by his contract and by the advances he had already received. On September 23, 1859, Malassis sent an urgent letter to Baudelaire after receiving a telegram in which the poet informed him that he had no money for him:

... my dear Baudelaire, it's as clear as can be: the problems will start up again a month from now, and will you have money then? According to the terms of his agreement, M. de Calonne is supposed to give you some, or rather, give *me* some, but will he?

It all seems very doubtful, and I wonder how you'll manage to pay off part of your debt, quarter by quarter, when you haven't found a way to do it *after nine months*.

You know my situation. I haven't a penny. I'm even poorer than you. If we experienced any difficulty in renewing the debt, even with amortisation, I really don't know what I should do.

... I don't need to tell you again that the situation is very serious for me, since, all told, with these personal promissory notes, I'm literally *discrediting* the firm, which doesn't belong only to me.[9]

Two days later, Baudelaire replied: 'You were much too quick to send me a whole pack of silly remarks.' His work for the *Revue contemporaine*, including the piece on opium, would bring in 1,000 francs, although he was also counting on two other articles which had been left in Honfleur. One of these may have been the article on 'L'Art philosophique'. They obviously belonged in any case to the optimistic list of works in preparation and could not be converted into cash. The situation was not improving. Malassis wrote on November 8:

You'd find it difficult to picture my position. I'm really not a living person. The slightest incident makes life with my family impossible. I have the feeling the whole time that they see me as an object of anxiety and suspicion.

Calonne rescued the two friends, but the merry-go-round continued: 'The Boyer (800.50),' wrote Baudelaire, 'which can be cashed with Asselineau, will be paid by a note from Christophe. The Christophe (750.75) will be paid by a note from Boyer.' Perhaps he was deriving a certain thrill from these alarming transactions. It was only when they threatened to encroach on his life in Honfleur that he began to take them seriously. But was he really considering the risks that Malassis was running, and which inevitably involved the publisher's mother and sister, not forgettng poor old De Broise? In examining Baudelaire's entangled affairs, one is forced to marvel maybe not at the way in which he managed to control them (one suspects that even he was sometimes lost in their intricacies), but at least at the influence he exerted over the friends he pressed into service – Poulet-Malassis, Asselineau, Babou, Monselet, the naive Christophe, the sculptor to whom he dedicated the poem, 'Danse macabre', and the even more innocent Philoxène Boyer. Chennevières was obviously correct in calling Baudelaire 'one of the great hypnotisers of our time'.

Writing to Malassis on September 25, 1859, Baudelaire dangled two other possible sources of income before his eyes – a play and a Poe translation. The translation was *Eureka*, which Baudelaire offered, strangely enough, to a new democratic and anticlerical review – the *Revue internationale*. The printer of the review made so many mistakes that the editors were obliged to publish a list of errata. Its director, Carlos Derode, having promised to pay for the whole manuscript in advance, decided instead to wait until each separate section was delivered. After January 1860, the *Revue internationale*, soon to disappear, ceased publication of *Eureka*. It was not the sort of tale to attract the readers. Even one of the review's own contributors attacked both the author and the translator: 'If the reader wishes to cry out in fright, "Am I an idiot?" he has only to venture into that gigantic charade signed by one of America's two great men (the other being Washington), and translated by the leading poet of the new France.'

For the play, Baudelaire had in mind the Théâtre Impérial du Cirque, which became the Théâtre du Châtelet in 1862. His intention was to write an adaptation of a short story by his friend, Paul de Molènes, entitled *The Sufferings of a Hussar*. The adaptation was meant to 'combine *literary qualities* with the *turbulent production* of the Boulevard theatres'[10] – the same thought that had inspired the earlier play, *The Drunkard*. The idea was excellent; only Hugo and Dumas had ever succeeded in combining the facile skills of a popular playwright with a graceful literary style; but Baudelaire was incapable of putting this into practice. Lyric poets rarely make good playwrights or producers. The play was never more than a plan – a great pity, since Baudelaire's story of passion and honour which sets partisans of the King against the supporters of Napoleon was one that might have appealed both to the general public and to connoisseurs. The theatre director, Hostein, could naturally give no firm assurances and, come the beginning of November 1860, Baudelaire was telling his mother: 'The theatre arouses in me such disdain that in order to shorten the task, I've been thinking of finding a collaborator – *as famous and as stupid* as possible. It would mean half as much work, and, consequently, half as much money.' He had been hoping to borrow three thousand francs on his unwritten play.

Despite occasionally threatening desertion, Baudelaire remained with Calonne and the *Revue contemporaine*. Journals which paid well and seemed destined to survive were hard to find. The *Internationale* folded and the *Revue française* barely had time to complete its publication of the *Salon de 1859* before it too disappeared on July 20. Baudelaire's great treatise on aesthetics was read by only a few people.

There was another review that made itself available to the poet, but it was very small and its contributors remained anonymous. The *Revue anecdotique*, founded in 1855, was bought up by a patron of the arts who liked to masquerade as a publisher – Ernest Bouju. 'Rich and self-effacing, he delights in surrounding himself with writers and artists. He provides them with a decent income and puts at their disposal luxury printing, engraving, and all the materials needed to make a fine edition.'[11] Baudelaire was obviously interested in this strangely modest little man, and suggested that Malassis might want to team up with Bouju and Michel Lévy's rival, Bourdilliat, to produce 'an edition of Edgar Allan Poe at 80 francs a copy'. This luxury edition would be illustrated by Constantin Guys. The idea never bore fruit, but Baudelaire's connection with Bouju did at least earn him a good relationship with the unfortunately very private *Revue anecdotique*.

Constantin Guys, like Ernest Bouju, was remarkable for his modesty – a very 'whirlwind of modesty', in fact, according to Baudelaire. 'He picked a quarrel with me when he found out that I wanted to write something about him.'[12] As an art critic, Baudelaire was extremely excited about his latest discovery and, at a time when he felt that he was not properly appreciated by Delacroix, Baudelaire saw in Guys an artist around whose work he might construct his new theory of art – a theory of the sketch that captures the fleeting instant and which received poetic expression in the sonnet, 'A une passante'.

When, in January and February 1861, Baudelaire applied to the Ministry of State for a grant, he asked that one be awarded also to Constantin Guys. On January 10, his letter included a lengthy 'Note on M. Constantin Guys, artist and man of letters', which informed the ministry that the artist had just been deprived of his long-standing post on the *Illustrated London News* by the accidental death of its founder, Herbert Ingram.[13] Baudelaire indicated that Guys – though his name was completely unknown to the French because of his bizarre 'aristocratic' habit of never signing works – was responsible for all the illustrations in the English press of the February revolution and the Crimean War. Many of these had become very popular in France.

Baudelaire was intending to show the minister a series of drawings by Guys, along with his own study of the artist, which, untypically, had already been written. (The first draft dates from the summer of 1860.) Reviews were reluctant to accept a piece on such an obscure artist and it was the frivolous *Figaro* that eventually published *The Painter of Modern Life* at the end of 1863. In accordance with the artist's emphatic request, he was referred to only as 'M. G.' This was the study that allowed Baudelaire at last to define the essence of modernity, which until then had found no champion among painters. 'He has sought out everywhere the transitory, fleeting beauty of present-day life,' he wrote, and 'has managed to distil in his drawings the sharp or heady taste of the wine of Life.' Along with Wagner, Guys was Baudelaire's last great admiration. The artist was 'the least accommodating and most whimsical of men' – he once asked Baudelaire to send him 'a note on all works and theories' concerning the Venus de Milo – but Baudelaire enjoyed his company. Together, they visited dens of iniquity like the Casino in the rue Cadet, or places of even worse repute. The artist and the poet were observing life.

Shortly before his discovery of Guys, Baudelaire had discovered the work of Charles Méryon, who came to represent for the poet of 'Les Sept Vieillards' the intrusion of the supernatural into modern life. Having obtained from Edouard Houssaye (brother of Arsène and director of the *Gazette des Beaux-Arts*) a copy of Méryon's collected aqua fortis prints, Baudelaire devoted a page to Méryon's Paris views in the *Salon de 1859*. For Victor Hugo, to whom he compared the engraver, Baudelaire transcribed his comments:

> I have rarely seen depicted more poetically the natural grandeur of an immense city ... But a cruel demon has touched the mind of M. Méryon; a mysterious delirium has muddled those powers that seemed to be as sound as they were brilliant ... we still anxiously await consoling news of this singular [naval] officer, who one day became a powerful artist, having said farewell to the grave adventures of the Sea in order to portray the dark majesty of that most unnerving of capitals.

Baudelaire, who was so partial to eccentricity (his own in particular), found it difficult to appreciate Méryon's strange behaviour. He told Malassis on January 8, 1860 that Méryon had written to him at the 'Hotel of Thebes' (instead of Dieppe). On one state of *The Pont-au-Change*, Méryon had replaced a small balloon with a flock of birds of prey. When Baudelaire pointed out to him that this was somewhat unrealistic, he replied that '*those people* (the Imperial Government) had oftentimes released eagles in order to study the omens according to the rite, and that that had been printed in the newspapers – even in the *Moniteur*'. Méryon spoke admiringly of Michelet's *Joan of Arc*, but was 'convinced that the book is not by Michelet ... After he left, I wondered how it was that I whose mind and nervous system have always had what it takes to go mad, never did so. Seriously, I gave thanks to Heaven like the pharisee.'

Méryon was causing Baudelaire no end of trouble: the publisher, Delâtre, had asked the poet to write an introduction for a new printing of Méryon's *Eaux-fortes sur Paris*:

> Good! here's a chance to write some musings of ten, twenty, or thirty lines on beautiful engravings – the philosophical musings of a Parisian *flâneur*. But M. Méryon, who doesn't see things in the same way, intervenes. One should say, 'On the right, you can see this; on the left, you can see that.' One should look up notes in old books. One should say, 'Here, there were originally twelve windows, which the artist has reduced to ten,' and finally, one is supposed to go to the Hôtel de Ville to inquire about the exact date of demolitions. M. Méryon talks, gazing at the ceiling, ignoring all remarks.

The project came to an abrupt end, as did Baudelaire's relationship with Méryon.

In the years which separate the two editions of *Les Fleurs du Mal*, Baudelaire kept up his old friendships. Notoriety also brought him new acquaintances. In Lyons, the critic Armand Fraisse had been expressing admiration for Baudelaire's poems and, in 1861, when reviewing the *Sonnets humouristiques* of his compatriot, Joséphin Soulary, he wrote courageously: 'I have read *Les Fleurs du Mal* twenty times, and shall often reread it in years to come.'[14] Baudelaire shared the critic's liking for Soulary's 'charming book of sonnets' and asked him to pass on his congratulations. In a letter from Lyons on February 22, 1859, Soulary called Baudelaire 'the leading poet of our time' and, though he was six years older than Baudelaire, addressed him as 'Cher Maître' – probably the first time that anyone had ever paid him the compliment.[15] Baudelaire wrote the very next day to congratulate Soulary on the new edition of his sonnets, adding, 'Neither you nor I are *stupid* enough to merit universal suffrage.' This was clearly an allusion to Hugo the democrat, but also to a certain category of popular, representative poets to which Baudelaire knew he would never belong. He admitted only two other exceptions to the rule – Théophile Gautier and Leconte de Lisle: 'One might say that we shall experience very strong and very subtle pleasures, which the common herd will never know.'

As for Sainte-Beuve, a change had taken place. Baudelaire was no longer the disciple addressing his master, but a recognised writer talking to his elder – recognised, that is, by all but Sainte-Beuve himself: despite Baudelaire's hints and requests, Sainte-Beuve reviewed neither *Les Fleurs du Mal* nor the Poe translations. Without consulting Baudelaire, the critic Hippolyte Babou took up his cause and attacked Sainte-Beuve in the *Revue française* on February 20, 1859. Sainte-Beuve was accused of having failed to defend the poems at the time of the trial: 'That respectable fellow will glorify *Fanny* and keep quiet about *Les Fleurs du Mal.*' Baudelaire vindicated himself in a letter and received in return a reassuring note from Sainte-Beuve; but one suspects that some doubt remained in the critic's mind and that he was embarrassed by the ambiguous reputation of the poet who saw his *Fleurs du Mal* as an extension of the poetry of *Joseph Delorme*. In the *Moniteur*, on February 20, 1860, Sainte-Beuve used Feydeau's *Catherine d'Overmeire* as a pretext for summing up the present state of literature and for settling accounts with Babou. He redeemed himself in part by quoting a section of the letter he had sent to Baudelaire in 1857. Baudelaire, 'one of the oldest of those I call my "young" friends', nevertheless came in for some disparagement. He was described as a 'subtle thinker' and lumped together with secondary or marginal writers. As Baudelaire told Soulary on the 28th: 'I feel very flattered to be put on a par with my friend Flaubert and with a man like yourself; but coming as it does in connection with M. Feydeau ... it's a little hard to take.' Baudelaire must have felt more bitter than his letter suggested.

In his relations with Delacroix, there was little improvement. He tried in vain to obtain permission for Malassis to publish an edition of the painter's collected essays. Delacroix thanked the poet for a glowing passage in the *Salon de 1859*: 'You treat me as only the "glorious dead" are treated. You make me blush and please me greatly at the same time.' The letter was kind, but also a little distant. Delacroix belonged to the *haute bourgeoisie* and was probably not very keen to be praised by a critic who had been dragged before the criminal courts. Baudelaire sent him a copy of his *Théophile Gautier*. The painter was some time in replying. He eventually thanked him for his 'attractive book', but complained: 'It has the drawback of several of your publications. It is of such a subtle nature that I find it very hard to read.' The rest of Delacroix's letter concerned his admiration for Gautier.

The translator of Edgar Allan Poe was faring somewhat better. The two volumes of *Histoires extraordinaires* and *Les Aventures d'Arthur Gordon Pym* had on the whole provided him with a solid reputation. And then the critic who was cursed with such reluctant masters made a discovery that came as a powerful consolation. Though he had hailed the composer in 1849 as 'one whom the future will honour as the most illustrious of the masters',[16] his knowledge of Wagner's music could have been no more than rudimentary. Wagner had already visited France several times – most recently in 1853, when the police kept him under observation as a dangerous revolutionary, and in January 1858. He returned in September 1859, to the joyful and admiring cries of his French supporters, Champfleury among them. This time, Wagner gave three concerts at the Théâtre-Italien, conducting the orchestra and choirs himself. On the programme were the overture to *The Flying Dutchman*, extracts from *Tannhäuser* and *Lohengrin*, and the prelude to *Tristan*. Baudelaire attended the performances and was thrilled: 'I daren't talk about Wagner any more,' he told Malassis. 'People have been pulling my leg about it. That music was one of the greatest pleasures of my life. It's been easily fifteen years since I felt such exhilaration.' On the 17th, Baudelaire wrote a long and passionate letter to Wagner himself:

... Above all, I want to tell you that you have given me *the greatest musical pleasure I have ever experienced*. I am past the age at which one enjoys writing to famous men, and I would have waited even longer before expressing my admiration in a letter, did not my eyes light every day upon outrageous and ridiculous articles in which no effort is spared to malign your genius. You are not the first, Monsieur, to make me ashamed of my country. Indignation finally spurred me to express my gratitude, as I thought: 'I wish to distinguish myself from all those imbeciles.'

... What I felt defies description, and if you would be so kind as to refrain from laughing at me, I shall endeavour to translate my impressions. At first, I felt as though I knew this music, and, as I reflected on it later, I realised the cause of this delusion. It seemed to me that the music was *mine*, and that I recognised it as every man recognises those things he is destined to love ...

Secondly, the quality that struck me most was its grandeur. It represents what is great, and is itself a spur to greatness. Everywhere in your works I found the grandeur of great sounds, the great sights of Nature, and the great passions of men ... The effect produced by *the introduction of the guests* and by the *nuptial feast* is tremendous. I felt the whole majesty of a life that is larger than ours. Another thing: I often experienced a feeling of a rather peculiar order – the pride and pleasure of understanding, of allowing myself to be penetrated and possessed – a truly sensual pleasure which resembles the joy of rising in the air or rolling upon the sea. And, at the same time, your music sometimes expresses the pride of life. Those deep harmonies generally conjure up in my mind those stimulants which quicken the pulse of the imagination. Lastly, I also felt – and I beg you not to laugh – sensations which probably stem from my turn of mind and from my frequent preoccupations. There is throughout something spirited and inspiriting, something that longs to climb higher, something transcendant and superlative. For example, to take images from painting, I imagine that I have before my eyes a vast expanse of dark red. If the red represents passion, I see it changing, little by little, and by every gradation from red to pink, to the incandescence of the furnace. It would appear difficult, even impossible to attain anything more ardent; and yet a final flare comes and scores a whiter trace on the whiteness of its background. It is, if you wish, the supreme cry of the soul that has climbed to its highest peak.

I had begun to write down some meditations on the passages of *Tannhäuser* and *Lohengrin* that we heard; but I recognised the impossibiliy of saying everything.

I could therefore continue this letter ad infinitum. If you have been able to read me, I thank you ... Ever since the day I heard your music, this thought is always on my mind, especially in times of trouble: 'If I could but hear a little Wagner tonight!'

Ch. Baudelaire

I shall not include my address, since you might then think that I had some favour to ask of you.

Wagner may have asked around for Baudelaire's address and gone to thank him in person, since no written reply to the letter has ever been found. Baudelaire managed to shape his meditations into a study which was eventually published on April 1, 1861 by the *Revue européenne*. Three days' writing in the printing house itself, he told his mother, had given him the impetus to see this strenuous task through to the end; but he was also spurred on by events. After rehearsals at the Opera – one of which Baudelaire attended at the composer's invitation – *Tannhäuser* was a resounding failure on March 13, thanks to the machinations of Wagner's French enemies.[17] When revising his article for the slim volume published in May under the title, *Richard Wagner et Tannhäuser à Paris*, Baudelaire added an epilogue in which he took his compatriots to task for their stupidity.

Wagner had already told Baudelaire how grateful he was for the study in the *Revue européenne*: 'Your article,' he wrote, 'honours me and ... encourages me more than anything else that has ever been said about my humble talent ... Might I not soon have the opportunity of telling you in person,' he continued, 'how excited I was to read those beautiful pages which, like the finest poem, described the impressions that I must pride myself on having produced on a system as superior as yours?' Wagner was also delighted to learn later in the year that his admirers, Champfleury and Baudelaire, had planned a trip to Vienna in order to hear *Tristan und Isolde*.

The 'inspiriting' effect of Wagner's operas may have helped remove the bad taste that Baudelaire's other contact with the world of music had left. A German–American composer, Robert Stoepel, had arrived in Paris in November 1860 with a 'Romantic symphony', *Hiawatha*. The libretto, based on Longfellow's epic poem, was to be translated into French. Banville, Philoxène Boyer and others were approached, but turned the job down. Baudelaire unfortunately accepted, with the promise of 1,500 francs for the thankless task of reducing 800 lines of English poetry to 300 lines of French. Stoepel then requested a prose translation instead. For once, Baudelaire set to work immediately; but, for once, it was a great mistake: Stoepel left for London without having paid for the translation. *Hiawatha* was performed at Covent Garden; the composer returned to New York and Baudelaire never heard from him again. All that remained were two manuscripts (eventually published in 1971) and a reworked fragment – 'Le Calumet de paix' ('The Peace-Pipe') – which appeared in the *Revue contemporaine*.[18]

In his letter to Sainte-Beuve on June 14, 1858, Baudelaire mentioned that one of the pleasures which allowed him to forget the cruelty of life was dining with his 'old mistress'. For Jeanne Duval, life had lost none of its cruelty. Paralysis was gradually taking over her body and she was admitted for a time to the *maison de santé* Dubois.[19] Baudelaire paid for the bed: 'I don't want my paralytic to be evicted. *She* might like that, but *I* want them to keep her there until they've tried every cure.' Jeanne took advantage of Baudelaire's visit to Honfleur to try to extract twice the cost of her treatment. 'In her unhappy mind,' wrote Baudelaire, 'she dreamt up this ingenious way of obtaining the money twice over, without considering how easy it would be to check.' Even when she was out of danger, Jeanne was still an invalid. Baudelaire became her 'guardian and nurse', or her 'daddy', as he told Malassis. In the one and only letter we know of from Baudelaire to Jeanne, he tells her not to go out unaccompanied now that the streets are slippery. He calls her his 'dear girl' and promises to return to Paris as soon as possible to keep her amused. There is no term of affection at the end of the letter, but it was probably meant to be read by Ancelle, since it authorised Jeanne to receive the money.

In the summer of 1860, Jeanne was moved into the apartment at Neuilly,[20] along with Baudelaire's furniture, and the rent was to be paid in his name. On October 11, in a moment of discouragement, he told his mother:

In spite of that diabolical courage which has so often kept me going, I might die before you do. For the last year and a half, only the thought of Jeanne has held me back. (How would she manage after my death, since you'd have to use whatever money I left to pay off all my debts?)

The remark is interesting in that it suggests that Baudelaire felt a stronger sense of responsibility towards Jeanne than towards his mother.

In the meantime, a long-lost 'brother' of Jeanne had turned up. When Baudelaire moved in with his mistress, in order to spend 'less money and be nice to a sick woman', he complained that the man was spending every day with Jeanne from eight in the morning to eleven at night: it was impossible to get any privacy. He suggested that the brother, who was not in debt to the tune of 50,000 francs, should help support his invalid sister. The brother retorted that Baudelaire was presumably quite accustomed to being hard up, that he should never have accepted a responsibility he was unable to meet and that he, personally, had never saved up any money and was not to be counted on. 'I have often justly accused myself,' concluded Baudelaire, 'of being horribly selfish; but, my God! I never went as far as that.' Baudelaire then left Neuilly and returned to the Hôtel de Dieppe.

This brother must surely have been some former lover of Jeanne Duval. Baudelaire stayed away for several weeks, only to learn that after his departure, the man had put Jeanne in the hospital and sold some of her furniture and clothes. Baudelaire continued 'to support and console' his mistress, even after leaving for Belgium.

Jeanne Duval satisfied Baudelaire's passion for charity. Marie Daubrun left his less charitable affections unrequited; and Mme Sabatier had become an old friend. But Baudelaire also enjoyed distractions of a lighter variety. It was at the home of Mme Sabatier that he encountered Elisa Neri, who, in her curious career, had been an actress, an adventuress and a spy.

As she bade me farewell, your extraordinary Mme Nieri [*sic*] committed an act of childishness worthy of a foreigner. Before I had time to give the coachman my address, she took it into her head to pay the fare, and when I got angry, she said, 'It's too late, I've already paid!' And then, with a swiftness as extraordinary as herself, she darted, skirts and all, up the grand staircase of the hotel.

This Amazonian figure inspired Baudelaire with the sonnet, 'Sisina'. Just before it was published in the *Revue française*, Baudelaire asked the director of the review to send a copy to Mme Elisa Gnerri (*sic*), adding, 'That's the Lady who drinks Van Swieten water to the health of Orsini.'[21] (The water was a prophylactic and a remedy for syphilis, and Orsini the failed assassin of Napoleon III.) Baudelaire also thought of writing a story about a 'rational fool' and a 'beautiful' and 'seductive adventuress'.[22] Like Lola Montès, Elisa was the female type that appealed to the poet's mind and senses: both women were a far cry from society ladies, or even *demi-mondaines*, and were especially unrelated to the diaphanous heroines of George Sand.

One mystery remains in Baudelaire's love life: the *Paradis artificiels* and the poem, 'L'Héautontimorouménos' were dedicated to a woman named only as 'J.G.F.'[23] When he copied down the poem in an album, Baudelaire inscribed it 'to M . . . J . . . ', which might possibly stand for Marie-Jeanne. But Marie Daubrun seems to have had only one Christian name. Could 'J.G.F.' have been Jeanne herself? The dedication of *Les Paradis artificiels* is addressed to a woman who, 'though ill, is still active and alive within me, and who turns now her every glance to Heaven, that place of all transfigurations'. If Jeanne is present in these lines, she is indeed transfigured. When composing the dedication, Baudelaire noted that he wished it to be incomprehensible. If he was referring to the initials 'J.G.F.', then he was entirely successful; the text itself is perfectly clear:

> You will see in this *tableau* a grim and solitary walker, plunged in the moving current of the crowds, and sending his heart and thoughts to a distant Electra who not long ago was wiping his perspiring brow and *refreshing his lips, parched with fever*; and you will sense the gratitude of another Orestes whose nightmares you have often watched over, and whose terrible sleep you dispelled with a light, maternal hand.

This 'grim and solitary walker' was quick to reprove himself for his 'wretched character'.[24] His frequent self-examinations revealed laziness, procrastination, regret for lost time, the temptation to commit suicide and fear of an early death; but he also found within himself 'diabolical courage'. 'Pride' sustained him, and – with a little exaggeration – 'hate for all men'. 'I still wish for the power to dominate, to take revenge, to be impertinent with impunity – and other childish things.' Childishness and deliberate provocation aside, Baudelaire was kept alive by unshakeable faith in himself: obstacles and remorse only served to strengthen it.

Every once in a while, Baudelaire decided that he ought to be awarded the Cross of the Légion d'Honneur. 'I don't know if I ever told you,' he asked his mother on August 22, 1858, 'that there was talk of it last year, but that the trial of *Les Fleurs du Mal* delayed discussion of the matter.' The names on the honours list consoled him. Later, when preparing a vengeful preface for the second edition of the *Fleurs du Mal*, he wrote:

Someone brought up the question of that ridiculous *croix d'honneur* again. I hope very much that the preface to the *Fleurs* will put that forever beyond the bounds of possibility; and anyway, as I boldly answered a friend of mine who approached me with the matter: '*Twenty years ago* (I know what I'm saying is absurd), it would have been fine! But now I want to be an *exception*. Let them decorate every Frenchman *except me*. I shall never change my behaviour or my style. Instead of the Cross, they ought to give me *money*, *money*, and nothing but *money*. If the cross is worth 500 francs, let them give me 500 francs; if it's only worth twenty, they should give me twenty . . . My pride increases with my unhappiness.

On another occasion, Baudelaire applied for the directorship of a theatre subsidised by the Government. But he was simply pretending to play the social game. These trifling honours meant no more to him than his school prizes had done.

Two other more serious projects which never came to fruition were the essay on *Machiavelli and Condorcet*[25] and the study of dandyism in literature.[26] The latter provided one of the chapters of *The Painter of Modern Life*. The former, not unrelated to the essay on dandyism, would have been connected, through Condorcet, with the early days of François Baudelaire. The younger Baudelaire saw similarities between himself and Machiavelli – not so much the great political schemer as the hermit of San Casciano in retirement. Of an evening, having hunted the thrush, supervised the work of his wood-cutters and visited the inn where his friends were a butcher, a carpenter and two limekiln stokers, Machiavelli withdrew to his little house, donned his finest robes and entered the society of the great men of antiquity.

The first project at one time bore the title, *Literary Dandyism* or *Greatness without Conviction*.[27] For Baudelaire, to be a dandy was to achieve greatness even in the midst of pessimism and solitude – the sustenance of the strong.

CHAPTER 20

'That strange classic...'

1861–1864

By 1858, Poulet-Malassis had become a Paris publisher of good standing. He and De Broise, still printers at Alençon, had rented premises on the Left Bank, at number 9, rue des Beaux-Arts. It was there, on January 1, 1860 – the day on which Paris gained eight new arrondissements and swallowed up Montmartre – that Baudelaire signed a new contract for a second edition of *Les Fleurs du Mal, Les Paradis artificiels* and two volumes of critical essays which were eventually published after his death by Michel Lévy.

It was not long before Malassis and De Broise moved again, this time to the heart of the Paris publishing world on the Right Bank. Malassis had great plans for the new bookshop: 'The Realist painters are to execute ceilings and frescoes,' reported the *Revue anecdotique*. 'The names of Courbet, Amand Gautier, and others have been mentioned. People will be able to visit the shop as they do the Librairie Nouvelle, to browse and look at the new books. It will be a centre where people can meet and hear the latest news.'[1]

Malassis did not share Baudelaire's allergy to Realism. He was the publisher of the militant Duranty, and of his co-religionist, Champfleury, one of whose books – *Les Amis de la Nature* – sported a frontispiece designed by Gustave Courbet. Other Realist painters were put to work on a series of medallions to be placed above the elegant oak bookcases. Each medallion depicted one of the house authors – Monselet, Hugo, Gautier, Champfleury, Banville, Baudelaire, Asselineau, etc.

Baudelaire's portrait, however, was not entrusted to a Realist, but to a former pupil of Ingres – Alexandre Lafond. It was based on a recent photograph by Nadar.

It shows Baudelaire's face at the age of forty – a powerful face, with deep hollows around the mouth and under the eyes. Clean-shaven chin, cheeks slightly flushed, a balding brow, hair long and wavy, pushed back. His alarming features are those of a tragic actor and of a priest who celebrates black masses. The haughty expression is enhanced by the corners of his mouth which fall in sharp folds, and by the wide-open eyes, ironical and searching.

The almost life-size head stands out against a greenish background which heightens its impressive gloom.[2]

When his business collapsed a few years later, Malassis would keep only one of the medallions – Lafond's rendition of Baudelaire. It was sold after the publisher's death along with his other possessions, a token of this friendship for the sake of which Malassis blithely took the road to ruin.

By moving into larger premises, he was taking a considerable risk. De Broise prudently dissolved the partnership and retained sole possession of the printing shop in Alençon. Even before the brothers-in-law parted – on cordial terms – Malassis had decided to use a different printer for the second edition of *Les Fleurs du Mal*. From the end of 1858, Baudelaire had been sending him poems as he wrote them. 'I'm beginning to think,' he wrote in a letter accompanying 'Le Possédé', 'that instead of six *fleurs*, I'll do twenty.' The number steadily increased until, at the end of January or beginning of February 1861, the second edition appeared with the following indication on the title page: 'Enlarged with thirty-five new poems, and adorned with a portrait of the author designed and engraved by Bracquemond.'

Félix Bracquemond was one of the engravers employed by Malassis for the decoration of the new bookshop; but the choice of Bracquemond for *Les Fleurs du Mal* soon proved to be more than a little unfortunate. Baudelaire had long had in mind an allegorical frontispiece for his book, though it had never occurred to him to entrust the job to Bracquemond.[3] When leafing through an illustrated essay on *danses macabres*, he had come across a sixteenth-century engraving which appealed to him immediately: 'An arborescent skeleton, with legs and ribs forming the trunk, arms stretched out in a cross bearing leaves and buds, and sheltering several rows of poisonous plants in little pots placed at intervals as in a gardener's greenhouse.' The plants were supposed to represent the different vices of mankind. This was the idea on which Bracquemond was invited to work. After two disappointing attempts, Malassis sent the artist a tracing of the plate, along with a few suggestions. Bracquemond brought his third attempt to show the poet, who sent it on to Malassis with the following remarks:

Here's Bracquemond's monster. I told him it was good. I didn't know what to say, I was so amazed. The skeleton is *walking,* and it's leaning on a *fan* of branches which *comes out of the ribs* instead of *coming from the arms.* What was the use of the tracing from Langlois [the author of the essay on *danses macabres*]? I shall not permit it to appear, and if I upset you too much, as one might a child who wants to eat what he's paid for, I shall do what I can to console you and make up for it in some way.

A few days later, still in a rage, Baudelaire decided that Bracquemond should simply copy the picture in Langlois's book: '*Nothing* or the *Servile Copy* of Langlois's macabre picture.' The idea was eventually abandoned, or rather shelved. The allegorical frontispiece was replaced with the engraved portrait of Baudelaire. But Malassis was determined to get his frontispiece. After the publication of the second edition, he tried to resurrect the project for the luxury edition he was hoping to produce in time for the 1862 Universal Exhibition in London; but Baudelaire stood his ground. Bracquemond wrote to Champfleury: 'I've just done the skeleton-tree for the fifth time; but that's still not it!' He asked Champfleury to lend him Langlois's book and Champfleury replied:

Have you thought about doing a hunchbacked skeleton? Baudelaire would probably subscribe to that idea.

A skeleton shitting in some corner of a wood would be something rather new.

Baudelaire, with a Greek skullcap on his head and a beautiful courtesan on his arm, could surprise the skeleton as it wipes its arse. The shamefaced skeleton would lower its eyes, and this frontispiece ... would, I am sure, satisfy the desires of Malassis ...

P.S. – I forgot – but you would have found it at the tip of your graver – a few Fleurs du Mal poking the buttocks of the poor skeleton as it answers the call of nature.

Baudelaire later discovered someone in Belgium who – so he thought – was capable of producing the impossible frontispiece. In the end, his preference for Félicien Rops was no more justified than his hostility to Bracquemond.

The second edition of *Les Fleurs du Mal* was published in a run of 1,500 copies. The foreman of the printing house graciously offered Baudelaire a special copy printed on choice paper. At first, Baudelaire refused: 'I didn't ask for that. I don't want a special edition ...' The poor man was completely thrown by Baudelaire's irritation[4] – particularly since the poet had asked him to print some copies on strong vellum. It was easier for Baudelaire to ask than to receive.

The 1861 edition is an original edition in its own right. Not only is it larger than the 1857 edition by about a third, but the poems are also arranged in a different order and their meaning is often affected by their altered context. Moreover, to the original five sections of the first edition – 'Spleen et Idéal', 'Fleurs du Mal', 'Révolte', 'Le Vin', 'La Mort', these too in a different order – Baudelaire added one more: the 'Tableaux parisiens'.

Between the two editions, the book had taken an even more pessimistic direction. It ended now with a long poem, 'Le Voyage', which announced the final voyage in a solemn but intimate tone:

> O Mort, vieux capitaine, il est temps! levons l'ancre!

Only one hope remained:

> Plonger au fond du gouffre, Enfer ou Ciel, qu'importe?
> Au fond de l'Inconnu pour trouver du *nouveau*!

Sure of his genius, but as severe with himself as he was with others, Baudelaire claimed to be satisfied with the collection: 'For the first time in my life, I'm almost content. The book is *almost all right*, and it will remain as proof of my disgust and loathing of all things.'[5]

The Ministry of the Interior remained on the alert. It obtained a copy of the new edition and produced the following report:

> Though the second edition of *Les Fleurs du Mal* by Charles Baudelaire contains a certain number of poems remarkable for the strangeness and licence of their thought and style, this magistrate [the Chief Justice] has found no clear evidence of any offence.
> I feel therefore, with M. Chaix d'Est-Ange, that we should in this case refrain from initiating proceedings the outcome of which would be uncertain and which would not fail to give the work in question some undesirable publicity.

Baudelaire knew nothing of the inquiry conducted by the Ministry. He would have been annoyed to see his *Fleurs du Mal* referred to as a '*brochure*'. 'The only praise I seek for this book', he told Vigny in December 1861, 'is that people understand that it isn't just an album, and that it has a beginning and an end.' Even enlarged, the book does in fact have only 319 pages.

Mme Aupick's reaction came rather late in the day and was not exactly what her son had hoped to hear: 'You're always armed to stone me with the crowd,' he wrote. 'That all goes back to my childhood, as you know.

How do you always manage to be for your son the opposite of a *friend*, except where money's involved?' Mme Aupick had apparently passed on the opinion of the local priest. Baudelaire replied:

> As for M. de Cardine, that's a serious affair, but not at all in the way you think. Amidst all my other sorrows, I don't want some priest coming along to vie with me in my old Mother's mind, and I shall set things straight, if I can and if I have the strength. That man's behaviour is monstrous and unaccountable. Burning books is not something that's done any more, except by lunatics who want to watch some paper going up in flames. And I, who stupidly deprived myself of a valuable copy, just to be nice to him and give him something that people have been trying to get hold of for three years! ... And he didn't even understand that the book is based on a Catholic idea!

To judge by reviews, the second edition was hardly noticed, even though the author had very carefully organised the distribution of press copies. *Les Fleurs du Mal* was sent to several British periodicals, including *The Times*, *Blackwood's Magazine* and *The Edinburgh Review*. Baudelaire's thoroughness was rewarded the following year with an enthusiastic article in *The Spectator* by his English disciple, Charles Algernon Swinburne.[6]

The *Revue anecdotique*, in which Malassis now had a hand, praised the 'grandiose dignity' with which the poet 'tackles the most daring effects'.[7] Other reviewers were less obliging. In the *Revue britannique*, Amédée Pichot shuddered at the 'bloody phantoms of the phantasmagorical poet'. The *Figaro*, having contributed to Baudelaire's downfall in 1857, was back on the warpath. Their critic recognised Baudelaire's 'vast, sometimes very lofty intelligence', whilst reproaching him with his 'umbilical', macabre poetry and its creation of 'an unholy mixture of pagan corruption and excessive, Catholic austerity'. In *La Causerie* – the review in which Baudelaire had published 'Le Cygne' and 'A une Madone' – Eugène Moret regretted the fact that 'Never did a man more violent sing of more worthless things in a more impossible style.' 'What a tragedy it is,' he went on, 'that M. Baudelaire will not take himself seriously, though, between you and me, that would be no simple matter.'

From this journalistic wasteland, only two articles of any value emerged – one in favour, one against.

Armand de Pontmartin was a conservative critic who, in 1856, had made some disparaging comments about Baudelaire's preface to the *Histoires extraordinaires*. Baudelaire held the United States responsible for the death of Edgar Allan Poe and France for the suicide of Gérard de Nerval;

but, retorted Pontmartin, did not those orphans, 'who complain of their abandonment, begin by abandoning themselves?'[8] Baudelaire may well have felt that he himself was included among those 'children of fantasy and dream'. In 1860, when adding an obituary note on Thomas De Quincey to the *Paradis artificiels*, he denounced 'the great madness of morality' which 'usurps ... the place of pure literature': 'Pontmartins and other drawing-room preachers are cluttering up American and English newspapers as much as ours.' The publication of the 1861 edition of *Les Fleurs du Mal* gave Pontmartin a chance to retaliate.[9] Without wishing to be as insulting as Baudelaire had been, the critic accused him of having a perverted sense of good and evil, and of turning love into 'something disreputable'. There was nothing really new in all this. However, Pontmartin's article, which appeared in the *Revue des Deux Mondes* – the review which had accepted some *Fleurs du Mal* in 1855 – highlighted the rift between those who, like Baudelaire, called for the autonomy of poetry and those who stood for bourgeois values in literature. Pontmartin's conclusion was very revealing: 'What sort of society or literature would adopt M. Charles Baudelaire as its poet?'

Pontmartin also pilloried Leconte de Lisle – one of the 'masters of that learned verse of voluntary isolation'. The offended poet gave a firm reply in the *Revue européenne* on December 1, 1861, denouncing this 'indecent and ridiculous passion for moral proselytism' and defending *Les Fleurs du Mal*: 'The whole work had a strange and powerful appearance, a new conception, indivisible in its rich and dark diversity, stamped with the strong seal of long meditation.' Baudelaire himself had only recently been singing the praises of Leconte de Lisle in the *Revue fantaisiste* on August 15. In this way, the publication of the 1861 *Fleurs du Mal* brought together those poets who waved the flag of *l'art pour l'art* – Gautier, Banville, Leconte de Lisle and Baudelaire – all of whom, to a greater or lesser degree, shared the same publisher: Poulet-Malassis.

The press did little to bring Baudelaire to the attention of the general public; but the poet found fame in literary circles, where, fortunately for him, he still had quite a few enemies. This is how Asselineau began the chapter of his biography entitled, 'Last Years in Paris':

When the second edition of *Les Fleurs du Mal* appeared, one might say that Baudelaire had conquered fame. The scathing and unjust criticism that met the book when it first appeared fell silent at this second coming. The author and his work had profited from those preliminary attacks which consolidate success by opposition. Those who saw Baudelaire at that point in his life, smiling, bright, still youthful under his long and greying hair, were able to detect the beneficial and calming influence of passing time and favour gained. Enemies laid down their arms; new, young friendships came his way. When, at the end of the day, he went down onto the boulevard, he found all hands offered as he passed, and he shook them all, calculating his exquisite politeness to fit the degree of acquaintance or familiarity.

With the *Fleurs du Mal* of 1861, Baudelaire became one of the leaders of the new generation of poets, as Sainte-Beuve noted, a little reluctantly. (Sainte-Beuve had not reviewed the book): 'When I read some new verses ... or even a selection of poems in a newspaper, I think almost immediately, "Ah! this is a bit of Musset" or "This is some more Lamartine (not quite so common)"' or, he continued, ' "some Hugo, some Gautier, Banville, or Leconte de Lisle, or even Baudelaire"'.[10]

Younger poets like Henri Cantel or Albert Glatigny dedicated poems to Baudelaire. In 1863, Albert Mérat wrote a sonnet, the first and last stanzas of which give a clear indication of Baudelaire's influence and legend:[11]

> O Poète amoureux des choses truculentes,
> Des breuvages visqueux et des cadavres verts,
> Et qui veux, pour trouver les viandes succulentes,
> Les sentir sous la dent ondoyantes de vers ...
>
> Poète opiacé, tu donnes la nausée,
> Pourtant quel art viril et quelle lyre osée,
> Si tu voulais chanter sans charogne à la clé.*

Another disciple, who later managed to make quite a living out of his encounter with Baudelaire, was Léon Cladel, a novelist from the Quercy region in the South. In the summer of 1861, Baudelaire discovered the manuscript of a short story, *Aux amours éternelles*, which the young writer had left in the offices of the *Revue fantaisiste*. The master offered to help his young disciple correct the proofs and clean up the text, which contained 'half a dozen malapropisms and a few expressions from beyond the Loire'.[12] The story was published with a dedication to Baudelaire, who recommended the author to the *Revue européenne* as a writer who might offer them some original work. In the meantime, Poulet-Malassis had been given the manu-

---

* 'O poet, lover of colourful things, / Of viscous brews and green cadavers, / You who find your meat most sweet, / When it sways with maggots under your teeth ...

Opium poet, you inspire with sickness, / And yet what virile art and daring lyre were yours / If you sang in a less putrescent key.'

script of Cladel's *Martyrs ridicules* – a novel about the disillusionment of youth. Baudelaire was asked to write the preface, which was published by the *Revue fantaisiste*. In keeping with the theme of the novel, the preface was an all-out attack on the different species of young person – even on youth itself: 'I experience, in my meetings with youth, the same feeling of discomfort as when I run into a forgotten school friend who has become a stockbroker and who is not prevented by the intervening twenty or thirty years from calling me "*tu*" or from tapping me on the belly. In short, I feel that I'm in bad company.' According to Malassis, who published the novel at the end of 1861, Baudelaire's contribution was not confined to the preface:

> On my recommendation, Baudelaire took an interest in the boy, though not for very long. This Southerner, like so many of his compatriots, was a red herring. The fact remains that *Les Martyrs ridicules* were *entirely rearranged and revised on Baudelaire's instructions*, and I suspect that their collaboration went even further than that.[13]

It has so far been impossible to determine the extent of Cladel's debt to Baudelaire. Certain sentences that seem to show the hand of Baudelaire might be due simply to the disciple's admiration for his master and to the poet's influence on the first draft of the novel, which may date from 1857.

Cladel, whom Baudelaire never mentioned again in writing, made the most of his rather brief encounter – notably in a short story, *Dux*, which appeared in 1879. He depicted the poet in his room at the Hôtel de Dieppe, surrounded by the dictionaries he was using. As Banville pointed out, it is difficult to imagine Baudelaire lugging these cumbersome volumes about from one hotel to the next. At the Hôtel Pimodan, all he had were about thirty books, placed in a cupboard along with his bottles of Rhine wine and his emerald-green glasses.

> As for the lexicons, dictionaries and encyclopedias, and all the other bits and pieces with which it has pleased the legend [for which Banville was partly responsible!] to surround Baudelaire, I must say that one might have searched without ever finding any trace of these . . . Baudelaire did indeed have every lexicon – but in his head, in his vast brain, and he never cluttered up his apartment with them.[14]

The only dictionary that Baudelaire is known to have possessed is a French-English dictionary published in 1846, which the translator of Poe scoured in vain for certain words peculiar to the southern United States.[15]

Banville's assertion was later confirmed by Félicien Rops:[16]

I lived with Baudelaire for two years, and often served him as a secretary. I never once saw him consult a dictionary. He didn't have any, and didn't want to have any. On several occasions, he gave me his opinion on the matter, saying, 'A man who looks up a word in a dictionary is like a conscript who, upon receiving the order to fire, looks for a cartridge in his pouch.'

Rops added that when Malassis wanted to tease Baudelaire, he used to accuse him of having a copy of the Academy's dictionary hidden in his mattress. Either Cladel was telling a story, or, more likely, Baudelaire had been pulling his leg.

Cladel was an exception. Baudelaire usually met his friends and acquaintances in the cafés where he sometimes went to work. Next door to the Hôtel de Dieppe was the Taverne St Austin where, as he told Vigny, the 'beer and stout are excellent and inexpensive'.[17] Near the Tuileries was the Café Robespierre, later knocked down to make way for the Avenue de l'Opéra. It was there that the chronicler Philibert Audebrand saw the poet:

Grown old, jaded, and heavy, though he was still thin, the white-haired eccentric with the perpetually clean-shaven face looked less like a poet of bitter-tasting pleasures and more like a priest from Saint-Sulpice. He was still in the habit of acting the misanthrope, and would sit alone on a stool, ordering a mug of beer and a pipe which he stuffed with tobacco, lit, and smoked, all without saying a word the whole evening ... Sometimes a novice would approach him with much ceremony, either to pay his respects or to read him some verses. Invariably, the smoker, retaining the altitude [sic] of an imperturbable Oriental, would allow the novice to continue, and stop drinking and smoking only after he had made a proper fool of his supplicant. Once, thinking to please him, one of them brought him the latest Figaro, in which there was an article on him.

'Eh! Monsieur,' cried Baudelaire with every mark of disdain, 'who asked you for that paper? I'll have you know that I never so much as glance at that rubbish.'

And he went back to his pipe.[18]

Charles Yriarte left a portrait of Baudelaire from the same period.

Baudelaire had the most courteous manners. He was a man of perfect poise, and when you talked with him, you felt that you were in the presence of something full-bodied and strong. But the writer was silent and reserved when speaking to someone with whom he was not intimately acquainted. At such times, he said very little, speaking quietly and slowly, carefully articulating his words, polishing his phrases, and rounding out his sentences. He read as others officiate – a little pompously, but with uncommon perfection, and it was a delight to hear him read his sonnets, some of which are masterpieces of style ... There was something of the priest and the artist in him, some strange and inexplicable thing rather connected with the nature of his talent and his extravagant habits.[19]

Baudelaire also frequented cafés further to the north, beyond the *grands boulevards*. The Brasserie des Fleurs was at number 9, Boulevard de Clichy, opposite the Montmartre cemetery. Its owner, Gabriel de Gonet, was also in his finer hours a publisher and a writer. Here is his description of the man who loved perfection in all things:

Baudelaire was passionately fond of billiards, and played with extreme elegance, holding the cue by his fingertips as if it were a quill pen, and constantly pushing back his muslin cuffs.

One day when he was playing around on an empty billiards table, he stubbornly kept trying to achieve an almost impossible cannon, and in his gentle anger at not succeeding, said: 'I've been repeating my attempt for ten minutes now but to no avail. If it had been a hemistich, I would long since have thrown my pen away.' At last he succeeded, and was as happy as a child.[20]

Baudelaire spent most of his evenings now on the Right Bank, where publishers, newspapers and reviews had their headquarters. The Casino Cadet – the Folies-Bergère of the time – stood on the road which led up from the Boulevards to Montmartre.[21] The casino had been known to regale its customers with extracts from Wagner's *Lohengrin*,[22] but on most nights it rang to the cries of revellers and cancan dancers. Baudelaire visited it with Champfleury and Constantin Guys. Champfleury would indulge his taste for practical jokes, and Guys would make sketches from life. Baudelaire 'wandered about looking sinister among the girls, who found him scary', according to Sainte-Beuve's secretary, Jules Troubat: 'There, he would expound literary and artistic theories. One evening, he told me about a girl who, on being asked if she knew his works (he did not tell her who he was), answered that she only read Musset!'[23] Baudelaire's reaction is not hard to imagine. The Lyons critic, Armand Fraisse, having rashly declared his admiration for Musset, received the following reply:

Except at the age of first communion, in other words at that age when anything connected with prostitutes and silken ladders looks like a religion, I have never been able to suffer *that master of popinjays*, who has the impertinence of a spoilt child, who invokes heaven and hell for the sake of some restaurant adventure, his murky stream of mistakes in grammar and prosody, and, finally, his complete inability to understand the labour by which musing becomes a work of art.[24]

In this 'cancan palace', Baudelaire would pass among the diners and the waltzing couples, looking solemn and superior. At other times, seated alone at a table, drinking beer, he watched 'the macabre procession of blurry-eyed revellers and pretty girls, their cheeks flushed with consumption'. Asked by Charles Monselet what he was doing, he replied, 'My dear friend, I'm watching the death's-heads pass!'[25]

For all his grave and priestly air, Baudelaire's pastimes were not entirely monastic. A notebook he used between July 1861 and November 1863[26] contains not only lists of works to be written, visits to be made, timetables and accounts, but also some useful addresses. First in alphabetical order comes Adèle, at number 9, Boulevard Saint-Denis – perhaps the girl whom Manet sketched for the poet in 1865;[27] then Aglaé, Anna, Bathilde, Blanche – the list is very long; a Rachel, whose address is that of the house adjoining the Casino Cadet, and other ladies of dubious means, most of them without a surname. There is nothing to show that Baudelaire knew all the women in the list, nor anything to indicate the sense in which that verb should be understood.

Occasionally, the names, addresses and accounts give way to longer notes. One of these describes the style in which Baudelaire would like to see Agathe dressed: 'Earrings, necklaces, bracelets, rings. A *décolleté* dress, arms bare. No crinoline.' On the same page one finds the name Debauve, one of the great French chocolate makers: perhaps this was to be Agathe's reward for satisfying the sartorial tastes of her temporary companion?

> Dis-moi, ton coeur parfois s'envole-t-il, Agathe,
> Loin du noir océan de l'immonde cité...?

But this Agathe with her secret longings to fly far away from 'the black ocean of the squalid city' appears in a poem published long before in 1855 and, unlike the Agathe in Baudelaire's notebook, she conjures up 'L'innocent paradis plein de plaisirs furtifs'.

Another of the notebook's mysteries is the name Féline. Baudelaire's prose poem, 'L'Horloge', which first appeared in 1857, mentions a woman with this name and there is also a copy of the 1861 *Fleurs du Mal* inscribed by the author 'to my very dear Féline'. Was Féline Jeanne Duval, as Jacques

Crépet suggested, or another woman?[28] By the 1860s, Jeanne was unlikely to inspire comparison with a cat.

Finally, among the other names, that of Louise stands out, recalling as it does the Louise Villedieu mentioned in *My Heart Laid Bare*:

> All the bourgeois fools who incessantly utter the words, 'immoral, immorality, morality in art', and other silly things, remind me of Louise Villedieu, a five-franc whore who, when accompanying me one day to the Louvre – where she had never been – started blushing and covering her face; and pulling all the time at my sleeve, she asked, before the immortal statues and paintings, how people could put such obscenities on public display.[29]

Baudelaire knew a third Louise in 1863 and she was rather more important in his life than the other two. Her poet friend wrote to several theatre critics, recommending his protégée, Louise Deschamps, who was to make her début at the Odéon on May 16 in the leading role of Racine's *Andromaque*. The letter Nestor Roqueplan received was embossed with the letters 'L. D.' 'Our friend Sainte-Beuve,' wrote Baudelaire, 'joins me in recommending this lady to you.' Sainte-Beuve had indeed sent the actress along to the *éminence grise* of the Parisian stage, Achille Ricourt, with a letter containing the interesting disclosure that she was the heroine of Feydeau's novel, *Catherine d'Overmeire*. To judge by the novel, Louise had had an unhappy childhood; she had been seduced by an older man and, with more courage than talent, was attempting to extricate herself from a difficult situation. It is quite possible that Feydeau, Sainte-Beuve and Baudelaire all took an interest in the actress independently of their relations, or, for that matter, of their charitable concerns. Gautier, who no doubt also received a letter of recommendation from Baudelaire, praised 'this pale, fair young woman' in the *Moniteur*. Louise was another Marie Daubrun, with her 'beautiful arms', 'her charming hands' and even 'well-expressed accents of motherly love'[30] – a role which perhaps came naturally to her? Gautier advised her, however, to lower her sights and to leave the dizzy heights of tragedy for the humbler realm of drama. Louise heeded this piece of advice only too well and sank to the depths of vaudeville. Baudelaire might have seen her again a few years later in Brussels. A Mlle Deschamps was playing there in October 1864 at the Théâtre Royal du Parc in a play entitled, *A Straw Hat from Italy*.[31]

In Brussels, Baudelaire's companion – his last mistress, in fact – was a woman known only by her first name, Berthe.[32] He gave her a poem, 'Les Yeux de Berthe', originally written for Jeanne, who may have used this as a stage name in the early 1840s. With her sharp, almost masculine features and brown-black hair, Berthe did in fact look much the same as Jeanne had done twenty years before. Baudelaire gave her the poem along with two drawings he had done of her, the first draft of the prose poem, 'La Soupe et les Nuages', and the following message: 'To a horrid little fool, with the regards of a big fool who was looking for a girl to adopt and who had studied neither the character of Berthe nor the law on adoption.' When, with Malassis, he was putting together the later collection of poems, *Les Epaves*, in which 'Les Yeux de Berthe' was included, the following note was written, though it was afterwards scratched out on the proofs – obviously this was no platonic relationship: 'We think we have heard of this Mlle Berthe. She doubtless has virtues (all except faith), but she possesses in particular that virtue which is the opposite of chastity. True enough, poets have their own special glasses and telescopes which allow them to see what other men cannot.' Baudelaire's last mistress disappears from view after 1864. This, and the photograph, are all we know of her.

'Why don't you talk to me a bit about marriage like everyone else's mamma?' Baudelaire wrote on November 4, 1859. Mme Aupick had little need of prompting. Whilst Charles was enjoying a few *'plaisirs furtifs'*, she was dreaming of finding a wife for him, forgetting that her son was syphilitic. She apparently told Laure Dulong – a very young girl she knew in Honfleur: 'I regret the fact that my son does not wish to marry; I should very much like it if he were to become your Petrarch.'[33] Mme Aupick had not of course seen her son's letter to Madame Marie in 1852: 'Like Petrarch, I shall immortalise my Laura.' Of the two clichés, Baudelaire's was the more accurate: Petrarch never married.

Neither did Mme Aupick consider Baudelaire's opinion of young girls as she daydreamed about the happy couple spending their weekends at Honfleur. 'The young girl. What she really is,' Baudelaire noted in *My Heart Laid Bare*. 'A little fool and a little bitch; the greatest imbecility joined to the greatest depravity. There is in the young girl all the turpitude of the hooligan and the schoolboy.' Baudelaire preferred prostitutes and some ladies – the wives of Edouard Manet and Paul Meurice, who, as they showed during his final illness, had real affection for this strange, seductive and unhappy being.

Edouard Manet was mentioned only in passing in the article Baudelaire published in the *Revue anecdotique* for April 1862 on painters and engravers.[34] In the second version, which appeared in *Le Boulevard*, there was praise for Manet's forthcoming 'Spanish' paintings. (Baudelaire must by then have paid a visit to the artist's studio.) The two men became firm friends. Manet twice loaned Baudelaire large sums of money, and when the poet was in Brussels, ran errands for him in Paris. Baudelaire also defended Manet against a prominent art critic, Théophile Thoré, who accused him of imitating El Greco and Goya. In May 1865, Manet complained that people were laughing at his work. Baudelaire tried to cheer him up:

> So now I have to talk to you about yourself again. I have to try and prove to you what you're worth. What you're asking for is really stupid. *People laugh at you; jokes annoy you;* nobody recognises your talent, etc., etc. Do you think you're the first man ever to be in that position? Are you a greater genius than Chateaubriand or Wagner? They were laughed at, weren't they? and they didn't die of it. And in case I fill you with too much pride, I shall tell you that both those men are models, each in his own genre and in a world that is very rich, and that *you are but the leader in the decrepitude of your art.* I hope you won't hold it against me that I treat you so casually. You know how fond of you I am.

Manet painted or drew his friend several times. In 1862, he included him in the crowded *Musique aux Tuileries.* In the middle distance, Baudelaire can be seen talking with two other men, one of whom is the Inspector of Museums, Baron Taylor. The poet wears a silk top hat with broad, flat brims, 'elegant, very carefully designed, splaying out at the bottom, and skilfully drawn out to taper off towards the upper board'.[35]

> This type of hat, which was made according to his instructions, and for which he had a special liking, was to be the despair of Baudelaire in Brussels. He never managed to find a Brussels hatter capable of making an exact copy of it. After various unfruitful attempts, he decided to have his hats sent from Paris. He bought them at Camus's ... where Eugène Delacroix, Théophile Gautier, Louis Bouilhet, the sculptor Etex, the publisher Poulet-Malassis and other celebrities also equipped themselves. Camus, with innocent pride, called himself the 'Hatter of the Literati'.

Manet also painted the picture known as *Baudelaire's Mistress.* Jeanne Duval is shown from the front, 'looking like an idol and a doll... Across the breadth of the canvas ripples the enormous and paradoxical expanse of a summer dress with white and violet stripes.' So Félix Fénéon described the portrait which he commented on with the following lines from Baudelaire's satirical poem, 'Le Monstre': 'Tu n'es certes pas, ma très chère, / Ce que

Veuillot nomme un tendron ... Tu n'es plus fraîche, ma très chère, / Ma vieille infante!'*

What sinister unkindness there is in Manet's painting! And how it contrasts with the glittering and vibrant portrait, painted that same year, of Lola de Valence! The second picture inspired Baudelaire with this quatrain which was affixed to the frame when the painting was first displayed:

> Entre tant de beautés que partout on peut voir,
> Je comprends bien, amis, que le désir balance;
> Mais on voit scintiller en Lola de Valence
> Le charme inattendu d'un bijou rose et noir.†

Emile Zola later claimed that Lola de Valence was 'famous because of Charles Baudelaire's quatrain, which was booed and slated as much as the painting itself'.

No artist did more than Manet to please Baudelaire, or give form to the ideas expressed in *The Painter of Modern Life*; but Baudelaire himself never publicly recognised Manet's originality. Baudelaire's last *Salon*, admittedly, dates from 1859, but, with a few minor exceptions, nothing in his published or personal writings gives any hint that Manet was ever put on the same pedestal as Delacroix or Constantin Guys. Those who think that biographies should be hagiographies might take comfort in the fact that, by 1863, Baudelaire was no longer at his peak and that Manet was just starting on his career. As for the man himself, Baudelaire liked him very much. Just before his stroke, he had some copies of *Les Epaves* smuggled through to Paris. One was meant for Manet – 'the last man [after Guys] for whom he felt passionate friendship'.[36]

Baudelaire had continued to write on Delacroix – an article on his murals at Saint-Sulpice, for which the artist thanked him, and, in 1862, a review of an exhibition at which Baudelaire was delighted to rediscover *The Death of Sardanapalus*:

> Many times, my dreams were filled with the magnificent shapes which move in that vast painting which is itself as wonderful as a dream. To see the *Sardanapalus* again is to rediscover youth. How far back into the past the contemplation of that picture casts us! Back to that marvellous

---

* 'You're certainly not, my dearest darling, / What Veuillot likes to call a sapling ... / You're no longer very fresh, my darling, / My old infanta!'

† 'With so many beauties to be seen everywhere, / It's understandable, friends, that desire hesitates; / But one sees all a-sparkle in Lola de Valence / The unexpected charm of a pink and black jewel.'

age when artists like Devéria, Gros, Delacroix, Boulanger, Bonington, etc. were reigning jointly – the great Romantic school – beauty, grace, charm, and the sublime!

The same nostalgia had already been apparent in the third part of Baudelaire's *Théophile Gautier* in 1859:

> No French writer who fervently desires the glory of his land can, without a feeling of pride or regret, cast his eyes back to that period of fertile crisis when Romantic literature was flourishing so vigorously.

And also in the poem which serves as the preface to *Les Epaves* in 1866 – 'Le Coucher du soleil romantique'. Nostalgia was perhaps not the surest road to innovation in art.

Delacroix died on August 13, 1863. Baudelaire attended the funeral. Starting on September 2, in three separate issues of *L'Opinion nationale*, he published *The Work and Life of Eugène Delacroix*. It contained several long quotations from his earlier study and was certainly a great eulogy; but it also betrayed a hint of bitterness.[37] Delacroix had not responded to Baudelaire's admiration in the way the poet wished and, for fifteen years, had persistently kept him at a distance.

Delacroix had been an occasional visitor to the home of the Lejosnes, whose salon was also frequented by Bracquemond, Manet, Barbey d'Au-revilly and Delacroix's favourite critic, Théophile Silvestre.[38] Later, when Baudelaire was in Brussels, Major Lejosne, along with Manet, became the poet's factotum in Paris. Baudelaire must have had great confidence in Lejosne to write him this letter on January 1, 1863:

> A while back, one of my friends told a monk from Solesmes that I might one day go and visit the monastery to be in retreat; and the fine fellow replied, 'If he comes, my God! we shall receive him. We'd even receive convicts.' At first sight it seems absurd that my name should be known to a monk, and that this monk should think me worthy of the galleys; but I discovered the explanation. – Raymond Brucker[39] had been to Solesmes a few days before.

The friend who had told the monk of Baudelaire's impending visit to the monastery was the young poet, Villiers de l'Isle-Adam, later to become one of the leading figures of the Symbolist movement. Villiers was a fervent admirer of *Les Fleurs du Mal*. Apologising for his inebriated state during an evening spent with Baudelaire and Gustave Mathieu, he went on to regret his consequent inability to tell Mathieu what Baudelaire had 'created':

'Baudelaire is the most powerful,' he should have replied, 'and therefore the most *whole* of all the despairing thinkers of this wretched century! He strikes, he lives, he *sees*! Too bad for those who can't *see*!'[40] It is interesting to note that Rimbaud's famous description of Baudelaire as a seer (a *voyant*) was not without precedent.

Villiers was also a musician: he read Baudelaire's *Richard Wagner* with enthusiasm and set some of his poems to music. One evening, a friend of his remembered, he 'improvised a prelude of solemn tenderness and began to sing "La Mort des amants". Never have I heard anything more soothing, more morbid, or more sweetly ethereal than that marvellous, simple sonnet set to the marvellous, simple music ... The tone and intonation of the singing voice perfectly matched the music and the words, and we were struck to the very heart.'

Baudelaire and his young admirer also sketched out a playlet based on the poem, 'Le Vin de l'assassin' – obviously another incarnation of *The Drunkard*; and, on the same theme, Villiers wrote a prose poem, 'L'Ivrogne'.

Baudelaire's own prose poems represent the last great phase of his creative life. With the *Fleurs du Mal* of 1861, he had reached the limits of verse poetry. To express the modernity of the sprawling metropolis and its mysterious existence, new forms were needed – 'a poetic prose, musical, but without rhythm or rhyme, flexible and uneven enough to adapt itself to the lyrical impulses of the soul, to the undulations of reverie, to the jolts of the mind'. This 'obsessive ideal', wrote Baudelaire, springs 'from the frequenting of enormous cities' and from 'the intersecting of their innumerable connections'.[41] Baudelaire had been pursuing a similar ideal since 1855 and the Fontainebleau *Festschrift* in which he published two prose poems, 'Le Crépuscule du soir' and 'La Solitude'; but it was after writing the last great poems of *Les Fleurs du Mal* that he turned more fully to the *poëme en prose* – a genre which allowed for endless permutations and which became his last laboratory of poetic experiment. The search continued in Belgium, where Baudelaire also returned to the older forms of satirical poetry which he had practised and enjoyed in his youth. In verse, the circle was complete; in prose, the possibilities were limitless.

Since the end of 1861, Baudelaire had been trying to interest Arsène Houssaye in this new poetic form. Houssaye, who had himself tried his hand at prose poetry, was then the literary editor of *La Presse*. He could not decide whether or not to accept the poems and suspected Baudelaire of having excluded him from the anthology being edited by Eugène Crépet. Hope came in the form of Pierre-Jules Hetzel – the great defender of French publishing against the menace of pirated editions from Belgium. Hetzel wanted to publish the poems as a book, but without depriving Baudelaire of the fruits of publication in a periodical, since this would also provide some good advertising. And so he wrote to Houssaye:

> Baudelaire is an old friend of mine – that means nothing, since I've got too many friends – but he's without a doubt the most original prose writer and the most distinctive poet of our time. No paper can afford to put off that strange classic of unclassical things.[42]

Hetzel's remarkable expression decided the matter: Houssaye did as requested, and twenty of Baudelaire's prose poems appeared in *La Presse* in August and September 1862. As for the book, Baudelaire had given Malassis the rights to all his works, past and future. But Malassis went bankrupt and on January 13, 1863, thinking that he was once again in possession of his own works, Baudelaire signed a contract with Hetzel. The publisher was given ownership of the *Poëmes en prose* and a third edition of *Les Fleurs du Mal* for a period of five years. Malassis found out about this two and half years later in Brussels, and was none too pleased.

On March 9, Hetzel asked for the manuscript of the prose poems. Baudelaire replied that *Le Spleen de Paris* (the title he eventually settled on) still needed reshaping. 'Thanks to my nerves, I don't think I'll be ready before 10 or 15 April, but I can guarantee you a *curious* book that will be *easy to sell*.'

In the end, the prose poems were published posthumously, not by Malassis or Hetzel, but by Michel Lévy: the *Petits Poëmes en prose* form part of the *Œuvres complètes* edited by Asselineau and Banville. Experimentation had its disadvantages. Of the one hundred poems planned by Baudelaire, only fifty were ever completed.

The contract with Hetzel also included some other unfinished pieces – a volume of short stories and the work entitled *My Heart Laid Bare*. Writing novels or short stories had been a lifelong ambition for Baudelaire. All he had to show for his endeavours, apart from *La Fanfarlo*, were long lists of titles and plans, though some of the longer prose poems might be considered as short stories. The other project grew into something much more important. The notes which make up *My Heart Laid Bare*, along with two other sets entitled *Fusées* and *Hygiène*, are usually lumped together with the notebook under the misleading title, *Journaux intimes*, despite the fact that Baudelaire never kept a diary. As Jacques Crépet and Georges Blin pointed out, these interrelated sections should be clearly distinguished. 'In *My Heart Laid Bare*, violence, vulgarity, personal attacks, cries of hate or despair, and longing for vengeance are given free rein, whereas in *Fusées*, the author, as disillusioned and world-weary as he seems to be, is still a psychologist and an artist, a moralist and a man of wit; in short, he steps back from himself, and speaks mostly in a "detached" tone.'[43] The *Hygiène* series deals with the physical and mental side of creation, the care the writer should take of his body and soul.

Fusées was offered to Houssaye for publication in *La Presse* under the title, *Fusées et Suggestions*, or *Sixty-Six Suggestions* – a title which comes from Edgar Allan Poe. The work is mentioned only once in Baudelaire's correspondence. *My Heart Laid Bare*, on the other hand, is described in greater detail. One of the apparently 'puerile' things which had saved him from suicide was 'a large book I've been dreaming of for two years – *My Heart Laid Bare*, in which I shall gather up all my anger. Oh! if it ever comes out, *Jean-Jacques's Confessions* will pale in comparison. You can see I'm still dreaming.' The dream was connected in Baudelaire's mind with his long-desired move to Honfleur, where he would find enough time and peace of mind to write his notes up into a coherent text. Fortunately, that was not to be. The fragments of *My Heart Laid Bare*, which Baudelaire took with him to Brussels, retained all their venom and virulence. Fitting them into a logical pattern would have deadened their sting and, in any case, the book would have been unpublishable during Baudelaire's lifetime. It was only twenty years after his death that his thoughts and aphorisms came to light in Eugène Crépet's edition of the *Œuvres posthumes*.

In writing those pages, Baudelaire rediscovered all his old incisiveness and pugnacity, all the power of his thought; and yet it was in those same pages that he recorded this unexpected and disturbing accident:

> Mentally, as well as physically, I have always been conscious of the abyss – not just the abyss of sleep, but the abyss of action, dream, memory, desire, regret, remorse, beauty, number, etc.
>
> I have cultivated my hysteria with terror and delight. Now I have vertigo all the time, and today, January 23, 1862, I suffered a strange warning. I felt pass over me *the wind of imbecility's wing*.

The passage that follows in *Hygiène* expresses that same feeling of urgency and foreboding:

> To Honfleur! As quickly as possible, before I fall any further.
>
> How many signs and presentiments God has sent already! It is *high time* to act, to consider the present minute as the most important of minutes, and to forge my *perpetual delight* from my ordinary torment – Work!

January 23, 1862: Baudelaire was then in the middle of campaigning for election to the French Academy. He told one of its members, Alfred de Vigny, of his 'physical accident', but still did nothing to lessen the chance of its recurring. Everything, it seems, including of course his electoral campaign, could be used to prevent the move to Honfleur, where he would have been able to lead a settled life with his mother. At this point in his life, it was too late to remove the threat of further attacks, but the final catastrophe might still be averted. Baudelaire was living with the thought of death, sometimes hoping it would come quickly. This morbid obsession was increased by the death of his half-brother on April 14, 1862. Alphonse died from a cerebral haemorrhage with hemiplegia. For this mediocre man, Baudelaire felt no affection, but his death must have contributed to the changing climate and horizon of the poet's world. Shortly after the publication of the second *Fleurs du Mal*, Baudelaire had turned forty. Ten years before to the very day, eleven poems from the future collection were appearing as *Les Limbes* in the *Messager de l'Assemblée*. Then, the future was full of possibilities; now only death stood before him. Baudelaire never reached, or even came near to his fiftieth birthday. The prose poem, 'Le Vieux Saltimbanque' surely expresses this anguish:

> Everywhere there was joy, profit, and debauchery. Everywhere the certainty of bread for the days to come. Everywhere the frenetic explosion of vitality. Here, there was absolute poverty – poverty dressed up, to complete the horror of it, in comical rags, which owed their contrasting colours to indigence, not to art. He wasn't laughing, the wretched man! He wasn't crying, he wasn't dancing, or waving his arms, or shouting. He sang no song, neither merry nor lamenting; he wasn't begging. He was mute and motionless. He had given up. He had abdicated. His destiny was done...
>
> And, as I turned around, obsessed by that vision, I sought to analyse my sudden grief, and said to myself: 'I have just seen the image of the old man of letters who has survived the generation whose brilliant entertainer he was – the old poet, friendless, without family or children, degraded by poverty and public ingratitude, and whose stall the forgetful world wishes no more to enter!

Baudelaire's old clown is an allegory – a symbol of the poet himself.[44]

CHAPTER 21

The Candidate:
The French Academy, the Odéon, the Crépet Anthology

1861–1864

Of these three projects, one soon came to an abrupt end; the other two were typical examples of the way Baudelaire conducted affairs which were not absolutely vital to him: a frantic bid to reach a goal followed by a dwindling of ambition or the negation of the desired object – sometimes even a wish to destroy that object.

Baudelaire had noted the favourable impression made by the second edition of *Les Fleurs du Mal* in certain literary milieux. Because of this positive reaction, as he told his mother on July 10, 1861, several people had urged him to take advantage of the current vacancy at the Académie Française. The seat in question had been occupied by Scribe – a popular, prolific and mediocre playwright who had passed away that February. 'But,' he added, 'the *Conseil Judiciaire*! I'll bet that even in that "impartial" sanctuary, that would be held against me.'

It was obviously very likely that the bourgeois and aristocratic Academy would indeed take note of the candidate's debts and extravagant life style. Baudelaire knew this and so his application was at first intended as an act of provocation. He would feign ignorance of the rules and pretend to have forgotten about all those writers, from Molière to Balzac, whose sinful lives had prevented them from joining the forty 'immortals'. By following in the footsteps of so many illustrious and ill-starred applicants, he too, with his legal incompetence, would show up the literary incompetence of the academicians. On December 11, he wrote to Abel Villemain, perpetual secretary of the Academy:

Monsieur,
   I beg to inform you that I wish to be enrolled among the candidates standing for one of the seats now vacant at the Académie Française, and I would ask you to be kind enough to convey my intentions in this respect to your colleagues.

I might, to men of extreme indulgence, appear to have a few qualifications to show. Allow me to remind you of *a book of verse* which caused
a greater stir than it intended; *a translation* which has popularised in
France a great unknown poet; a severe and detailed *study* of the joys and
perils of *Stimulants*; lastly, a great number of *booklets and articles* on the
principal artists and men of letters of my time.

But, in my own eyes, Monsieur, that is a perfectly insufficient sum of
qualifications, especially if I compare them to all those, more numerous
and more curious, which I dreamt of acquiring. Please therefore believe
me, Monsieur – and I beg you to pass this on to your colleagues – when
I say that my modesty is not feigned. It is modesty demanded, not only
by circumstance, but also by my conscience, which is as strict as the
conscience of all ambitious men.

To tell the truth, the thought that most encourages me to petition for
your votes at such an early stage is that if I resolved to seek them only
when *I felt worthy of them*, I would *never* seek them at all. I thought that
after all it might be better to start immediately. If my name be known
to some of those among you, perhaps my temerity will be taken in good
part, and I should consider a few votes, *miraculously* obtained, as a
generous encouragement and an order to improve . . .[1]

Charles Baudelaire

Baudelaire's allusion to the trial of *Les Fleurs du Mal* and the mention of
'Stimulants' (a reference to *Les Paradis artificiels*) were unlikely to win
support from Villemain.

The prospective academician was expected to pay a visit to each of the
forty members. Apart from Villemain, Baudelaire also called on Lamartine,
Legouvé, Patin, Sandeau, Viennet, Vigny and perhaps a few others. The
politicians, he deliberately neglected, 'the Thiers, the Guizots, and other
grave intriguers'.[2] Approximately half the Academy seems not to have
received him. Mérimée, whom Baudelaire admired, avoided him.

On the death of Lacordaire, the Catholic priest, Baudelaire – he who had
narrowly escaped conviction for blasphemy – decided to apply instead for
his seat. For Baudelaire, this was a logical choice; but his application was
seen of course as a scandalous gesture. On December 20, Baudelaire wrote
to Arsène Houssaye: 'Word has reached me that since my candidature is an
outrage to the Academy, several of those gentlemen have decided that they
won't be visible; but it's too fantastic to be true.' On the contrary, the
Lyons poet, Victor de Laprade, on receiving Baudelaire's letter, exclaimed:
'Trying to annex the Palais Mazarin [the home of the Academy] to Char-

enton [the lunatic asylum] is the greatest act of audacity ever seen.'[3] Baudelaire also wrote to Flaubert, asking him to put in a good word for him with Jules Sandeau. Flaubert obliged, although his recommendation did not exactly exude conviction: 'The candidate enjoins me to tell you "what I think of him". You must be familiar with his works. As far as I'm concerned, if I were a member of the honourable assembly, I'd love to see him sitting between Villemain and Nisard! What a picture that would be!'[4]

Sandeau pointed out in reply that Baudelaire was one of the representatives of *'pure literature'* – Banville, Flaubert, Leconte de Lisle and Gautier, who, as Baudelaire said, did not wish 'to compromise his dignity' by applying. That was a matter of little concern to Baudelaire, who was making his visits *'on foot* and in rags', and without enough copies of his own works to give to potential voters.[5] Then there was the added embarrassment of having to introduce himself to writers whom he had previously attacked in print – notably members of what he had dubbed 'the Common-Sense School' and the University professor, Saint-Marc Girardin, famous for having urged the youth of France to 'be mediocre'.

Baudelaire was not terribly unhappy, however, about creating such a sensation, and refused at first to take the advice of Lamartine and Vigny. Lamartine, of course, had known General Aupick. As for Vigny, he was the great discovery of Baudelaire's campaign:

> Lamartine tried to make me give up my plan by telling me that a man of my age should not leave himself open to a slap in the face. (It seems I look young.) De Vigny, whom I did not know, had his door closed to visitors so that we could be alone, and he kept me for three hours ... Like Lamartine, he tried at first to dissuade me, but when I told him that, acting on Sainte-Beuve's advice, I had begun by officially declaring my candidature to the Secretary, he told me that since the damage was done, I must continue at all costs.[6]

Sainte-Beuve had not given Baudelaire the very best advice. As for Lamartine's remark, one might suppose that he was hinting that Baudelaire appeared too *old* to be looking for insults. The poet was certainly no longer a young man. Baudelaire's interpretation seems to have been correct, however, since he told his mother in the same letter:

> Lamartine paid me such a monstrous and colossal compliment that I don't dare repeat it; but I don't think one should trust his fine words. He's a bit of a *whore*, a bit of a prostitute. (He asked after you. That's a

courteous thing to do, and I'm grateful to him. After all, he's a man of society.)

Baudelaire came away from his meeting with Vigny with a similar impression – that 'virtue comes with breeding, and great kindness with great talent'. Vigny himself recorded the meeting in his diary:

> December 22, 1861. I received M. Baudelaire. Interview from 2 till 4. He is very erudite, knows English well, has lived in and seen a lot of India at the age of 17. Knows, sums up, and discusses *Edgar Poe* very well. Seems to exist literarily only as the translator of this philosophical novelist. Has the distinguished and unhealthy look of a studious and hard-working person. He has been given some bad advice, and acted incorrectly – as I told him – by officially declaring his candidature at such an early stage.
> Too often people have said secretly, in an 'aside': 'We'll get *him* to do a lot of bowing and scraping and then we won't appoint him.'[7]

Baudelaire actually prepared his campaign very carefully in the early stages; but the joy of the game gave way to the more malicious pleasure of collecting material for a humorous book based on his visits to academicians. This he intended to publish during or just after the election. Baudelaire told his mother about this project with some relish: 'Alfred de Vigny, whom I had the effrontery to tell about this fine idea, informed me that I wasn't the first person to come up with it, and that Victor Hugo had once been similarly tempted, but that since he finally managed to get elected, he never published his book.'[8]

Baudelaire's book was never written; but it does exist in the form of notes and ridiculous quotations taken from the works of the perpetual secretary, and entitled, *The Thought and Style of M. Villemain*. There was also an open letter which Baudelaire sent, unsigned, to the *Figaro*, concerning a banquet commemorating the birth of Shakespeare. He took the opportunity to cut down a few academicians, including Saint-Marc Girardin, 'that hideous courtesan of mediocre youth'. And finally, while Baudelaire's campaign was still in full swing, the *Revue anecdotique* recounted the candidate's visit to Villemain:[9]

> No one has ever claimed that M. Villemain was entirely pleasant, but ill temper in the perpetual secretary is aggravated by his apprehension that the candidate for the vacant seat comes with the secret hope that his own seat will shortly be vacated. This doubt is shared by M. Viennet,

who, whilst secretly swearing a *sedet aeternumque sedebit** to himself, never neglects to see his visitor to the door with the ritual words, 'You won't have to wait very long for my seat, Monsieur, you won't have to wait very long.'

Two of M. Villemain's thrusts, with M. Baudelaire's ripostes will give the curious a general idea of the conversation those gentlemen had:

M. VILLEMAIN. – So you are applying to the Academy, Monsieur. How many votes do you have?

M. BAUDELAIRE. – The perpetual secretary knows as well as I do that the rule forbids academicians from promising their votes. I shall therefore have no vote until that day on which, no doubt, I shall receive none.

M. VILLEMAIN, *insistently*. – I, Monsieur, have never been an original.

M. BAUDELAIRE, *with innuendo*. – Monsieur, what do *you* know about that?

The visit to Viennet (one of the surviving representatives of dying classicism), during which academician and candidate were able to agree only on the subject of migraine,[10] produced this gem of pedantry: 'There are only five genres, Monsieur! Tragedy, Comedy, Epic Poetry, Satire ... and Fugitive Poetry which includes Fable, *in which I excel*!'[11]

There was one pleasant surprise – 'M. Patin, whom I had been warned about, was charming.'[12] Perhaps Baudelaire reminded the Sorbonne Latin professor that he had been examined by him for the *baccalauréat* back in 1839.

Sainte-Beuve wrote an article, 'On the forthcoming Academy elections',[13] in which he poked fun at a certain number of candidates, in particular young Prince Albert de Broglie who wanted to join his daddy, the Duke, in the Palais Mazarin. There was also a section on his young friend Baudelaire:

> ... It is not as easy as one might think to prove to the politicians and statesmen of the Academy that there are in *Les Fleurs du Mal* some very remarkable poems ... and that, when all's said and done, M. Baudelaire has found a way to build for himself at the furthest point of a spit of land reputed to be uninhabitable, and beyond the confines of known Romanticism, a bizarre pavilion, very ornate and very contorted, but charming and mysterious, where Edgar Poë [*sic*] is read, where exquisite sonnets are recited, where people intoxicate themselves with hashish to talk about it afterwards, where opium and a thousand abominable drugs are taken in cups of perfect porcelain ... One thing is certain, and that

---

* 'He sits and will sit forever' (*Aeneid*, Book VI, 617)

is that M. Baudelaire gains by being seen, and that where one expected to see a strange, eccentric fellow enter, one finds oneself in the company of a polite, respectful and exemplary candidate, a nice boy, refined in his language and perfectly Classical in his deportment.

Sainte-Beuve's astonishing condescension apparently went unnoticed by the poet. Baudelaire was delighted with the article:

A few words, my dear friend, to describe the special sort of pleasure you gave me. I have been very offended (but never said a word about it) at hearing myself being treated for quite a few years now as a werewolf, as an impossible and unprepossessing chap. Once, in a vindictive news-paper, I read a few lines about my repulsive ugliness which apparently prevents anyone from liking me. For a man who so much likes the smell of women, that was very hard to take. One day, a woman said to me, 'How strange, you're very proper. I thought you were always drunk and that you smelled bad.' She was talking about the legend.

Finally, my dear friend, you put a stop to all that and I'm grateful to you – I who have always said that being wise was not enough, and that one should more especially be agreeable ...

When I see your activity and vitality, I'm quite ashamed. Fortunately, I have jolts and crises in my character which replace, though very inadequately, the power of continuous will.

Baudelaire was obviously sincere. He promptly wrote an anonymous article on the subject for the *Revue anecdotique*: 'M. Charles Baudelaire, whose barbaric and unfamiliar name more than one academician has had to pronounce, was tickled rather than scratched.' On Christmas Day, he had been complaining to his mother about all the bother and fatigue of applying to the Academy. Sainte-Beuve's article spurred him on and on January 26 he was telling Vigny that he had definitely decided to put his name down for Lacordaire's seat. Vigny again attempted to dissuade him and, this time, succeeded. On February 10, the perpetual secretary received the sort of letter that might be written by 'a nice boy, refined in his language'. Baudelaire asked him kindly to strike his name from the list of candidates – with just a hint of irony:

Permit me also, Monsieur, to borrow your voice to thank those gentlemen whom I had the pleasure of meeting, for the very gracious and cordial manner in which they were kind enough to receive me. They can be certain that I shall treasure the memory of their welcome.

It was Prince Albert de Broglie, a contributor to the *Revue des Deux*

Mondes, who eventually took Lacordaire's seat in the Academy. Ironically, the other vacancy was filled by Octave Feuillet – Baudelaire's classmate at Louis-le-Grand.

His memories of the brief campaign were by no means bitter. The encounter with Alfred de Vigny, like his discovery of Wagner, had been one of those rare occasions on which Baudelaire met a kindred spirit. It happened none too soon. Vigny was suffering from cancer and died, a few days after Delacroix, on September 17, 1863.

Five letters from Baudelaire to Vigny have survived, as well as one from Vigny to Baudelaire. With one of his letters, Baudelaire sent copies of his latest publications, including *Les Fleurs du Mal, Les Paradis artificiels* and some prose poems which had appeared in a review. He also promised to send a copy of the old edition of the *Fleurs* if he was able to find one and presented Vigny with a spare copy of the poems of Edgar Allan Poe in English. He concluded: 'Monsieur, I thank you again for the charming manner in which you received me. Though I already thought very highly of you, it was quite unexpected. You are fresh proof of the fact that vast talent always implies great kindness and exquisite generosity.'

After another two letters in which Baudelaire recommended that Vigny take some English ale for his unsettled stomach, Vigny replied:

> Since December 30, Monsieur, I have continued to be very unwell, and have spent nearly all that time in bed. There, I read and reread you, and must tell you how many of those *fleurs du mal* are for me *Fleurs du Bien*, and how much they enchant me. Also how unjust I think you are to that bouquet, which is often deliciously scented with springtime odours, in giving it that unworthy title, and how cross I am with you for having poisoned it in places with certain emanations from Hamlet's cemetery.

Vigny then invited Baudelaire to come and hear what he thought of the poems, which he had been reciting with much pleasure to fellow poets, feeling that they were still being judged too lightly and not fully appreciated. Finally, he added a piece of advice:

> Though I do not yet know you, it seems to me that in many things you do not take yourself seriously enough. – Do not throw away your reputation like that, your very real and unusual talent, your letters and your words...

Vigny must have touched on this point again in his conversation, since

Baudelaire told him on January 30: 'I can surely put some sonnets in *Le Boulevard* if a poet like Banville is going to be keeping me company.' *Le Boulevard* was not as frivolous a magazine as its title suggests, though it was certainly no ivory tower. Vigny was perhaps unaware of the fact that Baudelaire's poetry, because of the trial and because of the poet's provocative attitude, was unacceptable to the so-called serious reviews. Nevertheless, one must admire Vigny's perspicacity, tact and moral authority in giving Baudelaire this piece of advice which no one else had ever given him.

Baudelaire frequently had two-edged opinions of other writers – one for the public and the other for close friends; but for Vigny he had nothing but praise. In his two studies on Poe (1852 and 1856), he sided with the author of *Stello* and *Chatterton* in asserting that society had no place for the poet; and it was with real emotion that in the obituary study on Delacroix, he deplored the disappearance of Chateaubriand, Balzac and Vigny: 'There is in a great national bereavement a weakening of general vitality, a darkening of the mind which resembles a solar eclipse – a fleeting imitation of the end of the world.'[14]

The feeling of solitude had increased; but Vigny, as he died, left Baudelaire with feelings of reassurance, whereas Delacroix's passing left him only with uncertainty.

Some of the warmth went out of his relations with Champfleury in 1863 – this in connection with an episode which is significant when seen in the light of Vigny's advice. Champfleury informed his friend that a woman painter, Mme Frédérique O'Connell, would be interested in talking with him about Poe's philosophical ideas and poetry, as well as about his own. Baudelaire declined the invitation; Champfleury insisted and received the following reply: 'I'm very fond of you, but you're terribly stubborn! I knew my letter would be shown. Are you really that set on compromising my dignity in circles in which you've compromised yours? ... When I wrote back to you, I'd done my research. You know how much I like prostitutes and how much I hate philosophising women.'[15] The word 'dignity' made Champfleury see red: 'Don't go to places of worse repute, try to imitate my life of hard work, be as independent as I am, don't ever have to rely on other people, and then you can talk about dignity.' Champfleury decided, however, to put Baudelaire's comment down to his 'artificial and innate eccentricity', and their friendship survived. Champfleury had long since said farewell to Bohemian life – something that Baudelaire was unable to do. The novelist was in the process of becoming an art historian; the poet had never gone far from his source of inspiration – the turmoil of life and the flowering of evil – though he still felt the occasional longing for bourgeois approval.

After dreaming of the Légion d'Honneur and the Académie, Baudelaire turned his thoughts to other profitable awards. This time, he was dreaming of becoming the director of an officially funded theatre – a post which would allow him to produce and present his own plays.

> There is in Paris [he told Mme Aupick] a theatre – *the only one in which it's impossible to go bankrupt*, and where it's possible to make a profit of 400,000 francs in four years. I want that theatre ... I want it and I'll get it. The years go by, and I want to be *rich*. What I call *wealth* would be so little! You probably realise that if this came about, in spite of all my plans for saving money, I'd have to have a maisonette furnished in Paris, and you'd have to come and spend a few months of each year with me. Also, I think the theatre has three months' holiday ... There's an enormous dream for you. I shall follow it through very carefully, and perhaps it will come true. And even with all the tribulations of running a theatre, I'd not neglect the cult of my own mind.

The theatre of Baudelaire's dreams was the Odéon. Its director was Charles Rouvenat de La Rounat whom Baudelaire had known at the *Corsaire-Satan*. There was no sign at all of his giving up the post, or even falling out of favour. La Rounat was about to be made a Chevalier of the Légion d'Honneur. In any case, the holder of the position had to submit to very close ministerial supervision. Each month, precise accounts had to be drawn up and reasons given for the choice of plays. It is difficult, not to say impossible to imagine Baudelaire bending to the rules and becoming an accountant.

The poet nevertheless needed a stage for his Machiavellian abilities. He found it in a work being prepared by Eugène Crépet, who selflessly intended to erect a monument to the glory of French poetry. Born in Dieppe in 1827, Crépet had remained true to the ideals of 1848 and was a staunch opponent of the imperial regime. Refusing to accept any job from the State, he devoted himself to literature and gave up what little fortune he had in order to make his compatriots aware of their literary heritage and to raise the level of education. Crépet's democratic convictions did not make for a smooth relationship with Baudelaire.

Crépet's anthology of French poetry was supposed to consist of a selection of poems, preceded by a short introduction on each poet and a few bibliographical notes. Begun in 1859, the anthology, entitled *Les Poëtes français*, was eventually completed in 1862.

The fourth volume was to be devoted to contemporary poets beginning with Lamartine. Publishing an anthology presents little risk – if the poets are no longer living. But the mere preparation of an anthology of modern poets, once the idea has been launched, becomes an event in itself. From the remotest corners of the literary world, poets emerge with their hopes, fears, pretensions, false modesty and envy. Baudelaire contributed material to this fourth volume, in which some of his own poems were to be presented with an introduction by Théophile Gautier. He saw in it a chance to exercise his genius for manipulation and earn a little money at the same time. It was also an opportunity to upset the bourgeois literary market place by putting into practice the evangelical idea that the first (or at least the second) shall come last and the hindmost be reinstated to their rightful place.

Crépet himself, in his general foreword, indicated that his aim was to restore certain neglected poets to favour; for example, Népomucène Lemercier, the author of *Pinto* and *La Panhypocrisiade* whose courageous efforts had been rewarded only by obscurity – perhaps because of his name? The baroque period, much disparaged by classical writers and by their eighteenth- and nineteenth-century successors, was also well represented – notably *Les Tragiques* by Agrippa d'Aubigné, from which Baudelaire had borrowed a few lines for the epigraph of the 1857 *Fleurs du Mal*. Crépet and his contributors were thus continuing the work begun by Gautier and Philarète Chasles among others in throwing light on important works which the pedantry of Boileau and Malherbe had cast into darkness.

The contributors themselves were chosen by a carefully selected team and by two critics in particular: Philoxène Boyer, who had a reputation for being omniscient and who dispensed his encyclopaedic knowledge at various Parisian venues, and Charles Asselineau, who had become a great collector and scholar. It may have been Boyer who brought Baudelaire into the team, thus allowing him to exert his powerful influence over the other members. Crépet himself, the director and owner of the whole enterprise, may have felt at times that he (though not his money) was being brushed aside. On May 15, 1862, Baudelaire gave Arsène Houssaye his version of what had happened. He was trying to explain to Houssaye why he had been left out of the anthology:

> I put your name forward ... *Crépet would not hear of it*, and don't hold it against him. He's an excellent fellow who doesn't know anything about anything, and who, precisely because *he's indecisive*, always wants to *assert* himself.
>
> I nevertheless prepared an article on you in case he changed his mind.

It would not have been accepted any more than were my 'Hégésippe Moreau' and my 'Auguste Barbier', which were turned down *because they contained a few critical remarks*. *Crépet*, who didn't want to hear about you, would have told me, if he had changed his mind: '*We can't print an article that isn't completely complimentary to the poet in question.*'

... I shall probably not be having any more dealings with that fine fellow – I'm very fond of him, but he has ended up by annoying me with his procrastination, his qualms and his awful fear of not appearing independent. Please keep all these trifles to yourself.

One can imagine why Baudelaire would have preferred to keep all this a secret. There is nothing to show that Crépet himself wanted to exclude Houssaye and Baudelaire's article, of course, was pure invention.

Baudelaire eventually had seven of his articles accepted by Crépet. Seven out of 157 introductory notes on modern and contemporary literature might not seem like much, until one takes into account the fact that eighty-five were written by three of Baudelaire's friends – Asselineau, Babou and Boyer – and thirty-eight by writers sympathetic to the poet. Thus, 130 of the articles come from Baudelaire's milieu. His dominant role in the whole enterprise is further indicated by a slip of the pen in his letter to the son of the poetess, Marceline Desbordes-Valmore: 'I'm the one who took on [crossed out] was given the job of doing justice to your admirable mother...'

The seven articles by Baudelaire were on Victor Hugo, Marceline Desbordes-Valmore, Théophile Gautier, Théodore de Banville, Pierre Dupont, Leconte de Lisle and Gustave Le Vavasseur. The three others, on Auguste Barbier, Pétrus Borel and Hégésippe Moreau, were rejected. Barbier was criticised by Baudelaire for having confused art with morality and for having succumbed to 'the heresy of *teaching*'. Hégésippe Moreau, whose reputation is based almost entirely on his untimely demise, was accused of lacking genius and knowledge, and also of indulging in a simplistic form of anticlericalism. In both cases, Crépet's objections were ideological. With Pétrus Borel, the ardent republican, it was a question of taste. Baudelaire told Boyer: 'He thinks I was playing a trick on him by doing a Pétrus Borel. He thinks *Borel* is a clown unworthy of a place in the *Crépet* anthology. As for circumstantial value, he's never heard of such a thing.'

Even the articles Crépet accepted came in for criticism. In the same letter to Boyer, on May 15, 1860, Baudelaire wrote:

You MUST, without making it look as if I put you up to it, give Crépet a THOROUGH dressing down. I'm furious, stunned, and exhausted. 'This opening is common, trivial, and there's no point to it anyway. You shouldn't devote so much space to so and so, because you gave so little to so and so (his fault). You're impertinent to this one (actually, it's a compliment), etc., etc., etc., etc., etc., etc., etc., etc., etc., etc., etc., etc., etc., etc., etc., etc., etc.'

I've already *ruined* three articles just to make him happy. It seems that they ALL need to be redone, and I've already changed them THREE TIMES. All that just so we don't sound like bourgeois. This is the conceit that makes him torment people who can read and write.

Particular difficulties arose with Baudelaire's piece on his friend from the good old days of the Pension Bailly – Gustave Le Vavasseur. This time, Crépet's democratic sensibilities were not at stake, but an almost Victorian prudishness and the tactful respect that was due to the writer being presented. The uncorrected proof of the article begins with an illustration of Le Vavasseur's astonishing agility in handling versification:

Many years have passed since I last saw Gustave Le Vavasseur, yet I always think back with delight to that time when I was a frequent companion of his. One morning, as I entered his room, I found him almost naked, standing dangerously balanced on a pile of chairs. He was trying to rehearse the feats we had seen performed the day before by some people who do it for a living.

Crépet, being a man of his time, was shocked by Baudelaire's 'almost naked' and insisted that he change his opening remarks for the sake of his friend. Baudelaire replied, 'I beg you, please don't go on about your "almost naked". In all my other articles, I agreed to omit whatever was too harsh or might have been offensive. This is different. I assure you that I know my Le Vavasseur.' One suspects that, having noticed Crépet's irritation, Baudelaire tried to make things worse. In the final version, the phrase was changed to: 'I remember how, more than once, as I entered his room, in the morning, I found him, almost naked ...' But did Baudelaire really know 'his' Le Vavasseur that well? Gustave had become lord of the manor of La Lande-de-Lougé (eighteen kilometres from Argentan) and Crépet was simply expressing Le Vavasseur's misgivings about being portrayed as a circus acrobat. Philippe de Chennevières, who wrote the article on Ernest Prarond, intervened and told Crépet that his friend Le Vavasseur was happy to leave the 'almost naked' since the gravity of one of the poems included in the anthology would act as a counterweight.

Baudelaire seems to have enjoyed being the secret organiser of Crépet's idea, and had already completed his seven articles on August 4, 1859. The money, however, was slow in arriving, since the fourth volume was not to appear until 1862. A contract was therefore drawn up between Crépet and Baudelaire which allowed the poet to publish the introductions he had written for the anthology, either in a book or in any review he pleased, except the *Revue européenne*. (Crépet was not keen to support the Government's new organ.) Baudelaire was in fact intending to publish his introductions under the title, 'Reflections on Some of My Contemporaries'. This would eventually form part of the posthumous collection, *L'Art romantique.*

The contract with Crépet enabled Baudelaire to publish his articles in a new review – the *Revue fantaisiste* – started by an enterprising young man from Bordeaux, who was on his way to becoming a famous poet: Catulle Mendès. His review survived only a few months, from February 15 to November 15, 1861, but found time to publish the seven pieces written for Crépet, along with two others which had been rejected. The article on Hégésippe Moreau was omitted for reasons that are unclear.

Even after signing the agreement with Crépet, Baudelaire was fuming. A little later, he wrote to Malassis: 'I never want to see Crépet again. After de Calonne, Stoepel; after Stoepel, Crépet. Without even observing the custom of being more polite on one's own ground than elsewhere, he treated me in a high-handed fashion ... I'm sick and tired of all these insults.'

The fourth volume of *Les Poëtes français* finally appeared in August 1862, published by Hachette. Baudelaire did not receive a copy and wrote to Hachette, who passed his letter on to Crépet. Crépet wrote back from Villers-sur-Mer:

> I deliberately left your name off the list of contributors and featured poets to whom I sent the volume in question.
>
> Before sending it to you, I shall wait for you to leave with my concierge the Poetry of V. Hugo which you borrowed from me about two years ago, and which you are being so slow about returning.
>
> E.C.

When I asked you recently for those books, you told me: 'When I go and see my Mother, I shall bring them back with me.' It seems to me it would have been much quicker and easier to have them sent immediately. Am I supposed to do without those books until you happen to feel like going to see your Mother?

Baudelaire replied on September 9:

My dear Crépet,

Your precious letter arrived too late; by which I mean that I now have the fourth volume of *Les Poëtes français*. I shall keep the invoice as carefully as your letter.

As for your books, your demand is only too just. It was puerile of you to be so imperious about it. I can remember clearly only *Les Contemplations* and *La Légende des siècles*. For fear of being wrong, I shall ask for anything by Victor Hugo I might have at my place.

Charles Baudelaire

The quarrel continued. Crépet answered on the 14th, claiming to be indifferent to the fact that Baudelaire had bought the fourth volume, since he had already been given free copies of the other volumes, to which he did not contribute. He went on to point out that the imperious tone of his letter was simply an imitation of Baudelaire's own stiffness: the absence of any friendly or even merely polite expression and initials instead of a signature were other characteristic features of the poet's style which Crépet had copied. 'Plagiarism might appear "puerile" to you, but it was the best way I had of making you see how offended I was by the almost incessantly disdainful, imperious and virtually dictatorial tone of your letters.'

Crépet's may not have been the last word. The fourth volume was a great success and was reprinted in 1863. The note on Baudelaire had been written by Théophile Gautier. Baudelaire must have been pleased with the praise he received. Seven of his poems were included – 'L'Albatros', 'Réversibilité', 'Le Crépuscule du matin', 'La Cloche fêlée', 'Le Guignon', 'Les Hiboux' and 'Les Petites Vieilles'. In the first reprint of the book, the frightening final stanza of the last poem was missing, replaced by a row of dots:

> Ruines! ma famille! ô cerveaux congénères!
> Je vous fais chaque soir un solennel adieu!
> Où serez-vous demain, Eves octogénaires,
> Sur qui pèse la griffe effroyable de Dieu?*

It seems most unlikely that Crépet was responsible for the deletion. Baudelaire must have requested it himself.

Baudelaire and Crépet were never meant to get on. Baudelaire was determined to see this affable and unselfish man as a bourgeois tyrant, a

---

* 'Ruins! My family! O kindred minds! / Each night I bid you a solemn farewell! / Tomorrow where will you be, you ancient Eves, / Over whom the horrid claw of God impends?'

weak-kneed pedant. Even a person of extreme equanimity would surely find it difficult to accept the following reaction to a few suggested changes – '*Everything I write is correct and irrefutable*'[16] – or to tolerate that tone of insolent superiority which the poet so easily adopted. Baudelaire was similar in this respect to the anti-Semitic novelist, Céline. Crépet and, later on, the Belgians, were to Baudelaire what Jews and Chinamen were to Céline. The myth was built up in order to be destroyed. Baudelaire's myth was the bourgeois and he had certainly seen some fine examples in his time: his mother and step-father, Alphonse, Emon especially; but with Crépet, he was mistaken.

Having done his best to become the invisible director of the fourth volume and having almost pulled it off, Baudelaire spoiled everything with his impatience. As the poem 'L'Héautontimorouménos' suggests, the poet was his own executioner, subject to sudden fits of violence directed against himself as well as against other people. Crépet was not a man to bear a grudge and seems to have been unaware that Baudelaire included his name in his notebook under the heading, 'FILTHY RABBLE'. When Malassis' possessions were sold after his death in 1878, Crépet bought up *My Heart Laid Bare, Fusées, Pauvre Belgique!*, other manuscripts and the letters from Baudelaire to Malassis, no doubt with a view to compiling the important work he was to publish in 1887: *Charles Baudelaire, Posthumous Works and Unpublished Correspondence, Preceded by a Biographical Study*. In his introduction, Crépet wrote:

> I myself was well acquainted with Baudelaire. In those days already so distant (1856–1863) when I was preparing and publishing the anthology entitled *Les Poëtes français*, he was one of the group of highly talented critics whose collaboration I obtained. Our relations, which ceased after the publication of the book, never went further than acquaintanceship – respectful on my part, discreet on his. But this is not the place for personal reminiscences ... I shall simply state that, having never been his friend in the true sense of the word, I have retained with respect to his reputation the same freedom of opinion I retained with regard to his person.

The 1887 biography is ample proof of Crépet's impartiality.

Baudelaire's article on Hugo is one of the finest he wrote for the anthology. Hugo is praised unreservedly as the poet of '*the mystery of life*', made perceptible through '*universal analogy*' – a '*génie sans frontières*'.

Baudelaire and Hugo had been on good terms since the prosecution of *Les Fleurs du Mal*. Baudelaire asked him for a letter to form the preface of his essay on Gautier which was coming out as a small book in 1859. Hugo sent the letter as requested on October 6. In a particularly inflated style, the symbol of exiled democracy drew a line between himself and Baudelaire. The essay he was being asked to preface contained a denunciation of the 'heresy' that art could be used to teach. Hugo's response was: 'I understand your whole philosophy (for, like every poet, you bear within you a philosopher). I do more than understand it, I accept it; but I keep my own. I have never said, "*l'Art pour l'Art*"; but always, "*l'Art pour le Progrès*" . . . It is for Progress that I suffer now and for Progress that I am ready to die.' Hugo added nonetheless: 'You love Beauty. Give me your hand.' This was the open letter in which Hugo coined the famous phrase so often used to describe Baudelaire's achievement as a poet:

> What are you doing when you write those striking verses – 'Les Sept Vieillards' and 'Les Petites Vieilles' which you dedicate to me and for which I thank you? What are you doing? You are marching; you are moving onward. You are endowing the heaven of art with some macabre ray of light. You are creating a new *frisson*.

In December, Baudelaire sent him an autograph copy of 'Le Cygne': 'Monsieur,' he wrote, 'Here are some verses written for you and with you in mind. They should not be judged with your stern gaze, but with your paternal eye . . . Please accept my little symbol as a very insufficient mark of the sympathy and admiration your genius inspires.' Hugo thanked him for his 'strong and penetrating' stanzas and later, on April 29, 1860, for his page on Méryon in the *Salon de 1859*: 'You have within you, dear thinker, all the notes of art. Once again you have demonstrated that law according to which, in an artist, the critic is always equal to the poet.' This was an idea Baudelaire later recalled in his essay on Wagner.

Baudelaire had also been in touch with Hugo in connection with Crépet's anthology, requesting permission to reproduce certain poems. Hugo's reply was rather cautious, but he expressed delight 'that my name will be uttered by you and embedded in one of those profound and beautiful pages that only you know how to write'. Hugo went on to congratulate him on *Les Paradis artificiels*. 'So, at last, thanks to you, I have read the famous *opium eater*. You bring that work to life with great power. To analyse in such a way is to create.' The author was invited then to come one day and visit the great man 'on his rock'.

Early in 1861, the second edition of *Les Fleurs du Mal* was put on the boat for Guernsey. Hugo again showered the poet with compliments. Baudelaire reciprocated the following year with a positive review of the first part of *Les Misérables*. Just one small piece of criticism: 'Does anyone enter the police force *out of enthusiasm*?' and a conclusion in which Baudelaire noted, even after so much 'progress', the persistent reality of Original Sin. Hugo wrote to thank him and morally 'shook his hand' in the name of 'progress through Truth'. Mme Aupick heard a different point of view: 'That book is vile and inept. I have shown in this that I know the art of lying. He wrote me an absolutely ridiculous thank-you letter. That proves that a great man can also be a fool.' Charles Asselineau was also treated to Baudelaire's opinion of *Les Misérables*:

> What sort of sentimental criminals are they, who feel remorse over a forty-sou piece, who argue with their conscience for hours, and who set up rewards for virtue? Do those people think like other men? *I* shall turn it into a novel in which I'll show a rogue – a real rogue, a murderer, thief, fire-raiser and pirate – and which will end with these words: 'And 'neath these shady trees I planted, surrounded by an adoring family – children who love me, and a worshipping wife – I savour in peace the fruit of all my crimes!'[17]

This is a fine example of Baudelaire's double-edged opinions, also apparent in these two classical images, the first from the anthology article, the second from *Fusées*: 'Like Demosthenes, he converses with the wind and the waves. Once, he prowled alone in places teeming with human life. Now, he walks in deserts peopled with his thoughts'; 'Hugo often thinks of Prometheus. He applies an imaginary vulture to his breast which suffers only the stabs of vanity's moxas ... Hugo the Priesthood always has his brow bent down – down so low that all he sees is his navel.' Sincerity is irrelevant here. One should probably talk instead of dual sincerity. Baudelaire could only admire Hugo the poet, though their poetics are irreconcilable; but Baudelaire the marginal writer and man was unable to tolerate some of Hugo's attitudes – his contentment in misfortune, his way of treating the poor as if he himself were a pauper.

Baudelaire's criticism was not always tacit or reserved for friends. In the 1846 *Salon*, Hugo was ranked below Delacroix as 'a craftsman who is far more skilful than inventive, a worker who is much more correct than creative' – in short, a simple orator. Some, like a journalist from the inevitable *Figaro*, liked to think that Baudelaire was envious. On June 6, 1858, the paper reported Baudelaire as having said, 'Hugo! Who's that? Who's ever heard of Hugo?' Baudelaire sent an open letter in reply:

> I think, Monsieur, that the writer of that article is a young man who is still unable to distinguish clearly between what is permissible and what

is not. He claims to watch my every move – obviously with great discretion, because I've never seen him.

The amount of energy the *Figaro* puts into persecuting me might make some people think ... that the paper is hoping to find great leniency in the Law on that day when I ask the court that condemned me to defend me.

The 'young man' replied on the same page of the paper claiming to have heard Baudelaire's public attack on Hugo in the café, Le Divan Le Peletier, four years ago – 'the very same time when his famous friend M. Courbet was saying (in the same place) that *Michelangelo does not exist*'. Once again, as in the trial, the prosecution was basing its case on Realism.

Hugo had his disciples in Paris and, on Jersey and Guernsey, his antennae were turned towards France. He must have been aware of a certain enmity on the part of Baudelaire. The mutual compliments hid suspicions. Hugo's would appear at the end of 1863 when Baudelaire asked him to intervene on his behalf with Lacroix, the publisher of *Les Misérables*.

Malassis was soon to be in exile himself. In 1861, his business was flourishing. His thirty-six-page catalogue contained works by some of the most original writers of the time. But this had also brought him several heavy fines and prison sentences. Furthermore, the risks he took in setting up the new bookshop had increased with his involvement in Baudelaire's debts. At the beginning of September 1862, he was declared bankrupt. One creditor alone – a printer, Poupart-Davyl – was owed 14,000 francs. Malassis went into hiding; but he was arrested on November 12, following a complaint lodged by Poupart-Davyl, and incarcerated in the Clichy debtors' prison. Creditors were expected to pay for the upkeep of their debtors in the prison which included 'gaming rooms, a café-restaurant, a tobacconist, a pastry shop, a reading room, and separate bedrooms, which the creditor rented for the debtor at the cost of five sous to two francs a day depending on the furnishings and how often the bedding was changed'.[18] Poupart-Davyl is unlikely to have kept Malassis there for very long.

Shortly after the arrest, Baudelaire went to see Poupart, who was also prosecuting another friend of the poet – possibly Catulle Mendès whose *Revue fantaisiste* he had printed.

Poupart refused point-blank, but he was quite calm about it, when all of a sudden the creature [his mistress] came in, and as soon as she saw me, she flew into an indescribable rage. Poupart, somewhat ashamed, tried to explain to her that we were talking about something else. It was no good. She kept provoking me with all kinds of insolent remarks. When she started saying insulting things about you, I coldly explained that well brought-up people, when they had something bad to say about someone, made sure they didn't say it in front of that person's friends, and that in any case I'd come about something else, etc...

But then suddenly, Poupart, who until that point had been calm, and even embarrassed, stirred up no doubt by the awful squealing of that old bitch, began shouting too, without knowing why he was doing it – because I hadn't gone there to talk about you, and hadn't said anything about you.

So then I got up, nodded to Poupart, and he saw me out. And then the door was slammed violently with vague curses in my direction. It was the girl again – probably furious because I hadn't said goodbye to her.

Baudelaire sent this letter to Malassis on November 18, 1862. On December 8, Malassis asked Asselineau, 'If you see Baudelaire, warn him that I'll have him called as a witness for the defence to recount the scene he had at Poupart's.' Baudelaire seems to have been spared this chore. Having borrowed fifty francs from Poupart, he was, not surprisingly, rather keen to pay him back.[19]

Towards the end of the year, Malassis was transferred from Clichy to the Madelonnettes prison in the Quartier du Temple. Regulations were strictly enforced and the publisher was kept in what was virtually solitary confinement. It should be remembered that at the height of the troubles in 1848 Malassis had produced his 'newspaper of the rabble' – *L'Aimable Faubourien* – and that, if not exactly a revolutionary in the recent sense of the word, he was a confirmed anarchist. This was made abundantly clear to the government of Napoleon III by a series of short texts, either serious or mocking, which signal the dawn of trade-union socialism (as opposed to its utopian predecessors). One of these tracts had already brought the publisher a fine of 500 francs.

This political affiliation might explain why Malassis received such harsh treatment at the Madelonnettes and also why he had to wait such a long time for his trial. In his letters, Baudelaire kept him in touch with life in the literary world and passed on the latest Paris gossip. He tried to visit the prison, but obtained permission to do so only at the end of March 1863. Perhaps this halfheartedness had something to do with the fact that on January 13 he had signed away his works to Hetzel.

The trial eventually took place on April 22, 1863. The publisher's friends were there *en masse*, and Sainte-Beuve and Théophile Gautier among others had apparently expressed the wish that an honourable solution would be found.[20] By this time, Malassis had already served five months in custody. The court no doubt took this into account when it sentenced him to one month in prison. As the review, *Diogène* reported, Malassis had been jailed for 'a very pardonable little sin'. Six months for negligence in book-keeping was indeed a little strange to say the least.

Soon after leaving prison and after putting his affairs in order, Malassis was in Belgium. He would stay in Brussels until 1870. Like other debtors – like other republicans too – he was glad to put a border between himself and the imperial authorities.

While Malassis was still in Paris, Baudelaire told him, in August 1863, that he would write in a few days, probably from the Hôtel du Grand Miroir in Brussels. It was not until April 1864 that he finally settled there, but the intervening months were filled with plans for departure. Debts were one reason for leaving, though, unlike Malassis, Baudelaire was protected to some extent by the *conseil judiciaire*. He also felt the need of a change, to see new faces and shake off his boredom. Vengeance was a powerful motive. *My Heart Laid Bare* was to be 'a book of rancour':[21]

> Certainly my Mother and even my stepfather will be respected. But in telling of my education, the way in which my thoughts and feelings were fashioned, I wish to demonstrate throughout the book how foreign I feel to society and its religions. I shall use my real gift for impertinence against *all France*. I feel a need for vengeance as a tired man needs a bath.
> ... I shall of course publish *My Heart Laid Bare* only when I have a fortune large enough to protect me, outside France if need be.

Baudelaire also intended visiting the rich art galleries of Belgium in order to write a book[22] (these were to prove a disappointment), to give some lectures, to write articles in *L'Indépendance belge* – read in Paris for its independent commentaries on French politics – and, finally, to offer *Les Paradis artificiels* and two volumes of critical essays to Victor Hugo's publishers – Lacroix and Verboeckhoven.

In those days, instead of the usual *conférences*, lectures were referred to as *lectures* (literally 'readings'). This was not so much an anglicism as a description of fact. Since Charles Dickens' lecture tour of the United States, it had become customary for writers to read to an audience from their works. The usual venue for such things in Brussels was the 'Cercle artistique et littéraire'. With the help of Arthur Stevens, the art dealer and younger brother of the painters Joseph and Alfred, Baudelaire was able to contact the President of the Cercle – D. J. L. Vervoort, who was also President of the Chamber of Deputies. In spite of Arthur's intervention, negotiations dragged on until just before Baudelaire's departure for Belgium.

Baudelaire was also in touch with the director of *L'Indépendance belge*, which eventually published only one poem of his, 'Les Bons Chiens'. However, writing to Mme Aupick in November 1863, he made it clear that one plan took precedence over the others: 'I think I'm being well paid for my lessons [i.e. lectures]; but you know my journey has a different goal – to sell *three* volumes of criticism to the firm that bought *Les Misérables*. Everyone tells me that they're unintelligent and very miserly people.' The lectures were supposed to allow Baudelaire to reach his prospective publisher. Thinking himself to be on good terms with Hugo, Baudelaire wrote on December 17 to request 'an *enormous* favour'. Hugo was asked to put in a good word for him with Albert Lacroix who would soon be visiting Guernsey. Unfortunately, as Baudelaire told his mother on the 31st: 'Storms in the Channel upset my scheme, and my letter arrived four days after the publisher left. Hugo said he'd put things right with a letter, but nothing can replace the spoken word.' When sending his letter to his faithful disciple in France, Paul Meurice, so that he could pass it on to Baudelaire, Hugo wrote: 'People say that he [Baudelaire] is virtually my enemy; but I'll do him the favour he asked.' Whether or not Hugo kept his word, Lacroix showed no interest in Baudelaire's work. And what if Hugo found out that Baudelaire was responsible for the article in the *Figaro* on April 14, 1864 in which the commemoration of Shakespeare's birth was denounced as an operation dreamt up by the Hugo clan to pave the way for the master's study of *William Shakespeare*, and to celebrate the beauties and virtues of democracy?[23]

The century's two greatest poets had seen each other only a few times. They were soon to meet in Brussels and discover their irreconcilable differences.

At the start of 1864, Baudelaire sank into what he called 'a hideous state of lethargy',[24] caused as much by his mental as by his physical condition. His illness was making silent progress. And what a series of disasters! On July 1, 1862, he sold all his works, past, present and future, to Poulet-Malassis who promptly went bankrupt. In September that year, *La Presse* ceased publication of *Le Spleen de Paris*. This book and *Les Fleurs du Mal* were sold the following January to Hetzel, but Baudelaire was unable to complete the prose poems. On November 1, he gave Michel Lévy sole ownership of his five volumes of Poe translations for 2,000 francs, thus losing a regular and reliable source of income. And now Lacroix was showing no signs of interest in his work.

'My trip augurs very ill,' he told his mother in November 1863. Finally, at the end of April, he left for Brussels. He was losing France and Belgium was certainly no gain. Baudelaire was now alone and on the road to death.

PART SEVEN

EXILE AND DEATH

CHAPTER 22

Brussels

April 1864 – March 1866[1]

Baudelaire left the train at the Gare du Midi in Brussels on April 24, 1864. Still quite youthful in appearance under his greying hair, he made his way to the Hôtel du Grand Miroir at number 28, rue de la Montagne. He was intending to stay only a few days, or, at the very most, a few weeks. Just before leaving Paris, he had told a creditor that he expected to be back by June 15.

The hotel, which owed its unusual name to its thirteenth-century founder, Engelbert de Speculo, had once enjoyed a good reputation, but now it had fallen on hard times and was beginning to show its age. The entrance was set in a cramped-looking façade, under a balcony to which the gold letters of the name were attached. It opened onto a quiet inner courtyard, which was large and lined with porticoes forming archways. A broad stone staircase with attractively wrought handrails led up to the foyer, where the traveller was greeted by a Parisian, Lepage, and his wife, a small, surly woman from Picardy, who kept a close eye on the customers' accounts, as well as on their personal correspondence.

Baudelaire was given room number 39 on the second floor, overlooking the courtyard. It was reached by a steep, narrow staircase. A quick inspection revealed the furnishings to be rather tawdry – an imitation mahogany bed with a green quilt, a cupboard, a chest of drawers, a threadbare couch, an armchair in a similar condition, two chairs with broken cane-work and a small rug. On the mantelpiece, instead of a clock, there was a lamp with a lampshade and, against the wall with its faded paper, a table.

The Grand Miroir was something of a disappointment; but Baudelaire was an old hand at doing without home comforts. The main thing was to see his business through as quickly as possible, with the least inconvenience. A few days after arriving, he was registered as a temporary alien at the Hôtel de Ville:

SURNAME: Baudelaire
CHRISTIAN NAMES: Charles
PROFESSION: Man of letters
AGE: 43
PLACE OF BIRTH: Paris
DOMICILE: Honfleur
DATE OF ARRIVAL: April 27
HOTEL: Grand Miroir

Baudelaire took advantage of the few days remaining before his first lecture to visit the city and discover the sights to which he would later return. Apologising for missing an appointment, he wrote: 'In a city one doesn't know, everything is beautiful and exciting. I spent all day yesterday just wandering about.'[2]

With its surrounding *faubourgs*, each like a little village, encircled by its boulevards built on the site of the old ramparts and crisscrossed by the muddy waters of the Senne which turned the large wheels of its water-mills, Brussels was a relaxed, provincial capital. From the central Grand-Place, its small, meandering streets spread out in a maze. Straddling the valley and the hills to the west, the city was divided into two parts – the *ville haute* and the *ville basse*. Steep roads and stairways joined the two sections, each of which possessed its own distinct population. In the upper town lived the aristocracy, property owners and the puritans of the *grande bourgeoisie*. The *ville basse*, where the lower classes lived, was the more colourful part of town, with its shopkeepers, merchants and craftsmen. Every street and alleyway, each cul-de-sac and vennel in the crowded areas had a character of its own: cafés, taverns and noisy beerhalls breathed out the stale smell of *faro*, the inns and restaurants exuded the rich aroma of their oily cooking, the shops and market stalls were brimming with produce. Here and there, one could find more silent, peaceful *quartiers*, slumbering at the foot of churches and chapels, or curled up around the convent courtyards.

This was no longer the busy, commercial city of Flemish history, but a town which went about its humdrum business with a strict eye to morality, a fondness for material possessions and regular church attendance (not to mention good cooking). Its hard-working population was a credit to the country, in all but one respect: intellectual pursuits were rare and interested only a certain élite. This élite consisted mainly of French writers who had been forced into exile by the Second Empire. The Cercle artistique et littéraire, for example, on which Baudelaire had set his sights, had enjoyed considerable success with its literary *soirées* ever since Napoleon III's *coup d'état* and the consequent arrival in Belgium of French refugees. Some of these exiled writers gave private lessons to the sons of the bourgeoisie and were thus able to inculcate a new generation with their republican ideals.

Arthur Stevens lived in a house in the upper town, near the Place Royale. It was probably he who first gave Baudelaire a tour of the city. After leaving the hotel and admiring the baroque Chapelle Sainte-Anne across the street, the two friends walked on up the rue de la Colline and came to the Grand-Place. The 'prodigious décor' of this 'attractive and ceremonious' square must have delighted Baudelaire, who mentioned in his notes the 'toy style' of its beautiful houses.[3] From a man who was thinking of the '*maison joujou*' at Honfleur, this was obviously meant as a compliment. The poet was to be introduced to the Cercle artistique, which had its home on the first floor of the Maison du Roi, facing the townhall. The Maison du Roi had at one time been the breadmarket and was a fine Gothic structure, though its original style had been changed over the years almost beyond recognition, with the addition of an ugly Mansard roof and hideous bosses which covered the façade. The ground floor and basement were taken up by bird sellers and seed merchants who set up their stalls every Sunday morning on the square.

Baudelaire and Stevens climbed the long stone staircase to the lecture room, where they met the president, D. Vervoort, and his two secretaries. The final arrangements were made, the newspapers informed and invitations sent out. On April 29 – a Friday – the *Etoile belge* announced that at eight o'clock the following morning, a lecture would be delivered on 'Eugène Delacroix, the Painter and the Man'. In fact, the lecture was postponed until Monday.

On the Saturday, Baudelaire sent an invitation to the publisher, Albert Lacroix, and another to Gustave Frédérix, a young critic who worked for *L'Indépendance belge*. Frédérix, who had just written an obituary article on Delacroix and who was an early admirer of Richard Wagner, attended the lecture. The publisher did not. Baudelaire, it should be noted, was not entirely unknown in Belgium. His classmate from Louis-le-Grand, Emile Deschanel (another political exile), had published reviews of the Poe translations and defended the poet at the time of the trial.

The evening of May 2 arrived. Baudelaire was speaking in public for the first time, and began his lecture with an ingenious and flattering exordium. It immediately won over an audience whose competence in things artistic was outweighed by its curiosity. 'Messieurs,' he began, 'I have for some time now been wanting to come among you and make your acquaintance.

I felt instinctively that I would be well received. Please excuse my com-
placency. You practically encouraged it without knowing it.'4 The lecturer
went on to vaunt the merits of his new surroundings which had restored
his 'intellectual health' and allowed him to enjoy this 'atmosphere of
bonhomie to which we Frenchmen are so little accustomed, especially those
of us who, like myself, have never been treated by France as spoilt children'.
After evoking the painter's death and describing the sale of the contents of
his studio, Baudelaire recited his study on 'The Work and Life of Eugène
Delacroix'.

Frédérix gave a very favourable review of the lecture in *L'Indépendance
belge*, noting Baudelaire's 'most brilliant and well-deserved success'. A later
reviewer confirmed the fact that everyone had gone away very pleased with
the evening and gave a revealing description of the poet as lecturer:

> M. Baudelaire is not an orator in the true sense of the word. He has
> neither the right flourishes nor the right delivery. He is nervous, and the
> listener is hard put to follow him; but he does have the tact to try and
> achieve oratorical effects, and is all the more successful for it. I am
> informed that M. Baudelaire is to give one more lecture before he leaves.

In the end, Baudelaire delivered four other lectures. His first attempt
may not have been a *tour de force*, but, for a trial run, it was certainly very
encouraging.

After the lecture, Baudelaire was invited by a friend of the Stevens –
Mme Léopold Collart – to spend two days in the country at Stalle-sous-
Uccle. Mme Collart was the wife of a wealthy cloth manufacturer. At her
large house, built in the grounds of a former convent, she enjoyed entertaining the republican exiles and indulging her taste for art and literature.

Uccle at that time was still a village of about fifty houses nestling on the
edge of the Soignes forest. Arthur Stevens had moved there as part of his
plan to marry one of Mme Collart's daughters. By offering his professional
services to the youngest girl, who was a keen artist, he had made some
headway, but was prevented from making any further progress by the fact
that he was in the process of obtaining a divorce. Undaunted by the father's
refusal to allow his daughter to marry, Stevens had taken out a lease on a
neighbouring house.

Baudelaire and Stevens left the day after the lecture in the coach for
Uccle, drawn by two horses (three for the steeper hills) and costing seventy
centimes. The journey lasted an hour and a half, and took the travellers out
of Brussels by the Barrière de Saint-Gilles. After a short stop at a country
inn, the coach set off again, with the horses pulling slowly up the long,

tree-lined hill of the Chaussée d'Alsemberg. On the right, overlooking the
valley of the Senne, Baudelaire was surprised to see a café with a sign
marked 'Cemetery View'. This discovery was the origin of the prose poem,
'Le Tir et le Cimetière'. Once over the hill, the road dropped down towards
Uccle. At the bottom of the slope, Baudelaire and Stevens left the coach,
walked along the riverside path and arrived at the Stevens' little house,
where Arthur lived with his sister-in-law and niece.

After introductions, Baudelaire was taken up the street to the home of
the Collarts. At first, conversation between the sworn enemy of democracy
and progress on the one hand and the friend of political refugees on the
other must have been a little strained. Baudelaire's hosts were admirers of
Victor Hugo and George Sand; but painting provided some neutral ground.
Marie Collart, the youngest daughter, had several canvasses to show the
poet – animal studies and portraits of her sister Elisa. One of her paintings
is remarkable for its colour and texture: the young woman is shown in a
long white dress, holding a parasol, admiring a bed of poppies. One is
reminded of an Impressionist painting. Baudelaire's curiosity was tinged
perhaps with some affection: Stevens later wrote to Marie, after the poet's
death, to congratulate her on buying a photograph portrait of 'that poor
Baudelaire . . . He had a great liking for your talent.' Baudelaire must also
have been touched by the Collarts' hospitality, since he later returned for
a second visit.

Back at the Grand Miroir in Brussels on the 5th, Baudelaire read the
review published by Frédérix – for which he thanked him – and also a letter
from his mother. He wrote back at once, enclosing a copy of the review:

> Here's a note that appeared about my first lecture. People here are
> saying that it was a huge success; but, between you and me, everything
> is going very badly. I arrived too late. There's a lot of greed here, and
> agonising slowness in all things – a great morass of empty brains. To
> tell the truth, these people are more stupid than the French.
>
> No credit – no credit at all; though that's probably very lucky for me.
>
> I'm giving a different lecture next Wednesday. The winter funds of
> the Cercle have been used up, so I was told, and since the real aim of my
> journey was to seduce the publisher Lacroix, I accepted the fee of 50
> francs per lecture (instead of 200 or 100). Unfortunately, Lacroix was in
> Paris. I have just *requested* permission to give *three more free of charge* when
> he returns, but I'm not telling anyone why I'm here.
>
> I've had letters sent to the Cercles in Anvers, Bruges, Liège, and Ghent
> to let them know that I'm in Brussels. I have yet to receive their replies.

Baudelaire had already formed his opinion of Belgium. He thought he was getting away from France, but had merely discovered a more revolting version of it. A bond of loathing was to form between himself and Belgium, and even now he was contemplating a longer stay – 'until the end of June', at least. The plan to tour the other major cities fell through. Liège was booked up and Anvers was rebuilding its lecture theatre.[5]

On May 11, invitations were sent out for the second lecture, which was to be given that same evening. The subject was Théophile Gautier. Baudelaire would read the text of the booklet he had published in 1859. May, if the weather was good, was not the ideal month for a lecture. The audience was no larger than the first time: about twenty people came and several left in the course of the talk. This was partly the fault of the lecturer, whose opening remarks went something like this:

> This is the second time I have spoken in public, and it was in front of you, at my first lecture, that I lost what might be called the virginity of the word, which, I might add, is no more of a loss than the other.[6]

The writer Camille Lemonnier remembered Baudelaire talking in a 'great nave' that was almost deserted, revealing to the assembled few a Théophile Gautier as glorious as 'the great popes of Art'.

> A little table occupied the centre of the platform. He stood there in his white cravat in the circle of light put out by an oil lamp ... His pale, clean-shaven face was darkened by the half-light of the lampshade. I could see his eyes move about like black suns. His mouth had a life of its own within the life and expression of the face; it was thin and trembling, delicately vibrant under the violin bow of the words. And the whole head looked down as from a tower on the intimidated listeners.[7]

At the end of his talk, Baudelaire apparently bowed 'as if he were standing before a real assembly'. 'A door banged quickly, and then an usher took away the lamp. I alone stayed behind in the returning darkness, in that night in which the echoless voice had risen and fallen – the voice of that Father of the literary Church.' Literature aside, it was a dismal failure.

The three other lectures, which Baudelaire had offered to give free of charge and which he devoted to Les Paradis artificiels, were equally unsuccessful.[8] At the end of the last lecture, Baudelaire thanked his audience for listening so patiently to his sometimes rather lengthy readings. One of those present described him as having 'terrible stage-fright, reading and stammering, trembling, with his teeth chattering, his nose buried in his manuscript. It was a disaster.'[9]

Baudelaire received one hundred francs from the Cercle artistique et littéraire. Forgetting that three of the lectures were given free of charge, he had been counting on 500 francs with which to pay the owner of the Hôtel de Dieppe back in Paris. Furthermore, the publisher he was hoping to contact had come to none of the lectures. He decided to make one last attempt and stake everything on 'a *lecture* organised by myself at a stockbroker's who will be lending me his drawing room'. Invitations were sent to Lacroix and to one of the King's ministers. 'I want some fine society,' he told his mother. This, he hoped, would also serve to dispel the rumours put about by 'someone from Hugo's gang' that he was in reality a spy from the French police.

The stockbroker, Prosper Crabbe, was the man who managed the Stevens' and Collarts' finances. On the first floor of his vast office building, Crabbe had three drawing rooms joined together in which he exhibited his collection of fifty paintings. Baudelaire invited Frédérix to come 'to a little literary *soirée*, of a very private nature' on June 13. Malassis, who by then was in Brussels, was asked to collect him at his hotel. Here is Baudelaire's description of the *soirée*:

> ... fifteen people invited by myself, five of whom came – the best, but quite without influence – and only two of whom – the Minister and the Director of *L'Indépendance belge* – wrote to excuse themselves; fifteen people invited by the master of the house, five of whom turned up. Just imagine *three enormous drawing rooms*, lit with *chandeliers and candelabras*, decorated with superb paintings, an *absurd* profusion of cakes and wine – and all for ten or twelve *very miserable* people.
>
> A journalist leant over and said to me: '*There is something* CHRISTIAN *in your works that has not been sufficiently noticed.*' At the other end of the room, on the stockbroker's settee, I heard a murmur: '*He's saying that we're* CRETINS!'
>
> There's an example of the Belgian mind and mores for you.
>
> When I saw that I was boring everyone, I interrupted my reading, and started eating and drinking. My five friends were ashamed and dismayed. I alone was laughing.[10]

Lacroix had not bothered to show his face. One of the shareholders of the publishing company was present and managed to arrange an interview for Baudelaire with the other partner, Verboeckhoven.[11] On June 23, Baudelaire learnt that the deal could not go through. Verboeckhoven was asking for a novel. 'What hypocrisy!' wrote Baudelaire. 'He knows I don't have one.' When Asselineau later suggested Lacroix as a possible publisher for the poet's complete works, Malassis told him the story behind Baudelaire's lectures in Brussels: 'He [Lacroix] never on any account wanted to meet Baudelaire, and always behaved towards him in the most stupidly vulgar fashion. Baudelaire detested him, and had every reason to do so.'[12]

'Everything's fallen through,' Baudelaire told Ancelle on July 14. The lectures had failed and brought in only one hundred francs; negotiations with Lacroix had led nowhere; the director of *L'Indépendance belge* already had his own Paris correspondents; and, finally, one senses that even the art galleries had been a disappointment.

The unwarranted violence of Baudelaire's comments on Belgium and the Belgians might cause the reader of his poetry and criticism some discomfort; but even genius is not immune to illness. The loathing and disgust which Baudelaire was beginning to express in his notes on Belgium were partly a form of mania, brought on by his syphilis, which by now was at an advanced stage, and aggravated by various excesses – notably alcohol. His arteries showed signs of premature ageing. To hate a few individuals is a sign of good health; hating a whole country is a symptom of serious disorders. Baudelaire's continued presence in Belgium was surely another sign of this obsession. If Brussels was so revolting, why not return to Paris? His reasons for staying on were specious.

Baudelaire was hoping to turn his notes into a series of satirical letters for the *Figaro* and then into a book, *Pauvre Belgique!* The book was to be enriched with poems ironically entitled *Amoenitates Belgicae*. To complete his documentation, Baudelaire had first to visit several other towns. On October 13, 1864, he wrote to Ancelle:

> The fragments I've already done are worth easily 1,000 francs; but I won't allow them to be published *as long as I'm still in Belgium*. – Therefore, I have to go back to France in order to get some money, and I need some money in order to leave, – and also to go on another excursion to Namur, Bruges, and Anvers (to do with art and architecture; six days at the most). So the whole thing's *a vicious circle*.

This curious mixture of folly and awareness of folly is typical of Baudelaire. The weeks passed and still he did not leave. On New Year's Day, 1865, after eight months in Brussels, he told his mother:

> You've probably guessed that I'm terrified of being in Paris with no money, of staying in Paris – my hell – for just six or seven days, without giving a few of my creditors some definite assurances. I do not wish to return to France until I can do so covered in *glory*.

Baudelaire continued to worry about returning to France. The book of vengeance was all but abandoned, and remained in the form of sometimes repetitious notes. In Paris, a literary agent, Julien Lemer, whom Baudelaire had known for about fifteen years, was given the job of finding a publisher for the poet's complete works. This was supposed to be another source of income, but neither Lemer nor Ancelle were capable of persuading any publisher to make an offer, whereas Baudelaire himself, had he been on the spot, might have been more persuasive.

Baudelaire had arrived in Brussels 'almost penniless'.[13] On August 30, 1864, he drew up a list of his daily expenses:

Room	2
Lunch	2
Dinner	
without wine	2.50
	6.50
with wine	3
	9.50

Even this rate of spending would have taken a large bite out of his monthly allowance from Ancelle. He was no longer receiving any royalties, and then there was the cost of travel and other minor expenses: 'tobacco, paper, stamps, repairs, etc. For example, my dream of having some quinine wine has become a real obsession with me, as the thought of a bath full of water would in the mind of a man with scabies.' Being poor in one's own country is bad enough, but being penniless and abroad is to be an object of suspicion as well as a pauper.

Why then did Baudelaire stay on in Belgium? Was it because, as he claimed, he was unable to pay his hotel bill? With each passing day, he became more and more 'stuck in the mud', as Malassis put it, 'going on about a country which isn't worth much, but which he doesn't understand much either'.[14] The whole of 1865 passed in this way and then the first three months of 1866. When making a flying visit to Paris and Honfleur in July 1865, Baudelaire ran into Asselineau, who told him what Théophile Gautier had said: 'That Baudelaire is incredible! How can anyone be so obsessed as to linger on in a country which makes him suffer? When I went off to visit Spain or Venice or Constantinople, I knew I'd like it there, and that when I returned I'd write a good book about it. But Baudelaire stays on in Brussels, where he's bored, just so he can have the pleasure of saying that he was bored there!'[15]

Baudelaire's answer was that he still had to visit other parts of Belgium in order to make notes for his book, but this was obviously a pretext: he already had his notes. Perhaps the wife of Paul Meurice was the only person to be given a straight answer to her straight question: 'Look. What are you doing in Brussels? Nothing. You're dying of boredom when people are looking forward to seeing you here. What strings are tying your feathers to that stupid Belgian cage?' Baudelaire replied on February 3, 1865:

> No, I assure you, I have no *particular* complaint. I'm still out of humour (that's a real disease), both because I'm suffering from the stupidity around me, and because I'm unhappy with myself. But I was suffering in France, too, where there's less stupidity, or at least where stupidity is more polite ... So whether I'm in Paris, Brussels, or a strange town, I can rest assured that I'll be sick and incurable. There is a form of misanthropy which comes, not from having a bad character, but from being too sensitive and too easily shocked. Why do I stay in Brussels when I hate it? *First of all, because I'm there*, and because in my present state I'd be uncomfortable wherever I was; secondly, because I'm doing penance. I'm doing penance until I'm cured of my vices (it's going very slowly), and also until a certain person to whom I've entrusted my literary affairs in Paris has settled certain questions.

Baudelaire knew a few remedies for boredom: one of these was provocation, at which he was a past master. Shortly after his arrival, he was suspected of spying on republican exiles for the French police. Despite finding this calumny extremely disagreeable, Baudelaire later spread rumours to the effect that he was a pederast and had been 'sent from Paris to correct the proofs of *infamous works*':

> *Exasperated* that people always believed what I said, I let it be known that I had *killed* my father and *eaten* him, and also that I had been allowed to escape from France because of the services I was rendering the French police, AND THEY BELIEVED ME! *I have taken to disgrace like a duck to water.*[16]

Baudelaire was putting back into circulation the very rumour which had caused him embarrassment when he first arrived. One can understand the perverse pleasure it gave him; one can also imagine the consequences of his behaviour. Everything was fuel to the fires of irony: Belgian women, Belgian French, Belgian architecture. Cholera, 'the sacred beast', was called down on the 'stinking banks of the Senne' that the poet might revel in 'the agony of that hideous race'.

He continued to visit the Cercle artistique, having perhaps overcome his

resentment. The Cercle was organising an International Exhibition of the
Fine Arts for October 1864. The exhibition included a painting by Gustave
Courbet which had been rejected by the Paris Salon. Entitled *Venus Pursuing
Psyche in Her Jealousy*, it was actually based on one of Baudelaire's two
'Femmes damnées'. A paper, *Le Sancho*, objected to the work and stated
bluntly that it showed 'two Gougnottes' (a slang word for lesbians) and
ought to be hung in a brothel. Baudelaire kept a cutting of the article as a
'sample of the subtlety of Belgian criticism'.

One of the members of the Cercle, Emile Leclercq, remembered seeing
Baudelaire holding forth at one of the meetings:

> His whole success as a writer and talker – or rather as an artist, for
> that is all he was – could be summed up in a single word: contradiction.
> In art, sensing that the modern movement was headed for naturalism,
> he would go into transports about David and his school. In literature,
> form and the bizarre were all that counted. He had neither convictions,
> nor common sense, nor any sincere enthusiasm. He posed as a religious
> man, but his whole life, which he talked about shamelessly, contradicted
> the mysticism of which he liked to make a great show ... The natural
> Baudelaire had disappeared under an artificial character who played his
> role very well and who probably faltered only when face to face with his
> Maker.[17]

Leclercq was a freethinker and a Realist – probably the one described by
Baudelaire in *Pauvre Belgique!* as 'a novelist who imitates the copyists of
Champfleury's apes'.[18] Leclercq's words nevertheless give some idea of the
irritation which Baudelaire tried, successfully, to provoke.

The taverns of Brussels provided the poet with other platforms – not
the pubs which dispensed *faro*, the 'twice-drunk beer', but English inns like
The Globe. These were rather rare at the time. The first had been opened
in 1815 by Thomas Bailey – a sergeant in Wellington's army at Waterloo.
The Prince of Wales, still run by an Englishman and his Belgian wife, stood
on the Place du Musée at number 8, rue Villa-Hermosa. There, Baudelaire
would spend time with Arthur Stevens and his brother Joseph, the animal
painter. As was the case with most of the old cafés in Brussels, one entered
through a narrow corridor which led to two rooms – one of them small
and smoky under its low ceiling, rather like a ship's cabin, the other more
spacious and decorated with hunting scenes remarkable only for their
naivety. English beer was served in pewter mugs and taken with pieces of
cheese dipped in a curious mixture known as pickle. It was there at The
Prince of Wales that the episode described in the prose poem, 'Les Bons

Chiens' took place. The poet admires Joseph Stevens' handsome waistcoat, 'of a colour both rich and faded which recalls the suns of autumn, the beauty of mature women, and Indian summers'. The painter impulsively takes off his waistcoat and gives it to Baudelaire, 'on condition that he write something on the dogs of poor people'.

Baudelaire also frequented the taverns with Malassis, who had not been long in forgiving the poet his treachery in selling his works to Hetzel. On June 9, 1864, Malassis sent news to Asselineau:

> I've seen Baudelaire again, not without pleasure as you can well imagine. All we had to do was see each other again, and everything was forgotten! He's sticking to his decision to remain in Brussels, not because of Lacroix, who's a literally chimerical publisher, but, I think, because he's so amazed at this city in which, with the exception of myself, he never meets a single creditor.

Malassis and Baudelaire enjoyed each other's company immensely. The latter told Sainte-Beuve in March 1865 that one of their great pleasures in discussion was pretending to be atheist and Jesuit, and went on to say of his friend: 'I marvel at his courage, his activity, and his incorrigible gaiety.' Baudelaire's words explain the inscription on the photograph of himself taken in 1864 or 1865: 'To my friend Auguste Malassis, the only being whose laughter lightened my sadness in Belgium.' Above the inscription is a phrase from Horace – 'Ridentem ferient Ruinae' – expressing Baudelaire's lucid and mocking despair: 'with laughter shall I see the ruins bear me off as they fall' – thinking in particular – optimistically – of the ruins of Belgium.[19]

Malassis had settled in the Faubourg d'Ixelles in the upper part of the town. He owned a drab little house, set back from the neighbouring houses, with a small garden in front. Malassis was leading a secluded life with a woman from Alsace, Françoise Daum, known to her friends as Miss Fanny. They eventually married in 1870. According to her companion, she had 'outstanding culinary ability' – a point of some interest to Baudelaire, who was constantly complaining about the blandness and stodginess of Belgian cuisine. 'Malassis,' he told his mother, 'has taught his cook to cook a little. If I didn't live so far away, I really think I'd pay him board so as to be able to eat at his place.' Baudelaire frequently made the journey to Ixelles. It was a long but pleasant walk along a road lined with small houses and one or two fine country residences – large, white, cubical houses surrounded by flowering gardens that could be glimpsed between the railings. There were also the open-air cafés to which the city dwellers flocked on Sundays.

The publisher was still practising his art. He and his new partner, Lécrivain, with the help of Belgian printers and booksellers, were producing pornographic books, as well as pamphlets directed against the Second Empire. These little books were smuggled over the border into France.

To illustrate his publications, Malassis had finally laid hands on the *rara avis* for which he had scoured all of Paris – 'an artist who understands what a typographical frontispiece is. My bird is called Félicien Rops, and he's quite well known.' Rops had indeed been introduced to Parisians as early as 1857 in an article which compared him to Daumier, even to Delacroix.[20] He was more commonly referred to, however, as 'the Belgian Gavarni' – an irritating expression for Rops, since the frivolous nature of Gavarni's engravings had little in common with the Belgian's macabre obsessions, which touched on the realm of the unconscious.

Baudelaire may already have seen a few works by Rops, but the two men had never met. Malassis, thinking that Rops and his talent would console the poet for Bracquemond's blunders, invited him to one of Baudelaire's lectures. Rops was unable to attend, but told Malassis how much he wanted to meet the poet with whom he shared 'a strange infatuation ... a passion for the skeleton'.[21] It was probably in Namur that they met for the first time. Baudelaire left Brussels immediately after his last lecture on May 23 to spend a week with Rops and his family – the first of several visits. On leaving Namur, he apparently told Rops, 'Life is beautiful, but unpredictable. Perhaps one of us is about to enter eternity. With the hope that we shall meet again soon and in happy circumstances, allow me nevertheless to bid you an eternal farewell.'

Félicien Rops, born in 1833, was twelve years younger than Baudelaire, but his great affection for the poet removed any barriers that age might have placed between them. In 1859, the handsome Félicien had married Charlotte Polet de Faveaux, by whom he had had a son and whom he deceived with such dedication that he was said to be married in Namur and a bachelor on the rest of the Continent. The artist's father-in-law was a judge. He owned the nearby Château de Thozé, as well as a handsome town house in the rue Neuve. This 'severe but jovial magistrate' found favour with the great hater of Belgians: 'He has written a book on hunting, and quoted verses to me from Horace and *Les Fleurs du Mal*, and some phrases from D'Aurevilly ... He's the only Belgian who knows Latin and is capable of conversing in French.'[22] Namur itself was spared in Baudelaire's notebook, partly because it was the home of Rops and partly because it was 'neglected by tourists'. Baudelaire had time to admire the cathedral – Saint Aubin – and the Eglise Saint-Loup, 'the masterpiece of Jesuit masterpieces',

the interior of which forms 'a terrible and delicious catafalque'. And it was
in Namur especially that Baudelaire experienced his last great aesthetic joy –
the discovery of what later came to be known as the baroque style of
architecture.

Many years later, Rops recalled some of the less conventional pleasures
of the Belgian tourist:

> I don't hold the record for half-naked Flemish girls. I did loads of
> them with Guys! We went all over the place, sketching the big fat hussies
> from the nether regions of the Rydeack which was still there in those
> days, and which doesn't exist any more. We got them to pose in the same
> room! And Baudelaire was presiding![23]

This is the only evidence we have of a trip made by Rops and Baudelaire
to Anvers in the company of Constantin Guys, who is not mentioned in
any of the poet's letters from Belgium. On May 11, 1865, Baudelaire
recommended Rops to Manet:

> If you see Rops, don't pay too much attention to some of his inor-
> dinately provincial airs. Rops likes you. Rops has understood the worth
> of your mind, and even imparted to me some of his observations on the
> people who hate you (for it seems you have the distinction of inspiring
> hate). Rops is *the only true artist* (in the sense in which I, and I alone
> perhaps, understand the word *artist*) I have found in Belgium.

In 1865, Rops printed a menu entitled *Le Grand Marmiton* for a dinner
given by the photographer Charles Neyt. The guests included Baudelaire,
Malassis, the poet Glatigny and Arthur Stevens. In Baudelaire's honour,
the wine served was 'Bordeaux Back-from-India 1842' and wine from the
Cape, which proves that the legend of Baudelaire's trip to the Indian
continent was generally believed – perhaps even by the traveller himself.
In a letter to Ancelle, he referred to his experience of Bourbon, Mauritius
and Calcutta: 'Just imagine then what I have to suffer in a country where
the trees are black and *where the flowers have no scent*!'[24]

This dreary insipidity was occasionally relieved by some interesting
events, notably the arrival of Nadar with his balloon, *The Giant*: 'If by
chance I'm still here on the 25th, which I doubt very much, I shall go off
with Nadar, who kindly offered me a place in his *nacelle*. To flee this filthy
race in a balloon, to go and land in Austria, or maybe Turkey – any sort
of folly sounds appealing, provided it relieves my boredom.'[25] In the end,
Baudelaire failed to join the ballooning party, which landed somewhere
between Ypres and the sea.

Nadar, who spent a few days in Brussels with his party, was an extremely exuberant and unrepining sort of person, and must have been a pleasant change from the soporific dullness that Baudelaire associated with Brussels.[26] But Nadar and his group of friends must also have been something of an encumbrance. In his present state of despair, Baudelaire was more and more a friend of silence. Nadar himself noticed the poet's increasing taste for solitude, 'and in particular an irritation, which exasperation turned ever more to bitterness, at that sweet and studious land whose welcoming retreat had smiled on many of our number at the time of the last Empire'.[27]

Baudelaire's friends were few: the Collarts, the Stevens brothers – Arthur and Joseph – Malassis, Rops, as well as two painters, Louis Dubois and Edmond Lambrichs – and two photographers, Louis Ghémar and Charles Neyt. The latter produced two of the most moving photographs of Baudelaire from this period. In one, the face expresses despair ironically defying fate; in the other, known as 'Baudelaire au cigare', the same irony is tinged with painful regret.

There was also the German-Hungarian, Kertbeny, whom Baudelaire had invited to one of his lectures on stimulants. Kertbeny was the man who had introduced the poetry of Petoefi to Germany and also, to a lesser extent, to the French. He had a reputation as a polyglot. One day, he left a visiting card with Baudelaire, full of excruciating mistakes in French: '*J'ai l'honneur d'attenter à vous jusqu'au midi, et j'étais bien heureux de pouver reçu aujourd'hui votre aimable visite*,' etc.[28] Baudelaire wrote on the card: 'This is the man who knows 52 languages. Obviously he only knows 51.'

Another passing figure of fun – and exasperation – was Alexandre Weill, a former '*petit crétin*' on the *Corsaire-Satan*. Unfortunately for Baudelaire, the garrulous Weill decided to stay at the Hôtel du Grand Miroir when coming to give a lecture at the Cercle artistique et littéraire – 'a first lecture,' wrote 'R'. (i.e. Malassis) in the *Petite Revue*, 'which will probably not be followed by several others'. 'In his brain, ideas follow one another with the same logic as the numbered balls in lotto.'[29] Weill had had some insulting things to say about Baudelaire's study on Gautier, published by Malassis, and was an easy target with his thick, German accent – hence a cartoon drawn by Baudelaire which shows a very hairy, bespectacled speaker uttering incongruous remarks in incomprehensible patois. The poet who devoted such time and effort to introducing Edgar Allan Poe to the French had, deep down, like many of his compatriots, a considerable fund of xenophobia and anti-Semitism.

Other acquaintances, like Albert Glatigny, were a consolation.[30] A great friend and admirer of Banville, Glatigny was a poet, improviser and wandering actor. Though poor and in bad health, he was always a gay and youthful figure, travelling between Paris and Brussels, where he spent his time in the company of Hugo, Malassis, Baudelaire and Rops. One day he arrived in the Belgian capital, 'dead tired'. Malassis and Rops were nowhere to be found. 'Without Baudelaire,' he wrote, 'I would have fallen prey to the republicans.'

The Hugo tribe was indeed unavoidable, even though the *pater familias* himself was still 'over there' on his island. Baudelaire perhaps felt some obligation to make contact with the Hugos and realised only very late in the day that Mme Hugo had a real liking for him. It was probably the young critic, Gustave Frédérix, who introduced Baudelaire to the family. The poet was often invited over, but, with his increasing misanthropy and reluctance to bathe in reflected glory, he seems to have declined politely most of the invitations he received. His excuses were at least expressed with a degree of originality: 'You know,' he told Victor's son, Charles, 'there are none so swamped with chores as the idle, when they have a sense of neglected duty.' Baudelaire nevertheless called on the Hugos early in 1865, and learnt that the great exile was shortly to arrive in Brussels. Here is how Baudelaire passed on this piece of news to Ancelle:

> It seems that he and the Ocean have fallen out. Either *he* was not strong enough to bear the Ocean, or the Ocean *itself* grew tired of him. – What a waste of time it was setting up a palace on a rock! I who am alone and forgotten by all, shall sell my Mother's maisonette only as a last resort. – But I have even more pride than Victor Hugo, and I sense, in fact I know I shall never be as stupid as he. – One can be happy anywhere (provided one is well, and that one has books and engravings), *even when faced with the Ocean.*

Hugo, however, remained on his rock for the time being. Had he decided to take up residence in Brussels, Baudelaire may well have decided to return to Paris. Brussels in the 1860s was too small a place for two stars of that magnitude, already so close that dark flares passed between them. Hugo was still in Guernsey when, at the beginning of May 1865, Baudelaire was invited to dinner:

> I was *forced* to dine yesterday with Mme Hugo and her sons. (I had to borrow a shirt.) – My God! how ridiculous a once beautiful woman is when she lets everyone see how much she misses adulation. – And those little gentlemen, whom I knew when they were very young, and who

want to control the world! They're just as stupid as their mother, and all three of them, mother and sons, are just as idiotic as their father! – They pestered me and plagued me for a long time, and I played along like a jolly old fellow. – If I were a famous man, and afflicted with a son who mimicked my faults, I'd kill him out of repulsion for myself. But since you don't know how ridiculous all those people are, you won't be able to understand my laughter or my rage.[31]

Another version of the same dinner, this time in a letter to Mme Meurice:

> ... Mme Hugo explained to me her majestic plan for *international education* (it appears to be the latest craze of that great party which has agreed to take on the happiness of the human race). Speaking does not come easily to me at the best of times, especially after dinner, and especially when I want to dream, and I had no end of a job trying to make her see that there were great men BEFORE *international education*, and that since children have nothing better to do than eat sweets, drink liqueurs in secret, and go off to visit prostitutes, there would not be any more great men AFTER it. Luckily for me, I'm considered insane, and should be treated with indulgence.

Hugo arrived in Brussels for a holiday in July 1865. On the 23rd, he sold Lacroix and Verboeckhoven *Les Chansons des rues et des bois* and *Les Travailleurs de la mer* for 120,000 francs – more than Baudelaire had received on his coming of age. Baudelaire had dinner with Hugo himself, who invited him to come and spend some time with him on Guernsey. 'He really bored me,' Baudelaire told his mother. 'This time,' (in his latest collection of poetry) 'he's tried to be gay and nimble, in love and young again. It's horribly heavy. All I see in such things, as in many others, is yet another opportunity to thank God for not bestowing so much stupidity on me. I keep saying the Pharisee's prayer.'

Baudelaire had indeed received a copy of Hugo's *Chansons*, bearing the inscription, 'To Charles Baudelaire, *jungamus dextras*'. This he interpreted for Manet in the following way: 'I don't think it just means, "Let's shake hands." I know the innuendoes of V. Hugo's Latin. It also means, "Let's join hands TO SAVE THE HUMAN RACE." But I don't give a damn about the human race, and he never noticed.'

Despite his undemocratic opinions, Baudelaire eventually became a regular visitor to the Hugos' home in the rue de l'Astronomie. Mme Hugo herself informed her husband of this when he asked her why Baudelaire had not written to acknowledge receipt of the *Chansons*: 'We see Baudelaire

very often, and, with Frédérix, he is our usual guest. I think that Baudelaire
is a little sick in the head. He digs up and resuscitates unknown talent, but
the brilliance and renown of the living offend him, and that, I think, is why
he's said nothing about the *Chansons des rues et des bois*.'[32]

At the beginning of 1866, Baudelaire was playing the role of go-between
for Mme Hugo and Sainte-Beuve, as if trying to stir up the old fires of
adulterous passion which had caused the rift between Hugo and the critic
back in the early 1830s. 'Mme Hugo alone, and in spite of her sons,' he
told Sainte-Beuve, 'hears your name and praise of you with pleasure.'[33]
Sainte-Beuve thanked Baudelaire for mentioning him to Mme Hugo: 'She's
the only faithful friend I've ever had in those circles.'[34] As for Hugo himself,
Sainte-Beuve was convinced that their old enmity was still only dormant.
Baudelaire copied down the positive part of Sainte-Beuve's letter for Mme
Hugo, adding, in his usual scheming way: 'He has not the slightest inkling
that M. Victor Hugo still harbours suspicion for his old friend.'[35] The affair
went no further than that. Baudelaire at least was finally pleased with the
thoughtful attention he was receiving from Mme Hugo. 'Mme Victor
Hugo,' he told his mother, 'who until now has only ever seemed ridiculous,
is decidedly a good woman. But she does enjoy mothering all her friends.
She has instructed her doctor to pay me a visit.'[36]

Baudelaire was also treated compassionately by another Hugo – Charles
Hugo's young wife, Alice. After dinner, Alice would sit down at her Erard
piano and the poet would say, 'Come on, then – what about a few noble
chords from Wagner?' This was his usual way of asking to hear some
excerpts from *Tannhäuser*, wrote Frédérix, 'the work he had defended and
described so well in Paris'.[37]

There was then some harmony at least in Baudelaire's relations with the
Hugos. His poetry, meanwhile, had struck a chord in the hearts of his
younger contemporaries:

> I sometimes receive [he told Ancelle], from very distant places, and
> from people whom I do not know, tokens of sympathy which touch me
> deeply, but which do not console me for my loathsome poverty, my
> humiliating situation, nor especially for my vices.

One of the distant places referred to was probably Rumania, where Ange
Pechméja, who had left France after the *coup d'état*, had published the first
article to appear on Baudelaire beyond the Danube. Pechméja was himself
a poet and had written a sequence of five sonnets strongly influenced by
Baudelaire: 'After a pious reading of *Les Fleurs du Mal*.' The following

passage is taken from the long and enthusiastic letter Baudelaire received from Bucharest:

Closely wrapped in its exquisite form, like the flower in its narrow sheath, the meaning of your verses makes the series of developments latently contained in their concise formulation explode in the reader's mind. And that, in my opinion, is what especially makes your book a book apart; for, to my knowledge at least, nothing like it exists to that degree in any other poet. With most, the thought, instead of strongly supporting the form, too often leaves it limp; with you, it bursts through its covering.

Another quality ... which you possess to *at least* the same degree as V. Hugo or Gautier, is that perfect sense of the relative value of sounds and their contrasting harmony, thanks to which a line of poetry can delight the ear like a piece of voluptuous music.

> Et comme un bon nageur qui se pâme dans l'onde,
> Tu sillonnes gaîment l'immensité profonde
> Avec une indicible et mâle volupté.*

Such verses crunch in the mouth like a delectable *dragée*.

That is not all, I am convinced that if the letters which go to make up verses like these were translated into the geometrical shapes and coloured tones which analogy assigns to each in turn, they would present the agreeable texture and beautiful shades of a Persian carpet or Indian shawl.

My idea will seem burlesque to you. Sometimes I feel like drawing and colouring your verses.

Pechméja was interested in analogies between sound and colour as he showed in *The Egg of Kneph, the Secret Story of the Zero*, published in Bucharest in 1864. Baudelaire was so touched by this expression of admiration that, even though it came after his stroke, he dictated a letter of thanks.

Admiration also came from France. It was on February 1, 1865, that *L'Artiste* published a text entitled *Symphonie littéraire*, written by a young writer, Stéphane Mallarmé:

In winter, when I'm tired of my torpor, I plunge with delight into the cherished pages of *Les Fleurs du Mal*. No sooner is my Baudelaire open

---

* 'And like a powerful swimmer who swoons in the waves, / You happily glide through the limitless deep / With inexpressible and virile delight.'

than I am drawn into a surprising landscape which lives in my eye with
the intensity of those created by profound opium.

At the end of 1865, the twenty-one-year-old Paul Verlaine published a
long, three-part study in the new review – *L'Art*.[38] It was a protest against
the popular image of Baudelaire as poet of the Carcass, and a declaration
that his 'profound originality' lay in his 'powerful and essential' depiction
of modern man, 'with his overexcited, quivering nerves, his painfully subtle
mind, his brain filled with tobacco, and his blood burnt with alcohol' –
modern man as the modern hero. Verlaine was alluding to Baudelaire's first
two *Salons* in which the poet had urged artists to extract from modern life
its beauty and heroism. The study also included references even to some of
Baudelaire's lesser known works.

Sainte-Beuve noticed the articles by Verlaine and told Baudelaire about
them. The avuncular critic went on, however, to bemoan these youngsters'
lack of experience and ignorance of tradition. 'If you were here,' he wrote,
'whether you liked it or not, you would become an authority, an oracle, a
consultant poet.'[39] Baudelaire asked Sainte-Beuve to send on copies of the
new review and, after receiving two of the three issues in question, enclosed
these 'trifles' in a letter to Mme Aupick:

> These young people have talent, but what a lot of silliness! What
> exaggeration and youthful infatuation! For a few years now, I've been
> discovering imitations and tendencies here and there which alarmed me.
> I know of nothing more compromising than imitators, and I like nothing
> better than being alone; but that is no longer possible, and it seems that
> *the Baudelaire school* exists.[40]

This was the school which Emile Deschanel dubbed the '*école fantaisiste*'
in the lecture he gave in Paris in 1866 on his old classmate from Louis-le-
Grand. Baudelaire himself read about this in a column in *Le Temps* written
by Henry de La Madelène. Deschanel was praised for his expert reading of
Baudelaire's poetry and criticised for presenting it with 'the attitude of a
startled bourgeois'. Ancelle had been obliging enough to attend the lecture.
Two days later, Baudelaire rebuked him for his report:

> And you were NAIVE enough to forget that the French HATE poetry –
> *true* poetry – that they only love pigs like Béranger and Musset, that
> *whosoever tries to spell correctly is considered to be a heartless man* (which is
> actually quite logical, since passion always expresses itself badly), and,
> lastly, that poetry which is profound, complicated, bitter, and casually

satanic (in appearance), is less suited than any other to appeal to never-ending frivolity!

Must I tell you – you who realised no more than anyone else – that in that *horrific* book, I put all my *heart*, all my *tenderness*, all my *religion* (disguised), all my *hate*? True, I shall write the exact opposite and swear to God that it's a book of *pure art*, of mimicry and juggling tricks, and I shall lie through my teeth . . .

That's quite enough, don't you think? You'll forgive me my diatribe. Don't deprive me of the only friend I can insult. But whatever gave you the idea of going to a lecture by Deschanel?'[41]

There is no record of how Baudelaire reacted to Mallarmé's piece. He clearly failed to take Verlaine's remarkable study seriously. It is all the more surprising, therefore, that he became so comradely with the much less gifted Catulle Mendès. Before very long, they were calling each other '*Mon cher*', and Baudelaire agreed to provide Mendès with poems for a new review which gave name and identity to a new poetic movement: *Le Parnasse contemporain*. The poems Baudelaire offered Mendès were the 'trifles' and '*bouffonneries*' contained in the volume soon to be published in Brussels by Malassis: *Les Epaves*. As Baudelaire warned Mendès, the book also 'contains, unfortunately, the six condemned poems from *Les Fleurs du Mal*, which means that it will be impossible to put it on sale or send it to the newspapers'.[42] The poet who was usually so careful about anything he published virtually gave Mendès *carte blanche* to choose any poems he wished, asking only that he be shown the proofs and paid the one hundred francs that were promised and which he needed to buy some medicine. Mendès also asked if there might be some unpublished verses to supplement the poems from *Les Epaves*. Baudelaire graciously offered some of his humorous anti-Belgian epigrams. Mendès was careful to omit any pieces that might lead to prosecution and the fifth issue of *Le Parnasse contemporain* appeared on March 31, 1866, devoted entirely to Baudelaire and these co-called 'Nouvelles Fleurs du Mal'. By the time the review reached the poet, it would be too late for him to express any opinion, or even make use of the one hundred francs.

In his state of sickness and fatigue, Baudelaire allowed himself to be led along by the forceful and handsome Mendès – a strange lack of irritation or impatience. With Malassis, things were different. Together, they had published four books – the two *Fleurs du Mal*, *Les Paradis artificiels* and the *Théophile Gautier*, and when they met up again in Brussels, both men dreamt of new projects. But the fruitful years at the end of the 1850s were already far in the past. The old enthusiasm had waned, and Malassis must still have felt some bitterness about Baudelaire's betrayal and his own uncalculating generosity.

Baudelaire was bored. He agreed to undertake a 'strange piece of work' – a translation from Latin about which no details are known. This, Baudelaire hoped, would encourage Malassis to entrust him with the job of translating Petronius's *Satyricon* (a project which dates back to 1862), as well as a critical work on Laclos, the author of *Les Liaisons dangereuses*. How unfortunate that Baudelaire's Petronius was never written! He alone was capable of inventing a language that could faithfully render that curious work in French. As for Laclos, his work was known to very few people at the time and was banned in any case. Baudelaire had often thought of devoting a study to the novelist, but it was February or March 1866 before he eventually jotted down some notes on the back of a prospectus for the *Parnasse contemporain*. These notes, made after a rereading of *Les Liaisons dangereuses*, are, according to a leading Laclos scholar, strikingly original. Baudelaire presents an entirely new image of the novelist – not the pornographic writer condemned by tradition, but one whose theme is the tragedy of man preyed on by evil.[43] The poet's remarks bear witness to the astonishing acuity of his mind during those rare moments when his syphilis gave him some respite.

Baudelaire's financial difficulties continued in spite of his friend's forgiving nature. It was thought until now that Malassis had remained unaware of Baudelaire's illegal contract with the unsuspecting Hetzel until mid-1865. In fact, he knew about it as early as the spring of 1864. From Brussels, he instructed a bailiff to inform Hetzel (who had himself perhaps told Malassis) that Baudelaire had already signed away his author's rights. Pressed by creditors, Malassis was thinking of selling Baudelaire's debts to a third party as a last resort, having loyally hidden this source of credit from the receiver in 1862. In order to avoid the worst consequences, he offered the debts to Hetzel. They amounted to 5,000 francs.

In the meantime, Baudelaire went to ask Ancelle for advice. The next day, he was in Honfleur, telling his mother the whole sad story. 'Thanks to you,' she replied, 'I'm very hard up. I can't pay 2,000 francs, let alone 5,000.' Nevertheless, at her behest, Ancelle paid out the 2,000 francs needed to avoid disaster. On the 9th, Baudelaire was back in Paris, where he stayed for five days, unable to pay for a train ticket. It was like returning to prison. He took a room at the Hôtel du Chemin de Fer du Nord. One day, Mendès, returning from a trip to the country, suddenly found himself face to face with Baudelaire at the station:

I saw the wretched state of his clothes – perfectly proper, no doubt, but worn and shiny in places – and, with his unshaven face, he looked almost menacingly sullen, the way he did on the days the bills came due ... He would certainly have preferred not to run into anyone. I was about to apologise and go away, when he turned pleasant and affectionate, and took me by the arm. We left the station together. He explained that he had come to Paris on business, that he was going back to Brussels, that he had missed the evening train, and would spend the night in a hotel, leaving the next day on the first train.

Mendès, who lived close to the station in the rue de Douai, offered to share his small lodging. Baudelaire did not sleep and stayed up reading. Suddenly, he dropped his book, turned to his host and said, 'Do you know, my boy, how much money I've earned since I've been working, since I've been alive?'

There was in his voice an agonising sharpness of reproach and something that sounded like protest. I shuddered. 'I don't know,' I said. 'I shall count it up for you!' he shouted ... Along with the amounts he had received for them, he reeled off a list of his articles, verse poems, prose poems, translations and reprintings, and, having added them all up in his head, with the suddenness of the Inaudis that are exhibited in music halls, he proclaimed, 'Total profit from all my life: fifteen thousand, eight hundred and ninety-two francs, sixty centimes!'[44] ... He burst out laughing, then extinguished the lamp. 'Now,' he said, 'let us sleep.'

When Mendès awoke, Baudelaire had gone.

Once the debt with Malassis had been settled, the rift between them should have disappeared; but Baudelaire was becoming an increasingly unpleasant companion. On August 30, 1865, Malassis wrote to Asselineau:

No news from this end. I hardly see Baudelaire any more. That doesn't bother me too much: even though it's always a pleasure to see him, he's become so slow, insistent, and rambling that it would be more than a little tiresome to have him over every day. He'll have wasted his time in Belgium, as you can well imagine. His studies consist of making everything fit in with his prejudice.[45]

The two friends had nevertheless managed to agree on the publication of the collection of poems from which Mendès had been allowed to choose. The title of *Les Epaves* – meaning 'wrecks' or 'remains' – referred to the condemned poems and the other pieces which Baudelaire had left out of

Les Fleurs du Mal. Only 260 copies were printed. The book was intended mainly as a private publication, pending successful completion of negotiations in Paris for a third edition of the *Fleurs.* It also allowed the poet to reproduce in a less compromising context the poems excised by the Courts – Malassis had already reprinted these poems in *Le Parnasse satyrique du dix-neuvième siècle,* which he was bringing out just as Baudelaire arrived in Brussels. This 'collection of titillating and bawdy verses by MM. de Béranger ... Baudelaire, Monselet, [etc]' was supposedly published in Rome, at the sign of the Seven Deadly Sins. Baudelaire was none too pleased to find himself placed in the company of Béranger!

Twenty-three poems make up *Les Epaves,* divided into five sections: 'Pièces condamnées', 'Galanteries', 'Epigraphes', 'Pièces diverses' and 'Bouffonneries'. In the opening poem – 'Le Coucher du soleil romantique' – Baudelaire expresses his nostalgia for a vanished age. The 'Epigraphes' include the quatrain on Lola de Valence and 'Verses for the Portrait of M. Honoré Daumier' which Champfleury had asked him to write for his *History of Modern Caricature.*

The frontispiece was entrusted to Félicien Rops. Baudelaire accepted the very ornate and complicated skeleton Rops produced, though it is far from certain that he saw in it the ideal image he had tried in vain to extract from Bracquemond. Malassis saw fit to accompany the engraving with an 'Explanation' and also inserted a note intended to relieve the poet of responsibility for the collection:

> The author will be apprised of this publication at the same time as its two hundred and sixty probable readers who, for its voluntary publisher, represent – more or less – the literary public in France, ever since beasts have decidedly usurped in that country the word of men.

Les Epaves was published in Amsterdam at the end of February or in March 1866, just a few weeks or days before its author collapsed, paralysed. Baudelaire had already drawn up a distribution list[46] for friends, journalists editors, publishers, painters and even, ironically, a judge – Ernest Pinard, who, after all, was indirectly responsible for the appearance in *Les Epaves* of the six condemned poems.

These copies were smuggled into France, addressed to Charles Asselineau – a prudent man who would not have appreciated the honour. Two years later, in fact, a publisher, Sacré-Duquesne, was sentenced to one year in prison and a 2,000-franc fine for having copies of *Les Epaves* brought into the country.[47]

Baudelaire's last book was severely judged by Albert Glatigny who was staying at that time in Belgium: 'Although the volume is very short it's still too long. Apart from the six poems removed from *Les Fleurs du Mal*, there are only three or four pieces at the most that are worthy of Baudelaire.'[48] There is, however, little doubt that even if *Les Epaves* had contained only those six *Fleurs du Mal*, the book would still have outshone the works of the Parnassian poets, with the notable exception of Verlaine's *Poèmes saturniens*, which appeared the same year.

Baudelaire's other important project – the publication of his complete works – had come to naught. *Pauvre Belgique!*, which he wanted to include in his collected works, existed only as a pile of notes, newspaper clippings, assorted documents and a few brilliant fragments.

On January 30, Baudelaire had written to Ancelle: 'I shall be returning this Sunday to Namur in order to see Rops and admire once again that Jesuit church of which I shall never tire.' But on the eve of his planned departure, he was obliged to call off the visit: 'I've been having frequent dizzy spells and vomiting of bile again. I have a fear of the train carriage, so please forgive my unpunctuality.'

Finally, around March 15, Baudelaire left for Namur where he stayed with the Rops family. During his visit to the Eglise Saint-Loup, he collapsed on the flagstones. Suffering from a cerebral disorder, he was taken back immediately to Brussels.

CHAPTER 23

The Final Voyage

Brussels, March 1866 – Paris, August 1867

Ever since the 'strange warning' of January 23, 1862, Baudelaire's health had been steadily deteriorating. His letters from Belgium – particularly those to Ancelle – were filled with worries about his physical condition.[1] (Baudelaire was hoping to spare his mother undue anxiety.) At first, he was tempted to put his discomfort down to that dreadful country with its damp soil and humid climate, the water that was splashed every morning over the pavements in large bucketfuls, the food, insipid and badly prepared, the 'heavy' atmosphere of the place and its way of slowing everything down.[2] But as the days and weeks went by, different explanations had to be found – explanations which might also account for the disturbing accidents that had occurred before he left for Brussels.

In February 1865, Baudelaire's state of health was already quite serious. He was suffering from colds, headaches and rheumatism, and from a persistent fever which had brought on insomnia.[3] On February 14, he went out for the first time in ten days, his head 'wrapped up in a kerchief', with 'a dull pain above the right eyebrow'.[4]

In addition to this physical pain, there was also the irritation caused by an article he had read the day before in *L'Indépendance belge*: Jules Janin had denounced the scathing irony of Heinrich Heine and all those other wretched foreign poets who left one longing for Béranger and the French poets who sing of 'the delightful exhilaration of being twenty years old'. Baudelaire, the poet of *spleen* and *ennui*, was disgusted by Janin's facile praise of happiness and angrily penned an eloquent reply in the form of an open letter.[5] Sickness and despair unfortunately sent this idea the same way as *Pauvre Belgique!* and all the other unfinished works.

In May 1865, his headaches suddenly returned, this time with stomach pains – and then again in December. In order to write, he was forced to wrap his head in a compress soaked every hour in sedative water; he was also taking tablets which contained opium, valerian, digitalis and belladonna. That Christmas, he wrote to Ancelle:

My head is a little hazy and befuddled, and I can't think straight. It's connected with the long series of attacks, and also comes from using opium, digitalis, belladonna, and quinine. – A doctor I called was unaware that I once used opium for a long period. That's why I had to double and quadruple the doses. I've managed to change the time the attacks occur, which is quite an achievement; but I'm very tired.

On January 1, 1866, he told his mother that he was faring much better; but on the 18th, Ancelle heard a different story:

I've been sick again – very sick. Dizziness and vomiting for three days. I had to remain on my back for three days, because even when I was crouched on the floor, I kept falling over, head first. I think it was an intoxication of the bile. The doctor prescribed only Vichy water – and I haven't a penny!

The doctor in question was probably a young practitioner, Oscar Max, who had been called by the hotel owner.[6] The patient must have revealed very little of his medical history for the doctor to prescribe such a mild course of treatment. Baudelaire nevertheless found it too strict – no beer, no tea, no coffee, no wine: 'No wine? God, that's cruel!'[7]

He was then examined by another young doctor, 'a very pleasant and well-educated man',[8] who had been recommended by Malassis. Baudelaire sent the doctor a detailed description of his attacks and was advised not to read or study, as he told Sainte-Beuve on January 15:

It's a funny sort of medicine that does away with the principal function! Another doctor I saw could think of no consolation but to tell me I was *hysterical*. Don't you think it's wonderful, the elastic use of those portentous words designed to hide our ignorance of all things?

The notes which Baudelaire prepared for the doctor referred neither to his syphilis nor to the treatment he had received and the doctors themselves appear to have made only a cursory examination. There was still no test which allowed a quick and accurate diagnosis of the disease.

Meanwhile, back in Paris, Baudelaire's friends were hearing alarming rumours. Asselineau wrote to reproach him for leaving everyone in the dark and asked him to send a report from the doctor or himself which might be shown to a Paris physician.[9] Baudelaire wrote back on February 5:

... It isn't very easy for me to write. If you had some good advice, I'd be very glad to hear it. Actually, for the past twenty months, I've been ill nearly all the time ... One evening, without having eaten or drunk anything, I started rolling about and falling over like a drunkard, grabbing pieces of furniture and pulling them over with me. Vomiting of bile or white froth. These are invariably the different stages: I'm perfectly well, and haven't eaten, and then all at once, without warning and for no apparent reason, I feel haziness, distraction, and stupor, followed by a terrible pain in the head. I absolutely have to fall over, unless I'm lying on my back when it happens. Then, cold sweat, vomiting, and protracted stupor. For the headaches, they gave me tablets made up of quinine, digitalis, belladonna, and morphine ... The illness persists; and the doctor pronounced the great word – hysteria.[10] In good French, that means I'm raving mad. He wants me to do lots and lots of walking. It's absurd. Apart from the fact that I've become so timid and clumsy that I can't bear to be in the street, it's impossible to take a walk here, because of the state the streets and roads are in, especially with this weather. For the first time, I've given in to the desire to feel sorry for myself. Do you know that sort of illness? Have you ever seen anything like it?

Thank you again for your good letter. Do me the pleasure of writing back. Greet Banville, Manet, and Champfleury for me if you see them.

Asselineau took this letter 'to that excellent Dr. Piogey – the physician, friend, and counsellor of us all, who had known Baudelaire for a long time and treated him more than once. Piogey was not terribly reassuring and found the symptoms very grave, but refused to express an opinion until he had seen the patient.'

Baudelaire was thinking of consulting Charles Lasègue – his former tutor from Louis-le-Grand. Lasègue, as Baudelaire told his mother, had become 'a famous doctor. He specialises in *madmen* and *hysterics*.'[11] Baudelaire decided to see him the next time he was passing through Paris.

Mme Aupick was growing worried. Baudelaire sent another long note to her doctor in Honfleur describing his symptoms and tried to reassure her on February 10 by claiming to have had neither dizziness nor vomiting for three days.

What's really *ridiculous* is that a man walking behind me, or a child or a dog going past make me feel like fainting. It is ridiculous, isn't it? Yesterday, I went to see an exhibition of drawings; but after a few minutes, as when I'm forced to apply my mind to something (*it won't last forever*), I felt some bad signs coming on, and despite the rain, I fled into the open air.

You can see that it's all purely nervous. The summer will chase it all away. The only sensible thing the doctor told me (in my opinion) was, '*Take cold baths and go swimming.*' But in this confounded city, there's no river. It's true they've invented swimming pools or artificial ponds in which the water is heated a little by a nearby machine. It's horrible just to think about it. I have no desire to bathe in an artificial lake polluted by all those filthy pigs. That piece of advice is as difficult to follow as the order to go out walking. – I'm going to go in search of some cold showers.

Two days later, Baudelaire was still talking about improvement. He was enjoying smoking again and felt 'not only great disgust with all the tablets, but also great hunger, which hasn't happened to me for three weeks now'. His timidity was disappearing and he was referring to his ailments now in the past tense: 'Very often during those endless days spent in bed, I said to myself, "Look! let's be reasonable! What if it's apoplexy or paralysis that's coming on? What shall I do, and how shall I put my affairs in order?" '[12] In mentioning paralysis, Baudelaire was making a more accurate diagnosis than his doctors.

Nonetheless, he followed the doctor's ineffectual diet, which was supposed to counteract 'a thinning of the blood': roast meat, tea (but no green tea), just a little wine, cold showers and walks. The worst part must have been the complete ban on coffee and brandy.[13] Baudelaire had become a great drinker of spirits, as Malassis told Jules Troubat, Sainte-Beuve's secretary, on April 9, 1866: 'Contrary to the doctors' advice and the pleas of his friends, [Baudelaire] continued to use and abuse stimulants. He so much lacked the will power to change his habits that we stopped putting brandy on the table at my place so that he wouldn't drink any; otherwise, he was incapable of resisting temptation.'[14]

During this brief remission, Baudelaire made his notes for a preface to *Les Liaisons dangereuses*, and wrote his long letter to Ancelle about Deschanel's lecture and the planned edition of his complete works. He was still able to muster strength for some things at least:

Except for Chateaubriand, Balzac, Stendhal, Mérimée, de Vigny, Flaubert, Banville, Gautier, and Leconte de Lisle, I can't stand any of the modern rabble. Your academicians, I detest. Virtue I detest. Vice I detest. The 'flowing' style I detest. Progress I detest. Never speak to me again about your sayers of nothing.

The trip to Paris was still a possibility and Brussels was still seen as a major cause of illness:

> As for these recurrences of rheumatism and headaches, and this stiffness [he told Mme Aupick on February 26], what else can you expect in such a humid climate, whose inhabitants are so fond of humidity that even when it's raining cats and dogs they wash their houses not only inside but also on the outside?

Here again, though, Baudelaire seemed to have some premonition of his imminent collapse: 'I hope very much I'll never be in the position of having to be carried off like an invalid.'

From March 5 to 20, there were no letters. Between those two dates, perhaps on the 15th, Baudelaire went to Namur on the invitation of Rops and his father-in-law. He was glad to see them and the Eglise Saint-Loup again. But it was there in the church that the inevitable accident occurred. Eugène Crépet's is the only existing account:

> As he was admiring the lavish carvings on the confessionals, and pointing out their beauty to Poulet-Malassis and M. Rops who were there with him, he suddenly went dizzy, tottered, and fell down onto a step. His friends picked him up; he seemed not to be alarmed, and claimed that his foot had slipped. They pretended to believe him; but when he rose the next morning he was showing signs of mental disorder. He was taken back quickly to Brussels. Just after entering the carriage, he asked for the door to be opened; but the door was already open. He had said the opposite of what he meant to say. Aphasia, of which this was an undeniable prodrome, set in soon after.[15]

Back at the Hôtel du Grand Miroir, despite what had obviously been a mild stroke, Baudelaire was still able to move and write letters. On March 20, he composed the last letter written in his own hand; it was addressed to his mother: 'I am neither well nor sick. I work and write with difficulty.' Unlike the preceding letters and the notes for *Pauvre Belgique!*, the words in this letter were clearly formed and only one was crossed out.

The following day, having spent all night reading Hugo's latest novel, *Les Travailleurs de la mer*, Baudelaire was able to visit Mme Hugo. He had made a few notes on the book, and was hoping to write them up into an article. Even after losing the ability to hold a pen, he still intended dictating the article to Arthur Stevens; but it was never written.

During the night of the 22nd, his condition seems to have worsened noticeably; but his mind was to remain intact for several days. Baudelaire apparently still had no idea of how desperately ill he really was, or perhaps he was simply trying to reassure his mother: 'All my friends and doctors are of the opinion that I should abandon all literary affairs for six months and go and live in the country.' When Baudelaire was an adolescent, he had received the same advice from Hugo, who clearly understood him no better than did these friends and doctors. To see Baudelaire pretending to accept this impractical suggestion is just as sad as what was about to happen.[16]

Dr Marcq had written to tell Mme Aupick of her son's condition, perhaps a little too optimistically. He stressed the need of a complete change of life style, with a strict diet and family to watch over him. In eight or ten days, he added, Baudelaire ought to be able to manage the journey to Honfleur. Without knowing that the catastrophe had already occurred, Mme Aupick suspected that all was not well. She copied down part of the doctor's letter for Ancelle on April 1 and admitted that she was very concerned:

> What does this 'nervous affection' mean, and why can't he move? ...
> His brother died in horrible convulsions brought on by the pain he
> experienced when an ulcer in his bladder (which the doctors did not
> know about) perforated. They were treating him for other things – gout
> and gravel: how ignorant they all are! Need I say once more how touched
> I am by your kindness! ... Oh! how much I need you and your advice!
>
> Your old friend
>
> C. Aupick[17]

By the end of March, Baudelaire was having to dictate all his letters – one to Mendès concerning the proofs of *Le Parnasse contemporain*, another to Ernest Prarond, thanking him for the copy of his *Airs de flûte* (in which he pointed out a few mistakes), one to Ancelle and another to Mme Aupick. It's 'useless, or at least premature', he wrote, 'for Ancelle to come to Brussels: 1. Because I'm in no condition to move; 2. Because I have debts; 3. Because I have six towns to visit – that will probably take a fortnight. I don't want to lose the fruit of so much work.'[18]

In the meantime, Malassis himself had sent a letter to Ancelle, who replied on March 29 that Mme Aupick's poor health was preventing her from travelling to Brussels and that she had asked him, Ancelle, to go in her place: 'I have written to Baudelaire to prepare him for seeing me, but I told him that he should first write to me so that I would be making the journey as far as possible with his consent. I am sending him one hundred francs in a registered letter.'

On March 31, Léon Marcq warned Malassis that Baudelaire's condition had deteriorated once again and that he wanted to call in Dr Crocq – a famous Brussels doctor – for a second opinion. The same day, Malassis informed Bracquemond of the latest developments:

> Baudelaire is in a very serious condition. I had to write ... to M. Ancelle – who is responsible for Mme Aupick's affairs. There were fears for a time that Baudelaire had hemiplegia and a disease of the spinal chord, but what it comes down to apparently is a general disorder of the nervous system which will necessitate a *purely vegetative* life for six months to a year. I believe that M. Ancelle will be coming to collect Baudelaire.

Before sending the letter, Malassis added a postscript:

> I am re-opening this letter to tell you that within the past few hours Baudelaire's condition has become *extremely serious*.[19]

Malassis sent a telegram to Ancelle. The next day, April 1, he informed Asselineau that Baudelaire was now paralysed on the right side.

It was on March 31 that the paralysis appeared, indicating that the illness had reached the point of no return. Mme Hugo wrote that day to Arthur Stevens: 'My son Charles has just returned from a visit to our friend Baudelaire, whom he found very ill – too sick to be left on his own.' She also sent a letter to her husband: 'Baudelaire is doomed. He had been in pain for some time ... The illness has taken over almost the whole brain. They have given up all hope for the invalid and the greatest fear now is that he might survive his intellect. It is very sad, for Baudelaire's was an uncommon mind.' During the final illness, the Hugo family let not a day go by without sending for news of Baudelaire.

On April 1, Malassis sent the following letter to Asselineau:

> My dear friend,
>   I want you to know that Baudelaire is very low. A week ago, we thought it was just a complicated nervous affection that would require a lengthy course of treatment. Yesterday, he was paralysed on the right side, and a softening of the brain became apparent. I'm probably explaining this very badly, but you'll understand.
>   There is virtually no hope of saving our friend. I've just come from his hotel. He barely recognised me.

It was impossible to keep Baudelaire in his room at the Grand Miroir and give him the proper treatment. Malassis, Arthur Stevens, Dr Marcq and perhaps also Félicien Rops transported him to the Clinique Saint-Jean et Sainte-Elisabeth on April 3.[20] The entry book shows that the patient was admitted with 'apoplexy'.

On April 4, Malassis wrote once again to Asselineau, announcing Ancelle's arrival in Brussels: 'Baudelaire is incapable of stringing two ideas together. In trying to join one to the other, he gropes for the words and cannot find them. The mental effort is too great.' With the illness, old secrets came to light. Malassis, who had been so close to the poet for so long, had been astonished to learn that Ancelle was Baudelaire's *conseil judiciaire* and that he still owned 'about forty thousand francs'. Furthermore, Baudelaire had apparently never mentioned Asselineau to Ancelle: 'He was very mysterious in his affections . . .'

The institution to which Baudelaire had been removed stood at number 7, rue des Cendres (!). The clinic was run by Augustinian nuns. It was a large, solid-looking building, plain and uninviting when seen from the outside, but the inner courtyard was more cheerful and led to a garden overlooked by a row of tall, sunny windows. The former *hôtel* which housed the clinic had been the scene of the 'Waterloo Ball' held by the Duchess of Richmond in 1815 to celebrate Wellington's victory. It had been a fine setting for the event, with its spacious corridors, broad, monumental stairways with carved handrails and large oak-panelled rooms with decorated ceilings.[21] The head doctor at the clinic was Dr Lequime, a Professor of Medicine at the University of Brussels. On Baudelaire's arrival, he noted simply the hemiplegia on the right side with motory aphasia, as did Dr Crocq when he was called to the clinic. After a talk with Ancelle, the doctor left him in no doubt as to the inevitable outcome, as Malassis told Asselineau on April 4: 'Now that Baudelaire is lost, the only question that remains is the literary one, and I consider that to be of prime importance.'

Malassis' concern was entirely disinterested. He, more than anyone else, including the doctors who examined his friend, saw clearly that Baudelaire was nothing more than a body, and that for the poet and for his friends the only matter requiring urgent attention now was posterity. Baudelaire's physical death, however, was still a long way off. Seventeen long months would pass before he was finally laid to rest in the Montparnasse cemetery.

This biography of Baudelaire is the story of his intellectual life, not the tale of that living death to which he was now condemned. It therefore seems appropriate to select from all the letters which now began to multiply like worms on a corpse only those elements which are strictly relevant to that story.

Baudelaire's behaviour was distinguished at first by refusals – an angry refusal to return to France or to live with his mother in Honfleur and a refusal to gratify the nuns at the clinic with some simple mark of piety. In this, his anger was shared by Mme Aupick. On April 9 – Baudelaire's forty-fifth birthday - she wrote to Malassis:

> From what you tell me, Charles is not happy with the food; and *I* am not happy with the boorish behaviour of the Sisters. There I was, thinking he was living among gentle, caring doves, as I always imagine Nuns to be. We cannot change the education they received, but I thought we might be able to change the food by paying extra, and I have just written to M. Ancelle about this. As it was he who arranged everything with the Mother Superior, I thought that he should be the one to settle that, and *quickly*.

The following day, she wrote again:

> I have received a letter from the Mother Superior to whom I had written to ask for news, and she wrote me a most upsetting letter. After informing me of my poor son's state of health, she told me *that he has no faith* and that it's *very hard for her having a man in her establishment who has no faith*, and she is asking me to come to her help.

But where could Charles be moved to if the Sisters refused to keep him? And weren't they tormenting him with their ministrations instead of leaving him in peace and allowing him to recover? Until now, her legs had prevented her from travelling to Brussels, but now she asked Malassis where she might find a small furnished apartment with a kitchen for herself and her maid, and on April 12, she set off from Honfleur. Perhaps to avoid exhaustion, perhaps because the 13th was a Friday, she spent the night in Paris. Ancelle sent a telegram to Malassis: 'Aupick and maid arrive tomorrow 1 p.m. Pick up at station. Take to hotel near son.' Being well acquainted with his ward, Ancelle advised Malassis to prepare Baudelaire for the surprise.

Mme Aupick could have had little notion of what slow, destructive progress the disease had made. She would be seeing her son for the first time since his flying visit to Honfleur nine months before. On April 14, 1866, the day on which Mme Aupick arrived in Brussels, Malassis passed on the latest news to Asselineau:[22]

> At the moment, Baudelaire's condition is as follows: in the space of eight days he has twice suffered an acute softening of the mind. I don't know if I'm expressing myself very well, but you've studied medicine and you'll know what I mean. It seems he might be taken from us

overnight by a similar sort of attack, but also that his present state might drag on for months or even years, which I hope will not be the case ...

The face is still intelligent, and thoughts seem to pass over it *in a flash*. I think that he experiences some pleasure when he hears a friend's name.

His mother is arriving in Brussels today. She really should have stayed at home, because it's a heart-breaking thing to see.

Despite my recommendation, Baudelaire has been placed in a clinic run by *unsupervised* nuns. Those people are over-zealous, and I fear they may have been pestering the invalid. So far, Baudelaire has refused to give them the satisfaction of even the most elementary signs of faith. Hence a great feeling of irritation in the place. Had I not received news tonight of Mme Aupick's arrival, I would have had Baudelaire transported on my own authority to a different clinic.

Not, my dear friend, out of cussedness or atheism – you know how much I respect freedom of choice – but you can understand that I who would go and fetch a priest if Baudelaire asked for one whilst fully aware of his condition, cannot stand by and see a man tormented and exasperated when he now has nothing more to ask of his fellow men than to be left in peace.

I receive letters every day about this – mostly from people I don't consider to be close enough friends of Baudelaire to be worth the bother of replying. I answered only Troubat who wrote to me on behalf of Sainte-Beuve, and today, Champfleury.

Yours truly,

A. P. Malassis

Mme Aupick put up at the Hôtel du Grand Miroir. From there, she wrote to Ancelle: the doctors had made no attempt to conceal the fact that her son was in a 'serious condition'.[23] But the explanation they gave was a charitable one: '*His mind has worked too hard*, he's worn out *before his time* ... His tongue is not paralysed, but he's lost *the memory of sound* ...' Mme Aupick had been telling her son stories from when he was a boy:

The doctors are of the opinion that his understanding is gone, and they want me to leave; but what makes him lose his temper is that he cannot speak ... He eats, he sleeps, he goes out in a carriage with Stevens and myself, or on foot, with a walking-stick, on the public promenade in the sun. But no more words. I shan't go away; I shall keep him *like a little child*.

He isn't insane as the doctors say. Malassis claims that the constitution of a poet is so different from that of other men that it can sometimes mislead the doctors. What an excellent young man that Malassis is! He was shedding tears. How good he is! That young man must have a fine soul!

I do not think he can read, or else there would always be a book in his hand. If he picks one up, he can't make out the letters, and throws it down.[24]

Mme Aupick's desire to have him all to herself '*like a little child*' might itself appear to be a sort of aberration. She went on to complain again about the nuns who were still badgering their patient: 'Whenever he eats, they want him to cross himself.'[25]

Obviously it was vital that Baudelaire be removed from this convent-clinic for the sake of his health. This was quickly accomplished, to the relief of both parties. According to G. Barral, who claimed to have heard this detail from Spoelberch de Lovenjoul,[26] the nuns, after Baudelaire's departure, 'threw themselves on their knees, shed abundant tears, sprinkled holy water on the spot that had been occupied by their terrifying patient, and felt their fears subside only when they saw the stole of the exorcising priest who had been summoned with great haste, happy at last, and sensing that they were delivered from the demon, as if Satan himself had left their bewitched establishment!' The Sisters and the Mother Superior had heard Baudelaire uttering oaths, like '*crénom*' ('confound it') and concluded that he was a blasphemer, but these were nothing more than a sign of suffering and 'impatience at being misunderstood'.[27]

On April 19, Malassis informed Asselineau that he and Arthur Stevens had taken Baudelaire over to the hotel where he would stay with his mother.

As the carriage was going along at a snail's pace, he took obvious delight in observing the shop fronts and the activity in the streets. He understands all the simple things we say to him, especially those concerning his condition, and he scarcely has a thought but it refers to that ... His vocabulary is reduced to the single syllable, *non*, which he seems to repeat as many times as it takes for him to believe that he has expressed his idea ...

He showed signs of great joy when he arrived in the hotel room we've put him in. It's large, nice and airy, and on the ground floor. Stevens made him a glass of orange water. He drank it. Stevens offered him another, and he refused. Stevens then indicated his own liking for orange blossom, and Mme Aupick asked him to have another one himself. Thereupon, Baudelaire got the giggles, which shows you that he has not lost his sense of humour and irony, and that he's capable of *conversation*.

A week later, Baudelaire's condition had barely changed. Malassis referred Asselineau to a book by Armand Trousseau in which there was a sobering and depressing description of this 'strange disease', aphasia. Asselineau looked it up and found the following passage:

> For aphasia with paralysis, when it is not associated with syphilis, as in the case of the Keller woman, I feel obliged to confess our utter incompetence. We can no more cure the aphasia than we can the paralysis that accompanies it. Nature alone is responsible for virtually any improvement, and this is never more than partial. The aphasic remains forever injured in his understanding as in half of one side of his body. His mind will ever be unsound.[28]

The case of Marie Keller is curious. Trousseau treated her for syphilis, and she recovered the power of speech. Why Malassis, who, unlike the doctors, knew that Baudelaire had syphilis, did not clutch at this straw is hard to say. In any case, the treatment would merely have retarded the disease and would not have restored the poet's creative mind.

'Trousseau's article is not reassuring,' Asselineau replied. Having 'read and reread' this article several times, Malassis eventually admitted to himself that nothing could stop 'this apparently absurd disease which allows a man to understand what he can no longer find in himself and express'.[29]

In Paris, friends were worried and journalists hungry for copy.[30] A rumour went round that Baudelaire was in danger not only of losing his mind but also his life. On April 14, in *L'Evénement*, Georges Maillard reported that Baudelaire had actually died and the same piece of news appeared in *Le Temps* the next day, announced this time by Henry de La Madelène. Banville quickly wrote a letter to *L'Evénement* denying the rumour and went on to say that the patient was enjoying 'every solace which affection and money can obtain'. Baudelaire, he wrote, is not a Gilbert or a Malfilâtre.

Banville's indiscreet reference to Baudelaire's personal fortune – which he put at 40,000 francs – was quite deliberate. Pierre Véron, who was otherwise sympathetic to the poet, had depicted him 'lying paralysed on a hospital bed.' Rops considered this a grave insult, and asked a friend in Paris to inform M. Véron that 'Charles Baudelaire has made friends in Belgium who are devoted enough ... never to allow him to resort to the hospital as long as they have even the smallest home, or, lacking that, the smallest roof under which to receive him'.[31]

Having reported Baudelaire's death, Henry de La Madelène prepared a

long study on his friend.[32] It was published by *Le Nain jaune* and began
with these words:

> The poet of *Les Fleurs du Mal* has just died sadly in Brussels in an
> obscure hotel room, and his devastating death has been the literary
> sensation of the week in Paris. From this moment, posterity has begun
> for Charles Baudelaire.

Or rather, it would have begun with these words, had La Madelène not
heard that Baudelaire was still alive. He quickly wrote a prefatory paragraph:

> As we were going to press, the Belgian newspapers were denying the
> rumour of Charles Baudelaire's death. May God grant that this happy
> news be true, and that the poet have many long days yet to live! As I
> have written nothing on Baudelaire when I thought him dead that the
> living Baudelaire cannot read, I shall change not a word of this article.

But Baudelaire was incapable of reading anyway. Malassis and Asselineau
judged the article idiotic – perhaps a little hastily. La Madelène may have
refused to recognise Baudelaire as one of the truly great poets (imitating,
even as he wrote this, some verses from 'Les Phares'), he may have described
him as a 'brother in indifference' of Alfred de Musset and swallowed the
legend wholesale – 'monstrous passions' and the voyage to India – but the
fact remains that by quoting long passages from Baudelaire's verse and
prose, he wrote what Raymond Poggenburg has called the first 'Baudelaire,
sa vie et son œuvre'.

Other articles appeared, some sympathetic, others revelling in the legend
and failing to understand the poet. Charles Yriarte asserted in the *Figaro*
that 'in his suffering, Baudelaire felt a certain satisfaction at being thus
afflicted with an extraordinary illness which defied analysis. It was another
example of his originality.' The second category of articles – those which
combined stupidity with malevolence – would reach a jarring crescendo at
the time of the poet's death.

It was May 1, 1866 and for Baudelaire, nothing had changed. Malassis
sent another report to Asselineau:

> Baudelaire's mother seems to love him very much, but with a childish,
> maternal sort of love. One of her topics of conversation is the time when
> she was a young woman and took him out walking when he was a pretty
> child. The dear lady has been graced for many years with a delightful
> vivacity which she says left her only last winter. This sprightliness still
> shows in her thinking but has gone out of her legs. All in all, she's a

young old woman, pleasant and kind, but too frisky for her seventy-two years. I left the fifth issue of the Parnasse with her [which Mme Aupick had previously refused], and she was forced to take a look at it. She liked one of the poems, the one which ends with the verse,

Entends, ma chère, entends la douce nuit qui marche.*

She read it to me, and I was surprised to hear that she reads very well, like someone who knows they read well. She enunciates the words *sharply* like Baudelaire, using just the right stress and intonation. He looks very much like her in his face, especially his mouth and forehead.

The disease had made little difference to Baudelaire's temperament, but only emphasised what was already there. He was 'brusque, impatient, and irascible – the way he's always been', wrote Malassis, 'only more so'. Mme Aupick was complaining to Malassis about her son's violent temper tantrums. On one occasion, Malassis was supposed to take his friend for a drive in the country:

I went over at nine o'clock, and we took the opportunity to cut his hair. Once the ceremony was over, he conveyed his desire to be given a hairbrush. His mother handed him one that was very dirty which she had probably already offered to him, and which he had already refused. He flew into a rage, gnashed his teeth, and flung it into a corner of the room. I explained to her that the extreme care which Baudelaire had always taken of his person and toiletry articles explained his anger, which might easily have been avoided. Five minutes later, he lost his temper again, once more because of a brush. He had been given a great big clothes-brush, almost a scrubbing brush for his hat. Finally, we left. We walked through the fields, lunched at a small inn, and I had the most cheerful conversation I could with him, and brought him back without his ever having shown anything but joy at being alive and happiness, except for once or twice when he raised his eyes to heaven with a resigned expression, after a vain attempt to speak.

Baudelaire could not be kept in Brussels. The plan at first was to move him to Honfleur, but mother and son could not agree to this. Neither of them wanted to live together in the *maison joujou*. 'The poor lady confessed to me that to return with her son in such a state would be a very hard blow for her pride. Her circle of acquaintances in Honfleur is made up of former friends of General Aupick, who, as you well know, never showed any

* 'Recueillement'

sympathy for Baudelaire.' Baudelaire, too, had his pride: 'We're having a
lot of trouble trying to get him to make his mind up to leave. He did not
want to return to Paris because of his condition – he's still partially aware
of it.'

From the end of May, correspondence increased between Paris and
Brussels, with both parties – Ancelle and Asselineau, Malassis and Mme
Aupick – trying to obtain a free train pass for the invalid from the French
and Belgian railways. Malassis would be unable to accompany his friend.
The publication of Baudelaire's condemned poems in *Le Parnasse satyrique*
made him *persona non grata* with the French authorities; the same court
which condemned *Les Fleurs du Mal* had found him guilty for this later
collection. It was Arthur Stevens who offered to make the journey with
Mme Aupick and her son. At the other end, Ancelle looked for a suitable
hotel near the Gare du Nord.

Baudelaire's return to Paris took place on Friday, June 29. His mental
capacity had again diminished, although, a few days before departure, his
clarity of thought momentarily returned:

> He remembered various minuscule things: that he had a watch at
> the pawnbroker's, a passport for Paris, some small debts with friends,
> restaurants, and cafés in Brussels – having managed to obtain credit in a
> country where credit is never given to anyone – a few sheets of the *Poëmes*
> *en prose* which were still with the copyist. It meant a whole series of cross-
> examinations, because I couldn't understand what he wanted, as you can
> well imagine, and after a very long time, having tried every possible
> explanation of his discontent, I finally hit on this one: 'Were the manu-
> scripts you sent to be copied returned?' Thereupon, a great outburst of
> joy, and I recovered the manuscripts . . .
> Before we parted, I spoke to him at length about how he might enjoy
> putting his works in order with a friend – you, for example – until the
> day when he is able to get back to work. I told him that we had to start
> printing the definitive edition of *Les Fleurs du Mal* with everything ready
> and prepared. He nodded; but my impression is that . . . it will be difficult,
> not to say impossible to get Baudelaire to agree to the publication of his
> works while he still possesses the degree of intelligence he does now.
> The hope of completely recovering his mental health has definitely not
> left him.

The journey was uneventful. Baudelaire was happy to find waiting for
him on the platform 'M. Ancelle, and especially M. Asselineau'. In his 1868

biography of Baudelaire, Asselineau remembered the scene:

> When I saw him walking towards me, supported by M. Stevens, leaning on his *left* arm, with his walking-stick tied to his coat-button, it wrung my heart, and tears came to my eyes. He caught sight of me, and laughed a long, resonant, drawn-out laugh which made my blood run cold. Was he mad after all? I had scarcely spent half an hour with him when I was – alas! – completely reassured on this point. I became convinced that Baudelaire – for whom this must have been a sorry advantage – had never been more lucid or more acute. As I watched him, while he dressed, listen to the conversations that were going on quietly just a few feet away, losing not a word, as I could tell from the signs of approval or impatience that he gave, exchanging smiles with me, shrugging his shoulders, nodding his head, giving, in a word, marks of the most sustained attention and the keenest intelligence, I had no doubt that that part of him which the illness had spared was perfectly fit and active, and that his mind was as free and as nimble as when I had seen him the year before.

The mysterious trunk containing Baudelaire's manuscripts and books arrived on the same train. This trunk had been packed by Malassis in the presence of Ancelle when Baudelaire was being taken to the hospital. It was supposed to contain not only the books and papers he had taken to Brussels, and some other books sent by friends – Champfleury's *Histoire de la caricature*, for example – but also a copy of *Les Fleurs du Mal*, 'all ready for the printing of the definitive edition', some prose poems in manuscript form and his notes for *Pauvre Belgique!*. The contents of the trunk were later used for the preparation of Baudelaire's *Œuvres complètes*. But was that priceless copy of *Les Fleurs du Mal* ever found and was it really 'all ready', as Malassis claimed, with the new poems inserted amongst those of 1861 in the order that Baudelaire intended?[33] The third, posthumous edition of the poems shows no evidence of any definite plan. With that remaining lucidity detected by Asselineau, Baudelaire was probably trying desperately to settle what for him was a problem of the utmost importance, but one which, for himself as for his friends, was now insoluble.

After spending his first few days back in Paris in a hotel near the station with Mme Aupick, Baudelaire was examined by three doctors – Piogey, Lasègue and Blanche, who recommended that he be placed in a nursing home. The clinic chosen was Dr Emile Duval's 'établissement hydro-thérapique de Chaillot', near the Arc de Triomphe, offering 'spring water, baths and showers of every sort, gardens, gymnastics, electricity', etc.

Baudelaire moved in on July 4, 1866 and would stay there until his death, more than a year later.

He was given a ground-floor room in the pavilion which stood at the bottom of the garden. It was adequately furnished and well ventilated, with a high ceiling. The window looked onto the garden. Its main decoration consisted of two paintings by Manet, one of which was a copy of Goya's portrait of the Duchess of Alba, which Baudelaire greatly admired. The room also contained the trunk, to which Baudelaire had the key. The books were taken out and placed in a bureau – twenty-six in all, including an English-French dictionary, four volumes of Poe and the poetry of Sainte-Beuve. There was also a desk in lacquered wood which Baudelaire of course could not use and some photographs and engravings, one of them probably a *danse macabre* by Rethel. For obvious reasons, this was not displayed.

Baudelaire seemed to be quite happy, as the *Petite Revue* told its readers – most of whom were friends of the poet: 'He welcomes his visitors cheerfully, and enjoys making them talk.' But, as Asselineau pointed out, the expense of staying in the clinic would soon exceed Baudelaire's income and his mother's savings. It was time to apply to the ministry for a grant. A petition was drawn up, calligraphed, and sent to the Ministre de l'Instruction Publique, who received it on August 25.

> ... In these sad circumstances, the friends of M. Charles Baudelaire address themselves spontaneously to Your Excellency, and beg you to accord him a pension in relation to the cost of the care which his condition demands. This favour would moreover be justified by the works of a writer who has revealed to France the finest literary genius of the New World, and who for twenty years has been contributing to the most important Reviews and Journals – the *Moniteur*, the *Pays*, the *Revue contemporaine*, the *Revue des Deux Mondes*, etc.

The petition was signed by Champfleury, who had taken the initiative, as well as by Banville, Leconte de Lisle and Asselineau. (Théophile Gautier was away from Paris at the time.) Furthermore, three members of the Académie Française added notes – Jules Sandeau, Mérimée, who expressed esteem for Baudelaire's work, and for his 'kindness and candour', and Sainte-Beuve, who, like Mérimée, was now a Sénateur:

> M. Baudelaire is one of the most refined and distinguished talents to have appeared in the last fifteen years. I shall take the liberty of pointing out that M. Baudelaire is the son (by a first marriage) of Madame la Générale Aupick. His Mother, who loves him dearly, has no other

livelihood than a pension of 6,000 francs granted her by the Emperor as the widow of a former Ambassador. At present, *more than half* of this pension must be used for the treatment and upkeep of her dear invalid son.

No mention was made of *Les Fleurs du Mal* – probably a deliberate omission. The petitioners emphasised instead the Poe translations, which were in fact the only part of Baudelaire's work which ever earned him any government grants.

On October 4, the minister signed a decree awarding Baudelaire the provisory sum of 500 francs – 'a rather miserable amount', wrote Champfleury in a letter to Banville, 'but they keep all their money for schoolmasters'. Champfleury went to the nursing home to give Baudelaire the news: 'He was *very happy*, and pronounced with me the word *Mé-ri-mée*, as if astonished at the support which had come from that quarter.' Baudelaire must have been pleased at this show of loyalty, but Champfleury was unfortunately right about the sum granted by the minister – board and lodging in Dr Duval's establishment came to more than 5,200 francs.[34]

Mme Aupick took a long time to realise that her son was exasperated by her presence – something that Malassis had already noticed in Brussels:

The poor woman – she's a real scatterbrain, as you've been able to see – never noticed the unfortunate effect of her behaviour, and the way she acted with her son. She knows him less well than anyone else, and I can easily imagine her living for thousands of years without ever understanding the first thing about him. She wanted to fondle, pamper, and comfort him; and with all her motherly love, she went about it in such a way as to keep him in a constant state of irritation.

In Paris, Asselineau had many an opportunity to observe for himself this extreme possessiveness. On July 23, Mme Aupick remarked that her son was 'gentle and polite with everyone', and saved his anger for her. His latest tantrum had to do with *Les Epaves*:

Lately, picking up that unhappy book again, he thrust it in my face so that I had to step back, and getting into a furious rage which I failed to comprehend, and stamping his foot with all his might, he eventually threw himself on his couch, completely worn out, waving his legs in the air and roaring like a savage beast. When I recounted this scene to M. Duval, he said: *That is to be avoided; it could easily give him a stroke. I have been wanting to tell you for some time now to stop your visits, because you are the only person with whom he gets worked up and angry.*

In spite of the doctor's advice, Mme Aupick stayed on in Paris and saw her son again a few days later: 'He was nicer to me, even affectionate now and then.' After finally deciding to return to Honfleur, she made two other short visits to the nursing home in the autumn and spring, and then came back to Paris in July 1867. She was there when her son died.

There were plans to take Baudelaire to Nice: perhaps the warmer weather would do him good. Even Honfleur seemed a possibility while his condition was stable, but this plan was more likely to have been the result of a misunderstanding. Ancelle chided his ward for having failed to make it clear that he wanted to go there:

> He looked at me in a rather melancholy way, and when I asked if he did indeed want to go to Honfleur where his Mother would be happy to receive him, he answered no, very gently. I then had him confirm his reply by repeating the same question several times, but he did not change his mind.

Baudelaire probably had no real desire to leave Paris. At Duval's nursing home, there were visitors to take his mind off things. Of course, he was no longer capable of reading; the paralysis had affected his eyes – 'he doesn't even know his letters'. Asselineau took over from Malassis and kept him in touch with the slow, inexorable progress of the disease.

Mme Aupick mentions several visitors welcomed 'joyfully' by her son: Sainte-Beuve, Du Camp, Henry de La Madelène, Banville, Hetzel, Leconte de Lisle. Others included Nadar and his wife, Champfleury, Cladel, Troubat, Mme Meurice, Edouard Manet and Mme Manet. In the last few weeks of her son's life, Mme Aupick wrote to Asselineau to say that Charles was hoping to see M. Manet the painter; 'unfortunately, I do not know his address and cannot write and tell him that his friend is calling out for him'.

The wife of Paul Meurice was also a great consolation. On August 15, 1866, Champfleury told Malassis that, trusting in the beneficent influence of music, he had suggested that she go and play the piano in the clinic:

> Mme Meurice gallantly brought along the score of *Tannhäuser*, and it had the result I expected. I was not there at the performance, but Mme Meurice told me of the strong impression it made on Baudelaire. Unfortunately, she has just left for the seaside, and so has Mme Manet, who might have been prevailed upon to take her place, and now Baudelaire will be without music until the end of autumn.[35]

Asselineau takes up the story of Baudelaire's last year:

In the early months, he enjoyed going for rides, visiting people in town, and dining out. Nadar, who cherished him as an old and excellent friend, and whose affection was mingled with sincere admiration, dreamt up the idea of entertaining him and breaking the Lenten fast of the clinic by collecting him one day every week and taking him to dinner at his place with a small number of guests, all old friends who were used to his sign language, and who would give him a jolly time. Baudelaire seemed delighted at first with these little get-togethers, and when his host came to fetch him, he would find him ready and dressed, impatient to climb into the carriage. Soon, however, to our great astonishment, he refused to come. He conveyed the idea that these reunions were tiring him out, and that he paid for the pleasure of an evening with insomnia and over-excitement followed by depressions which hindered his treatment. It is clear to see that he had lost neither awareness of his condition, nor hope of a cure.[36]

Even if Baudelaire believed he might still recover, he was incapable of writing. His main preoccupation for many years and the dream that had led him to Brussels became his single, serious concern – the publication of his complete works. At the end of the summer of 1866, he intimated to Asselineau that he wished to reach an agreement with Michel Lévy, not for some, but for *all* his writings. In order to ensure he was understood, Baudelaire took a volume from his shelf published in the Lévy collection and underlined the name of the publisher, pointing at it and fixing his eye on it so as to make his intention as clear as possible. Having heard this, Malassis replied on September 27:

> Baudelaire would like to get a contract for all his works, just as he did before his aphasia. He spent all his time chasing after that contract, lining up figures next to his products, but he wouldn't get down to finishing his books. Actually, it must be said that Baudelaire was incapable of finishing them. His intermittent mental impotence, which he must have spoken to you about quite often as he did to me, had become continuous, or nearly so.[37]

Malassis believed that, given the unfinished state of Baudelaire's works, a contract with Lévy or with any other publisher would be a dead letter. And indeed, when one considers the present *Œuvres complètes*, with all their notes, outlines and fragments, Malassis was obviously right. But then Baudelaire was right, too, and Lévy, to some extent, agreed with him. The poems in verse and prose, the *Paradis artificiels*, the articles of literary criticism, the *Salons*, the essay on Wagner and a few other texts could form a corpus of four or five volumes to be added to the Poe translations, which already belonged to Lévy. This is what Asselineau, and eventually Malassis too, tried to achieve.

One day in January 1867, Michel Lévy went along with Asselineau to the nursing home. Using his friend as a go-between, Baudelaire talked about the publication of his works; but when Lévy proposed starting work immediately on a new edition of *Les Fleurs du Mal*, Baudelaire refused obstinately and showed him an almanac on which March 31 was marked with a dash. As Asselineau observes, 'this date was the limit of his hopes'. Up until the very last, Baudelaire was determined to supervise the printing of the new edition himself.[38]

During his excursions from the nursing home, Baudelaire went several times himself to the Librairie Michel Lévy Frères.

> I still have before my eyes the scene that occurred between him and Ernest Feydeau during Baudelaire's last visit to the bookshop in the rue Vivienne.
> I was chatting with Feydeau, who was leaning on my desk, when Baudelaire opened the door and entered.
> He recognised Feydeau, but instead of offering a handshake, he took his beard in both hands, and for at least ten minutes, which must have seemed an age to Feydeau, he kept saying, 'hm? hm?' as he pulled at his beard ...
> We tried our best to understand what he meant and reply.
> It was heart-rending.
> Finally, he let go of the beard, and went away, taking his leave with a gesture which he tried to make as graceful as possible.[39]

On January 21, 1867, Jules Troubat described Baudelaire's condition to Malassis. He had realised that the poet's memory was still intact: 'he showed me all the things he used to enjoy – Sainte-Beuve's poetry, the works of Edgar Allan Poe in English, a small book on Goya, and, in the garden of the Duval nursing home, a succulent exotic plant which he pointed out so that I could admire its jagged outline ... When I spoke to him of Richard Wagner and Manet, he smiled with delight.'
Malassis replied:

> Asselineau gave me news the other day of our poor friend, Baudelaire, which fits in with what you told me. Baudelaire is in a condition which deceives those who see him, but his true mental state is very uncertain,

and very mysterious. He has lost his memory of language and figurative signs, and no one can tell to what extent his whole mind has been affected by his partial paralysis. Trousseau's *Clinique médicale* has something very sad to say about his condition: 'Remember,' he says, 'when you see an aphasic who appears to be in possession of his mental faculties, though he has lost the ability to express himself, how many times you have said of certain animals, "If only they could speak." '[40]

Ever since noting the effects of the stroke in Brussels, Malassis had been convinced that his friend was beyond help. Asselineau was less certain for a time that the disease could not be halted. The doctors had tried to reassure Mme Aupick. She clung to a few words and expressions which her son had been taught to pronounce, and was delighted when she heard that he was able to say '*La lune est belle*', and '*Passez-moi la moutarde.*' After the end of November 1866, there was no further mention of these dubious signs of improvement.

Baudelaire apparently refused to abandon hope until that fateful day he had marked on the almanac – March 31, 1867. He continued to toy with the idea of travelling, without being particularly keen to leave Paris. The deadline arrived and nothing had changed.

He then adopted a resigned and gloomy attitude. No more songs or bursts of anger, no more scenes or any of those sudden vigorous and urgent entreaties which compelled one to attend, and which set those present thinking. It was obvious that Baudelaire had relinquished all hope and abandoned every illusion. He was yielding to the foe he had struggled with so valiantly and for so long. Soon, he lost all desire to leave his bed. There he spent his days, watched over by his mother. His will was broken; but the mind was still awake. He never ceased to welcome his friends or stretch out his free hand to the visitor. Until his final days, he continued to take an interest in the conversations that went on at the foot of his bed, and took part in them only by making small signs with his head or his eyelids. Whenever you looked his way, you found his eye intelligent and attentive, though darkened by an expression of infinite sadness, which those who glimpsed it will never forget. The last months must have been for him the most painful of all. He had outlived himself, and was living now only to sense all that he had lost.[41]

Little is known of the progress of the disease between February and August 1867. At the beginning of August, Asselineau wrote to Malassis:

Dear friend, now it's my turn to give you bad news of poor Baudelaire, not that I've ever been able to give you any good news, but, for some time now, the illness has been gathering momentum. He probably won't last out the month.

Mme Aupick is still deluding herself. She's talking about a possible improvement. But the doctors and we, his friends, who do not see him every day, notice each time that he has declined a little more. For two or three months now, Baudelaire has not wanted to leave his bed. He's still and as if asleep, and shows only by glances – which are, alas! quite sad – that he still notices when his friends are there. Yesterday, after an absence of three weeks, he recognised me only with a distressingly vacant look, and was able to give me his hand only after I had pulled it out from under the covers.

He is watched over every night. It's Albert the publisher who has taken on that job, and he's performing it, I must say, with quite untiring devotion.[42]

From always lying in the same position, a sore has formed on his back, and it's threatening to become gangrenous. It is probable, then, that the next letter you receive from me will be to announce the inevitable news.

During his last two days and nights, Baudelaire's mother stayed at his bedside. He seemed to sleep with his eyes open.[43]

On Sunday, September 1, 1867, Asselineau wrote to Malassis:

It's all over. Baudelaire died yesterday at eleven o'clock in the morning after a long death-agony, but one that was gentle and painless. He was so weak in any case that he wasn't struggling any more.

We, like Poulet-Malassis, have had before our eyes 'the image of Baudelaire living in physical decomposition'; and, with him, we can answer Charles Asselineau: 'Though I was prepared, your letter gripped me by the throat, and I felt anguish, even tears. You know how much I loved him.'

EPILOGUE

Baudelaire died 'quietly and without any apparent suffering, on Saturday, August 31, 1867, at about eleven o'clock in the morning'.[1] He was forty-six years and four months old. His creative life appears long only if one compares it to that of Rimbaud; compared to Victor Hugo's, it was very short – 1841 to 1859.

Baudelaire received the last sacraments – a fact recorded by the death announcement and confirmed by Charles Asselineau. Louis Veuillot, editor of the Catholic review, *L'Univers*, wrote to Mme Aupick on 23 September 1867: 'M. Asselineau's kind note informed me that he requested and received the last sacraments, and this gave me one of the greatest joys I have ever experienced. I thought not of his death, but saw only the resurrection, and, without being very surprised, thanked God for his great mercy.' Others, like Estelle Gautier, one of Théophile Gautier's daughters, were astonished: 'They claim that at the time of death, he called for a confessor, which seems incredible, considering he could only say Crénon [*sic*]. In his last days, they managed to get him to say *bonjour* like a little child, but that is all.'[2] Estelle was insinuating that since Baudelaire was senile, his act was meaningless; but we know that his mind never entirely succumbed to the disease. It is impossible in any case to imagine Baudelaire's work without its Christian dimension, even if his peculiar form of Christianity is one from which the Redeemer is absent. One should also remember that in his hostility to the contemporary world, with its blind faith in material progress, Baudelaire was eager to be seen as a Catholic. He admired Jesuits and their art, and even played the Jesuit with Malassis, though, as he admitted to Sainte-Beuve, this little game was designed to satisfy a taste for self-contradiction.[3] More significant is the letter written to Sainte-Beuve's secretary, Jules Troubat, a few weeks before the stroke. Baudelaire dated it 'Ash Wednesday', knowing that Troubat, like his employer, was strongly anticlerical and anti-Catholic.

When Veuillot told the readers of *L'Univers* that Baudelaire had received the last rites, Pierre Véron of *Le Charivari* retorted that Veuillot was trying to get his Catholic hands on Baudelaire's coffin and ignoring the fact that Baudelaire was a devotee of intellectual freedom; only when 'his powerful mind was struck down by paralysis' did he deny his convictions. Véron had obviously not read Baudelaire's notes on freethinkers in *Pauvre Belgique!*.

Nadar, who was a freethinker himself, in the best sense of the word, but also a friend of Veuillot, gave an account of his last conversation (if that is

the word) with Baudelaire. It took place at the nursing home; its subject –
the immortality of the soul:

> 'Look here, how can you possibly believe in God?' I insisted.
> Baudelaire moved away from the rail on which we were leaning, and
> pointed to the sky. Before us and above us, setting all the clouds aflame,
> and surrounding the powerful outline of the Arc de Triomphe with gold
> and fire, was the magnificent glory of the setting sun.
> '*Crénom! oh! crénom!*' he protested again, chiding me indignantly as he
> repeatedly punched towards the sky.[4]

The most accurate comment on Baudelaire's last wish came from Arthur
Stevens:

> Baudelaire was certainly a believer, but he hated religious *ritual*. In
> any case, he was too well brought-up not to die in the religion of his
> Mother, when his Mother was standing there beside him.[5]

As Nadar told the readers of the *Figaro* on September 10, Baudelaire
believed in God; but it was a very personal and particular form of belief,
without which *Les Fleurs du Mal* would not have been what they are.

Baudelaire had died at the worst possible moment – at the height of
summer and on a Saturday. The body could not be left any longer in the
nursing home and so the burial was arranged for Monday, September 2.
There was little time to warn all friends and acquaintances, some of whom
would receive the announcement only after returning to Paris from a
weekend in the country.

With the help of Edmond Albert, Asselineau sent messages to a few
people – notably Veuillot, Nadar and Philarète Chasles. The death was
registered at the townhall of the sixteenth arrondissement by Ancelle and
Asselineau. Baudelaire was described on the certificate as a 'man of letters'.

After a service at the Eglise Saint-Honoré d'Eylau – a service which was
probably reduced to an absolution – the cortège set off for the Montparnasse
Cemetery, where Charles Baudelaire was laid to rest, not with his father,
whose ashes had disappeared, but in the family vault with General Aupick.
Their remains were later joined by those of Mme Aupick in August 1871.
It was a touching and specious reconciliation.

Banville addressed those who stood at the graveside, praising the poet and
emphasising his originality. Of all the extravagant texts Banville devoted to
his friend, this oration is the most interesting, the most courageous. Ten
years after the first edition of *Les Fleurs du Mal*, it indicated the extent of
Baudelaire's achievement whilst Hugo was still seated on the poetic throne:

Continuing the ancient tradition, though he was also a pioneer, Victor Hugo has always transfigured Man and Nature in the image of a certain premeditated ideal; Baudelaire, on the other hand, like Balzac, Daumier, and Eugène Delacroix, accepted all of modern man, with his failings, his pallid grace, his ineffectual aspirations, his triumphs mingled with so much discouragement and so many tears!

Asselineau spoke next for the friends of Baudelaire:

Too much has been said about the 'legend' of Charles Baudelaire, heedless of the fact that this legend was but the echo of his disdain for stupidity and pretentious mediocrity.

I speak in the name of those who loved him faithfully, followed and understood him, and I declare on this solemn occasion, with the gravity and conviction that death inspires: Yes, that great mind was a good mind too; that great heart was also a good heart.

Asselineau made a point of stating that 'until the end ... in that sick, paralysed, and voiceless body', the mind had remained 'lucid'. He was hoping thus to disarm the critics.

On September 6 or 7, he described the funeral in a letter to Malassis:

Baudelaire's funeral had the same curse on it as those of Alfred de Musset and Heinrich Heine. First, the season was against us – many people were away from Paris – and then the day of the week – we had to send out the invitations on the Sunday, and as a result, many people received theirs only the following day when they returned from the country. There were about one hundred people at the church, and fewer at the cemetery. The heat prevented a lot of people from following to the end. A thunderclap which boomed out as we entered the cemetery nearly sent the others running. The Society of Men of Letters was not represented, though I had written as early as Saturday to its President, Paul Féval, to say that I was counting on him and his committee. Neither was there anyone from the Ministry, neither Doucet nor Dumesnil. The speeches were read out in front of sixty people, and the reading of them betrayed our disappointment. Théodore was very moved, and myself even more, and angry, too. We hurried things along as if impatient to get it over and done with. Among those present I noticed Houssaye and his son, Nadar, Champfleury, Monselet, Wallon, Vitu, Manet, Alfred Stevens, Bracquemond, Fantin, Pothey, Verlaine, Calmann Lévy, Alphonse Lemerre the publisher, Ducessois the printer, Silvestre, Veuillot, etc.[6]

Gautier and Michel Lévy were both away from Paris. Sainte-Beuve was ill and wrote to Mme Aupick on the day of the funeral to express regret that he was unable to attend: 'Now at last he has entered the undefiled regions of memory and poetic remembrance ... His profile must forever be engraved among the medallions of our time.' Sainte-Beuve, who had only two years left to live, left the engraving of Baudelaire's medallion to others. He was expressing once again the embarrassment and discomfort he felt when faced with that 'very talented eccentric'.[7]

'Several men of letters,' wrote Eugène Crépet, 'notably Philarète Chasles and Emile Deschamps, Ernest Prarond and François Coppée, made their excuses to Asselineau in affectionate and emotional letters.'[8] Hugo's reaction is not known, though he later thanked Asselineau for sending him his biography of Baudelaire.[9]

Alfred Stevens had written to his brother Arthur on the 3rd. Arthur replied:

> The incident you recounted, about Baudelaire's coffin, as it entered the cemetery, battered by the wind and strewn with the leaves that fell from the trees, moved me deeply. Like you, I find it very poetic, and am certain that Baudelaire would have desired no better accompaniment for his entry into death.[10]

The thunderclap that was heard as the cortège entered the cemetery and the coffin, battered by the wind and strewn with leaves, seem to be present in an unfinished painting by Edouard Manet, who was present at the funeral. With its Parisian cemetery, the angry sky and small flock of figures, *L'Enterrement*, which shows the Pantheon (near the Pension Bailly) and the Val-de-Grâce, does at least have a symbolic value.

Baudelaire's grave was still fresh when the newspapers grabbed the body: it was the silly season for the Paris press.[11] 'All of them, large and small alike,' wrote Asselineau, 'are quick to tell their readers how well they knew Baudelaire, and how they know for a fact that he was insane ... But it seems that a certain M. Vallès of *La Situation* takes the cake. I haven't read the article, but I know from Monselet and Wallon that it's despicable.' Vallès was not the only hostile critic. Victor Noir had already reeled off all the lurid details of the legend for the *Journal de Paris* on September 3: Baudelaire went on a voyage to India that lasted five years; while he was there, he took up with an Indian woman who later came to be known in Paris as 'the Black Monster'. When sailing in the Indian Ocean with Mieroslawski, the brother of the Polish hero, Baudelaire decided to live in the hold of a ship that was carrying ice, and left it only for the hospital.

During the trial, Pinard read out 'Les Femmes damnées' and brought the house down: 'The defendant was very nearly carried in triumph.' An English writer is now busy translating the Poe translations into English, because the 'Yankees' claim that in order to appreciate their compatriot, 'one must read him in Baudelaire's translations'. The stupidity of this article was matched by the malevolence of the insults published two days later by Jules Vallès. Victor Noir's only claim to fame is that he was killed in a duel by Prince Pierre Bonaparte; but Vallès is an important writer and his extremely acrimonious words were destined to reach a wider audience:

> I was introduced to him.
> He blinked his eyes like a pigeon, puffed out his chest, and leaned over:
> 'Monsieur,' he said, '*When I had scabies . . .*'
> He pronounced *gale* [scabies] the way dandies say *cha-a-rming*, and stopped.
> He was counting on making quite an impression and thought he had entirely succeeded with his unusual opening remark.
> I replied without batting an eyelid:
> 'Are you cured?'
> He was speechless, and took a minute at the very least to recover. I observed this man with the bogus mange, and noticed immediately that he had the head of an actor – his face clean-shaven, pinkish and swollen, his nose fat and bulbous at the tip, his lips simpering and pursed, his expression tense; his eyes, which Monselet described as 'two drops of black coffee',[12] seldom looked straight at you; he seemed to look for them on the table as he talked, with his body swaying to and fro, speaking in a drawl . . .
> There was something of the priest, the old woman, and the ham actor in him – especially the ham actor.

Vallès' cruel insistence managed to make faults out of what others might have seen as redeeming features: Baudelaire was a believer, but his was a pathetic sort of mysticism 'in which the angels had the wings of a bat and the face of a whore'; was he really addicted to hashish and opium, or was it just a pose?; he liked to act the immoralist, but with women he was 'timid' and 'clumsy'. In his depiction of Baudelaire paralysed on his death-bed, babbling like a child, Vallès reached an ecstasy of insult:

> *Crénom!* Maybe it was also the cretinous grunt of despair! – Who knows?

Perhaps it meant: 'Oh! why have I been an actor all my life! I've made myself insane, I know it and cannot say it, and even if I could, my pride would hold me back!'

Oh! I pity him, I swear to you! yes, I pity him.

The reason for this blind rage appears between the lines. Baudelaire was a 'cleric' and did not belong to the category – or class – of the workers. He was thus denounced as a reactionary, which indeed he was in his later years. It is curious to note that this reactionary has now been rehabilitated by Marxist critics, following in the footsteps of Walter Benjamin. The independent nature of a work of art apparently makes it extremely difficult for any artist to remain true to himself in what he has created.

Gautier's article, which later became the preface of Baudelaire's *Œuvres complètes*, gave a broader and more detailed picture of the poet; but it was Nadar who answered Vallès directly: 'One should not and cannot remain silent in the face of certain attacks on that man who can no longer reply.'[13] Nadar went to the very heart of the anger that Baudelaire inspired:

This man who, as a born gentleman, appeared to be so cold, and, in many things, so sceptical, took to the point of fervent admiration and joyful enthusiasm his respect for a thing well made. He had that rarest and most estimable of qualities – conscientiousness in his work, religious devotion to duty. A life which got off to a bad start ... and a literary output which by necessity was meagre never made him falter or forget for an instant what he owed to his work and to himself. He was painstaking to the point of obsession. Baudelaire's life, and that of Gérard de Nerval, will remain as examples to other writers of professional dignity – two fine examples, which will be of no use whatsoever.

Before ending his article, Nadar quoted the poem, 'La servante au grand coeur ...', asking if that was the work of a degenerate and a pervert. He concluded:

That man who lived in perpetual torment, feverish, unappeased and undefeated, that hysteric, that maniac, that werewolf, never harmed a soul. He did not even stoop to hate.

In this, however, Nadar was surely mistaken.

Baudelaire had died without making a will. An inventory was drawn up on September 6, 1867 at the request of Mme Aupick. Then, following the advice of Ancelle, who was not yet aware of the full extent of the debts left

by the deceased, she accepted the succession without liability to debts
beyond assets descended. This allowed her to uphold her own claims
without being able to sell off any of the property she had inherited. It also
meant that a court order would be needed before the right to publish
Baudelaire's work could be sold. The sale would be by auction – a prudent
and efficient solution, since the settling of the estate would finally be
completed only a few days before Mme Aupick's death in 1871. Various
complications arose. An eligible party of the eighth degree had turned up
on the paternal side. The demands of creditors necessitated negotiations
and even court hearings. The credit column, once all the accounts had been
examined, showed a total of only 11,300 francs, of which the distant relative
received 3,800. Mme Aupick was to receive 7,500 francs, with 19,200 francs
as a reimbursement of monies paid to her son. This sum eventually went
to her inheritors.

In 1868, Mme Aupick gave Asselineau a certain number of books,
engravings and objects which he was to distribute among Baudelaire's
friends. Dr Piogey received a Persian desk and, from Asselineau himself,
Deroy's portrait of the young poet; Banville received a Persian casket and
a cane; Sainte-Beuve 'a charming Algerian sachet' with a photograph
for which he thanked Asselineau. Mme Aupick asked Ancelle to give
Champfleury an engraving of *The Dance of the Dead* by Rethel which
Baudelaire had had in his room. Asselineau was to receive Baudelaire's
photograph of Mme Paul Meurice, two Rethel engravings and an ink
drawing by Baudelaire relating to the poem, 'Les Yeux de Berthe'. Works
by Legros went to Malassis and Bracquemond, watercolours by Guys to
Nadar and Ancelle, and paintings by Manet were returned to the artist. Dr
Piogey also received some Jongkinds and Banville some Devérias. As a
reward for his devotion to Baudelaire and to the preparation of the *Œuvres
complètes*, as well as for his book, *Charles Baudelaire, sa vie et son œuvre*, Mme
Aupick left Asselineau 'the sum of ten thousand francs, as a mark of
gratitude, in the name of his friend'.

Asselineau had indeed shown great devotion in preparing the publication
of his friend's complete works. He and Malassis clearly understood that
Baudelaire had settled on Michel Lévy as his publisher, after negotiations
with Lacroix had failed, and despite his bitterness at Lévy for paying so
little for his Poe translations. Malassis was no friend of Lévy, but shortly
after the poet's death, he recognised that 'Lévy is part of *his last wishes*. For
that reason, it seems to me we should give up on Lévy only if his offer
proves to be decidedly inadequate.'

Lévy was a long time returning to the city and it was already October when Asselineau was able to see him. He found the publisher in a difficult mood:

'I'm just back from a trip, and my office is full of things to do. I'm going crazy. It's enough to give me a stroke. *If Guizot himself offered me a book I wouldn't take it.*'

'I haven't come here to beg,' I told him. 'I've been waiting to see you before anyone else so as to carry out Baudelaire's intentions. We have four volumes of *Works* to offer you, plus an optional fifth volume.' 'We'll see.' 'No, we won't see. There's a seventy-five-year-old Mother who's in a hurry to settle the matter. We must decide within a week and bring the edition out in January. In any case, it's a good deal.' 'A very good deal, but I'm snowed under. Well, show me the whole manuscript, then we'll look at it together, and *discuss* it.'

I returned the next day with the whole bundle, and we went through it. He asked me to leave it with him for a few days. I made a list of all the items; and we're supposed to meet again next week to conclude. As I was leaving, I said, 'Should I tell Mme Aupick, who is leaving for her home in Honfleur, that the deal is settled?' He answered, 'No, not yet; but I'd be sorry if someone else were to do it. I was so fond of Baudelaire!'[14]

Negotiations with Lévy were long and difficult, partly because of the limit set by the publisher: Lévy was determined to pay no more than 2,000 francs[15] (the same amount he had paid in 1863 for the Poe translations) and partly because of Ancelle's refusal to be hurried. There was also the question of the poems from *Les Epaves*, some of which were to be inserted in *Les Fleurs du Mal*. These poems belonged to Malassis, who tried at first to assert his rights. Lévy refused to pay him any more money, and so Malassis gave him the poems of his own free will in the interests of Baudelaire's work and in memory of the man whom he considered 'as an adopted brother'.[16] One thinks of all the other small publishers who discovered so many great writers, only to be robbed of their discovery, often in the interests of the writer. The only two reliable editions of *Les Fleurs du Mal* were published by Poulet-Malassis and there can be no question that the masterpiece of modern French poetry owes its existence to a publisher who was revolutionary in every respect, bankrupt, exiled, penniless and proud – proud enough to relinquish his rights on part of Baudelaire's work in favour of Michel Lévy. When Baudelaire designated Lévy as his publisher, he was acting in the best interests of his work. Malassis acquiesced in this desire, which derived from a sort of inviolable egoism which does not or should not take account of gratitude or recognition.[17]

Ancelle realised that the sale of rights to the work should take priority. He obtained a court order on November 22, 1867 which allowed the rights to be auctioned off, thus putting them beyond the reach of any creditors. The reserve price was set at 1,000 francs. Asselineau put in a bid of 1,750 francs. His was the only bid.

Asselineau had neglected to inform Malassis that the auction was taking place. He later explained that the auction was a mere formality intended to strengthen Mme Aupick's position as heiress.[18] The edition, he added, would comprise four volumes:

1. *Fleurs du bobo.**
2. *Beaux-Arts. Salons.*
3. *Paradis artificiels. Poëmes en prose.*
4. *Variétés.*

The second and fourth eventually appeared as *Curiosités esthétiques* and *L'Art romantique* respectively. The former title had been chosen by Baudelaire; the second was invented by the editors while work was in progress.

Claiming to have an aversion to responsibility in all things, Asselineau asked Banville to join him in his task.[19] The choice was approved by Malassis who would have been the most competent editor, as his opinion of the Lévy edition was soon to show.

Malassis remained the owner of the six condemned poems, which were not officially publishable in France until 1949. Using two other poems from *Les Epaves*, which might have drawn the courts' attention to the new edition of *Les Fleurs du Mal* – 'Les Promesses d'un visage' and 'Le Monstre' – along with three 'Bouffonneries' from the same collection, Malassis published a booklet entitled *Complément aux Fleurs du Mal de Charles Baudelaire (édition Michel Lévy, 1869)*. It went on sale in Brussels during the summer of 1869.

Meanwhile, the publication of the first volume of the *Œuvres complètes*, containing 152 *Fleurs du Mal*, had not gone off quite as smoothly as planned. 'After a long night of insomnia' in November 1867, Mme Aupick told Asselineau of her misgivings, and asked him to expunge 'Le Reniement de Saint Pierre' from this so-called *'Edition définitive'*:

As a Christian woman, I cannot and must not allow that poem to be reprinted. If my son were alive, he would certainly not have written it now, having had religious sympathies for quite a few years...

*'Bobo' is the childish equivalent of *'mal'*.

The two poems which follow 'Le Reniement de Saint Pierre' are not very Christian either; perhaps I am deluding myself, but it seems to me that they might pass, *à la rigueur*, as an orgy of the imagination, as the ramblings of an exasperated and unhappy poet, whereas the 'Reniement' is quite plainly irreligious – it's a profession of faith. Maybe my indulgence for the other poems has something to do with the admiration I have for the 'Litanies de Satan'. It is an exceptional work with respect to talent, form, and the verses which have such a harmonious rhythm, like a piece of music, for one seems to sing as one reads them, perhaps because of that sad refrain, that woeful lament that comes at every third verse:

> O Satan, prends pitié de ma longue misère!

At the beginning of the poem, there is something I like very much:

> O toi qui de la Mort, ta vieille et forte amante,
> Engendras l'Espérance, une folle charmante!

What a happy find '*folle charmante*' is, applied to Hope! But I shall not detain you any longer with this wish of mine, to which I attach great importance.

Asselineau wrote to Malassis:

> Can you believe it? Mme Aupick wrote last Saturday to suggest we expunge 'Le Reniement de Saint Pierre'. I'm not entirely comfortable about my reply. I fear it may be a little on the stiff side; but my God![20]

Asselineau, who had threatened to have nothing more to do with the edition, had done well to be strict with Mme Aupick; there might otherwise have been no end to her misgivings. She replied to say that she had 'sacrificed her doubts before the image of her son' and promised that his thought would remain intact, signing her letter, 'Your old friend and mother'.[21]

Asselineau was quick to put Malassis' mind at rest: 'My letter to Mme Aupick had a tremendous effect . . . She answered with alarmed submission. Of course, I sent her a soothing reply.'[22] As Malassis pointed out in conclusion: 'She has nothing in common with her son's writing, and she must have become aware of that a long time ago.'[23]

These differences of opinion did nothing to alter the affection she felt for Asselineau, her 'dear friend', or even her 'dear son', as she called him.[24] On March 16, 1868, she invited him and Banville to come and spend the summer in Honfleur: 'You really should get to know this place where

Charles lived, which he adored, and which he called the *toy* house because it's so small.' Banville was unable to go and sent his regrets.[25]

Mme Aupick wanted to invite Malassis as well, but in the end, Asselineau made the journey to Honfleur alone. The following autumn, Mme Aupick saw him again in Paris and then received him once more at Honfleur in the summer of 1870.

Whilst he was there on the spot in 1868, Asselineau was able to help her organise the papers and articles which Charles had left behind, and which were needed to make up the *Œuvres complètes*. Questioned by Asselineau, she would go in search of a particular letter or piece of writing, full of uncomprehending goodwill, not knowing if she would be able to find what he and Banville were looking for.

They remained in touch up to and beyond the Franco-Prussian War. In 1870, Banville dedicated a short story to her – *Eudore Cléaz* – in his usual dithyrambic style:

TO MADAME
CAROLINE AUPICK

Should I not tremble, Madame, at daring to offer such a modest work to the Mother of the great poet Baudelaire, to the ambassadress who so brilliantly represented abroad the wit and elegance of France? The dedication of *Eudore Cléaz* will at least convey to you my humble admiration and profound respect.

Th. de Banville

In June 1871, Félicité Baudelaire was at the bedside of Mme Aupick. Having already met Asselineau in Paris and in Honfleur, it was she who sent him the news:

So now I am here with her, trying to guess what she is saying, for without being as stricken as her poor son, she seems to have the same affliction. She talks about everything, and understands everything; but the word she wants to use refuses to come ... As her reason is not affected, you can understand how distressing her condition is ...

We speak of you every day, dear Sir, and our poor friend keeps saying all the time, 'How amazed he will be!' You know she likes you very much, and would love to see you; but her desire is suppressed by a feeling of shame at letting herself be seen when not at her best.

On July 25, 1871, Félicité told Asselineau that their 'dear friend' had suffered another attack: 'She is watching her faculties die off even as she lives.' The neighbours, said Félicité, were being wonderful – Charles Michaud and, of course, the Emons.[26] It was Michaud who informed Asselineau of the death on Wednesday, August 16. The funeral took place in Honfleur on the 19th and the same evening, the coffin was transported to Paris to be buried in the Montparnasse Cemetery. The man who accompanied her remains to their final resting place was Emon. In her will, Mme Aupick had written: 'If I die here in Honfleur, my mortal remains should be taken to Paris to the tomb in which my husband, General Aupick, and my son, Charles Baudelaire lie in the Mont Parnasse Cemetery.'[27]

Her possessions, which included what was left of her son's inheritance, were shared out, apart from a few gifts, between Ancelle, Emon and Félicité Baudelaire. Thus it is that the widow of Alphonse Baudelaire, who survived until 1902, received the letters which Charles had written in his childhood and youth to his mother, the General and Alphonse. These she kept hidden away, probably afraid that the honour of the family which she alone now represented might be tarnished by references to the venereal disease which Charles had contracted in 1839.

When one thinks that this priggish woman inherited part of Baudelaire's estate – his money and more importantly his personal papers – which then were handed down to people who otherwise had no connection with the poet and who were ashamed even of this small tie, it becomes a real pleasure to replace these 'relatives' with Baudelaire's true family – Mallarmé, Verlaine, Rimbaud, T. S. Eliot, Pierre Jean Jouve, Pierre Emmanuel, Yves Bonnefoy.

Ruines! ma famille! ô cerveaux congénères!

A strange family, or rather a strange poet, born into a family devoted to prejudice and all the more loyal to social conventions for their having been, on Mme Aupick's side at least, a serious breach of etiquette.

Malassis wrote to Asselineau on November 27, 1867: 'Mme Aupick speaks of her first husband only in a perfectly detached tone. It was the General who was her *man*.' It was indeed the General who saved her from the mediocrity in which she would otherwise have lived. Malassis judged her harshly, accusing her of a 'lack of artlessness': 'Mme Aupick', he wrote at the end of one of his letters, 'no longer favours me with her correspondence that is so full of the spirit of conformity.'[28] Asselineau, who did not possess his friend's ironic wit, was inclined to be more lenient: 'She's really a good, kind soul.' But even Asselineau was made to realise that a veritable abyss separated Baudelaire from his family. The following letter was written while Baudelaire was still in Brussels:

I dined yesterday with M. Ancelle, and with Baudelaire's sister-in-law, who was once an attractive woman, and who's extremely stiff and starchy. I was even granted the honour of taking her home, since she's my neighbour. There I was, in short, in the heart of the enemy – what a lot of reservations, and cautious, qualifying remarks! Those fine, upstanding people haven't the faintest notion that dear old Baudelaire is the glory of his family and one of the most completely remarkable minds of our time. They seemed quite flabbergasted when they heard me talking about him the way we do.

I can't say for certain that I wasn't taken for a charlatan and a *poseur*. There was only one person there who really likes Charles, and that was old Ancelle; he's a good chap. He has some odd misconceptions about our friend, but he does love him. He talks about him every day and with great warmth. I gave him a hearty handshake.

Mme Baudelaire irritated me: she has the self-importance you might expect from the wife of a magistrate. As I listened to her, I understood all that poor Charles has had to suffer from his family.

The general opinion is that Mme Aupick adores her son, but that she would have liked to see him turn his work to greater profit. Old Ancelle told me naively: 'It would never have occurred to him to capitalise on it.'[29]

Asselineau was right. Within the limits imposed by his role as *conseil judiciaire*, Ancelle was the one who best loved and best served Baudelaire. When thanking Eugène Crépet for having sent him the *Œuvres posthumes*, he added:

> I spent much of my life with Baudelaire, and that period (about thirty years) has left me with vivid memories of an affectionate relationship which are infinitely precious to me. Baudelaire did not always behave in the way I expected of him and which my care and attention merited, but I shall never forget the happy times he gave me with his brilliant conversation and the genuine affection he always showed me.[30]

Before she died, Mme Aupick had the pleasure of reading the biography written by her adopted 'son', Asselineau, as well as the Lévy edition of the *Œuvres complètes*. These seven volumes, three of which contained the Poe translations, were produced at an unusually rapid rate. The last volume appeared in the spring of 1870, less than eighteen months after the first.

Poulet-Malassis, the expert, regretted the fact that the volume devoted to *Les Fleurs du Mal* contained too many poems borrowed from *Les Epaves*:

'I have always wondered, and still do, whether Baudelaire would have added any of these poems to his book.' He also disapproved of the inclusion of a sonnet addressed to Banville which had obviously been slipped in by the addressee. Banville had been given the sonnet in July 1845 and had kept it in his files. As for the *Curiosités esthétiques*, Malassis was satisfied with the organisation of the volume, but added that 'Baudelaire would have changed many things, and corrected quite a few mistakes'. The mistakes, he wrote, might still have been corrected by the editors, but would Lévy have allowed enough time for the work to be completed? Perhaps the decision to reproduce the texts as they were had been the best solution after all.[31]

Such as they are, the *Œuvres complètes* immediately gave Baudelaire a place in contemporary literature. At the beginning of 1870, a reader whose interest had been aroused by the legend was able to put on his shelves the seven volumes of *Œuvres complètes*, the biography by Asselineau, and a first bibliography prepared by Albert de La Fizelière and Georges Decaux. Malassis, who had assisted the authors of the bibliography in their work, wrote to Ancelle: 'You will be glad to see, as I am, Monsieur, that with this publication [and with the others mentioned] Baudelaire is treated, and so he should be, as a classic of French literature.'[32] Malassis would certainly have agreed with Hetzel, who, when urging Arsène Houssaye to publish the prose poems, declared that no newspaper should wait to publish Baudelaire – 'that strange classic of unclassical things'.

Friendship had allowed the poet of 'Le Voyage' to reach the open sea without delay.

APPENDIX 1

Baudelaire's financial situation
from 1844 to 1864

Baudelaire's income can be divided into five categories:

1 Annual allowance paid by Ancelle
2 Deductions from the capital
3 Grants awarded by the Ministre de l'Instruction Publique and the Ministre d'Etat between 1857 and 1862
4 Financial assistance from Mme Aupick
5 Royalties

The sums indicated under headings four and five are inevitably approximate; the three other sources of income are therefore shown separately. These figures cover the period from the setting up of the *conseil judiciaire* to Baudelaire's departure for Belgium.

Each heading is explained below:

1 *Annual allowance.* The annual interest on Baudelaire's capital was 2,629 francs. It was decided that he should be paid 2,400 francs per year, the remaining 229 francs to be kept in reserve. The civil service payscale between 1840 and 1860 suggests that a salary of 2,400 francs would have provided a young unmarried man with a comfortable living. The salary of a deputy chief clerk in a ministry, for example – a position open only to men of over thirty – was between 2,000 and 2,700 francs. A head clerk earned between 4,000 and 5,000 francs a year.

2 *Deductions from the capital.* On three occasions, Baudelaire received large sums which were not reinvested but used to pay off urgent debts. His allowance was reduced accordingly as the table below indicates.

3 *Ministerial grants.* On December 20, 1855, Baudelaire wrote to his mother:

> I can't bear the idea of asking a minister for money, and yet it's virtually common practice. They have funds for such things. I myself have always been too proud and too cautious to resort to that expedient. Never will my name appear in the wretched files of any government. I prefer to owe money to

everyone I know. I'd rather argue with you, and torment my Mother, however painful it may be.

As Jacques Crépet noted, 'Baudelaire was probably sincere in his declaration, but his needs were soon to overcome his repugnance.' On June 4, 1857, Baudelaire reluctantly applied for a grant to the Ministre de l'Instruction as a member of the Society of Men of Letters. Between that date and April 2, 1862, he received nine '*indemnités littéraires*' totalling 2,500 francs. Most of these were obtained through the intervention of his friend at the ministry, Armand Du Mesnil. He also received five '*secours*' or '*encouragements*' from the Ministère d'Etat totalling 950 francs. Three of these were paid to him as an '*auteur dramatique*'. The following table groups these sums in their yearly totals.

SUMMARY OF KNOWN ANNUAL INCOME

I   Annual allowance paid by Ancelle
II   Deductions from the capital
III   Ministerial grants

Year	I	II	III	Total
1845	2,400			2,400
1846	2,400			2,400
1847	2,400			2,400
1848	2,400			2,400
1849	2,400			2,400
1850	2,400			2,400
1851	2,400			2,400
1852	2,400			2,400
1853	2,400			2,400
1854	2,400			2,400
1855	2,200	7,000		9,200
1856	2,100	5,500		7,600
1857	2,100		200	2,300
1858	2,100	3,000	250	5,350
1859	2,100		750	2,850
1860	2,100		1,650	3,750
1861	1,900		300	2,200
1862	1,900		300	2,200
1863	1,900			1,900
Total from 1851 to 1863	28,000	15,500	3,450	46,950

4   *Assistance from Mme Aupick*. The following estimate of sums paid to her son by Mme Aupick is based on family records and on Baudelaire's correspondence:

Before 1851	10,000 (estimate)
1851	1,000
1852	500
1853	460
1854	
1855	
1856	
1857	7,313
1858	
1859	
1860	
1861	
1862	500
1863	700
	20,473

5 *Royalties*. The following table is a summary of income from Baudelaire's Poe translations:

a) Publications in periodicals:	
Le Pays	700
Le Moniteur	1,800
Revue internationale	620
Various (estimate)	1,000
	4,120

b) Volumes:	
Histoires extraordinaires	1,383
Nouvelles Histoires extraordinaires	916
Aventures d' Arthur Gordon Pym	467
	2,766

To these totals should be added the 2,000 francs paid by Michel Lévy to Baudelaire on November 1, 1863 for the rights to all his translations from Poe. The sum total is therefore 8,886 francs – considerably more than Baudelaire earned from all his other works put together.

Baudelaire's earnings from original works published as books can be deduced from his contracts with Poulet-Malassis:

Les Fleurs du Mal, 1857	250
Les Fleurs du Mal, 1861	300
Les Paradis artificiels	300
Théophile Gautier	30
	880

Approximately 1,600 lines of *Les Fleurs du Mal* were first published in periodicals. If one applies the fee paid by Calonne at the *Revue contemporaine* – four francs per stanza or 0.75 per line – the total is 1,200 francs. However, since not all reviews paid their poets as well as Calonne, it would be wise to round this figure down to 1,000 francs.

For the prose poems, to take the fee offered by Arsène Houssaye for the twenty poems which appeared in *La Presse*, Baudelaire would have received approximately 800 francs.

To this total of 1,800 francs should be added royalties received for articles of criticism published in various newspapers and reviews, as well as Baudelaire's contributions to Crépet's anthology, *Les Poëtes français*. These can be put at 2,400 francs, giving a total of 4,200 francs for publications in periodicals.

SUMMARY
(Totals are rounded up or down to the nearest hundred.)

Translations		8,900
Original works		
– books	900	
– in periodicals	4,200	5,100
		14,000

The total resulting from our investigations and estimates thus lies close to the figure mentioned to Catulle Mendès by Baudelaire himself, when he put his total earnings at 15,892 francs.

APPENDIX 2

Emile Deschanel's notes for his 1866 Paris lecture on Baudelaire

He himself, whilst still at school, was a poet, in Latin or in French. I remember one of his masterpieces in Latin verse. It was a good topic, and he turned it to very good account. It was about the strange form of torture devised by a Roman emperor who wished to rid himself of those he feared. He invites them to dinner; they accept. During the feast, a few rose petals fall softly from the cracks in the ceiling. Oh! what a pretty and elegant shower of rain! ... what a gallant idea! They are enchanted, they applaud ... roses rain down on their faces, into their cups, onto the tables. The guests, bedecked with roses, drink to Caesar's health ... And the roses continue to fall, and the rain falls harder ... Little by little, the roses on the floor form a pile which rises imperceptibly. They eat, drink, laugh, and talk. The roses engulf the tables and the feasting couches ... and now they cover the guests ... Amazement sets in ... They look at each other ... Caesar has gone! ... Some begin to worry; they rise and try to leave ... the doors are closed! The deluge of rose petals keeps on falling. Finally, it covers the heads of the guests, higher and higher, and slowly suffocates them. They perish beneath the mass of roses that gradually climbs to meet the roof!

Baudelaire worked wonders with that. He wrote the most brilliant Latin verses, adding his own dazzling variations.

Even then, in *rhétorique* or in *philosophie*, French verse came just as easily to him. From one end of the class to the other, from the boarders' to the day boys' part of the school, he used to get people to pass on his improvised poems to me as they came to his pen, while the mathematics teacher was at the blackboard with his back turned. Of course, they were the verses of an adolescent, limply and charmingly constructed. Here are some that I've managed to remember since 1839:

> Ecoutez une histoire, et simple et sans apprêts
> D'amour d'adolescents d'amour timide et frais,
> Tel que chacun en eut dans ses jeunes années,
> Et qui pour moi ressemble aux premières journées
> D'un printemps pur et beau, lorsque plein de tiédeur
> Chaque soupir du vent fait éclore une fleur.

N'est-ce pas qu'il est doux, maintenant que nous sommes
Fatigués et flétris comme les autres hommes,
De regarder parfois à l'orient lointain,
Si nous voyons encor les rougeurs du matin,
Et, quand nous avançons dans la rude carrière,
D'écouter les échos qui chantent en arrière
Et les chuchotements de ces jeunes amours
Que le Seigneur a mis au début de nos jours? . . .

C'était donc une douce et belle adolescente,
Pour tous ceux qui l'aimaient et bonne et caressante.
Et tous deux s'en allaient jouer sous les lilas,
Couraient à perdre haleine, et, lorsqu'enfin bien las,
Lui pour appui prêtant son épaule abaissée,
Elle offrant le contour de sa taille enlacée,
Ils revenaient, les vents printaniers et joyeux
Mêlaient les cheveux bruns avec les blonds cheveux.

Sérieux, ils restaient une heure sans rien dire,
Et puis se regardaient et se prenaient à rire.
Et ce silence avait d'ineffables douceurs,
Et ce rire charmant était tout près des pleurs.

. . . Il aimait à la voir, avec ses jupes blanches,
Courir tout au travers du feuillage et des branches,
Gauche et pleine de grâce, alors qu'elle cachait
Sa jambe, si la robe aux buissons s'accrochait . . .

Le soir, dans le salon, il aimait à l'entendre
Chanter parfois un air mélancolique et tendre,
Quand sa gorge, oppressée en de vagues désirs,
Ainsi que l'instrument se gonflait de soupirs . . .
Etc.

The poem ended suddenly (perhaps deliberately so) with these four verses, dry and prosaic in their realism:

> Mais, plus tard, à Paris lorsqu'il revint enfin,
> Riche, elle demeurait au faubourg Saint-Germain ...
> ... Maintenant, sans rougir, il l'appelle *Madame*,
> Trouve cela tout simple, et n'a plus rien dans l'âme.*

* 'Listen to a tale, uncontrived and artless, / Of adolescent love – a youthful and timorous affair, / Like those we all knew in our earlier years, / And which I would compare to the very first days / Of a pure and beautiful Spring, when, filled with warmth, / Each sigh of the wind brings a flower to bloom.

Is it not a sweet delight, now that we / Like other men are tired and worn, / To cast our eyes at times to the distant East, / If still we see the morning's blush, / And as we progress in our harsh career, / To listen to those echoes which sing behind us / And the whisperings of those young loves / Which the Lord has placed at the dawn of our days?

She was, then, a sweet and lovely young girl, / Kind and tender to all who loved her. / And they both went off to play in the lilacs, / Ran till they were breathless, and when, at last, quite weary, / He offering his lowered shoulder for support, / She yielding the contour of her waist which he held, / They returned, the joyful, springtime winds / Mingled brown hair with fair curls.

Solemnly, they remained for an hour without a word, / Then they looked at each other and started to laugh, / And their silence was one of ineffable sweetness, / And that enchanting laugh was very close to tears.

... He loved to watch her in her white skirts, / Running through the leaves and branches, / Clumsy and full of grace, when she tried to hide / Her leg, if the dress had caught on the bushes ...

Of an evening, in the drawing-room, he loved to hear her / Sometimes sing a tender, melancholy air, / When her breast, weighed down with vague desires, / Swelled like the instrument with sighs ...

But later, in Paris, when he finally returned, / She was rich, and residing in the Faubourg Saint-Germain ... / Now, without blushing, he calls her *Madame*, / Finds that perfectly natural, and has no more heart.'

NOTES

ABBREVIATIONS

Unless otherwise stated, the place of publication is Paris

Bdsc: *Baudelaire devant ses contemporains*. Edited by W. T. Bandy and Claude Pichois. Le Monde en 10/18, 1967.

BET: Claude Pichois. *Baudelaire, études et témoignages*. Revised edition. Neuchâtel: La Baconnière, 1976.

CPl: Baudelaire. *Correspondance*. Edited by Claude Pichois and Jean Ziegler. 2 vol. Gallimard, 'Bibliothèque de la Pléiade', 1973.

EJC: Eugène and Jacques Crépet. *Baudelaire*. Messein, 1906.

ICO: *Iconographie de Charles Baudelaire*. Edited by Claude Pichois and François Ruchon. Geneva: Pierre Cailler, 1960.

LAB: *Lettres à Charles Baudelaire*. Edited by Claude and Vincenette Pichois. Neuchâtel: La Baconnière, 1973.

OC: *Œuvres complètes*. Edited by Claude Pichois. 2 vol. Gallimard, 'Bibliothèque de la Pléiade', 1975–1976.

1   *OC*, I, 661.

2   Letter to Mario Uchard, Jan. 17, 1863.

3   See Dominique Julia, 'Les Années de formation de Joseph-François Bau-delaire', *Bulletin baudelairien*, XV, 2 (winter 1980).

4   Georges de Nouvion, 'La Famille de Charles Baudelaire', *Bulletin de la Société historique du VIe arrondissement* (1901). The author of this article obtained his information from Félicité Baudelaire, the widow of Charles Baudelaire's half-brother, Alphonse.

5   Letter to Asselineau, March 24, 1868.

6   On this stage of François Baudelaire's career, see J. Ziegler, 'François Baudelaire (1759–1827), peintre et amateur d'art', *Gazette des beaux-arts*, March 1979.

7   Published by Marcel Ruff, in *L'Esprit du Mal et l'esthétique baudelairienne* (Armand Colin, 1955), p. 462.

8   *Souvenirs de la fin du XVIIIe siècle et du commencement du XIXe, ou Mémoires de R. D. G.* [Baron René Desgenettes] (Firmin Didot, 1835–1836). Quoted by J.-F. Desjardins, 'Les Origines familiales de Baudelaire', *Revue des Deux Mondes*, Dec. 15, 1964.

1   See J.-L. Bonnet, 'Un ancêtre audois de Baudelaire', *Bulletin baudelairien*, XX, 2 (Aug. 1985).

2   St Pancras Church, Pancras Road, County of Middlesex, Parish Register of Baptisms, 1793–1801. Greater London Council P 90 (PAN 1/8). Photocopy kindly supplied by Michael Packenham and Harry Cockerham. A 'Certificate of Baptism' was published by M. Ruff in *L'Esprit du Mal et l'esthétique baudelairienne*, p. 463. St Pancras was one of the churches in which Catholic ceremonies were conducted.

3   Documents relating to the Relief Committees (Public Record Office, Kew).

4   *OC*, I, 794–785.

5   Probably Crébillon *père*, the dramatist.

6   On François Baudelaire's known work, see Claudie Bertin, 'François Bau-delaire (1759–1827), peintre à la gouache', *L'Estampille*, 1987.

7   It is not known what became of François's remains: cemetery plots held in perpetuity date only from 1832.

CHAPTER 3

1   Our thanks to Kathleen O'Flaherty and Barbara Wright for research into Aupick's Irish origins.

2   The following account of Aupick's early career is based largely on Cl. Pichois, *Le Vrai visage du général Aupick, beau-père de Baudelaire* (Mercure de France, 1955).

CHAPTER 4

1   Ernest Prarond remembered hearing Baudelaire recite this poem in 1843 (*BET*, p. 25).

2   Private collection.

3   Aupick, letter to General Durrieu, Oct. 1, 1829: 'The little household is very well. Charles is going off to boarding-school and there are two red eyes.' Published by W. T. Bandy in *Du romantisme au surnaturalisme. Hommage à Claude Pichois* (Neuchâtel: La Baconnière, 1985).

4   Georges Barral claims that Baudelaire told him in 1864: 'I'm sick, constitutionally sick, and was born with an execrable temperament because of my ill-matched parents ... That's what comes of being the child of a twenty-seven-year-old mother and a sixty-two-year-old father!' From *Cinq journées avec Ch. Baudelaire* (Liège, 1932), p. 25.

CHAPTER 5

1   This and the following letters are quoted by Arthur Pougin in *La Jeunesse de Mme Desbordes-Valmore* (Calmann-Lévy, 1898).

2   Letter to Sainte-Beuve, May 4, 1865.

3   The reports of the school inspectors are held in the Archives Nationales, F^{17} 2491 (Lyon: 1832–1845).

4   Letter to Mme Aupick, Feb. 6, 1834.

5   Archives Nationales, F^{17} 2491.

6   'Charles Baudelaire, sa vie, ses œuvres, souvenirs personnels', *Revue du Lyonnais*, June 1892.

7   See the article by E. Hardouin-Fugier, 'Lyon, bagne de la peinture', *Bulletin baudelairien*, XVIII, 2 (Aug. 1983).

8   The Hospice des Antiquailles is mentioned in the uncorrected proofs of the prose poem, 'Le Crépuscule du soir'.

CHAPTER 6

1   As Mme Aupick told Charles Asselineau in 1868.

2   Baudelaire's work for the *Concours général* was discovered in the Archives

Nationales by Jules Mouquet and published by him in *Vers latins* (Mercure de France, 1933). Texts and translations in *OC*, I, 225 ff.

3 *Journal des Débats*, Aug. 24, 1917.

4 *Choix de matières et pièces de vers latins, recueillis par M. Chardin, ancien professeur de seconde au lycée Louis-le-Grand* (Delalain, 1864).

5 On Jacob Rinn, see the dissertation by David Pellow, *Charles Baudelaire. The Formative Years* (Vanderbilt University, 1971).

6 Gaston de La Tour. Letter dated Feb. 10, 1878.

7 Letter to Mme Aupick, Aug. 8, 1864.

8 Letter to Alphonse Baudelaire, Oct. 23, 1838.

CHAPTER 7

1 Letters to Alphonse (Oct. 23) and Mme Aupick (Oct. 19, 1838).

2 Jules Simon, *Premières années* (Flammarion, 1901).

3 Cousin's friend, Louis Ménard, gave Baudelaire a copy of his *Prométhée délivré* which contains a printed dedication to Cousin. It was later found in one of the boxes on the *quais* ... Cousin's interpretation of Baudelaire's expulsion was refuted by Philippe Berthelot in his study of *Louis Ménard et son œuvre* (Juven, 1902). Nevertheless, it is worth noting that in a letter to Ernest Prarond in 1886, Eugène Crépet wrote: 'I shan't ask you why Baudelaire left Louise-le-Grand without having completed his studies. I think I know the real reason, but I think also that I ought to keep quiet about it, and I know that there was no trace of it in the Louis-le-Grand school archives (at least that's what a letter from the present headmaster tells me).'

4 Baudelaire later sketched an amusing caricature of 'The Late M. Pierrot' in Philoxène Boyer's album.

5 H. Hignard, *Lettres de l'Ecole normale (1838–1841)* (Lyons, 1898).

6 Published by Jean Pommier, *Dans les chemins de Baudelaire* (Corti, 1945).

7 Jean Pommier and Cl. Pichois, 'Baudelaire et Renan à l'ombre de Saint-Sulpice', *Mercure de France*, Sept. 1958. This is a more satisfying explanation than the one advanced by Eugène and Jacques Crépet in their *Charles Baudelaire*: 'Tradition has it that Baudelaire owed his success in this insignificant test to his collusion with a housekeeper of one of the examiners.'

CHAPTER 8

1 *OC*, I, 784.

2 *BET*, p. 27–28.

3 Hugo's play was first performed in 1831. Baudelaire must have attended one of the performances given at the Comédie-Française (Nov. 11, Dec. 22 and 31, 1839, and Feb. 1, 1840).

4 On this much-neglected writer, see the chapter in Pierre Boyé's *Esquisses romantiques* (Debresse, 1937).

5 *BET*, p. 19.

6 See the thesis by Mgr. Pierre Jarry, *Un artisan du renouveau catholique au XIX⁰ siècle: Emmanuel Bailly (1794–1861)* (Université Catholique d'Angers, 1971).

7 This description is taken from R. P. Kokel, *Vincent de Paul Bailly, un pionnier de la presse catholique* (Editions B. P., 1957).

8 Letter dated Nov. 21, 1839. Prarond archives.

9 Henry de Chennevières, 'L'Ecole Normande', *L'Artiste*, Oct. 1893. This article was written in fact by Henry's father, Philippe.

10 In 1843, the Salon jury refused three paintings by Buisson, perhaps because he claimed to be a pupil of 'Nobody'. Buisson later became a conservative *député* in the Assemblée Nationale. He died in 1909.

11 The sonnet was published for the first time by 'an emeritus bibliophile, M. Antony Bruno, to whom it was given in 1840', in the *Monde illustré*, Nov. 4, 1871. See *OC*, I, 202 and 1229–1230.

12 'Un chapitre d'art poétique. La Rime. A mon ami Prarond', dated 1846–1875 in Le Vavasseur's *Poésies complètes*, vol. I (Lemerre, 1888).

13 Chennevières (not the one from the Pension Bailly), in *L'Abeille de Fontainebleau*, Oct. 22, 1869.

14 *BET*, p. 18.

15 This, and the following letter published by J. Crépet, *Mercure de France*, March 15, 1937.

16 *L'Esprit du mal et l'esthétique bauderlairienne*, p. 166.

17 *BET*, p. 37.

CHAPTER 9

1 *OC*, I, 784. The principal articles on Baudelaire's voyage are those published by Charles D. Hérisson in the *Mercure de France* (Oct. 1956, April 1959, March 1960) and the *Revue des Sciences humaines* (Jan.–March 1969). Hérisson proves conclusively that Baudelaire never set foot in India.

2 *BET*, p. 14–15.

3 Private collection.

4 See the article by Cl. Pichois in the *Revue d'Histoire littéraire de la France*, Oct.–Dec. 1957.

5 *Mémoires d'un critique* (A la Librairie illustrée, n.d.), p. 96.

6 Letter published by E. Crépet in his biography of Baudelaire, p. 221–226.

7 Published by Maurice Levaillant in *Le Figaro*, Aug. 12, 1930. 'When [the Captain] was detained on board or at the shipyards, my uncle Duranteau would take his place. I seem to remember hearing that he was the one who went ashore with Baudelaire and acted as his mentor ... He introduced him in particular to a family of wealthy planters whose seven daughters were remarkably beautiful.' One

of these daughters later married the architect of the Suez Canal, Ferdinand de Lesseps.

8 The 'B ...' might stand for Baritault, one of Baudelaire's fellow passengers. This letter was published in the Port-Louis newspaper, *Le Cernéen*, June 22, 1866.

CHAPTER 10

1 Published by J. Crépet, *Bulletin du bibliophile*, Aug. – Sept. 1939.
2 *BET*, p. 35.
3 The *Revue de Paris*, to which Baudelaire was to submit his 'book on painting'. See p. 119.
4 May 6, 1861. *CPl*, II, 152.

CHAPTER 11

1 Henri (i.e. his father, Philippe) de Chennevières, art. cit.
2 *OC*, I, 784.
3 Prarond archives.
4 Dupont probably included parts of this book in *Les Deux Anges*, published in 1844. His portrait was painted by Emile Deroy at about the same time as Baudelaire's and, later, by Gustave Courbet.
5 Prarond archives. Letter dated Aug. 20, 1886.
6 *Bdsc*, p. 133–135.
7 On Privat d'Anglemont, see J. Ziegler's 'Essai biographique' in *Etudes baudelairiennes* VIII and his article in the *Bulletin baudelairien*, XII, 1 (summer 1976).
8 J. Ziegler, 'Emile Deroy (1820–1846) et l'esthétique baudelairienne,' *Gazette des beaux-arts*, May–June 1976. In a letter to Poulet-Malassis dated Aug. 15, 1866, Champfleury claimed that Deroy was Baudelaire's 'only close friend at that time'.
9 *Mes souvenirs* (Charpentier, 1883), p. 94.
10 According to Nadar, in a letter dated Aug. 26, 1896.
11 *Mes souvenirs*, p. 89.
12 Cl. Pichois, 'La Jeunesse de Baudelaire vue par Ernest Prarond (documents inédits)', *Etudes littéraires* (Quebec), April 1968.
13 *Mes souvenirs*, p. 98.
14 Letter to E. Crépet, Oct. 1886. *BET*, p. 15–16.
15 These verses were discovered in *L'Artiste* (May 1890) by J.-Fr. Delesalle and published in the *Bulletin baudelairien*, XVIII, 2 (Aug. 1983).
16 Charles Cousin, letter to the publisher René Pincebourde, who was preparing the volume entitled *Charles Baudelaire, Souvenirs – Correspondances* (1872).
17 *LAB*, p. 138.
18 Jules Buisson, letter to E. Crépet. *BET*, p. 39.
19 *OC*, I, 694.
20 Letter sold at Drouot, Nov. 20, 1984.

21 'La Maladie de Baudelaire', *BET*, p. 219–238.

22 Quoted by P. W. Lasowski, *Syphilis. Essai sur la littérature française du XIXe siècle* (Gallimard, 1982), p. 63.

23 Champfleury, *Contes choisis. Les Quatuors de l'île Saint-Louis*... (Hetzel, 1855).

24 *BET*, p. 21.

25 R. de Beauvoir, 'Une visite à l'hôtel Pimodan', *La Quotidienne*, Dec. 2, 1845.

26 Asselineau, in his biography of Baudelaire, reprinted in *Baudelaire et Asselineau: textes recueillis et commentés* by J. Crépet and Cl. Pichois (Nizet, 1953). See p. 67.

27 *BET*, p. 36.

28 Asselineau's notes for his biography, in *Baudelaire et Asselineau*, p. 170. Most of the following details also come from Asselineau's notes.

29 Banville, *Mes souvenirs*, p. 80.

30 Banville, in *La Renaissance littéraire et artistique*, April 27, 1872.

31 *BET*, p. 26–27.

32 *Mes souvenirs*, p. 74–75.

33 *BET*, p. 27.

34 In the poem entitled 'L'Héautontimorouménos'.

35 Note by Ernest Prarond. Prarond archives.

36 See p. 108.

37 *De quelques écrivains nouveaux* (Michel Lévy, 1852), p. 16.

38 'I can't remember if I was the one who took Baudelaire to see Sainte-Beuve. What makes me think I did is the fact that, in those distant days – 1843 or 44 to 1848 – Sainte-Beuve never ran into me without asking for news of Baudelaire.' (*BET*, p. 33).

39 *CPl*, I, 116–118.

40 See *OC*, I, 205–206 for a description of this poem.

41 For a discussion of Baudelaire's early poems, see Felix Leakey, 'Baudelaire-Cramer: le sens des *Orfraies*', in *Du romantisme au surnaturalisme. Hommage à Claude Pichois* (Neuchâtel: La Baconnière, 1985).

42 Letter to E. Crépet, 1886. *EJC*, p. 39.

43 This and the following letter are in the Prarond archives.

44 Letter dated May 10, 1887. Crépet's biography had already appeared when he received this information.

45 Constant was later known under the name Eliphas Lévi as an expert on the occult.

46 Flora Tristan, *Lettres*, ed. S. Michaud (Seuil, 1980), p. 193.

47 *OC*, II, 985. Arondel is cheekily compared here to the collector of antiquities, Thomas Howard, Earl of Arundel (1585–1646).

48 Baudelaire et ***, *Mystères galans des théâtres de Paris*, ed. J. Crépet (Gallimard, 1938), p. viii-ix.

49 *CPl*, I, 103. Probably written at the end of 1843.

50 See Cl. Pichois, 'Un ami de Baudelaire: Edmond Albert, éditeur en placard', *Etudes baudelairiennes* II.

51   J. P. van der Linden, *Alphonse Esquiros. De la Bohème romantique à la République sociale* (Nizet, 1948) and Anthony Zielonka, *Alphonse Esquiros (1812–1876): a Study of his Works* (Geneva: Slatkine, 1985).

52   Asselineau, in his biography of Baudelaire. *Baudelaire et Asselineau*, p. 65. For the following quotation, see p. 69–70.

CHAPTER 12

1   See the index of Baudelaire's signatures in *CPl*, II.

2   *BET*, p. 19–20.

3   *BET*, p. 21.

4   Two paintings purchased by Baudelaire for 400 francs were sold in 1844 for eighteen francs.

5   See Cl. Pichois, 'Baudelaire jeune collectionneur', *Humanisme actif. Mélanges d'art et de littérature offerts à Julien Cain* (Hermann, 1968).

6   'Baudelaire jeune collectionneur'. Baudelaire mentions, for example, in *Quelques caricaturistes français*, 'Les tableaux de Bassan qui représentent le carnaval de Venise'. Jonathan Mayne, the English translator and editor of Baudelaire's art criticism, has found only one painting by Bassan depicting 'le carnaval de Venise' – a painting which is in the Kunsthistorisches Museum in Vienna.

7   Graham Robb points out that this was also a deliberate choice. In 1846, Baudelaire told the old art critic of *Le Corsaire-Satan*: 'It doesn't seem to me to be at all necessary to know classical art in order to write about modern art, which is completely different. I quoted the names of these old masters just so as not to appear lacking in erudition, and a little, I must admit, in order to please a few readers who are infatuated with anything old.' ('Le *Salon de 1846*: Baudelaire s'explique', *Nineteenth-Century French Studies*, XV, 4 (summer 1987).

8   *BET*, p. 21.

9   *OC*, I, 701 and 785.

10   *CPl*, I, 112. Baudelaire was not the only writer to visit the gaol. See Cl.-M. Book (Senninger), 'Théophile Gautier et l'hôtel des Haricots', *Revue d'Histoire littéraire de la France*, April-June 1965.

11   J. Ziegler devotes a chapter to Marix in *Gautier. Baudelaire. Un carré de dames, Pomaré, Marix, Bébé, Sisina* (Nizet, 1977).

12   *Baudelaire et Asselineau*, p. 167, and the following quotations: p. 167–169.

13   Rediscovered and edited by J. Ziegler in the series, 'Publications du Centre W. T. Bandy d'Etudes baudelairiennes' (Nashville: Vanderbilt University, 1976).

14   Champfleury, *Souvenirs et Portraits de jeunesse* (Dentu, 1872), p. 137.

15   Letter to Banville, July 6, 1845.

16   *Bdsc*, p. 73–80.

17   In another (more plausible) version, the offending wine is Bordeaux (see *La Fanfarlo, OC*, I, 575).

18 See G. Robb, 'Baudelaire à l'hôtel Corneille: du nouveau sur *La Fanfarlo*', *Mélanges de littérature en hommage à A. Kies* (Brussels: Facultés universitaires Saint-Louis, 1985).

19 *CPl*, I, 131.

20 From the prose poem 'La Chambre double'.

21 Notably by Jules Mouquet: Baudelaire, *Vers retrouvés* (Emile-Paul frères, 1929). See *OC*, I, 1259–1269.

22 Baudelaire generally uses the word 'tribades' to designate lesbians in the modern sense. An early version of 'Femmes damnées' discovered by Yoshio Abé and published by him in his Japanese translation of *Les Fleurs du Mal* begins with the verse: 'Les Tribades en rond sur le sable couchées . . .'.

23 See J. Ziegler, *Un carré de dames*.

24 *OC*, I, 548.

25 See Cl. Pichois's introduction to *Les Paradis artificiels* (Folio, (1983)), p. 11–13.

26 *Correspondance*, ed. R. Pierrot, vol. V (Garnier, 1969), p. 69–72.

27 Most of the following details come from a series of satirical articles on *Le Corsaire-Satan* published by the rival *Silhouette* in 1846. These have been edited with an introduction and notes by G. Robb: *Le Corsaire-Satan en Silhouette: le milieu journalistique de la jeunesse de Baudelaire* (Publications du Centre W. T. Bandy d'Etudes baudelairiennes, 1985).

28 Champfleury, *Les Aventures de Mademoiselle Mariette* (Lecou, 1853). The 'Saint-Charmay' of Champfleury's *roman à clé* is Lepoitevin Saint-Alme.

29 *Baudelaire et Asselineau*, p. 81.

30 *La Silhouette*, 24 May 1846. *Le Corsaire-Satan en Silhouette*, p. 64. The book Baudelaire refers to is his *Salon de 1846*.

31 See G. Robb, 'Lola Montès et la Fanfarlo', *Etudes baudelairiennes* XII (1987).

32 Lola Montès, *Aventures de la célèbre danseuse racontées par elle-même, avec son portrait et un fac-similé de son écriture* (Chez tous les libraires, 1847).

33 *OC*, I, 570–571.

34 *Le Corsaire-Satan*, March 8, 1845.

35 *La Presse*, March 11, 1845.

36 Private collection.

37 *Baudelaire et Asselineau*, p. 73.

38 In the preface to *Hernani*.

39 See Armand Moss, *Baudelaire et Delacroix* (Nizet, 1973).

40 See the study by J. Ziegler on Deroy (*Gazette des beaux-arts*, May–June 1976).

41 *Baudelaire et Asselineau*, p. 69 and 71.

42 Prarond archives.

43 The articles which are most likely to have been written by Baudelaire – in part at least – can be found in *OC*, II, 1012–1027.

CHAPTER 13

1   See Cl. Pichois, 'Baudelaire en 1847. Petit essai de sociologie littéraire', *BET*.

2   *Les Libres Penseurs* (1848).

3   Introduction to Dupont's *Chants et Chansons* (1851). The words in italics come from the *Song of the Workers*.

4   Champfleury, *Souvenirs et Portraits de jeunesse*, p. 132–133.

5   *Baudelaire et Asselineau*, p. 93–95.

6   See Nori Kameya, *Un conteur méconnu, Charles Barbara, 1817–1866* (Minard, 1986).

7   Théophile Gautier, in his preface to *Les Fleurs du Mal*. Gautier was supposedly describing his first meeting with Baudelaire, but seems to have been remembering Courbet's portrait rather than Baudelaire himself.

8   E. Crépet, 'Etude biographique', in his edition of the *Œuvres posthumes*, p. xxxiii.

9   Charles Toubin, quoted in *Bdsc*, p. 34–35.

10   Charles Bataille, quoted in *Bdsc*, p. 35.

11   *EJC*, p. 26.

12   Letter to Mme Aupick, March 26, 1853.

13   Letter to Mme Aupick, Dec. 4, 1847.

14   Charles Monselet, quoted in *Bdsc*, p. 148–149. See also J.-Fr. Delesalle, *Bulletin baudelairien*, XVI, 3 (autumn 1981). On the Café Momus: J. Crépet, 'Une farce de la bande à Murger', in *Propos sur Baudelaire*, ed. Cl. Pichois (Mercure de France, 1957).

15   *Baudelaire et Asselineau*, p. 181–182.

16   See Cl. Pichois, 'Autour de *La Fanfarlo*, Baudelaire, Balzac et Marie Daubrun', *Mercure de France* (Dec. 1956), and *CPl*, I, 804.

17   *Baudelaire et la Belle aux cheveux d'or* (Yale University Press, 1941).

18   A. Moss, *Baudelaire et Delacroix*, p. 149.

CHAPTER 14

1   A typed copy of these *Souvenirs* was given to Cl. Pichois by Toubin's niece, Mlle Eugénie Toubin. The pages concerning Baudelaire can be found in *Bdsc*.

2   Alphonse Promayet (1822–1872) was a childhood friend of Gustave Courbet, and appears in many of Courbet's paintings, notably *L'Atelier*.

3   J. Crépet was unable to find any such article in *La Presse*.

4   The Duc d'Abrantès was a writer, composer, gastronome and dandy. See Banville's *Mes souvenirs*, p. 143–155.

5   Fargue, 'Mémoires d'un conscrit', *Mercure de France*, Feb. 1, 1929. Reprinted by Jules Mouquet and W. T. Bandy in *Baudelaire en 1848. La Tribune nationale* (Emile-Paul frères, 1946).

6   Charles de Freycinet, *Souvenirs*, vol. I (Delagrave, 1912), p. 6–7 (courtesy of W. T. Bandy).

7 *Baudelaire et Asselineau*, p. 85–86.

8 Letter to E. Crépet, 1886. *BET*, p. 40–41.

9 *OC*, I, 455.

10 The figure is a composite symbol of worker and bourgeois (if the top hat represents the bourgeoisie). Courbet's vignette is reminiscent of Delacroix's *La Liberté sur les barricades*.

11 J. Mouquet and W. T. Bandy, *Baudelaire en 1848*, p. 12–16.

12 Articles from *La Tribune nationale* are reproduced in *Baudelaire en 1848*.

13 Lamartine, *Histoire de la Révolution de 1848* (Perrotin, 1849), vol. II, p. 162–163 (courtesy of W. T. Bandy).

14 Letter to E. Crépet. *EJC*, p. 82.

15 *La Petite Revue*, March 11, 1865.

16 *Figaro*, Jan. 19, 1889. *EJC*, p. 85–86. A different account is given by Maxime Rude in *Confidences d'un journaliste* (Sagnier, 1876).

17 *Baudelaire et Asselineau*, p. 92.

18 *CPl*, I, 157–158.

19 Information from Michel Brix.

20 Pierre Dufay, 'Un restaurant de Baudelaire: la mère Perrin', *Mercure de France*, Jan. 15, 1937.

21 *Correspondance*, ed. J. Bruneau (Bibliothèque de la Pléiade), vol. I, p. 718.

22 Du Camp, *Souvenirs littéraires*, vol. II (1892), p. 57–58.

23 Théophile Gautier gives a description of the Summer Palace in his book, *Constantinople*.

24 Private collection.

25 See Cl. Pichois, 'Baudelaire devant la sociocritique ouest-allemande', *Etudes baudelairiennes* IX.

CHAPTER 15

1 See Houssaye (*Confessions*, II, 252) and Sainte-Beuve's preface to *Chateaubriand et son groupe littéraire*.

2 *Baudelaire et Asselineau*, p. 173–174. The 'refutation of Locke's system' refers to the sixth of De Maistre's *Soirées de Saint-Pétersbourg*.

3 *OC*, I, 669.

4 *EJC*, p. 296–297.

5 *EJC*, p. 293–294.

6 Asselineau's notes, published in *Baudelaire et Asselineau*, are the main source of information on Philoxène Boyer.

7 Monselet, *La Lorgnette littéraire* (Poulet-Malassis et De Broise, 1857), p. 27.

8 Boyer's album was auctioned at Drouot on May 22, 1985.

9 See Philibert Audebrand, *Lauriers et Cyprès* (Calmann-Lévy, 1903).

10 Discovered by Raymond Poggenburg: 'Un nouvel aperçu de Baudelaire en 1853', *Du romantisme au surnaturalisme. Hommage à Cl. Pichois* (Neuchâtel: La

Baconnière, 1985). On Henry de La Madelène, see R. Poggenburg's study in the *Bulletin baudelairien*, XVIII, 3 (Dec. 1983).

11   Cl. Pichois, 'Un carnet d'Asselineau utilisé par Baudelaire', *Quaderni francesi*, I (1970).

12   Luc Badesco, 'Baudelaire et la revue *Jean Raisin*. La première publication du *Vin des chiffonniers*', *Revue des Sciences humaines*, Jan.–March 1957.

13   Audebrand, *Derniers Jours de la Bohème* (Calmann-Lévy, n.d.).

14   *LAB*, p. 407.

15   *Journal pour rire*, April 9, 1852. The blasphemous poetry alluded to is probably 'Le Reniement de Saint Pierre'.

16   Du Camp, *Souvenirs littéraires*, II, 62.

17   See L. Badesco, art. cit., and J. Crépet and Cl. Pichois, 'Baudelaire au *Moniteur de la cordonnerie*', in J. Crépet, *Propos sur Baudelaire*, p. 33–42.

18   According to a note by Champfleury dated July 29, 1853. Quoted by W. T. Bandy in the *Bulletin baudelairien*, X, 2 (winter 1975).

19   See G. Jean-Aubry, *Un paysage littéraire. Baudelaire et Honfleur* (Maison du livre, 1917).

20   Quoted by Cl. Pichois in his study of Alphonse Baudelaire. *BET*, p. 54.

21   *BET*, p. 17.

CHAPTER 16

1   At number 60, a short step from Mme Sabatier's apartment at 16, rue Frochot, as R. Poggenburg points out (*Du romantisme au surnaturalisme. Hommage à Claude Pichois*, p. 205).

2   Letter to Mme Aupick, May 6, 1861.

3   See M. Monnier and Cl. Pichois, 'La Maladie de Baudelaire', *BET*, p. 219 ff.

4   See 'Une femme à enterrer', in J. Crépet, *Propos sur Baudelaire*, p. 149–155.

5   *Souvenirs des autres* (Crès, 1917), p. 139.

6   *Souvenirs d'un septuagénaire*, quoted in *Bdsc*, p. 122.

7   *CPl*, I, 792.

8   There are numerous books on Mme Sabatier, most of them trivial or inaccurate. For example, *Madame Sabatier. Apollonie au pays des libertins*, by Louis Mermaz (Lausanne: Editions Rencontre, 1967) boasts on its cover a picture of the wrong Mme Sabatier ... André Billy's *La Présidente et ses amis* (Flammarion, 1945) is interesting in that it contains the memoirs of Edmond Richard, Mme Sabatier's last friend. See also Armand Moss, *Baudelaire et Madame Sabatier* (Nizet, 1975; revised edition, 1978), and Pierre Dufay, *Autour de Baudelaire* (Au Cabinet du livre, 1931).

9   Judith Gautier, *Le Collier des jours. Le Second rang du collier* (Librairie Félix Juven, 1909), p. 182.

10   According to E. Richard (A. Billy, op. cit., p. 118).

11   'Baudelaire-Cramer: le sens des *Orfraies*'. See chapter 11, note 41.

12 *OC*, II, 59.
13 'Vieux souvenirs d'un étudiant de 1852'. *Le Journal*, Sept. 1, 1924. See the article by J.-Fr. Delesalle, *Bulletin baudelairien*, IV, 2 (April 1969).
14 *EJC*, p. 295.
15 *Baudelaire et la Belle aux cheveux d'or* (Yale University Press, 1941), p. 34.
16 *CPl*, I, 139.
17 Letter to Mme Aupick, Nov. 4, 1856.
18 Letter to Asselineau, end of December 1855.

CHAPTER 17

1 Firmin Maillard, in *Le Présent*, July 2, 1857.
2 This hotel, now the Hôtel du Quai Voltaire, was also inhabited at different times by Sibelius, Wagner and Oscar Wilde.
3 *Baudelaire et Asselineau*, p. 96–97.
4 *Baudelaire et Asselineau*, p. 187.
5 Henri Plassan, 'Un homme fatal', *Gazette de Paris*, Aug. 16, 1857.
6 *OC*, I, 187.
7 Baudelaire, letter to Malassis, March 9, 1857.
8 Malassis, letters to Asselineau, Bégis and Mouravit collections, Archives départementales de l'Orne.
9 On July 9, Baudelaire told his mother that, 'appalled' at the 'horror' he was about to inspire, he deleted one third of the poems at the proof stage.
10 See the list drawn up by Maurice Chalvet, *Bulletin du bibliophile* (1975), p. 245–265.
11 *EJC*, p. 300.
12 Quoted in *OC*, I, 1177.
13 Letter published by J. Crépet, *Bulletin du bibliophile* (1945), p. 207.
14 *Ibid.*
15 See *CPl*, I, 937.
16 See the edition of *Les Fleurs du Mal* by J. Crépet, G. Blin and Cl. Pichois, vol. I (Corti, 1968), p. 541 ff.
17 *LAB*, p. 45.
18 See the edition of *Les Fleurs du Mal* quoted above, p. 438–439.
19 Quoted by P. W. Lasowski, in *Syphilis*, p. 127.
20 H. Plassan, art. cit.
21 Quoted by J. Crépet in the Conard edition of *Les Fleurs du Mal*, p. 319–320.
22 *LAB*, p. 152–153.
23 See *OC*, I, 1186–1205.
24 According to A. Billy, *La Présidente et ses amis*, p. 138.
25 *Revue des grands procès contemporains* (1885), quoted by J. Crépet, ed., *Les Fleurs du Mal* (Conard), p. 330.

26 *Baudelaire et Asselineau*, p. 114.

27 Malassis, letter to Asselineau, May 15, 1868. Published by J. Marsan, *L'Archer*, Sept.–Oct., 1936.

28 See Cl. Pichois, 'Montalembert, le substitut Pinard et Charles Baudelaire', *BET*, p. 133–140.

29 Published by J. Crépet, *Bulletin du bibliophile* (1945), p. 200–202. The article referred to was published by Léon Plée in *Le Siècle* on Aug. 20.

30 *Souvenirs et Portraits de jeunesse*, p. 138.

31 *Correspondance* de Flaubert, ed. J. Bruneau (Pléiade), vol. II, p. 659–660.

32 Baudelaire intended to write the 'history' of this 'misunderstanding' (*OC*, I, 685).

33 Letter to Mme Aupick, July 9, 1857.

34 Letter to Malassis, Oct. 9, 1857.

35 See *LAB*, p. 321–325.

36 Perhaps those which tied Baudelaire to Jeanne?

37 Quoted by Maurice Chalvet, art. cit.

CHAPTER 18

1 *Journal*, ed. R. Ricatte, vol. II (Monaco, 1956), p. 164. The café, now called 'Au Petit Riche', stands at number 5, rue Le Peletier.

2 M. Monnier and Cl. Pichois, 'La Maladie de Baudelaire', *BET*, p. 233.

3 Letters from Deschamps, Flaubert, Hugo, and Sainte-Beuve in *LAB*.

4 This is the expression used by Baudelaire in his letter to Malassis on Nov. 11, 1858.

5 *OC*, II, 338–339.

6 See Cl. Pichois and François Ruchon, *Iconographie de Charles Baudelaire* (Geneva: Pierre Cailler, 1960).

7 Most of the following details are taken from *Bdsc*.

8 *Baudelaire et Asselineau*, p. 169.

9 *LAB*, p. 146.

10 Another of Feydeau's novels – *Sylvie* (1861) – has a hero, Anselme Schanfara, who may be modelled in part on Baudelaire, as P. Martino revealed in 1923 (*Revue d'Histoire littéraire de la France*, p. 568).

11 Feydeau's annotations were published by G. E. Lang in *Charles Baudelaire jugé par Ernest Feydeau* (Ronald Davis, 1921).

12 Letter dated Feb. 26, 1858.

13 Unpublished letter kindly supplied by Pierre Berès, in which Baudelaire states that a certain Monsieur Semé has lent him 100 francs. Semé was a secondhand clothes dealer in the rue de l'Ecole-de-Médecine.

14 These words are underlined three or even five times in the original letter.

CHAPTER 19

1   Prarond archives.

2   As described in the prose poem, 'Le Port'.

3   Mme Aupick later told Malassis: 'I used to give him lessons, but only for pronunciation, since he knows the language better than I.' (Letter published by J. Crépet, in *La Nouvelle Revue française*, Nov. 1932.)

4   Charles Bréard, *Vieilles rues et vieilles maisons de Honfleur du XVe siècle à nos jours* (Honfleur, 1900).

5   L. Lemonnier, *Enquêtes sur Baudelaire* (Crès, 1929), p. 21. This chemist was the father of the future humorist, Alphonse Allais.

6   A. Schanne, *Souvenirs de Schaunard* (Charpentier, 1886), p. 230–231.

7   See J. Crépet and Cl. Pichois, 'La Mort de la "Belle aux cheveux d'or"', in *Propos sur Baudelaire*. Marie Daubrun died in poverty in 1901.

8   *OC*, II, 94.

9   Private collection. This is one of the very few letters from Malassis to Baudelaire to have survived.

10   *CPl*, II, 98.

11   *Revue anecdotique*, Nov. 1859.

12   Letter to Malassis, Dec. 16, 1859.

13   Letters and notes discovered and published by Pierre Duflo in the *Revue d'Histoire littéraire de la France*, July–Aug. 1983.

14   The articles by Fraisse on Baudelaire have been published by Cl. and V. Pichois in *Sur Baudelaire* (Gembloux, Duculot, 1973).

15   *LAB*, p. 357.

16   Letter to an unnamed correspondent, July 13, 1849.

17   Wagner wrote to Baudelaire about this conspiracy (*LAB*, p. 397–398).

18   On this sad incident, see *Etudes baudelairiennes* II (1971).

19   Now the Hôpital Fernand Widal where Nerval was treated in 1852 and where Henry Murger died in 1861.

20   The house in which Baudelaire rented an apartment stood on the site of the present Neuilly post office.

21   Letter dated April 1, 1859.

22   See *OC*, I, 588, 591, 595–596 and 650. On Elisa Neri, see J. Ziegler, *Un carré de dames*.

23   For the latest speculations (but not the last), see *Bulletin baudelairien*, XII, 2 (winter 1977), and XIV, 2 (winter 1979).

24   Letter to Mme Aupick, Oct. 11, 1860.

25   First mentioned on Nov. 15, 1859.

26   First mentioned on Feb. 4, 1860.

27   Letter to Malassis, Feb. 4, 1860.

CHAPTER 20

1   *Revue anecdotique*, Nov. 1–15, 1860.

2   'Notes pour une Iconographie du poète Charles Baudelaire', in the *Tombeau de Charles Baudelaire* (Bibliothèque artistique et littéraire, 1896).

3   The long history of this frontispiece is told in detail in *ICO*, p. 100–120.

4   Paul Mariéton, letter to E. Crépet, Aug. 14, 1886. Private collection.

5   Letter to Mme Aupick, Jan. 1, 1861.

6   See Patricia Clements, *Baudelaire and the English Tradition* (University of Princeton Press, 1985). For the few reviews of the 1861 *Fleurs du Mal*, see W. T. Bandy, *Baudelaire Judged by his Contemporaries* (Columbia University, 1933).

7   Feb. 1–15, 1861.

8   *L'Assemblée nationale*, April 12, 1856. Quoted by J. Crépet in the Conard edition of the *Histoires extraordinaires*, p. 377.

9   'Les Poètes et la poésie française en 1861', *Revue des Deux Mondes*, Aug. 1861.

10   'De la poésie en 1865', *Le Constitutionnel*, June 12, 1865.

11   For the three poems on Baudelaire, see *Bdsc*, p. 176–180.

12   See *CPl*, II, 184–185. The original letter has not been found.

13   Malassis, letter to A. de La Fizelière, March 24, 1868. On Baudelaire's relations with Cladel, see Judith (daughter of Léon) Cladel, (*Maître et disciple, Charles Baudelaire et Léon Cladel* (Corrêa, 1951).

14   *Mes souvenirs*, p. 81.

15   Catalogue of the Baudelaire Exhibition at the Petit Palais, 1968–1969, no. 240. Baudelaire had particular difficulty with the words 'hickory' and 'red bud' (*CPl*, II, 337 and 834).

16   Letter dated Aug. 25, 1886. The addressee may have been Cladel, or, in view of the date, E. Crépet.

17   Letter dated Jan. 30, 1862.

18   *Un café de journalistes sous Napoléon III* (Dentu, 1888), p. 295–296.

19   Le Marquis de Villemer (pseudonym), *Les Portraits littéraires* (Lachaud, 1870), p. 124.

20   *Bdsc*, p. 154.

21   See Cl. Pichois, *Baudelaire à Paris*, photographies de Maurice Rué (Hachette, 1967), p. 26.

22   *CPl*, II, 13–14.

23   *Bdsc*, p. 155–156.

24   Letter dated Feb. 18, 1860.

25   Jules Claretie, 'Le Monument de Baudelaire', *Le Journal*, Sept. 4, 1901. *Bdsc*, p. 156–157.

26   *OC*, I, 711–779.

27   *LAB*, p. 230.

28   *Les Fleurs du Mal*, ed. J. Crépet and G. Blin (Corti, 1942), p. 354–355.

29   *OC*, I, 707.

30   *Le Moniteur universel*, May 18, 1863.

31   On Louise Deschamps, see *CPl*, II, 297–298, and *Bulletin baudelairien*, VIII, 1 and 2 (Aug. 1972 and April 1973).

32   See *BET*, p. 59–79, and *OC*, I, 1139–1141. Photographs of Berthe in *ICO*.

33   Laure Dulong, born in 1847, was later known to Edmond de Goncourt, who recorded her description of Mme Aupick: 'That small, delicate, dainty woman, ever so slightly round-shouldered,' who 'had a high opinion of her son's intelligence', but who didn't dare express it 'because of the authority a certain M. Hémon [*sic*] had over her. He saw her son as a rogue who was always talking about coming to see his mother, but never came, and wrote to her only in order to ask for money.' (*Journal*, June 3, 1895).

34   On Manet's relations with Baudelaire, see *CPl*, II, and *LAB*, p. 228–239.

35   Georges Barral, 'Entretiens avec Baudelaire', *Le Petit Bleu* (Brussels), Aug. 31, 1901. The following quotation comes from the same article.

36   Malassis, letter to Champfleury, April (?) 1866.

37   See in particular *OC*, II, 744, 760 and 768.

38   See J. Crépet, *Propos sur Baudelaire*, p. 74–78, and the article by Cl. Pichois in *L'Avant-scène Théâtre*, April 1–15, 1985.

39   Close friend of Barbey d'Aurevilly who reconverted him to Catholicism.

40   *LAB*, p. 387.

41   Letter-Preface to *Le Spleen de Paris*.

42   *Catalogue Exposition Charles Baudelaire* (Bibliothèque Nationale, 1957), no. 436.

43   *Journaux intimes* (Corti, 1949), p. 181.

44   As Jean Starobinski shows in *Portrait de l'artiste en saltimbanque* (Geneva: Skira, 1970).

CHAPTER 21

1   The only known copy of this letter seems to be a rough draft. Baudelaire's file has mysteriously 'disappeared' from the Academy's archives.

2   Letter to Mme Aupick, Christmas 1861.

3   *CPl*, II, 755.

4   *CPl*, II, 766.

5   Letter to Mme Aupick, Christmas 1861.

6   Letter to Mme Aupick, Christmas 1861.

7   Text kindly supplied by André Jarry.

8   See, however, *Victor Hugo raconté par Adèle Hugo*, ed. A. Ubersfeld and G. Rosa (Plon, 1985), p. 602–628. Hugo was elected to the Académie in 1841.

9   Jan. 1, 1862.

10   Letter to Vigny, Jan. 26, 1862.

11   Reported by Asselineau, in *Charles Baudelaire, Souvenirs – Correspondances* (Pincebourde, 1872), p. 73.

12   Letter to Mme Aupick, Christmas 1861.

13   *Le Constitutionnel*, Jan. 20, 1862.

14   *OC*, II, 769.

15   March 4 (?), 1863.

16   *CPl*, II, 21.

17   Asselineau, quoted in *EJC*, p. 300.

18   J. Hillairet, *Dictionnaire historique des rues de Paris* (Editions de Minuit, 1964).

19   Letter to Mme Aupick, Jan. 3, 1863.

20   Catalogue of the Malassis Exhibition at Alençon, 1957, no. 260.

21   Letter to Mme Aupick, June 5, 1863.

22   Letter to Victor Duruy, Aug. 7, 1863.

23   *OC*, II, 225–230.

24   Letter to Mme Aupick, March 3, 1864.

CHAPTER 22

1   This chapter was written in collaboration with Dr Edmond Henrotin (1916–1981), grandson of Marie Collart and an expert on the Brussels of Baudelaire's day. The main sources of information on the earlier part of Baudelaire's stay in Brussels, apart from the poet's own correspondence, are the book by Maurice Kunel, *Baudelaire en Belgique* (Liège: Soledi, 1944), based on the memoirs of Georges Barral, and the chapter 'Baudelaire et l'opinion belge de son temps', in Gustave Charlier's *Passages* (Brussels: La Renaissance du livre, 1947).

2   *CPl*, II, 360.

3   *OC*, II, 940.

4   *OC*, II, 773–775.

5   Kunel, *Baudelaire en Belgique*, p. 31.

6   Léon Dommartin, in *Bilboquet*, May 29, 1864. A slightly different version was published by Malassis in *La Petite Revue*, Jan. 21, 1865.

7   C. Lemonnier, *La Vie belge* (Fasquelle, 1905).

8   Malassis, who attended all five lectures, told Asselineau that there was an audience of eight at the last lecture (letter dated April 13, 1868).

9   Kunel, p. 36.

10   Kunel claims that Baudelaire talked on this occasion about *Les Fleurs du Mal* and about the prose poems he was writing.

11   Letter to Mme Aupick, July 31, 1864.

12   Letter dated Sept. 18, 1867.

13   Letter to Ancelle, May 7, 1864.

14   Letter to Champfleury, Oct. 10, 1865.

15   *Baudelaire et Asselineau*, p. 139–140.

16   Letter to Mme Meurice, Jan. 3, 1865.

17   Article published in *Le Libre Examen* (Sept. 10, 1867) on the occasion of Baudelaire's death.

18   *OC*, II, 879.

19   *ICO*, no. 57.

20   Léon Fuchs, in *Rabelais*, Oct. 17, 1857 (courtesy of G. Robb).

21   Pierre Dufay, 'Dix-huit lettres de Félicien Rops à Poulet-Malassis', *Mercure de France* (Oct 1, 1933), p. 48.

22   *OC*, II, 951.

23   Letter published by Kunel, *Mercure de France*, Sept. 1957. The 'riddeks' of Anvers were dancehalls frequented mainly by sailors.

24   Oct. 13, 1864.

25   Letter to Ancelle, Sept. 2, 1864.

26   Nadar's visit recounted by G. Barral, *Cinq journées avec Charles Baudelaire* (1932), p. 38.

27   Nadar, *Charles Baudelaire intime. Le Poète vierge* (Blaizot, 1911), p. 117.

28   *OC*, II, 918–919.

29   *La Petite Revue*, Jan. 7, 1865.

30   See Guy Chastel, ed., *Lettres d'Albert Glatigny à Théodore de Banville* (Mercure de France, 1923).

31   Letter to Mme Aupick, May 8, 1865.

32   Quoted in *CPl*, II, 936.

33   Jan. 2, 1866.

34   *LAB*, p. 346.

35   Jan. 12, 1866.

36   Feb. 16, 1866.

37   *L'Indépendance belge*, June 20, 1887.

38   Nov. 16 and 30, Dec. 23, 1865.

39   *LAB*, p. 346–347.

40   March 5, 1866.

41   Feb. 18, 1866.

42   Jan. 19, 1866.

43   René Pomeau, *Laclos* (Hatier, 1975), p. 8.

44   Baudelaire was slightly over-optimistic! See p. 382.

45   Letter published in *Les Derniers mois de Charles Baudelaire* (see note 1 below), p. 19.

46   *CPl*, II, 624.

47   *Gazette des Tribunaux*, May 9, 1868.

48   Undated letter to Banville, in *Lettres d'Albert Glatigny à Théodore de Banville*, p. 19.

CHAPTER 23

1   For the first part of this chapter, see M. Monnier and Cl. Pichois, 'La Maladie de Baudelaire', in *BET*. Unless otherwise indicated, letters from Mme Aupick, Malassis and Asselineau can be found in J. Richer and M. A. Ruff, *Les Derniers*

mois de Charles Baudelaire et la publication posthume de ses œuvres, Correspondances – *Documents* (Nizet, 1976). The reader should note, however, that the text of letters published in this volume is extremely unreliable and that we refer to it only for the sake of convenience. Letters quoted in this chapter have been checked against the originals.

2   Letter to Mme Aupick, March 9, 1865, and *Pauvre Belgique! (OC*, II, 852).

3   Letter to Ancelle, Feb. 8, 1865.

4   Letters to Mme Aupick, Feb. 15 and March 9, 1865.

5   *OC*, I, 231–240.

6   On Oscar Max, see the article by Armand Colard, *Revue médicale de Bruxelles*, XVIII, 5 (May 1971).

7   Letter to Sainte-Beuve, Jan. 15, 1866.

8   Malassis, letter to Asselineau, April 19, 1866.

9   *Baudelaire et Asselineau*, p. 140–142.

10   P. W. Lasowski indicates the connections that were believed to exist between syphilis and hysteria (*Syphilis*, p. 159).

11   Letter to Mme Aupick, Feb. 12, 1866.

12   Letter to Mme Aupick, Feb. 12, 1866.

13   Letter to Mme Aupick, Feb. 17, 1866.

14   *EJC*, p. 190. Baudelaire had probably been using alcohol for many years, though Le Vavasseur described him in his youth as 'naturally sober. We often drank together, and I never saw him drunk.' (*EJC*, p. 194).

15   *EJC*, p. 188.

16   In the early 1840s, Hugo advised the young poet 'to go and stay in the country, to work in solitude, to go on a sort of retreat' (*BET*, p. 19).

17   Private collection.

18   April 30, 1866.

19   *BET*, p. 199.

20   Kunel, p. 163.

21   Description courtesy of Dr Henrotin.

22   Unpublished letter. Drouot, June 9–10, 1983.

23   *EJC*, p. 197.

24   *EJC*, p. 197–198.

25   *EJC*, p. 199.

26   'Souvenirs sur Baudelaire. La Maladie et la Mort de Baudelaire', *Le Petit Bleu*, Oct. 31, 1907.

27   *EJC*, p. 199.

28   Armand Trousseau, *Clinique médicale de l'Hôtel-Dieu de Paris*, 2nd ed., vol II (Baillière, 1865). Trousseau links aphasia to a 'softening of the mind' – a common expression at the time.

29   Malassis, letter to Asselineau, Sept. 3, 1866.

30   The following quotations are taken from W. T. Bandy, *Baudelaire Judged by his Contemporaries*.

31   *EJC*, p. 189.

32   Published by R. Poggenburg in the *Bulletin baudelairien*, XVIII, 3 (Dec. 1983).

33   Malassis, letter to Asselineau, Sept. 27, 1866.

34   *CPl*, I, lxxv.

35   *EJC*, p. 202.

36   *Baudelaire et Asselineau*, p. 147–148.

37   *Baudelaire et Asselineau*, p. 148.

38   *Baudelaire et Asselineau*, p.148–149.

39   Calmann-Lévy archives. J.-Y. Mollier, author of *Michel et Calmann Lévy ou la Naissance de l'édition moderne* (Calmann-Lévy, 1984), believes this document to be written in the hand of Michel Lévy's brother, Calmann.

40   *EJC*, p. 204–205.

41   *Baudelaire et Asselineau*, p. 149–150.

42   Edmond Albert was the brother-in-law of Georges Mathieu, one of the authors of the *Mystères galants*. See Cl. Pichois, 'Un ami de Baudelaire, Edmond Albert, éditeur en placard', *Etudes baudelairiennes*, II (1971).

43   Mme Aupick, letter to Malassis, Sept. 16, 1867.

EPILOGUE

1   *Baudelaire et Asselineau*, p. 150.

2   Published by Lois Hamrick in *Baudelaire par Gautier*, ed. Cl.-M. Senninger (Klincksieck, 1986).

3   *CPl*, II, 491.

4   Nadar, *Charles Baudelaire*, p. 139.

5   Published by J. Adhémar in 'Baudelaire, les frères Stevens, la modernité', *Gazette des beaux-arts*, Feb. 1958. Quoted here from the original.

6   *EJC*, p. 275–276. Fantin is the painter, Fantin-Latour, whose *Hommage à Delacroix* includes a portrait of Baudelaire. Ducessois was the brother of Félicité Baudelaire.

7   Malassis to Asselineau, Sept. 23, 1867: 'Sainte-Beuve has always been too inclined to see Baudelaire above all as a very talented eccentric.' (*Derniers mois*, p. 121).

8   *EJC*, p. 276.

9   *Baudelaire et Asselineau*, p. 165.

10   Published by J. Adhémar, art. cit. Quoted from the original.

11   See W. T. Bandy, *Baudelaire Judged by his Contemporaries*, and *Bdsc*.

12   In fact, this is how Baudelaire describes Samuel Cramer (and thus himself) in *La Fanfarlo*.

13   *Figaro*, Sept. 10, 1867.

14   Asselineau to Malassis, *Derniers mois*, p. 128.

15   Asselineau to Malassis, *Derniers mois*, p. 130.

16 Malassis to Ancelle, *Derniers mois*, p. 118.

17 For a different interpretation of Baudelaire's dealings with Lévy, see the detailed study by J.-Y. Mollier, in *Etudes baudelairiennes*, XII (1987).

18 *Derniers mois*, p. 149–151.

19 *Derniers mois*, p. 94.

20 *Derniers mois*, p. 134.

21 *EJC*, p. 270–271.

22 *Derniers mois*, p. 137.

23 *Derniers mois*, p. 135.

24 Letters from Mme Aupick and Félicité Baudelaire to Asselineau published by Auguste Auzas, *Mercure de France*, Sept. 16, 1912.

25 Letter published in *Le Manuscrit autographe* (1927), p. 107–109.

26 Emon's nephew – who spent a summer in Honfleur shortly after Baudelaire's death – was Gustave Moreau. There is a painting by him of Mme Aupick's garden (*ICO*, no. 79).

27 Mme Aupick's will has been published in the *Bulletin baudelairien*, XX, 3 (Dec. 1985).

28 *Derniers mois*, p. 108 and 75.

29 Asselineau to Malassis, April 22(?), 1866. *Derniers mois*, p. 34–35.

30 Private collection.

31 *Derniers mois*, p. 184.

32 *Derniers mois*, p. 164.

Index

B = Baudelaire

NAMES